Consumer Behavior Knowledge
for Effective Sports
and Event Marketing

Consumer Behavior Knowledge for Effective Sports and Event Marketing

Edited by

Lynn R. Kahle
University of Oregon

Angeline G. Close
University of Nevada, Las Vegas

Routledge
Taylor & Francis Group
New York London

Routledge
Taylor & Francis Group
270 Madison Avenue
New York, NY 10016

Routledge
Taylor & Francis Group
27 Church Road
Hove, East Sussex BN3 2FA

© 2011 by Taylor and Francis Group, LLC
Routledge is an imprint of Taylor & Francis Group, an Informa business

Printed in the United States of America on acid-free paper
10 9 8 7 6 5 4 3 2 1

International Standard Book Number: 978-0-415-87357-4 (Hardback) 978-0-415-87358-1 (Paperback)

Library of Congress Cataloging-in-Publication Data

Consumer behavior knowledge for effective sports and event marketing / edited by Lynn R. Kahle, Angeline G. Close.
    p. cm.
    ISBN 978-0-415-87357-4 -- ISBN 978-0-415-87358-1
    1. Consumer behavior. 2. Sports--Marketing. 3. Special events--Marketing. 4. Communication in marketing. I. Kahle, Lynn R. II. Close, Angeline.

    HF5415.32.C65866 2011
    796.06'98--dc22   2010012561

Visit the Taylor & Francis Web site at
http://www.taylorandfrancis.com

and the Psychology Press Web site at
http://www.psypress.com

To Debi Eisert, who is always a good sport, and

To Ben Scheinbaum, who continues to nurture the passion for sports

Contents

SECTION II   Building Relationships With Consumers
Through Sports

SECTION III　Providing Service to Consumers Through Sports and Event Sponsorship

Foreword
"Consumers: Alpha and Omega of Marketing"

Stephen A. Greyser
Harvard Business School

"The consumer is the alpha and omega (the starting point and ending point) of marketing."

As a marketer trained in consumer behavior, I long ago put forth this statement as my mantra for both the study and the practice of marketing. It constitutes a core connection between behavioral science and marketing. It encompasses both *understanding* and *influencing* consumer behavior.

Sports Permeate Society

This book focuses on the study of consumer behavior in the realms of sports and events. In perhaps no facet of American life is there more public engagement than sports. Sports energize widespread conversation, debate, even argument (but rarely of a violent nature). Sport is the lingua franca of 21st century workplaces and gathering spots. Indeed, interest in sports has spawned sports bars—often branded multiple-TV-screen venues providing entertainment and refreshment for followers of different sports and different teams as well as attracting interested fans in general. Some fans "wear their fandom" (not just at games) in the form of team or player apparel. At the 2009 Major League Baseball All-Star game, the stadium crowd (and much of downtown St. Louis) was a sea of Cardinal (host team) red.

Sports have become a secular religion. Sunday NFL football on TV is a weekly appointment much as church attendance has been. Like religion (for many), sports and sporting events provide a social fabric that knits people together into brand communities (e.g., fans of particular teams) and communities at large beyond fandom per se. Witness the massive community impact of and sense of representation by the New Orleans Saints as they marched through January on their way to the Super Bowl—and captured the NFL championship "on behalf of the New Orleans and Gulf Coast community" (while most of the nation cheered them on).

This phenomenon of community enthusiasm beyond traditional sport-alone fan support has manifested itself in other cities during other post-season runs. The quest of the Boston Red Sox in October 2004 for their first baseball World Championship in 86 years generated late nights and tired next-day workplace environments in New England and beyond. Fatigued but effusive fans and extended media coverage converted legions of nonfans ("beyond the periphery of the circles of fandom," in my analytic framework) into Red Sox supporters, at least for that month.

The point: "Sports bind a community together," according to National Hockey League commissioner Gary Bettman (personal conversation, August 2009). Businesses that provide sponsorship support for sports properties (teams, leagues, events) recognize the significance of enthusiasm and followership for the sports property and try to harness it in cobranding. Bank of America sponsorship head Ray Bednar described it as "connecting [the brand] to the passion of fans." And, sports (talk) radio provides an opportunity for fan experience-sharing through arguing their opinions with people fans know only via the airwaves: "Sports is a powerful dynamic in the community," stated Julie Kahn, who heads Entercom New England, home of the nation's top sports talk station, WEEI.

Super Bowl Sunday constitutes the largest venue for experience-sharing via sports—and for the simultaneous *other* big game, the "Super Bowl of Advertising"; it is the "national fairgrounds for commercials," where many consumers actually pay attention to the ads. Just like the game itself, this competition is extensively publicized before the event, actively discussed by many during the game (only 9% of Super Bowl viewers say they plan to watch alone), and widely commented on afterward. The 2010 Super Bowl attracted the largest viewership (106.5 million) of any program in U.S. television history.

Sports entail a further role for fans and the public as the context and vehicle for causes, corporate social responsibility, and philanthropic endeavor. Over 60 years ago, the then-Boston Braves helped create the

Jimmy Fund as the team's "good works" initiative to raise money for research to address cancer in children. The Red Sox have actively continued the effort over many decades, and their team radio and TV outlets are major participants. Millions of contributed dollars have helped build a premier institution (Dana Farber Cancer Institute) to serve this cause. Many teams (including the Red Sox) have their own foundations, and leagues have their own cause-oriented public service programs (e.g., "NBA Cares"). Athletes' foundations to support community entities are legion, and athletes speaking (via promotional announcements) on behalf of their own cause-based organizations (and others) are frequently seen, heard, and read in sports and nonsports media (including Web sites) alike. More broadly, nonprofit sports entrepreneurs use sport as a basis for improving people's lives via engagement in sport; Northeastern University's Center for the Study of Sport and Society studies and disseminates examples of these endeavors all over the world.

In a different realm, sports also provide a major platform for gambling—both legal and social. "March Madness bracketology" is a staple of workplace and school site pools and maintains fan interest through the weeks leading to the NCAA (National Collegiate Athletic Association) basketball championship game.

In short, sports are *entertainment* (sometimes diversion) for fans, who welcome the "unscripted drama" of live sports. It is *competition* for the athletes. It is *business* for the teams, leagues, and event owners—and their broadcasters. And, it is an *experience* for everyone involved, sometimes (as noted) reaching people beyond everyday fans.

Pervasiveness of Sports as Business

Beyond fans and the fan experience—or perhaps driven by it—the now-multibillion-dollar business of sports has become a pervasive element in our economy and our society. By way of a print media analogy, major business elements of sports regularly move from the sports pages (where the focus is dominantly on competition) to the business pages (often about major sponsorships, ticket price hikes, new types of merchandise, arena or stadium naming deals, etc.) and occasionally to the front page (e.g., league strikes or lockouts, threats of franchise transfers, plans for new stadiums, signing of superstar free-agent players, and the like). Also, treatment of sports business has become global, reflected in worldwide coverage of the business dimensions of megaevents such as the Olympics and the World Cup.

Beyond the competition and the playing of the games themselves, the business of sports has grown significantly in both size and financial stakes, always related to sports consumers directly or indirectly. Illustratively, there are

- more professional leagues/collegiate conferences and sports competing for fans' time and money and for marketing or sponsor support
- more big events seeking fan attention, sponsor support, and broadcast exposure
- more broadcast channels and hours providing opportunities for league and team rights fees but requiring corporate marketing and/or advertising support
- more opportunities for company or brand sponsorship of leagues, teams, events—"the official (product/service) of the (league/team/event)"—with pressures for more dollars and for measurable return on investment
- more licensed manufactured branded equipment, apparel, and other merchandise (for leagues, teams, colleges, events, players)—plus the memorabilia and autograph industry—and more distribution channels and retail space devoted to it, all competing for consumer purchases
- new financial paradigms for franchises in terms of new stadiums, more revenues from season ticketholders, and more corporate sponsorships, but with more complex relationships (e.g., team revenue sharing and luxury taxes, a more powerful role for players/agents, etc.)
- more contentious relationships between Players Associations (unions) and leagues
- more attention to and concern over the business of intercollegiate sports, including conference realignments, broadcast rights fees, and implications for both the "student" and "athlete" dimensions of the players
- more Web-powered products, including streamed athlete or team competition

In addition, effective management in the sports and events industry calls for addressing the traditional needs to attract in-stadium fans, broadcast audiences, and advertisers and to market merchandise that consumers see as appropriate. Understanding the enlarged landscape for the business of sports calls for recognition of the possible *limits to growth* in money or time on the part of fans, broadcast viewers or listeners, merchandise consumers, and sponsors or advertisers. For example, how does an economic downturn have an impact on event sponsorships, ticket pricing, luxury box sales, support for tournaments (e.g., in golf and tennis), sponsorships, and more?

Core Elements of the Business of Sports

The world of the business(es) of sports is vast. In *The Business of Sports: Text and Cases on Strategy and Management* (Foster, Greyser, & Walsh, 2006), I described in some detail a "model" of the area.[1] Here, let me simply point out the three principal elements and an additional major component:

1. First is *competition*—"the game." This encompasses entities such as leagues, teams, and events (e.g., the Olympics and the World Cup, "March Madness," etc.). It also includes players, which means unions and agents as well.

2. Next are *ways to leverage revenues* if a league, team, or event has the competition part right. Examples are the NFL business model with its extensive structured revenue-sharing among teams and a team with a successful "product" on the field, court, or ice. These revenue sources encompass broadcasting rights fees, sponsorships, arena or stadium naming rights revenues, licensed merchandise, branded retail stores, and so forth.

3. There are also other components, such as branded athletic equipment companies (think Nike), sports video games, sports gambling, financing firms for teams and leagues, and athlete training venues.

4. Beneath it all, supporting the entire apparatus are ... *fans*: fans—via bodies at games, eyeballs on TV, and opened wallets for tickets, merchandise, and so forth. Fans provide *time and hearts* for the sport of sports and for the business of sports.

   If one asks who sustains the business of sports, one need look no further than sports consumers—fans themselves. Of course, the business of sports is owned by leagues, teams, and event proprietors, who create the opportunities for competition; by broadcasters and sponsors, who significantly finance it; and by the players, without whom there would be no competition or event to market. But, ultimately paying for the system, as emphasized, are the fans—with time, hearts, and money.

In this book, Kahle and Close bring together conceptual and theoretical insights, along with the results of empirical research, to illuminate myriad dimensions of consumer behavior in sports and events. Some of the contexts treated are "big" sports; some are less-well-followed ones. Both attendance and participation are encompassed. In addition to improved

---

[1] Stephen A. Greyser, "The Business of Sports: A Perspective from Harvard," in *The Business of Sports: Text and Cases on Strategy and Management*, pp. 11–24.

marketing for leagues, teams, or entrepreneurial situations, sponsorship and its components (e.g., hospitality) are explored. Prosocial aspects of sport are examined, as is its larger setting of the contributions of sport to society. Fan behavior, from service at events to spectator rage, is the explicit focus in several chapters and a relevant component of many others.

As a whole, this book reflects the core idea of this Foreword: the consumer is the alpha and omega of marketing. To *influence* consumer behavior in terms of the time, money, and emotional attachment to brands and products, one must first *understand* the behavior, whether within the arena of sports and sporting events (as here) or beyond it in the broader world of marketing.

Reference

Foster, G., Greyser, S. A., & Walsh, B. (2006). *The business of sports: Text and cases on strategy and management.* Mason, OH: South-Western.

Preface

The relations among sports marketing, events, and consumer behavior embrace cutting-edge topics in the professional application of marketing thought. The growing complexity and importance of sports and event marketing have pushed scholars and practitioners to apply sophisticated marketing thinking and applications to these topics. The fundamental issues of communication and consumer response differ meaningfully from other types of marketing. This book not only presents some of the latest thinking for scholars but also deals with professional development in the sense that sports and event marketing can be viewed as a professional application of consumer behavior research. Readers will learn about new opportunities in using consumer behavior knowledge effectively in the areas of (a) influencing behaviors and society in sports, (b) building relationships with consumers through sports, and (c) providing service to consumers through sports and event sponsorship. This book includes comprehensive reviews, innovative conceptual pieces, and rigorous attention to data consistent with what readers have come to expect from the best scholarly publications. It draws attention to diverse topics and perspectives.

This book is unique in that it provides scholars and practitioners the opportunity to (a) gain rich insights on the newest avenues in consumer behavior as it relates to sports and event marketing, (b) accommodate a number of quality chapters, and (c) bridge practitioner trends with the latest scholarship. The idea for this book emerged from a "preconference event" at the American Marketing Association (AMA) Summer Educators' Conference, cosponsored by two AMA special interest groups (SIGs): Consumer Behavior (CBSIG) and Sports and Special Events Marketing (SPORTSSIG). We (Lynn Kahle, SPORTSSIG; and Angeline Close, CBSIG) have been the presidents of those SIGs and organized that event as a platform for scholars to share emerging works. These two subgroups of the AMA academic community represent approximately 500 members and attendees of the group programs.

We expect that this book should interest scholars both in consumer behavior and in sports marketing and management. The primary audience is academics in departments of advertising, marketing, psychology, physical education, leisure studies, management, and communication-related fields. They and their students, including master's students, will find an excellent collection of high-quality essays on this topic. As with many business books, the potential to inform a sophisticated professional audience of people who work for the media, advertising agencies, and corporate sports marketing departments also exists. Because of the newness of this topic, its explosive growth, the economic relevance, and the international and interdisciplinary audience, we expect interest may span a number of substantive fields.

We wish to thank the many people who helped us develop and refine this project, especially our colleagues and students in Oregon and Nevada, who continually inspire and challenge us. We deeply appreciate the encouragement we received from the AMA, especially that of Lynn Brown. Likewise, our friends at Psychology Press/Routledge/Taylor & Francis, especially Anne Duffy and Erin Flaherty, have provided priceless support and assistance. We also wish to acknowledge the support of a Pat and Stephanie Kilkenny Research Grant through the Warsaw Sports Marketing Center in completing this project. Finally, we want to thank our significant others, without whom we undoubtedly would have finished this project more quickly but less enjoyably.

Lynn R. Kahle
University of Oregon, Eugene, Oregon

Angeline G. Close
University of Nevada, Las Vegas, Nevada

About the Editors

Lynn R. Kahle (PhD, University of Nebraska, postdoctoral study University of Michigan) holds the Ehrman Giustina Professorship (endowed, tenured chair) in marketing and has been the department chair in the Department of Marketing at the University of Oregon, Eugene. He has been on the faculty in the Lundquist College of Business since 1983. As department chair, he was instrumental in founding the highly regarded James H. Warsaw Sports Marketing Center. He served as the founding director of the center, which *Sports Illustrated* described as the "best sports management school" (October 7, 2002, p. 27). He has chaired his university's Intercollegiate Athletic Committee and has been active in civic affairs as well, serving, among other things, as the head of the City of Eugene Human Rights Program.

He has held positions in several places around the world, including Technion University in Haifa, Israel; Griffith University, Gold Coast, Australia; Norwegian School of Economics and Business Administration, Bergen; University of North Carolina at Chapel Hill; Singapore Management University; Copenhagen Business School, Denmark; and Hanyang University, South Korea.

He has been a productive scholar. Topics of his research embody consumer and fan attitudes and values, public policy, sports marketing, international business, and communication. He has published more than 150 books, chapters, and research articles in such journals as the *Journal of the*

Academy of Marketing Science, Journal of Personality and Social Psychology, Sport Marketing Quarterly, Journal of Consumer Research, Journal of Consumer Psychology, Public Opinion Quarterly, Child Development, and *Journal of Marketing.* His 10 books include *Creating Images and the Psychology of Marketing Communication* (with C. H. Kim), *Sports Marketing and the Psychology of Marketing Communications* (with Chris Riley), and *Values, Lifestyles, and Psychographics* (with Larry Chiagouris).

Professor Kahle has received numerous awards. He is a Fellow in the American Psychological Association, the American Psychological Society, and the Society for Consumer Psychology, for which he has completed a term as president. He currently is president of the Sports and Special Events Special Interest Group of the American Marketing Association. He is an executive member of the American Marketing Association. *Who's Who in the World* and *Who's Who Worldwide* have included his biography.

Angeline G. Close (PhD, University of Georgia) researches, teaches, and serves the marketing community. Her expertise is in *event marketing,* namely, how consumers' experiences at sponsored events influence attitudes and consumer behavior. Current studies explore engaging consumers with events, uncovering drivers of effective event sponsorships, how entertainment impacts affect events/purchase intention toward sponsors, and why consumers may resist events. Synergistically, she studies consumers' experiences with *electronic marketplaces*—consumers' online experiences and how they interplay with on-ground events. Her research ties theory with implications for consumers, society, or consumer-focused business practice. She has contributed peer-reviewed studies in the *Journal of the Academy of Marketing Science, Advances in Consumer Research, Journal of Advertising Research,* and *Journal of Business Research,* among other articles and book chapters.

Experienced as an educator, Dr. Close has taught marketing management, advertising/integrated marketing communications (IMC), international marketing, and sales/promotions courses. Dr. Close engages her students' thinking in marketing theories and applications, especially in the local entertainment economy. In addition to research and teaching, Dr. Close serves the marketing and academic communities. Nationally, she serves as president of the American Marketing Association's Consumer Behavior Special Interest Group (http://www.cbsig.org). Involved with doctoral education, she serves on the board as advisor of the doctoral student group of AMA. She serves various leadership roles for the Association for Consumer Research, Society for Marketing Advances, and Academy of Marketing Science. Locally, she is a member of the Las Vegas Professional Chapter of the AMA.

Dr. Close has experience as a marketing research consultant and has contributed research projects for Hallmark, Coca-Cola, Dodge, Ford, Cingular, the New Media Institute, Harvey's Grocery, United Community Bank, AT&T, the Fashion Show Mall, Suzuki, the Tour De Georgia, and Road Atlanta. A recent project took place at the Petit LeMans race in the fall of 2008. In addition to marketing, other passions include volunteering with the Junior League, playing on tennis and softball teams, hiking, and visiting home in Atlanta.

About the Contributors

Steven J. Andrews is a doctoral candidate in consumer behavior in the Lundquist College of Business at the University of Oregon. In addition to degrees in marketing and psychology, he has a master's degree in exercise and sport science. He has coached tennis at all ages and skill levels since 1996 and is a competitive tennis player. In addition to studying sports-related consumer behavior topics, his research interests include visual persuasion and the influence of emotions on risky choice.

Matt Biggers is the senior vice president of marketing and communications for the New Orleans Hornets of the NBA. In this role, Biggers has responsibility for a wide range of disciplines for the Hornets, including all of the marketing, advertising, branding, creative services, events, game operations, media relations, and broadcasting. Prior to coming to the Hornets, he spent 12 years with another NBA franchise, the Orlando Magic. With the Magic, he served in several capacities in the marketing department, including director of marketing, where he led the marketing, advertising, creative services, events, and game operations for the club. Biggers graduated with a master of science degree in sport management from Georgia Southern University and a bachelor of science in business administration from Appalachian State University.

Carl S. Bozman (PhD, Washington State University) is professor of marketing at Gonzaga University. His current research focuses on the sustainability of not-for-profit organizations and how they can utilize new product development as a means to diversify and reinforce the resources available to fulfill their community service objectives.

Rick Burton is the David B. Falk Professor of Sport Management in the College of Human Ecology at Syracuse University. Burton previously worked as the commissioner of the National Basketball League

(Australia, New Zealand, Singapore) and as chief marketing officer of the U.S. Olympic Committee through the Beijing 2008 Summer Olympics. Prior to that, Burton served as the executive director of the Warsaw Sports Marketing Center while teaching in the Lundquist College of Business at the University of Oregon.

Joshua J. Clarkson (BA, MA, University of North Florida; PhD, Indiana University) is a postdoctoral fellow in the Marketing Department of the Warrington College of Business Administration at the University of Florida. His research interests focus broadly on the social and meta-cognitive processes that underlie human behavior, and his research offers specific contributions to the areas of attitudes/attitude change, attitude strength, self-regulation, and choice behavior. His work has appeared in various outlets, including the *Journal of Marketing Research*, the *Journal of Personality and Social Psychology*, and the *Journal of Experimental Social Psychology*. He enjoys watching soccer, football, and surfing—although most especially basketball—and remains an avid fan of the Indiana University Hoosiers, the Jacksonville Jaguars, and Kelly Slater.

T. Bettina Cornwell (PhD, University of Texas) is professor of marketing and sport management at the University of Michigan. Prior to joining the School of Kinesiology at the University of Michigan, she was pro-fessor and cluster leader in marketing at the University of Queensland in Australia. Her research focuses on marketing communications and consumer behavior, especially with regard to sport marketing and inter-national and public policy issues. Her articles on the topics of sponsorship-linked marketing have appeared in the *Journal of Advertising, Journal of the Academy of Marketing Science, Journal of Consumer Research*, and *Psychology and Marketing*.

R. Zachary Finney is associate professor of marketing at the Mitchell College of Business at the University of South Alabama. He earned a doc-toral degree in marketing from the University of Alabama in 2001. Dr. Finney's research in the areas of marketing strategy and sports has been published in journals, including *Journal of Business Research, Journal of Advertising Research, Journal of Marketing Theory and Practice*, and *Marketing Management Journal*, among others.

Dan A. Fuller is a professor of economics in the John B. Goddard School of Business and Economics, Weber State University, Ogden, Utah. His research interests include topics related to the economics of industry and education in economics. His research has been published in various journals, including *The Rand Journal of Economics, Energy Economics, Eastern Economic Review,* and *Journal of Economic Education.* He has been a lifelong skier and a member of the Professional Ski Instructors of America since 1995.

Stephen A. Greyser is the Richard P. Chapman Professor of Business Administration (Marketing/Communications) Emeritus at Harvard Business School (HBS), where he specializes in brand marketing, advertising/corporate communications, sports management, and nonprofit management. A graduate of Harvard College, he has been active at HBS since 1958. His association with the *Harvard Business Review* included 5 years as an editor and research director and subsequently as editorial board secretary and as board chairman. He was also a member of the Harvard Professional Sports Panel, advising undergraduates considering professional sports careers. For 8 years (to 1981) he was executive director of the Marketing Science Institute (MSI), a nonprofit research center for which he continued to serve as a trustee and is now on the Executive Directors Council; he is a charter member of MSI Hall of Fame. In 1993, he was elected Fellow of the American Academy of Advertising, honoring his career-long contributions to advertising and advertising education. In 2009, the Institute for Public Relations honored him with its award for "lifetime contributions to public relations education and research" for his work in corporate communications.

He is responsible for 16 books and monographs; is a frequent contributor to journals on marketing, advertising, and business/consumer attitudes (including 15 *Harvard Business Review* articles and two articles in the *Journal of Advertising Research*); and has published some 300 Harvard case studies. Others among his publications on branding are in *California Management Review, European Journal of Marketing, Journal of Brand Management,* and *Management Decision* (2009).

Greyser's marketing and advertising books include *Advertising in America: The Consumer View* (with Raymond A. Bauer), a study of the public's attitudes toward advertising; three editions of *Cases in Advertising and Communications Management*; several casebooks and other volumes in marketing; and the coauthored *Managing Cooperative Advertising: A Strategic Approach,* the first managerially oriented treatment of this topic. He also developed the *Harvard Business Review* reprint series *Advertising: Better Planning, Better Results.* He co-edited *Improving Advertising*

Budgeting (1999). He has conducted major surveys of executive opinions on advertising and on consumerism for articles in *Harvard Business Review*.

In addition, he has been a leading commentator on advertising's public policy dimensions, having twice been invited to address the Federal Trade Commission on advertising's social impacts. His public service in the advertising field includes two terms as a public member of the National Advertising Review Board, the industry's self-regulatory vehicle. He served on the Advertising Hall of Fame Selection Committee and is a member of the board of judges for ARF's Ogilvy Award for excellence in advertising research.

Professionally, he has been active with many organizations in the marketing field. He has served as a national director of the American Marketing Association (AMA) and chairman of its Publications Board; on the Advisory Council of the Association for Consumer Research; and as past president and chairman of the American Academy of Advertising, the national association of advertising educators. He was the first academic on the board of the Advertising Research Foundation and the first academic to serve as a director of the Advertising Educational Foundation, for which he also chaired its Academic Advisory Committee. He was a trustee of the Society of Consumer Affairs Professionals (SOCAP) Foundation and is a member of the Market Research Council. In addition, he has been a member of the Editorial Board of the *Journal of Marketing*, of *Marketing and Public Policy*, of the AMA management and application journal *Marketing Research*, of the AMA's *Marketing Management*, and of the European-based *Marketing Management* and *International Journal of Sports Marketing and Sponsorship*.

Greyser is a longtime contributor to the nonprofit management field. He was a founding faculty member and research director of the Institute in Arts Administration at Harvard. He coauthored *Cases in Arts Administration*, edited a Harvard University Press collection of international perspectives titled *Cultural Policy and Arts Administration*, and wrote several articles on better marketing of the arts and social programs. He was founding chairman of the Trustees Marketing Committee for the Museum of Fine Arts (Boston), of which he is an overseer, and has served on the Getty Trust's Advisory Committee for the Museum Management Institute. He has spoken to the Association of Art Museum Directors on leadership training and to the Museum Trustee Association. He was also an overseer of WGBH and is a trustee of the Sports Museum (Boston). He has cochaired the HBS Executive Education leadership seminar for nonprofit CEOs/COOs (chief executive officers/chief operating officers).

He conceived and developed the HBS MBA elective course "The Business of Sports," reflecting his lifelong fandom and longtime business involvement in sports. The course has generated over 25 new cases. He is coauthor of a cases-and-text volume, *The Business of Sports* (2006). In March 2006, HBS Working Knowledge published his "Winners and Losers at the Olympics," a treatment of Olympics-based marketing and endorsements. In 2006, he also organized seminars on "The Business of Olympics" and "Fifty Years of Change in Intercollegiate Athletics." He coauthored an article on ambush marketing (*Journal of Advertising Research*, 2005) and on internal company use of sponsorship (*Harvard Business Review*, 2007). For *Harvard China Review*, he organized, moderated, and spoke at seminars in 2006 and 2008 on "Sports in China" and presented "The Branding of China: Beijing 2008" (the role of the Olympics in branding a nation). He has also been on the selection committee for the Boston Red Sox Hall of Fame and wrote their 30th anniversary souvenir pamphlet for "The Impossible Dream" 1967 pennant winners. He was a board member of the BoSox Club, a Red Sox booster organization. He is a former sports broadcaster of three sports and a radio-TV producer, including a Red Sox pregame fan quiz program for 7 years.

He is a frequent speaker, television panelist, and commentator on advertising, consumer marketing, sports management, crisis communications, and consumer issues both in the United States and abroad. His views on the meaning of the Olympics for China were seen by millions in China on CCTV after the August 8, 2008, opening ceremonies.

His most recent HBS MBA teaching assignments included electives on corporate communications and the business of sports. He has also taught executive education sessions in the two HBS nonprofit management and governance seminars and in "Managing Brand Meaning," and has taught at Harvard Divinity School on branding for faith-based entities and at the Education School's Media and American Democracy program on the impacts of media ownership on content. He supervises HBS MBA field studies and is faculty advisor to its Business of Sports Club. He teaches the business of sports at Harvard's Extension School and formerly in Harvard Law School Professor Weiler's Sports and the Law course. Known as "the Cal Ripken of HBS," in over 40 years of teaching he has never missed a class.

Stephen J. Grove (BA, MA, Texas Christian University; PhD, Oklahoma State University) is a professor of marketing at Clemson University. He has published in *Journal of Retailing, Journal of the Academy of Marketing*

Science, Journal of Public Policy and Marketing, Journal of Macromarketing, Journal of Business Research, Journal of Services Research, Journal of Personal Selling and Sales Management, Journal of Advertising, The Service Industries Journal, European Journal of Marketing, Journal of Services Marketing, Managing Service Quality, Marketing Management, Journal of Marketing Education, Journal of Sport Behavior, International Journal of Sport Psychology, and several others. He is coauthor of the text *Interactive Services Marketing* (Houghton-Mifflin), now in its third edition, and the book *Services Marketing Self-Portraits: Introspections, Reflections and Glimpses from the Experts* (AMA). He has also twice served as chair of the AMA Services Marketing Special Interest Group (SERVSIG) and as a member of the AMA's Academic Council. His research interests lie in interactive aspects of the service encounter, environmental issues, and promotion of services.

Edward R. Hirt (BS, University of Dayton; PhD, Indiana University) is a Professor of Psychological and Brain Sciences at Indiana University. He has published in *Journal of Applied Social Psychology, Journal of Consumer Research, Journal of Experimental Psychology: Human Perception and Performance, Journal of Experimental Social Psychology, Journal of Personality and Social Psychology, Personality and Social Psychology Bulletin, Social Cognition,* and several others. He served as associate editor for the *Journal of Personality and Social Psychology* from 2000 to 2005 and is currently an associate editor for the *Journal of Experimental Social Psychology.* His work on fan behavior has been featured in such media sources as *ESPN* magazine, ESPN.com, NPR (National Public Radio), as well as a variety of newspapers (*Boston Globe, New York Times, Washington Post, Chicago Tribune* and *Chicago Sun-Times, Los Angeles Times, Atlanta Journal-Constitution, Philadelphia Inquirer, Wall Street Journal*), and he frequently conducts radio and TV interviews on related topics. He has also served as an expert witness for three trials dealing with trademark infringement. His research interests lie in the areas of self-concept and self-protective behaviors, judgment/decision making, sports psychology, group identification and allegiance, mood effects, attitude change, compliance, and the effects of physical and mental depletion. He enjoys watching baseball, basketball, football, track, and tennis and is an avid fan of the Indiana University Hoosiers, the St. Louis Cardinals, and LeBron James.

Scott Jones (BS, Florida State University; MBA, University of Tampa; PhD, University of Oregon) is an assistant professor of marketing in the

School of Business Administration at Stetson University. His research has been published in numerous marketing/business journals, including the *Journal of Public Policy and Marketing, Journal of Entrepreneurship Education, Journal of Internet Commerce,* and *Sport Marketing Quarterly.* His current research efforts are broadly focused on consumer interpretations of brand alliances; sport marketing issues, specifically spectator rage; and consumer interpretations and response to sport sponsorships.

Ekaterina (Kate) V. Karniouchina is an assistant professor of marketing at Chapman University. Her research interests include a broad range of topics related to media, tourism, and entertainment. Karniouchina's research concentrates on interdisciplinary issues, in particular, she aims to improve managerial decision making by synthesizing insights from marketing, finance, and strategy domains. Her research has been published in various academic journals, such as the *Journal of Marketing, Journal of Product Innovation Management, Marketing Letters,* and the *European Journal of Operational Research.*

Pamela A. Kennett-Hensel is professor of marketing at the University of New Orleans. Dr. Kennett-Hensel's research interests include sport and event marketing, services marketing, corporate social responsibility, and the impact of Hurricane Katrina-induced stress on consumer behavior. Her research has been published in such journals as *Marketing Letters, Journal of Business Research, Journal of Services Marketing, Journal of Business and Industrial Marketing, Journal of Marketing Education, Journal of Customer Service in Marketing and Management,* and *Journal of Targeting, Measurement and Analysis of Marketing.* Kennett-Hensel's research has also been presented at numerous national and international marketing conferences.

Jesse King attended Montana State University in Bozeman, where he studied marketing and psychology. Before beginning his doctoral degree, he worked in industry as an ethnographic researcher for a product development company, contributing to the design and usability of numerous medical, scientific, and consumer products. He is currently a doctoral candidate at the University of Oregon, where his research focuses on new product development, decision making, product innovation, and sports marketing.

Lada Helen V. Kurpis (PhD, University of Oregon) is an assistant professor of marketing in the School of Business Administration, Gonzaga

University. Her research interests include cross-cultural differences in consumer behavior, perception of foreign brands, influence of social values on sport consumption, and business ethics.

Russell Lacey is associate professor of marketing at the University of New Orleans. He received his doctoral degree in marketing from the University of Alabama in 2003. Prior to beginning his academic career, Lacey gained more than 12 years of marketing experience, holding a variety of corporate marketing positions for Baylor Health Care System and Blue Cross and Blue Shield of Kansas City. Dr. Lacey's research has been published in many peer-reviewed marketing journals, including *Journal of Service Research, Journal of Business Research, Marketing Letters, Journal of Advertising Research, Journal of Marketing Theory and Practice, Journal of Business and Industrial Marketing, Journal of Consumer Marketing, Journal of Relationship Marketing,* and *Health Marketing Quarterly,* among others.

Seung Pil Lee is a doctoral student in sport management at the University of Michigan, Ann Arbor. His research interests include sport sponsorship marketing and sport sponsorship public policy for sustainable development. Seung Pil Lee earned a master's degree in sport management at the Ohio State University and a bachelor's degree in statistics at Korea University.

Tamara Masters is a doctoral student in marketing in the David Eccles School of Business, University of Utah. Her research interests include consumer behavior, specifically judgment and decision making, as well as health-related consumer issues. Her previous industry experience includes consulting domestically and internationally for firms in retail, sports, health care, and high-tech arenas.

Scott Owen is a doctoral candidate at the University of Oregon. Prior to that, he earned his MBA at the University of Missouri and worked as a marketing researcher. His research interests include sustainability and new product innovation.

Gregory M. Pickett (BS, MBA, PhD, Oklahoma State University) is professor and chair of Clemson University's Department of Marketing. His research has been widely published in numerous marketing/business journals, including *Journal of Business Research, Journal of Services Research, Journal of Services Marketing, Services Industry Journal, Journal* *of Marketing Education, Journal of Advertising, European Journal of Marketing, Journal of Personal Selling and Sales Management, Sport Marketing Quarterly,* and *Journal of Public Policy and Marketing.* Pickett has served as the chair of the AMA Sport and Event Special Interest Group (SPORTSIG). His current research efforts are focused on sport marketing issues, specifically spectator rage; the downside of sponsoring teams and/or individual players that engenders strong feelings among fans; and the perceived pricing fairness of sport concessions.

Thomas J. Reynolds is a retired professor emeritus from the School of Management at the University of Texas (Dallas). During his academic career, he served on the faculties of the University of California (Berkeley), Michigan State University, and the University of Notre Dame. His academic career spans three areas: mathematical statistics, psychology, and marketing, with publications in *Psychometrika, Multivariate Behavioral Research, Applied Psychological Measurement, Organizational Behavior and Human Decision Processes, Psychology and Marketing, Journal of Marketing Research, Journal of Business Research, Journal of Consumer Research, Journal of Public Policy and Marketing, International Journal of Research in Marketing,* and the *Journal of Advertising Research.* Reynolds was on the 1966 Notre Dame national championship team.

Florian Riedmueller (PhD, University of German Federal Armed Forces in Munich) is a professor of marketing at the Georg Simon Ohm University in Nuremberg, Germany, prior to which he was professor of sports management at the Ostfalia University in Salzgitter. Before beginning his academic career, he acquired six years of marketing experience, holding a variety of marketing positions in the sporting goods industry with Adidas and Nike. He is editor of the *German Management-Handbook: Sport-Marketing* (second release in 2008) and has published in several German marketing journals. His research focuses on sport marketing and marketing communication.

Debra L. Scammon is the Emma Eccles Jones Professor of Marketing in the David Eccles School of Business, University of Utah. Her primary research interests relate to consumers' ability to navigate in the marketplace. Recent work has focused on consumers' perceptions of and reactions to risk, especially risk-protective behaviors. Current projects relate to recovery from disasters, consumer coping, and the inclusion of a broad set of stakeholders in the development of sustainable marketing strategy.

Scammon's research has been published in *Journal of Marketing, Journal of Public Policy and Marketing, Journal of Advertising, Journal of Business Research,* and *Journal of Consumer Affairs.* Scammon is an avid skier and enjoys traveling abroad.

John Tripodi is the managing director of Twenty3 Sport + Entertainment, a sport and entertainment strategic consultancy based in Melbourne, Australia. He previously held senior marketing and general management positions with Mars Inc. and the L'Oreal Group. Tripodi has a bachelor of commerce degree from the University of Melbourne and first class honors in marketing from Monash University. His sponsorship research has been published in numerous international journals.

1

Introduction
The Study of Sports and Events Consumer Behavior

Jesse King, Lynn R. Kahle, and Angeline G. Close

The integration of marketing principles and theory in the study of sport and sport event consumption and sport promotion has generated an increasing number of insights. Coinciding with this budding union, a mounting volume of literature has begun to detail the special aspects inherent in the sport and sport event consumption experience. This research is now more important than ever as the amount of money spent on sports, events, and sports marketing has escalated over the last several decades to position the sports industry as a major segment of the U.S. economy ("Advertise With Us," 2009).

In this introduction, we first consider the special attributes that distinguish sport and sport event consumption from a consumer perspective. An accompanying discussion outlines the theoretical underpinnings that give rise to these distinctions. The second section focuses on the status of sport consumer behavior research. Evidence shows that the study of sport consumption has the potential to contribute to consumer behavior knowledge in general, but that it also warrants study as a discipline in its own right. The third section presents a conceptual overview of the use of sport and sporting events as a promotional tool. After reviewing current sponsorship theory, we conclude that the particular attributes that help to define sport consumption also underlie its capacity to be employed in event marketing and the promotion of other goods and services. Current research into the impact of event sponsorship on brand image and firm value is also considered. Recommendations for advancing the study of sport and sport event consumer behavior are interspersed throughout the text. Finally, we introduce the sections of this book.

Attributes That Characterize Sport Consumption

Sports and Sporting Event Consumption: Intensity and Self-Definition

A number of dimensions separate sports and sporting event consumption from other consumption experiences. Fundamentally, sport is a form of nonfiction entertainment that unfolds in real time. The consumption of sport encompasses both the viewing of sports action in the attendance of a live event and the consumption of sport through traditional and new media (Shoham & Kahle, 1996). In addition, the concept includes actual participation in sporting activities (cf. Funk, 2008). This broad definition encompasses participation in sporting competition against rivals, such as in cycling, tennis, or soccer, but it also includes a fan's participation in or viewing of sporting activities, such as snowboarding, skiing, hunting, climbing, and rafting, that challenge the participant but whose challengers are often intrinsic or ambiguous (Shoham, Rose, & Kahle, 1998).

Sports can be distinguished from other forms of consumption, less in form than by degree. Although the sporting experiences share common elements found among other forms of experiential consumption and entertainment, they differ in magnitude along two primary axes. Both the level of emotion and depth of affiliation found in sport consumption often transcend other types of consumption. Sports have the potential to fuel our fantasies and dreams (Jensen, 1999; Preuss & Troelsen, 2010). Because of these differences, the study of sport consumption deserves more focused research in its own right (Kahle & Riley, 2004).

Self-Concept, Sports, and Sporting Events

A particular person's self-concept can be composed of many components. For example, a person's profession, faith, and gender each have a varying influence on how a person defines who he or she is. Further, the contribution of each influence may fluctuate depending on the context. This patchwork of social memberships and the importance given to each influence underlies many of the conceptions individuals have about who they are and how they should behave (Hogg & Abrams, 1988). Few associations inform an individual's self-concept to the extent found in sports. Only fundamental affiliations such as professions, family, and culture rival the importance of sport in many people's lives. Fans define themselves as supporters of teams and as individual athletes. Self-definition through sports is apparent in the many significant social categorizations related to sports affiliations. Consider the importance to many people of defining themselves as a hunter, cycler, fisher, runner, NASCAR (National Association for Stock Car Auto Racing) fan, football fan, snowboarder, or skier. This self-realization often begins in childhood or adolescence. Evidence of the importance sport consumers place on these associations can be found in the broadcast images of fans with letters painted on their chest, the prevalence of team logos affixed to supporters' cars, and the multitude of team and athletic merchandise purchased each year by sport consumers ("Advertise With Us," 2009). Whole patterns of values and lifestyles can cluster around sports and fan bases (Kahle, Duncan, Dalakas, & Aiken, 2001).

Sport consumption serves as a means of self-definition partly because sport presents challenges that help individuals determine their own limits while providing accessible comparisons to others. Through participation in games and sports as children, we begin to develop an understanding of our relative strengths and weaknesses; however, the role of sports in an individual's social self-concept is not limited to actual participation. Fans also view and attend sporting events and reference their affiliations to specific teams, sports, and athletes to inform their self-concept (Funk, 2008; Kelley & Tian, 2005; Madrigal, 2004; Madrigal & Dalakas, 2008). The affiliation consumers have to the sports they view or consume can act to fulfill needs for inwardly directed feelings of belonging and self-understanding as well as outward social expression of distinctiveness (Brewer, 1991; Troelsen, 2007).

The intensity of consumer affiliation with sports and sporting events exists along a continuum. As fans become more involved with a sport, the consumption experience can become increasingly prominent in their definition of self. Funk (2008) presented a hierarchy of sports consumption stages by which a consumer first becomes aware of a sport, then develops an attraction to the sport. As the hierarchy progresses, consumers become increasingly attached, defining themselves in terms of their relation to the sport. In the final level, the consumer forms an allegiance to the sport, internalizing the values of the sport, and continuously draws on his or her relation with the sport in the course of everyday life.

A similar pattern has been developed, using functional theory (Kelman, 1958), to understand fan motives and attitudes (Bee & Kahle, 2006; Kahle, Kambara, & Rose, 1996). Initially, weakly associated fans may turn out in support of local sports teams as an act of public compliance or internal obligation. The early stages of affiliation with a sport are often the result of normative social expectations of a desired group. As fans develop positive attitudes toward the sport over repeated exposures, their relation to the sport undergoes a transition. Fans progress from attending events because of private feelings of obligation to support a team and public displays to the broader community to which they feel affiliated, into an intrinsically rewarding part of their self-concept. The internalization of a fan's membership among a group of supporters or participants leads many sport consumers to use that membership as an outlet for distinguishing themselves as an individual. Thus, a consumer's involvement with sports can function for identification as a means of self-understanding, of fostering intragroup relationships, and of expressing one's self as a special individual by emphasizing intergroup differences.

Identification and Internalization

The functional model of sport fan motivation (Kahle et al., 1996) also describes internalization of the values of a sport by which consumers adopt a common set of beliefs and values shared by members of the particular sport consumption community (Jones, Bee, Burton, & Kahle, 2004; Shoham & Kahle, 1996). These attributes and the meanings they convey about a member's identity are created in sport from the ongoing communal development of sport narrative. All sports have dramatic histories shaped by stories of accomplishments, misfortunes, and intrigue among teams, coaches, and individual athletes (cf. Deighton, 1992). For highly identified and internalized fans, access to these meanings is gained with an increasing knowledge of the past history and present challenges that exist in their favored sports (Kelley & Tian, 2005). As a consequence of developing an understanding of the symbolic meanings affixed to particular players, teams, and sports, consumers employ these meanings to develop their own self-definitions (Kahle et al., 1996) and to express desired attributes to others.

Consumers rely on their affiliations with sports to express aspects of their self-concept to others. The sporting equipment and licensed paraphernalia industries totaled $47.76 billion in 2008 in the United States ("Advertise With Us," 2009), with many of those sales for items not actually used in sport competition. Fans wear jerseys and other sports-related merchandise both to express their membership to a group of supporters and to distinguish themselves as individuals with special preferences and characteristics. The meanings conveyed by using such symbolic attire extends beyond the current standings of the team during the season. The dramatic decline and eventual discontinuance of jersey sales following allegations of illegal behavior by Michael Vick (Weisman, 2003; WSBTV, 2007) demonstrated that the image consumers associate with athletes extends beyond their athletic performances.

The three main ascending levels of involvement in functional theory—compliance, identification, and internalization—correspond to the three macrotheories of psychology: behaviorism, neopsychoanalysis, and humanism. The fact that different fans relate to sport at different levels implies that dealing with those fans may require different theories. The way to reach fans whose connection with a sport is based on compliance will require different approaches and different theories from dealing with internalized fans.

The Social Role of Sports Consumption

Consumption of sports is often a social activity. Sports bring people together in supporting a team with the common goal of winning. During the consumption of a sport experience, the presence of others is important for enjoyment of the game and in the production of the overall experience (Deighton, 1992; Kelley & Tian, 2005). The collective cheers and admonishments of a crowd amplify the suspense of a competition. Sport provides an opportunity to socialize with others and to work together in the production of a shared experience (Kahle, Aiken, Dalakas, & Duncan, 2003). These shared experiences further provide fans common ground for establishing and maintaining relationships. The stories that result from sports dramas provide ubiquitous topics of conversation, about which almost all members of society have at least some knowledge (Kahle, Elton, & Kambara, 1997).

The social aspects of sports help define both inter- and intrapersonal relationships. Fans who support the same team may feel a bond with other fans of that team. People united at tailgate parties or skyboxes use sport to activate their interpersonal relations and business dealings (Kahle et al., 1997). The golf course can sometimes replace the boardroom as the preferred venue for negotiating a contract.

Sports and Self-Esteem

The level of affiliation sports consumers feel toward the teams, sports, and athletes they support have implications for the attributions that are made about the events that unfold on the field. A long-standing finding is that fans of winning teams tend to bask in the reflected glory (BIRG) of the team's accomplishments (Cialdini et al., 1976). Following a victory, Cialdini et al. (1976) found that fans are more likely to wear team paraphernalia and refer to the accomplishment in inclusive, first-person terminology, such as "We won!" Conversely, the opposing phenomena of cutting off reflected failure (CORF) occurs when a favored team suffers a loss (Snyder, Lassegard, & Ford, 1986). Fans CORF in an effort to disassociate and to protect themselves from the loss. As such, those fans affiliated with losing teams are more likely to reference the team in the third person (e.g., "They lost!"; Cialdini et al., 1976). The BIRGing and CORFing phenomena have been conceptualized as methods of enhancing and protecting self-esteem, respectively (Cialdini et al., 1976; Dalakas, Madrigal, & Anderson, 2004; Snyder et al., 1986).

The extent to which sport consumers BIRG and CORF further appears to be moderated by the level of affiliation felt toward a team. Wann and Branscombe (1995) demonstrated that, although highly self-defined sports fans engaged in more BIRGing behavior than fans with lower levels of identification following a win, those same highly identified individuals did not CORF to the same extent as lesser-identified fans following a loss. Several possible explanations have been suggested for this result. In one view, more highly identified fans hold their relation to the team as an integral part of their self-concept. These fans use BIRGing as a way to boost self-esteem by reinforcing their association with the winning team; however, CORFing is a devaluation of the team, and any distancing by highly identified fans would be equal to a devaluation of the self; hence, such actions are circumscribed. Only people who hold a weak attachment with a team would be likely to CORF because such distancing poses little risk to their self-concept (Wann, 1990). A complementary explanation holds that highly identified fans of a defeated team may refrain from CORFing because they see the potential for their team to improve in the future (Madrigal, 2004). Additional differences in the perception of inter- versus intragroup members and the attributions assigned to team actions are also moderated by the level of team identification (see Madrigal, 2004; Madrigal & Dalakas, 2008; Wann & Branscombe, 1995). Overall, it appears that as a sport becomes a more important part of a person's self-concept, individuals have greater difficulty distancing themselves from the fates that befall their team. For people who are more highly identified fans, evaluations and attributions regarding their favored team appear to become biased as if they were evaluations of the self rather than evaluations of a separate other. This merging of self-identity with that of the team has a number of interesting research implications, which could greatly benefit from continued empirical investigation.

Sports, Sporting Events, and Emotion

The hedonic and emotional nature of sports has been repeatedly documented in research. Hirschman and Holbrook (1982) reported on the fantasy, multisensory, and emotive nature of hedonic experiences and noted that each of these aspects is readily found in sports consumption. In many respects, attendance at sporting events and participation in sport serves as the prototypical representation of experiential consumption. The close association many fans feel toward the teams they support combined with the inherently competitive nature of sport meld to produce strong emotions among fans. This extreme emotional intensity is another aspect that separates sport consumption from other forms of consumption.

The consumption of sports is inexorably laced with emotion. Anxiety, beauty, uncertainty, hope, and the drama associated with a struggle to achieve the restricted outcome of winning or witnessing a win underlie the appraisals that drive the often-intense emotions that fans experience during and subsequent to sport consumption (Hirschman & Holbrook, 1982; Jones et al., 2004; Madrigal & Dalakas, 2008). These emotions cover a wide gamut of both positive and negative emotions. The ability of the sporting context to elicit emotion has attracted consumer behavior researchers investigating the pathology leading to their elicitation. The inherent richness of sporting contexts has been exploited to study fan rage, shame, joy, euphoria, awe, pride, gratitude, suspense, schadenfreude, anger, fear, and relief, among others. Sporting events have also been used as a context for exploring distinctions in the role of attributions and appraisals in the elicitation of emotions (Madrigal, 2008).

Suspense fuels much of the emotional intensity that surrounds sport consumption. Conceptually, suspense arises from a fan's concern over the possible outcome of an unresolved event (Zillmann, 1996). The enjoyment that fans experience from suspense may be the direct result of relief felt following the successful resolution of a contest. Thus, the emotions experienced during sport consumption and at sporting events are partially responsible for the enjoyment of the experience. Winning by a preferred team or the personal accomplishments of an athletic participant can trigger feelings of enjoyment and euphoria resulting from relief. In contrast, disappointment, anger, and frustration can arise following defeat or witnessing defeat.

Although the role of emotion in sport is well documented, less-empirical evidence surrounds the heightened intensity of emotions experienced from sports consumption in contrast to other products; however, conceptualizations of sport consumption consistently suggest that the emotions experienced by fans during and following a sporting event can be extremely intense (Madrigal, 2004). Evidence of these emotional extremes can be seen in the requirements for security features enacted during live events. Large professional sporting events routinely hire security personnel and often implement physical barriers, such as moats, in an effort to separate fans from each other and from the action on the field. For example, there are moats surrounding soccer fields in Brazil and Germany. As another example, the University of Georgia football stadium has "the Hedges" to separate emotional fans from the athletes.

The competitive nature of sports often requires an antipodal assignment of victory and defeat. Riots and citywide celebrations following important victories suggest that the intense emotion experienced from viewing a sporting event continues well beyond the confines imposed by the game clock, although more research is needed to understand fully why the intensity of these emotions often transcend the ones found in other consumption contexts. The key to effective sports and event marketing is to harness this arousal and direct it to rub off onto sponsors' agendas.

The valence of emotions experienced during and following a competition depend on the team (or athlete) a consumer chooses to support. These contrasting expressions of emotions, between those fans supporting winning versus losing teams, demonstrate the dramatic influence of appraisals on the elicitation of emotion.

The BIRGing and CORFing phenomena appear prevalently in sports because of a combination of elements special to the sport consumption experience. First, expressions of BIRGing and CORFing are driven by appraisals based on a fan's affiliation with each team or performer. The stronger an affiliation, the more *identified* the fan, the stronger the BIRGing phenomena after a win, and the weaker the CORF following a loss (Wann, 1990). Second, BIRGing and CORFing arise from *emotions* experienced as a consequence of winning or losing (Dalakas et al., 2004). Individuals tend to distance themselves from negative emotions and seek positive emotions. Supporters of winning teams have elevated moods following a game (Hirt, Zillmann, Erickson, & Kennedy, 1992) as well as greater reported happiness (Slone, 1989). An opposite pattern of emotions has been observed in fans following a losing performance, with increased anger and suppressed mood evidenced even on the physiological level.

Summary: Special Aspects of Sport Consumption

Sport consumption is a special form of consumption distinguished both by the intensity of emotions and by the heightened level of self-definition found among followers. This section has outlined research documenting both of these distinguishing aspects. The next section suggests that these same attributes that differentiate sport consumption also create two opportunities for researchers. First, sport and sporting events usually provide a powerful context for developing and testing theories that inform the field of consumer behavior in general. Second, sport consumption and consumer behavior in the context of events merit additional research as a field of study distinct from other hedonic consumption experiences.

The Study of Sport Consumption

Consumer behavior researchers have only recently begun to fully consider theories pertaining to low-involvement products. The majority of studies remain applicable only to fairly high-involvement products. In reality, most purchase occasions and attitude changes occur under conditions of low involvement. Although many brand managers would like to think that their brand of toothpaste is selected based on the deeply held beliefs of a consumer, the principal drivers are more often contextual. In contrast to the low level of involvement displayed in many purchase decisions, sport consumers are often highly involved. Linking a lower-involvement product with a higher-involvement sporting activity can sometimes cause a rub-off effect in which the product comes to share the compelling lifestyle attributes that attract fans to sport.

Much could be gained from testing and validating current and future consumer behavior and marketing theories in the sports and sporting event context. The majority of consumer behavior research is conducted under mundane conditions in carefully controlled environments. While studies involving sports can also be closely controlled, they have the added benefit of allowing the researcher to elicit strong emotions and demonstrate the effects of varying levels of involvement. The context offers the potential to test theories under extreme conditions to explore for possible boundary conditions. Although sports offer the ability to stretch some aspects of consumer behavior theory, they also share many of the elements found among all service and experiential products. Sports are also intangible, inseparable, variable, and perishable, making findings from sports largely generalizable to other contexts.

Sports have been employed to study discrete emotions (Madrigal, 2008) and the role of values (Kahle et al., 2001). They have also been used to study message source effects on attitude change (e.g., Close, Finney, Lacey, & Sneath, 2006; Haugtvedt & Kasmer, 2008; Kahle & Homer, 1985; Kahle & Kahle, 2006) and numerous other topics.

While the study of consumer behavior phenomena as applied to the sport context has supplied considerable insight, the potential for sports consumer behavior as an independent field of study has yet to be fully realized. The special aspects of sports consumption signify a distinction separating sport behavior from the mainstream theories of marketing and consumer behavior. These differences create fertile ground, much of which remains to be explored. Future research must acknowledge the special aspects of consuming sport and seek to advance understanding of sport consumption behavior as a field in its own right, tangential to the study of consumer behavior as a whole. If the study of the consumer behavior of sport is to become a legitimized, independent field, researchers must be willing to study the consumptive phenomena that exist only in the sports and sporting event context and explore topics and constructs that are specific to sports.

Evidence of sport consumer behavior and consumer behavior at sporting events as viable fields and contexts already exists. Kelley and Tian (2005) suggested that sports marketing will develop as a field when it begins to develop its own metrics. A number of such metrics focused specifically on assessing different aspects of the sport consumption experience already exist. Sukhdial, Aiken, and Kahle (2002), for example, have proposed a scale measuring a fan's perspective on sports as either a product or a process. Respondents were categorized as either appreciating traditional notions of sportsmanship such as loyalty to a team, altruism, and cooperation or as subscribing to an emerging view of sports in which winning at any cost is valued over fair play. In addition, Mahoney, Madrigal, and Howard (2000) introduced a scale to measure a fan's psychological commitment to a sports team. Pons et al. (2006) have introduced a scale to segment fans based on sensation, cognition, and socialization motives, and

Madrigal (2006) has introduced a scale to measure aspects of the sports consumption experience. Kahle et al. (1996) developed theoretically based scales to measure fan motivation. A number of other scales have also been developed to give researchers the tools needed to measure constructs of interest; however, more work remains to be done.

The Role of Sports in Event Marketing and Promotion

Thus far, the special aspects of sports consumption have been referenced only in their potential to inform an academic understanding of consumer behavior. This final section considers the remarkable use of sport as an event marketing strategy and a promotional tactic.

In many respects, the application of marketing to sports is intuitive. Sports managers can implement classic segmentation and differentiation strategies to increase sales of tickets and sporting event programming. Yacht racing appeals more to wealthy fans, bowling typically to less-privileged fans. Figure skating appeals more to women, auto racing more to men. The New England Patriots are more popular in New England than in Miami. The sports product can be modified to satisfy the demands of consumers by adjusting elements of the service environment, such as the seating or JumboTron screens (Kahle et al., 2003), the ticket prices, or even the game itself. A rational case can also be made for the use of professional sports teams or athletes in the promotion of sports equipment or merchandise. For example, an obvious relation exists in the leveraging of a fan's involvement with a professional NASCAR team to promote sales of the brand of car used in the race; however, many corporate sponsors are often far removed from the actual competition of the sport. Viagra sponsors a NASCAR team, as does Pedigree dog food, and Office Depot. Many sporting event sponsorships are abstruse in that the brands and products that are promoted often have little to do with the sport. Most Fortune 500 companies engage in some form of sports marketing, even if they have few products necessarily linked to sports.

Sporting event sponsorships are often expensive. Official Olympic sponsorships can cost upward of $300 million over a 4-year period (Davis, 2008) when fully activated; however, the high costs of many sponsorships appear justified as a number of studies have evidenced the positive effects of sponsorship on firm value (Pruitt, Cornwell, & Clark, 2004), on brand recall (Close et al., 2006; Lacey, Close, & Finney, in press; Levin, Joiner, & Cameron, 2001; Sneath, Finney, & Close, 2005), and on purchase intentions

(Close et al., 2006; Lacey et al., in press; Madrigal, 2000). Not only does sporting event sponsorship appear to be highly effective, but also consumers of sport comprise highly desirable demographic segments (Close et al., 2006; Jones et al., 2004), making sponsorship as a promotional tactic even more attractive.

Fundamentally, sports sponsorship involves the sanctioned promotion of the affiliation of a firm with a sports team (Cornwell, Weeks, & Roy, 2005). The initial fee paid by a firm to become a sponsor is often only a small part of the overall cost of activating or leveraging (promoting) the event sponsorship. Firms can spend millions of dollars trying to make their affiliation to a sports team known to consumers. Without proper promotion of the sponsorship, sponsoring firms risk wasting their money on rights fees without fans recognizing them as a sponsor.

Sponsorship has functions beyond simply attracting the awareness of a fan or improving a consumer's attitude toward a firm or product, both domestically and internationally (Cornwell & Maignan, 1998). In much the same way as consumers use their affiliation with a sports team to express elements of their identity to others, firms use sports to communicate aspects of their brand image (Close et al., 2006; Cornwell et al., 2005; Keller, 1993). Athletes and teams transfer meaning and provide information to customers about the products they endorse (Lacey et al., in press; McCracken, 1989). The concept that endorsers are capable of conveying meaningful information forms the basis of the matchup hypothesis (Kahle & Homer, 1985), under which a sponsorship is hypothesized to be most effective when the images of the sport and the sponsoring brand are congruent. This congruency can exist between a sponsor and event (Close et al., 2006; Lacey et al., in press; Roy & Cornwell, 2004), an endorser and brand (Boyd & Shank, 2004; Schaefer & Keillor, 1997), or the attendee (consumer) and the event (Close, Krishen, & LaTour, 2009). An incongruent matchup produces only weak associations in memory and is less likely to be remembered, although there is some indication that a moderately incongruent fit between the sporting event and sponsor, if resolved, may also be effective because the effort needed to overcome the incongruence results in more elaborate processing (Homer & Kahle, 1986; Mandler, 1982). The promotion of a sponsorship makes consumers aware of the relationship, but the structure of the sponsorship and the activation messaging should strive to highlight areas of congruence between the positive aspects of the sport and the brand to increase the effectiveness of the sponsorship (Becker-Olsen & Simmons, 2002; Close et al., 2009; Weeks, Cornwell, & Humphrys, 2006).

A number of other theories have also been forwarded to explain why sponsorship is effective. Cornwell et al. (2005) reviewed the psychological mechanics of sponsorship and noted that, although much remains to be understood about the nature of sponsorship, the majority of theories currently rely on some form of associative memory model (see Keller, 1993). Associative network models conceptualize memory as a network of associations linking concepts to one another with varying strength. Companies use sponsorships as a persuasive tactic in an effort to develop or strengthen favorable associations, in memory, between a sport property (team, player, league, etc.) and a product or brand. One associative memory theory commonly applied to sponsorship is balance theory (Heider, 1958), which suggests that the positive attitudes held by the consumer toward a sports team will balance out less-positive attitudes initially held toward the sponsoring firm when a relation between the firm and the sport is made known. The balancing of attitudes between the two nodes should lead to an improvement in the consumer's attitude toward the sponsoring firm. The beneficial effects of sponsorship congruency also fit nicely into an associative memory model as congruent sponsorships would be expected to more easily fit into existing associative mental networks.

A social perspective suggests that highly involved fans may also choose to patronize firms that sponsor sporting events and teams in an effort to conform to group norms (Close et al., 2009; Hogg & Abrams, 1988; Madrigal, 2004). That is, sports fans who value their relation to the sponsored team may feel social pressure to purchase products that are consistent with their perceived stereotypes regarding the types of products a loyal fan ought to purchase. The stereotypic norms referenced by the consumer are likely to be influenced by other group members and outside communications from sponsors with goals and values that appear to be aligned with (in support of) those of the team. This "referent informational influence" perspective has been supported by Madrigal (2000, 2001) in two studies, both of which found evidence that group norms strongly effect purchase decisions regarding a sponsor's products among those fans most highly identified with a team.

Both of these perspectives suggest that sponsorships require pervasive communication emphasizing the association between the sponsor and the sport to be persuasive in the mind of the consumer. If the association is not well known, the sponsor has little chance of having the positive associations held toward the sport transfer to the product or in being considered as a normatively correct purchase for a loyal supporter of a team. While conscious awareness of the relation between a sponsor and an event has been shown to improve sponsorship effectiveness, such awareness is not a necessary requirement for sponsorship activities to result in attitude change. In this regard, the combination of the two special attributes separating sport from other forms of consumption (high levels of identification or internalization and emotion) discussed offer a further explanation for why sport sponsorship may be effective.

Live sporting events are entertaining because they provide a blur of activity, captivating both to the packed stadia of loyal fans and to television audiences, who become caught up in the suspense and drama of the moment. Into these emotionally charged environments, highly aroused fans, many of whom consider their support of a team to be an important component of who they are as a person, are presented with suggestions of corporate sponsorship. As a persuasive tactic, sponsorship reaches fans when they are vulnerable because they are both cognitively overwhelmed and socially committed.

The emotional intensity with which fans experience a sporting event has been offered as both a potential facilitator and a possible inhibitor of sponsorship effectiveness. Information-processing theories suggest that increased arousal may facilitate the processing of peripheral information such as sponsorship messaging because fans are more engaged in the event (Kroeber-Riel, 1979). However, if fans are too aroused by the action on the field, they may not have the cognitive resources to process nonessential information (Pavelchak, Antil, & Munch, 1988; Pham, 1992). There may be an optimal (moderate) level of arousal in which the greatest amount of peripheral information is processed (Cornwell et al., 2005). Interestingly, even if highly aroused fans do not form an explicit memory of the sponsorship, it may still have an effect on their attitudes toward the sponsoring brand (Campbell & Kirmani, 2000; Janiszewski, 1990; Pham, 1992).

The actual substance of sponsorship is typically an "impoverished communication stimuli," such as a simple logo or brand name embedded within the event. Because communicative capacity of these messages is minimal, the effects of sponsorship on attitude change are likely to manifest via peripheral route processes (Cornwell et al., 2005; Petty & Cacioppo, 1986). One low-level processing theory, mere exposure effect, suggests that simple repeated exposure, even if subconsciously processed, can produce favorable attitudes toward a stimulus (Zajonc, 1980). Many sponsorships undoubtedly rely on this principle to strengthen brand associations in memory.

Further, many fans may not categorize sponsorship as a persuasive attempt, reducing the likelihood that they will be able to effectively cope with the attempt (see Friestad & Wright, 1994). Most sponsorships are typically less structured and controlled than other forms of promotion in that they are usually embedded within an event (Cornwell et al., 2005). Whereas consumers can easily discriminate between television commercials and television content, sponsorships are more difficult to separate from the actual experience of a sporting event, much in the same way that product placements can be difficult to separate from the media into which they are embedded. The logos of corporate sponsors are not limited to the sidelines and television transitions between replays. They can also be found on the jerseys, hats, and other paraphernalia collected by fans. The ability of a consumer to categorize a sponsorship as a persuasive tactic is further hampered by this extensive emphasis on the relation between the event and the sport. Theorists have suggested that sponsorships are effective partly because of an implied endorsement mechanism (Pracejus, 2004) by which the consumer infers that the sports property has actively engaged in screening or qualifying sponsors. In essence, the consumer infers that any sponsor who is allowed to become an "official partner" of a sport property must be a reputable company. It is as if the team that was paid by the sponsor has in turn endorsed the brand or product as acceptable for its fans. This implied endorsement is likely to extend to other "in-group" members who don paraphernalia with logos in support of their team. Fans who perceive the relation between the sports property and the sponsor as an endorsement of the brand rather than a promotional attempt by the sponsor would be expected to be less able to effectively cope with the attempt. The difference is similar in form to the difference between a salesperson pitching a product and a trusted friend making a recommendation. Consumers are likely to recognize and to actively cope with the former but are expected to subject the latter to less scrutiny. Currently, much further research is needed to understand better the role of persuasion knowledge in sponsorship. Cornwell et al. (2005) shared this view when they noted that current research has not "considered how individuals perceive sponsorship and related collateral communications as persuasion attempts." They further claimed that, "This is a potential valuable area of future research" (p. 39), a perspective that we would echo.

Other sports-specific research topics also exist beyond sport sponsorship, such as the somewhat-underappreciated topic of sports talk (Kahle et al., 1997). Talking about sports provides a common topic that can be helpful in establishing relationships. These conversations are typically low risk and can serve as an entry point for establishing a basis of shared values and beliefs among potential business partners. Although sports talk is not always persuasive, it does serve to increase each participant's knowledge of the other and helps to facilitate relationships. Kahle et al. (1997) noted that many businesses prize the NFL (National Football League) skyboxes because they facilitate relationship marketing efforts, allowing prospective partners to rehearse interaction patterns before engaging in more formal business discussions. The level at which these "sports talk" discussions occur is influenced by the extent to which social values are shared among individuals as well as their internalization of values shared with the sports object; however, sports talk also extends beyond one-on-one communication to include other forms of media and social commentary (e.g., radio sports shows, Internet fan sites). This sharing of information facilitates the diffusion of current, historical, and symbolic sports knowledge, which consumers use to adjust their relation with the sport. It is also likely that sports talk plays a role in the continuation of normative social pressures felt by the as-yet-unaffiliated consumers. Sports talk represents just one of the many other sports-specific marketing and consumer behavior research topics remaining to be explored.

The purpose of this overview is to provide an outline of the special attributes that separate the sports consumptive experience from other consumption experiences. Sports consumption is special both in the level of self-concept that consumers have to sports, teams, and athletes and in the intensity and emotions that surround the consumption experience. A discussion of the theoretical mechanisms that underlie both of these attributes was presented, as was a small sampling of topics that provide empirical support for these ideas. Finally, the psychology of sport sponsorship and the use of sport as a promotional tool were examined. The high levels of identification, internalization, and emotion that define the sport experience are likely to influence consumers' processing of sponsorship-related information.

Sport consumer behavior represents a fascinating and fertile area of research with surprising depth. Although the tendency in the past has been to characterize this field as a subdiscipline or specific instance of consumer behavior, the research presented demonstrates that the study of sport consumption is a topic area deserving study in its own right. Although much of the current theory has been coopted from other disciplines, much could be gained from the development of theory specific to the sports context. The development of native theory has the potential to reverse this trend, feeding findings from the sport context back into more generalized disciplines. One prime example is the BIRGing phenomenon (Cialdini et al., 1976), which was originally observed and studied among sports fans but has influenced social psychology theory more generally.

Because sport consumption lies at the intersection of both social and emotional acmes, it offers the potential for uncovering a number of interesting phenomena and equally interesting theoretical explanations.

The Chapters of This Book

The chapters of this book make significant additional contributions to the understanding of consumer behavior in sports and events marketing. Here, we comment on the issues raised by these chapters.

Section I: Influencing Behaviors in Society and Sports

Chapter 2: A Framework for Measuring the Contributions of Sport to Society: Actors, Activities, and Outcomes

Although contemporary businesses seek to expand their contribution to society, these firms must maintain a delicate dance of contributing to society while maintaining utmost responsibility to their financial stakeholders; hence, businesses have a need to align with mutually beneficial partnerships. With this need in mind, in Chapter 2 Lee and Cornwell knit together theories and findings from sport management and consumer behavior marketing in the management, economics, and marketing literatures. In this chapter, Lee and Cornwell blend divergent literatures to portray a macroview of how sport and sports-oriented firms can contribute to society. With a transformative approach, the authors depict how better measurement of intangibles, including image and reputation, can bring about a broader participation of corporate social responsibilities programs and partnerships involving sport. Lee and Cornwell share an analytical framework that includes examination of (a) types of cross-sector relationship mechanisms, (b) motivations and objectives for actors to work together through sport, (c) evaluation of collaborative activity outcomes, and (d) benefits of measurement to actors.

Lee and Cornwell review nine cross-sector relationship mechanisms and discuss the form each takes, noting the power balance suggested in the relationship. The mechanisms covered include philanthropy/patronage, sponsorship, cause-related marketing, brand alliance/cobranding, social partnerships, social alliances, and corporate social responsibility. They then discuss the social contribution of sport and the societal contribution via sport. In sum, sport's contribution to society can take many forms. There is an escalating use of sport as a communications vehicle. In many ways, the already-positive values of sport are utilized in both communication and action.

Chapter 3: The Psychology of Fandom: Understanding the Etiology, Motives, and Implications of Fanship

Any effort to describe the psychology of the sports fan is a complex, multilayered process. In light of this complexity, Hirt and Clarkson contribute Chapter 3 on the fundamental aspects of fandom. First, the authors note the label of "sports fan" along with definitional issues related to sports fandom. The authors discuss a variety of methods and measurement techniques employed to research fanship in the marketing and sports-related literature. Further, Hirt and Clarkson highlight a broad etiology of fanship. Following this review, the authors denote various motivations that underlie sports fanship. When a fan identifies with a favorite player or team, the fan receives both costs and benefits, which the authors discuss. A major contribution of this chapter is a new taxonomy of the fundamental needs by which these various motivations for fanship are categorized. This taxonomy comes with important managerial implications for improving market strategies designed both to escalate commitment from incumbent fans and to entice more consumers to fandom.

Chapter 4: Spectator Rage: An Overview

Customer rage is violent and uncontrolled anger, and in the context of sporting events, customer rage is synonymous with the aggression or verbal or physical behavior intended to control or harm another person (Coakley, 1998). In Chapter 4 on spectator rage, Jones, Grove, and Pickett note that this form of rage incorporates a range of consumer behaviors. The authors overview both physical and nonphysical behaviors, including taunting (e.g., opposing players, coaches, or officials); physical acts (e.g., throwing objects on the field or at other spectators); destruction of the setting; and obscene gestures. Although such rage occurs in many industries, acts of sports rage at professional events are often subject to mass media hype, scrutiny, and even notoriety. In turn, publicized rage at a sporting event is a catalyst for many other actions as precursors for all other sport-related products and business decisions, including endorsement contracts, broadcast rights, event sponsorships, and licensing agreements. Such important entities are contingent on a successful professional execution of the sporting event; hence, a nonprofessional or publicized act of rage undermines the professional standard and prestige often attributed to sporting events. In turn, acts of rage bring negative consequences to the stakeholders of the team and damage spectator sport. Namely, fan rage can harm fan loyalty and repeat patronage (e.g., in the form of season ticket sales) and extended contractual agreements (e.g., event sponsorships and media partnerships) as each is often the subject of considerable media scrutiny. Although sports marketers attempt to prevent fan rage, some motivators of fan rage are inadvertently prompted by sport marketers' desire to hype the events, to provide an intense experience for spectators, and to maximize ticket sales and revenue opportunities. In sum, Jones, Grove, and Pickett discuss various factors that have an impact on spectator rage at professional sporting events. The authors then suggest recommendations on how marketing strategies influence such factors that have an impact on spectator rage. Of particular interest throughout the chapter is how legitimate concerns about spectator rage conflict with the goals of providing a lively, intense, engaging, and exciting atmosphere for event attendees.

Section II: Building Relationships With Consumers Through Sports

Chapter 5: Sports-Related Subculture as a Useful Basis of
Market Segmentation: Insights for Ski Area Managers

While skiing continues to grow, there is intense competition among ski areas, in part intensified by the steady rise of the snowboarding segment. In this chapter, Scammon, Fuller, Karniouchina, and Masters use consumer behavior knowledge to understand trends in the ski industry. The authors conducted a Web-based survey of 792 skiers and snowboarders with participants from skier and snowboarder e-bulletin boards, and Web marshals of skier and boarder clubs, and in person at ski areas in New Zealand, designed to be representative of skiers and boarders in North America, Europe, and Australia/New Zealand. The data were analyzed according to pure skiers versus snowboarders and further broken down as participants who do stunts versus those who do not do stunts. The research showed the relative impact of many consumer-behavior-oriented variables, including motivations to ski or board, risky behaviors, sources of learning, and informal "rules of thumb" on and off the snow.

Although both skiers and snowboarders are learning to share snow, each group maintains recognizable differences in clothing, lingo, and style. On a broader level, snowboarders and skiers maintain different motivations, attitudes, and behaviors related to their sport. Findings showed that boarders are more prone to have experience doing stunts, while over 70% of skiers do not have stunt experience. The stunters tended to crowd in to move up in line more quickly, jump ahead on the top of a run, ignore control signs, and duck under ropes to seek opportunities to get through crowds quickly. Also, boarders tended to let more skilled boarders take the lead. Boarders tended to listen to music while boarding. Boarders, however, did not give beginner boarders more room, in contrast to skiers, who do. In sum, different ways of segmenting users may suggest different strategies for ski areas, event venues, leisure marketers, and retailers, each of whom can leverage this consumer behavior knowledge.

Chapter 6: The Impact of Corporate Social Responsibility on
NBA Fan Relationships: A Conceptual Framework
In this chapter, two marketing scholars with interests in event marketing in the realm of sports (Kennett-Hensel and Lacey) team up with a sports marketing professional (Biggers) with the New Orleans Hornets basketball team. In few areas is consumer social responsibility (CSR) taken more seriously than in the National Basketball Association (NBA). Namely, through its NBA Cares program, the NBA league, along with its teams and players, has donated more than $100 million and over 1 million hours of community service and volunteer work (NBA Cares, 2009). Just as with any for-profit operation, the NBA and its teams strive to balance CSR initiatives against other internal (i.e., players, front office employees, and owners) and external (i.e., fans and customers, community, and environment) stakeholder responsibilities. Kennett-Hensel, Lacey, and Biggers propose the following questions: Does one implement a CSR plan that ultimately leaves all stakeholders better off? How do these initiatives help a team achieve its more financially oriented objectives? To help address these key questions, the authors propose a framework that explains how corporate social responsibility initiatives contribute to the success of NBA teams through better fan relationships. In particular, the efforts of the New Orleans Hornets are highlighted given the authors' familiarity and work experience with this NBA franchise.

Chapter 7: And a Child Athlete Will Save Us: Marketing Psychosocial and
Physical Benefits of Sport to Children, Adolescents, Coaches, and Parents
In a call for growing minds and bodies in the name of health, Andrews shares a chapter that links, in a multitier ecological framework from the perspective of a young person's developmental environment, micro- and macroissues surrounding youth sports participation in the United States.

In addition, Andrews provides a marketing viewpoint and weaves in cues from sociology and psychology on how to encourage children to participate in sports, to become more active, and to get engaged in organized physical activity. Andrews overviews barriers and social challenges to youth-oriented physical fitness. Andrews then covers broad issues surrounding declining sports participation along with ways to increase social dynamics. These methods include improving relationship dynamics with parents, coaches, and other players along with ways to enhance the young athlete's individual and internal dynamics as evidence links improved sports performance (and therefore presumably increased participation) with enhanced self-protective psychological strategies such as self-esteem and self-efficacy.

In sum, Andrews' chapter develops a sense of urgency for children and their parents to become more active in youth sports as a means to help overcome potential obesity epidemics in the United States while improving children's self-esteem, confidence, and efficacy.

Chapter 8: The Motivations Associated With Attendance
and Participation in an Amateur Sporting Event
In Chapter 8, Kurpis and Bozman integrate research on social values and embed research on Hoopfest, a unique basketball sporting event. This chapter gives an overview of sport marketing research on values and motivations for sport participation and spectatorship. Understanding various aspects and properties of social values is a continually ascending domain of sport motivation research. Defined, a *value* is "an enduring belief that a specific mode of conduct or end-state of existence is personally or socially preferred" (Rokeach, 1973, p. 8). Given this definition, understanding values and how values relate to motivation in sports can assist sports marketers to concentrate marketing communications to targeted segments of consumers (Kahle & Xie, 2008). Furthermore, Kurpis and Bozman's research on values enables sports marketers to help design sporting events that best meet the desires of attendees. Long-term outcomes of the research presented in this chapter can help sports marketers to foster sport subcultures and to ensure viability of the promoted sport.

The authors present a case for treating social values (Kahle, 1996) as motivational constructs and thereafter relate these motivational constructs to the consumption of amateur sporting events, specifically Hoopfest, a large amateur basketball tournament. The authors discuss findings from Hoopfest as a means to reveal the utility of using social values to discern the motivations of event participants and spectators. Furthermore, the authors uncover how such an understanding, coupled with articulated community needs, contributed to a successful strategic reorientation of the Hoopfest event. The authors conclude with a discussion of potential outcomes of a values-based strategic reorientation along with recommendations for sports marketers who seek to incorporate an understanding of consumer values into their event-marketing strategies.

Section III: Providing Service to Consumers Through Sports and Event Sponsorship

Chapter 9: Hospitality: A Key Sponsorship Service in Sports Marketing

The growing use of hospitality to leverage sponsorship investments is now thought by some sponsorship experts to differentiate sponsors from each other and, in some cases, to make the difference in measuring return on sponsorship investment. Many people would prefer to avoid a 4-hour meeting with a salesperson but would gladly go to a sporting event with that person for essentially the same purpose. Hospitality is an underresearched but important tool in establishing relationships that characterize sports marketing. Burton, Tripodi, Owen, and Kahle, who represent both the academic and the practitioner sides, take a serious look at hospitality from the perspective of functional motives to guide practitioners and to inspire researchers to heed this growing phenomenon.

Chapter 10: Assessing the Existential Validity of the Bowl Championship Series Rankings

In this chapter, Reynolds presents a meaningful analysis of the controversial topic of the Bowl Championship Series rankings. Reynolds employs an R-methodology to ascertain the series rankings. He presents a strong case for how college football could handle the coronation of its champion in a manner that improves fan perceptions and sense of fairness.

Chapter 11: Service Quality Perceived by Fans at Professional Sporting Events

The authors of various meta-analyses covering all types of sports have classified the factors leading to the success of such an event into the following categories: (a) economic factors (e.g., income, ticket price); (b) sociodemographic factors (e.g., number and composition of spectators at the venue); (c) quality-related factors (e.g., performance of players or teams, comfort of the seats); and (d) residual factors (e.g., weather, time of match).

Riedmueller develops an alternative, theory-driven approach to evaluating the service quality of sporting events called the PROSPORT model. The chapter cogently illustrates how marketing theories can be applied to sports in general, especially to the illustration of quality at professional sporting events.

Chapter 12: Event Marketing and Sponsorship: Lessons
Learned From the Tour de Georgia Cycling Races

Even in difficult economic times, sponsorships continue to grow at a remarkable pace that far exceeds the growth of other integrated marketing communications (IMC) methods (International Events Group, 2009). In spite of the rosy picture, practitioners have begun to raise questions about the effectiveness of sport sponsorships and event marketing amid associated rising cost and sponsorship clutter concerns. So, at present, spending on sport and event marketing continues to increase without sufficient empirical evidence to support such an occurrence.

To help address these issues, in the final chapter, Finney, Lacey, and Close overview event marketing and sports sponsorships with a focus on a compilation of their 5 years of consumer fieldwork at the nation's premier professional cycling event. Specifically, from 2004 to 2008, Finney, Lacey, and Close conducted survey research at the five Tour de Georgia cycling races. Thus far, the five surveys have yielded seven research studies, which are overviewed in this chapter. The authors' research stream begins to move sports sponsorships from lay theories to empirically supported best practices of sports event sponsorship effectiveness. In doing so, new roles of attitude, motivations, emotion, affective forecasting, and cognition/product knowledge are illuminated.

Specifically, in the closing chapter Finney, Lacey, and Close review findings from each Tour de Georgia title sponsorship and synthesize themes. First, the authors provide background on the Tour de Georgia and efforts to gather data at the races. Second, they include an overview and synthesis. Finally, they conclude with suggestions for theory in the realm of consumer behavior and future research directions.

References

Advertise with us—The sports industry. (2009). Retrieved August 25th, 2009, from http://www.sportsbusinessjournal.com/index.cfm?fuseaction=page. feature&featureId=1492

Becker-Olsen, K., & Simmons, C. J. (2002). When do social sponsorships enhance or dilute equity? Fit, message source, and the persistence of effects. In S. M. Broniarczyk & K. Nakamoto (Eds.), *Advances in consumer research* (Vol. 29, pp. 287–289). Provo, UT: Association for Consumer Research.

Bee, C. C., & Kahle, L. R. (2006). Relationship marketing in sports: A functional approach. *Sport Marketing Quarterly, 15*, 101–110.

Boyd, T. C., & Shank, M. D. (2004). Athletes as product endorsers: The effect of gender and product relatedness. *Sport Marketing Quarterly, 13*(2), 82–93.

Brewer, M. (1991). The social self: On being the same and different at the same time. *Personality and Social Psychology Bulletin, 17*, 475.

Campbell, M. C., & Kirmani, A. (2000). Consumers' use of persuasion knowledge: The effects of accessibility and cognitive capacity on perceptions of an influence agent. *Journal of Consumer Research, 27*(1), 69–83.

Cialdini, R., Borden, R., Thorne, A., Walker, M., Freeman, S., & Slone, L. (1976). Basking in reflected glory: Three (football) field studies. *Personality and Social Psychology Bulletin, 34*, 366.

Close, A. G., Finney, R. Z., Lacey, R., & Sneath, J. (2006). Engaging the consumer through event marketing: Linking attendees with the sponsor, community, and brand. *Journal of Advertising Research, 46*, 420–433.

Close, A. G., Krishen, A., & LaTour, M. S. (2009). This event is me!: How consumer-event congruity leverages sponsorship. *Journal of Advertising Research, 49*, 271–284.

Coakley, J. J. (1998). *Sports in society: Issues and controversies.* (6th ed.). St. Louis, MO: Times Mirror/ Mosby.

Cornwell, T. B., & Maignan, I. (1998). An international review of sponsorship research. *Journal of Advertising, 27*, 1–21.

Cornwell, T. B., Weeks, C. S., & Roy, D. P. (2005). Sponsorship-linked marketing: Opening the black box. *Journal of Advertising, 34*(2), 21–42.

Dalakas, V., Madrigal, R., & Anderson, K. (2004). "We are number one!" The phenomenon of basking-in-reflected-glory and its implications for sports marketing. In L. R. Kahle & C. Riley (Eds.), *Sports marketing and the psychology of marketing communication* (pp. 67–69). Mahwah, NJ: Erlbaum.

Davis, J. (2008). *The Olympic game effect.* Hoboken, NJ: Wiley.

Deighton, J. (1992). The consumption of performance. *Journal of Consumer Research, 19*, 362–372.

Friestad, M., & Wright, P. (1994). The persuasion knowledge model: How people cope with persuasion attempts. *Journal of Consumer Research, 21*(1), 1–31.

Funk, D. (2008). *Consumer behaviour in sport and events: Marketing action.* Amsterdam: Butterworth-Heinemann.

Haugtvedt, C. P., & Kasmer, J. A. (2008). Attitude change and persuasion. In C. P. Haugtvedt, P. M. Herr, & F. R. Kardes (Eds.), *Handbook of consumer psychology* (pp. 419–435). New York: Erlbaum.

Heider, F. (1958). *The psychology of interpersonal relations.* New York: Wiley.

Hirschman, E. C., & Holbrook, M. B. (1982). Hedonic consumption: Emerging concepts, methods and propositions. *Journal of Marketing, 46*(3), 92–101.

Hirt, E., Zillmann, D., Erickson, G., & Kennedy, C. (1992). Costs and benefits of allegiance: Changes in fans' self-ascribed competencies after team victory versus defeat. *Journal of Personality and Social Psychology, 63*, 724–738.

Hogg, M., & Abrams, D. (1988). *Social identifications: A social psychology of intergroup relations and group processes.* London: Routledge.

Homer, P. M., & Kahle, L. R (1986). A social adaptation explanation of the effects of surrealism on advertising. *Journal of Advertising, 15*(2), 50–60.

International Events Group. (2009). Retrieved June 2009 from http://www.sponsorship.com

Janiszewski, C. (1990). The influence of nonattended material on the processing of advertising claims. *Journal of Marketing Research, 27*, 263–276.

Jensen, R. (1999). The dream society: How the coming shift from information to imagination will transform your business. New York: McGraw-Hill.

Jones, S., Bee, C., Burton, R., & Kahle, L. (2004). Marketing through sports entertainment: A functional approach. In L. J. Shrum (Ed.), *The psychology of entertainment media: Blurring the lines between entertainment and persuasion* (pp. 309–322). Mahwah, NJ: Erlbaum.

Kahle, K. E., & Kahle, L. R. (2006). Sports celebrities' image: A critical evaluation of the utility of Q scores. In L. R. Kahle & C. H. Kim (Eds.), *Creating images and the psychology of marketing communication* (pp. 191–200). New York: Erlbaum.

Kahle, L. R. (1996). Social values and consumer behavior: Research from the list of values. In C. Seligman, J. M. Olson, & M. P. Zanna (Eds.), *The psychology of values: The Ontario Symposium* (Vol. 8, pp. 135–151). Mahwah, NJ: Erlbaum.

Kahle, L. R., Aiken, D., Dalakas, V., & Duncan, M. (2003). Men's versus women's collegiate basketball customers: Attitudinal favorableness and the environment. *International Journal of Sports Marketing and Sponsorship, 5*, 145–159.

Kahle, L., Duncan, M., Dalakas, V., & Aiken, D. (2001). The social values of fans for men's versus women's university basketball. *Sport Marketing Quarterly, 10*, 156.

Kahle, L. R., Elton, M., & Kambara, K. (1997). Sports talk and the development of marketing relationships. *Sport Marketing Quarterly, 6*, 35–39.

Kahle, L. R., & Homer, P. M. (1985). Physical attractiveness of the celebrity endorser: A social adaptation perspective. *Journal of Consumer Research, 11*, 954–961.

Kahle, L., Kambara, K., & Rose, G. M. (1996). A functional model of fan attendance motivations for college football. *Sport Marketing Quarterly, 5*(December), 51–60.

Kahle, L. R., & Riley, C. (Eds.). (2004). *Sports marketing and the psychology of marketing communication.* Mahwah, NJ: Erlbaum.

Kahle, L. R., & Xie, G. X. (2008). Social values in consumer psychology. In C. P. Haugvedt, P. M. Herr, & F. R. Kardes (Eds.), *Handbook of consumer psychology* (pp. 275–285). Mahwah, NJ: Erlbaum.

Keller, K. L. (1993). Conceptualizing, measuring, managing customer-based brand equity. *Journal of Marketing, 57*(1), 1.

Kelley, S., & Tian, K. (2005). Fanatical consumption: An investigation of the behavior of sports fans through textual data. In L. R. Kahle & C. Riley (Eds.), *Sports marketing and the psychology of marketing communication* (pp. 27–65). Mahwah, NJ: Erlbaum.

Kelman, H. C. (1958). Compliance, identification, and internalization: Three processes of attitude change. *The Journal of Conflict Resolution, 2*(1), 51–60.

Kroeber-Riel, W. (1979). Activation research: Psychobiological approaches in consumer research. *Journal of Consumer Research, 5*(March), 240–250.

Lacey, R., Close, A. G. & Finney, R. Z. (in press). The pivotal roles of product knowledge and corporate social responsibility in event sponsorship effectiveness. *Journal of Business Research.*

Levin, A. M., Joiner, C., & Cameron, G. (2001). The impact of sports sponsorship on consumers' brand attitudes and recall: The case of NASCAR fans. *Journal of Current Issues and Research in Advertising, 23*(2), 23.

Madrigal, R. (2000). The influence of social alliances with sports teams on intentions to purchase corporate sponsors' products. *Journal of Advertising, 29*(4), 13–24.

Madrigal, R. (2001). Social identity effects in a belief-attitude-intentions hierarchy: Implications for corporate sponsorship. *Psychology and Marketing, 18*(2), 145–165.

Madrigal, R. (2004). A review of team identification and its influence on consumers' responses toward corporate sponsors. In L. Kahle & C. Riley (Eds.), *Sports marketing and the psychology of marketing communication* (pp. 241–255). Mahwah, NJ: Erlbaum.

Madrigal, R. (2006). Measuring the multidimensional nature of sporting event performance consumption. *Journal of Leisure Research, 38*(3), 267–292.

Madrigal, R. (2008). Hot vs. cold cognitions and consumers' reactions to sporting event outcomes. *Journal of Consumer Psychology, 18*(4), 304–319.

Madrigal, R., & Dalakas, V. (2008). Consumer psychology of sport: More than just a game. In C. P. Haugvedt, P. M. Herr, & F. R. Kardes (Eds.) *Handbook of Consumer Psychology* (pp. 857–876). Mahwah, NJ: Erlbaum.

Mahoney, D. F., Madrigal, R., & Howard, D. (200). Using the psychological commitment to team (pct) scale to segment sport consumers based on loyalty. *Sport Marketing Quarterly, 9*(1), 15–25.

Mandler, G. (1982). The structure of value: Accounting for taste. In M. S. Clark & S. T. Fiske (Eds.), *Affect and cognition: The 17th annual Carnegie Symposium* (pp. 3–36). Hillsdale, NJ: Erlbaum.

McCracken, G. (1989). Who is the celebrity endorser? Cultural foundations of the endorsement process. *Journal of Consumer Research, 16*, 310–321.

National Basketball Association. (2009). NBA Cares. Retrieved from http://www.nba.com/nba_cares/

Pavelchak, M. A., Antil, J. H., & Munch, J. M. (1988). The Super Bowl: An investigation into the relationship among program context, emotional experience and ad recall. *Journal of Consumer Research, 15*, 360–367.

Petty, R., & Cacioppo, J. (1986). The elaboration likelihood model of persuasion. *Advances in Experimental Social Psychology, 19*(1), 123–205.

Pham, M. T. (1992). Effects of involvement, arousal, and pleasure on the recognition of sponsoring stimuli. *Advances in Consumer Research, 19*(1), 85.

Pons, F., Mourali, M., & Nyeck, S. (2006). Consumer orientation toward sporting events: Scale development and validation. *Journal of Service Research, 8*(3), 276–287.

Pracejus, J. (2004). Seven psychological mechanisms through which sponsorship can influence consumers. In L. R. Kahle & C. Riley (Eds.) *Sports Marketing and the Psychology of Marketing Communication* (pp. 175–189). Mahwah, NJ: Erlbaum.

Preuss, H. & Troelsen, T. (2010). *Place branding through mega sport events and the impact on stakeholder communities.* Paper presented at Vancouver Olympic Conference, February, Vancouver, Canada.

Pruitt, S. W., Cornwell, T. B., & Clark, J. M. (2004). The NASCAR phenomenon: Auto racing sponsorships and shareholder wealth. *Journal of Advertising Research, 44*, 281–296.

Rokeach, M. (1973). *The nature of human values.* New York: Free Press.

Roy, D., & Cornwell, T. (2004). The effects of consumer knowledge on responses to event sponsorships. *Psychology and Marketing, 21*(3), 185–207.

Schaefer, A., & Keillor, B. (1997). The effective use of endorsements in advertising: The relationship between "match-up" and involvement. *Journal of Marketing Management, 7*(2), 23–33.

Shoham, A., & Kahle, L. R. (1996). Spectators, viewers, readers: Communication and consumption communities in sport marketing. *Sport Marketing Quarterly, 5*, 11–20.

Shoham, A., Rose, G. M., &. Kahle, L. R. (1998). Marketing of risky sports: From intention to action. *Journal of the Academy of Marketing Science, 26*, 307–321.

Slone, L. R. (1989). The motives of sports fans. In J. H. Goldstein (Ed.), *Sports, games and play: Social and psychological viewpoints* (2nd ed., pp. 175–240). Hillsdale, NJ: Erlbaum.

Sneath, J. Z., Finney, R. Z., & Close, A. G. (2005). An IMC approach to event marketing: The effects of sponsorship and experience on customer attitudes. *Journal of Advertising Research, 45*, 373–381.

Snyder, C. R., Lassegard, M., & Ford, C. E. (1986). Distancing after group success and failure: Basking in reflected glory and cutting off reflected failure. *Journal of Personality and Social Psychology, 51*, 382–388.

Sukhdial, A., Aiken, D., & Kahle, L. R. (2002). Are you old school? An investigation of the sports fans' attitudes and values. *Journal of Advertising Research*, *42*(July/August), 71–81.

Troelsen, T. (2007). The Sports Dream Society—starting now. Lecture, Copenhagen Business School.

Wann, D. L. (1990). Die-hard and fair-weather fans: Effects of identification on BIRGing and CORFing tendencies. *Journal of Sport and Social Issues, 14*(2), 103.

Wann, D. L., & Branscombe, N. R. (1995). Influence of level of identification with a group and physiological arousal on perceived intergroup complexity. *The British Journal of Social Psychology, 34*, 223–235.

Weeks, C. S., Cornwell, T. B., & Humphrys, M. S. (2006). Conceptualizing sponsorship: An item and relational information account. In L. R. Kahle & C. H. Kim (Eds.), (2006). *Creating images and the psychology of marketing communication* (pp. 191–200). New York: Erlbaum.

Weisman, L. (2003, August 15). Sky's the limit for Vick, Falcons. *USA Today*. Retrieved from http://search.ebscohost.com/login.aspx?direct=true&db=aph&AN=J0E166364189103&loginpage=Login.asp&site=ehost-live&scope=site

WSBTV. (2007, August 21). Bottom falls out of Vick jersey market. *WSBTV*, p. 1. Retrieved from http://www.wsbtv.com/news/13937947/detail.html

Zajonc, R. B. (1980). Feeling and thinking: Preferences need no inferences. *American Psychologist, 35*, 151–175.

Zillmann, D. (1996). The psychology of suspense in dramatic exposition. In P. Vorderer, H. J. Wulff, & M. Friedrichsen (Eds.), *Suspense: Conceptualizations, theoretical analyses, and empirical explorations* (pp. 199–231). Mahwah, NJ: Erlbaum.

Section I

Influencing Behaviors in Society and Sports

Consumer behavior research seeks to understand how to influence behavior, both on an individual level and on a societal level. The chapters in this section illustrate a cross section of approaches targeted at this goal. Lee and Cornwell knit together theories and findings from sport management and consumer behavior marketing in the management, economics, and marketing literatures to blend divergent literatures and to portray a macroview of how sport and sports-oriented firms can contribute to society. Lee and Cornwell review nine cross-sector relationship mechanisms and discuss the form each takes, while noting the power balance suggested in the relationship.

Hirt and Clarkson contribute a chapter on the fundamental aspects of fandom. Following a review, the authors denote various motivations and etiologies that underlie sports fanship. A major contribution of this chapter is a new taxonomy of the fundamental needs by which these various motivations for fanship are categorized.

Jones, Grove, and Pickett deal with fan rage. Acts of rage bring negative consequences to the team's stakeholders and damage spectator sport, although some motivators of fan rage are inadvertently prompted by sport marketers' desire to hype the events, to provide an intense experience for spectators, and to maximize ticket sales and revenue opportunities. The authors then suggest recommendations on how marketing strategies influence such factors that have an impact on spectator rage.

2

A Framework for Measuring the Contributions of Sport to Society
Actors, Activities, and Outcomes

Seung Pil Lee and T. Bettina Cornwell

Introduction

Increasingly, sports are becoming popular means, a "ride-along" vehicle in many instances, for social contributions to society. These collaborative ventures, often involving corporations, NPOs/NGOs (nonprofit organizations/nongovernmental organizations), governments, and sport organizations, take many forms. The following are some examples:

> UNICEF and FC Barcelona signed a five-year partnership to raise awareness and funds to benefit children affected by HIV and AIDS. FC Barcelona donates €1.5 million per year over five years to help fund projects aimed at combating HIV and AIDS in Africa and Latin America. Along with the funding, the football club is featuring the UNICEF [United Nations Children's Emergency Fund] logo on its 2006–2007 jersey, the first placement of its kind in the club's 107 year history. This commitment to UNICEF and the world's children reinforces FC Barcelona's motto, "More than a club." (UNICEF, 2009)

> Children's Healthcare of Atlanta is one of the designated charities of the AT&T Classic Golf Tournament. Including the 2007 donation, the tournament has now contributed more than $15 million to its primary charity, Children's Healthcare of Atlanta. Children's, formerly known as Egleston Children's Hospital, has been the primary recipient of tournament proceeds since 1981. (PGA TOUR, 2009)

> The world's largest corporate running series is continuing its long-standing tradition of supporting charities and institutions that contribute to an overall quality of life in the communities served by JPMorgan Chase. In 2009, the Series will donate more than $600,000 to charities and organizations in host cities around the world. The JPMorgan Chase Foundation makes a donation for each entry in the Corporate Challenge Series. (JPMorgan Chase and Co., 2009).

The Prostate Cancer Charity and the Tour of Britain, the UK's premier professional cycling race, have joined forces to create two mass participation events—
the first of their kind in the UK. Cyclists of all abilities will take to their bikes
and raise money to help this important cause. As the official car partner, Honda
will provide a fleet of around 40 more Honda Civics, CR-Vs and Insights for the
event. This partnership with Honda is also testament to the fact that the Tour of
Britain is an ideal platform for brands wishing to align themselves with Britain's
best Olympic sport, while also addressing their corporate social responsibility
needs. (Tour of Britain, 2009)

While sports in and of themselves have always been seen as a positive societal force, new cross-sector collaborations are creating new challenges and opportunities. In fact, these collaborative activities that seek to
support social good have become commonplace since the 1980s. Austin
(2003) argued that cross-sector collaboration will be much more prevalent
in this new century for several reasons. First, "the growing complexity of
the socioeconomic problems facing societies transcends the capabilities
of single organizations and separate sectors, Second, boundaries between
business, civil society, and government are increasingly blurred. Third,
societal expectations of business to contribute to the resolution of social
problems are rising" (Austin, 2003, p. 37). We, however, note that little
research has been done to date on these collaborative initiatives and their
functioning. The challenge and opportunity is that while business may
seek to expand their social contribution, they must still be responsible to
shareholders. There is a need to align partners in ways that lead to mutual
benefit. With this objective in mind, we bring together literatures from
marketing, management, economics, and more specifically sport management and consumer behavior. We intend to provide an analytical framework that includes examination of (a) types of cross-sector relationship
mechanisms, (b) motivations and objectives for actors to work together
through sport, (c) evaluation of collaborative activity outcomes, and (d)
benefits of measurement to actors.

The emphasis on measurement and benefit to partners is important
because it takes a transformative consumer orientation. Mick (2006)
explained that in transformative research, investigations are "framed by a
fundamental problem or opportunity ... and ... strive to respect, uphold,
and improve life in relation to the myriad conditions, demands, potential-
ities, and effects of consumption" (p. 2). Because sport involves production
and consumption and because ultimately we measure the consumption
activities in communities (e.g., in the donating behavior of individuals,
the participation of individual athletes, the awareness of audiences, and

the health and welfare decisions of people), we have consumer as well as organizational benefactors in mind. Thus, it is important that clear theoretical support and objective measurements of sport-related outcomes will encourage corporations, NPOs/NGOs, and governments to participate in collaborative sports initiatives that are supportive of societal goals.

Types of Corporate Cross-Sector Relationship Mechanisms

Corporate cross-sector activities oriented toward social good usually take already established forms, including sponsorship, philanthropy, corporate social responsibility (CSR) activities, cause-related marketing, corporate social marketing, cause branding, cobranding, mission marketing, social partnership and social alliances (Drumwright & Murphy, 2001, p. 162). We briefly review seven of the most popular mechanisms and comment on the form they take as well as the power balance suggested in the relationship: philanthropy/patronage, sponsorship, cause-related marketing, brand alliance/cobranding, social partnerships, social alliances, and CSR.

Philanthropy/patronage. Drumwright and Murphy (2001) categorized philanthropy as either traditional or strategic. While the former is referred to as "the paradigmatic case of a company initiative with low emphasis on economic goals," the latter "represents the tying of the philanthropy function and budget to the company's strategic objectives and markets" (p. 165). Seitanidi and Ryan (2007) defined corporate philanthropy as corporate contributions to NPOs in cash, products, material, or labor with no or little expectation of public recognition for its behaviors. The balance in this relationship between corporations and NPOs is not symmetrical because corporate motivation for those behaviors is based on one-way giving (Seitanidi & Ryan, 2007). Patronage, a similar concept, is referred to as "a more altruistic and less commercial form of business support than sponsorship" by the Association for Business Sponsorship of the Arts (ABSA, 1997, p. 3). As it originated from a class-based ancient Roman arts society, the "patron" also has an asymmetric relationship with the NPO (Seitanidi & Ryan, 2007).

Sponsorship. While modern-day sponsorship may have roots in philanthropy, it has evolved to become a market-driven phenomenon. Sponsorship is defined as "a cash and/or in-kind fee paid to property (typically a sports, entertainment, non-profit event or organization) in return for access to the exploitable commercial potential associated with that property" (International Events Group, 2000, p. 1). Seitanidi and Ryan

(2007) subdivided sponsorship as commercial sponsorship and sociosponsorship. Both supposedly have symmetric relationships with properties based on exchange compensations such as sales promotion, advertising, reputation, and image. While commercial sponsorship is motivated as "tools of sales promotion and advertising" to expect predominantly tangible benefit, sociosponsorship is related to CSR and intangible outcomes. Sociosponsorship aims to increase intangible benefits such as reputation and image with limited tangible benefits (Seitanidi & Ryan, 2007). Also, sociosponsorship is defined as "the vehicle through which resources are justifiably allocated from the profit to the non-profit sector, when the company's primary intent is the attainment of social responsibility, accompanied by compensation rewards" (Seitanidi, 1999, p. 33). Following these definitions and observation of enacted sponsorships, this is a major form of CSR through alignment with sports.

Cause-related marketing. Varadarajan and Menon (1988) defined cause-related marketing as "the process of formulating and implementing marketing activities that are characterized by an offer from the firm to contribute a specific amount to a designated cause when customers engage in revenue providing exchanges that satisfy organizational and individual objectives" (p. 60). There is also argued to be a symmetric relationship between corporations and NPOs based on mutual benefits, such as increased sales for the company and increased funds for the NPO (Seitanidi & Ryan, 2007). This accepted definition of cause-related marketing is narrower than the constituent terms suggested because it is limited to transactional exchanges. Narrowed to transactional exchanges, cause-related marketing activities may have limited scope in international projects.

Brand alliances/cobranding. Rao, Qu, and Ruekert (1999) defined brand alliances as "all circumstances in which two or more brand names are presented jointly to the consumer." It includes joint promotion, dual branding, and cobranding (Washburn, Till, & Priluck, 2004). Joint promotion is referred to as the circumstances when partner brands are presented as complementing one another (Rao et al., 1999). Dual branding describes when two brands share the same space, such as in the case of Tim Hortons and Wendy's (Levin & Levin, 2000). Cobranding involves the physical integration of two brands (Levin & Levin, 2000). "Brand alliances build brand equity by transferring new associations between partner brands or involving a short- or long-term association between two or more individual brands or other distinctive proprietary assets" (Dickinson & Barker, 2007, p. 77). In many instances, associations between nonprofit and commercial entities are designed to develop the reputation of the commercial ally because nonprofit brands have higher levels of trust and confidence that can be transferred (Austin, 2000). One could, however, imagine a charity being the recipient of corporate reputation, such as when a small local charity, which might be little known to the public, receives support from a major corporate brand. This could easily be the case in cross-sector partnerships for sport.

Social partnerships. Since arising in their modern form, with high social awareness of activities, social partnerships have been recognized as a popular collaboration method between corporations and NPOs (Brehm, 2001). Waddock (1988) defined social partnership as "a commitment by a corporation or a group of corporations to work with organizations from a different economic sector (public or non-profit) in terms of resources, time and effort to benefit all partners by addressing social issues beyond traditional boundaries and goals of corporations" (p. 18). The term *partnership* suggests equality in the relationship, but resource contributions may determine the power balance. Social partnerships are a natural form for many social sport investments since they frequently involve public-private collaborations for sport facilities. Sport facilities are commonly supported by corporations seeking goodwill in the community and brand awareness for products (Cornwell, 2008).

Social alliances. Andreasen and Drumwright (2001) defined social alliances as

> any formal or informal agreement between a non-profit organization and for-profit organizations to carry out a marketing program or activity where:
>
> a. Both parties expect the outcome to advance their organization's mission;
> b. The corporation is not fully compensated for its participation;
> c. There is a general social benefit expected. (Andreasen & Drumwright, 2001, p. 100)

Drumwright and Murphy (2001) referred to social alliance as "collaborative efforts between companies and nonprofits that encompass close, mutually beneficial, long-term partnerships designed to accomplish strategic goals for both entities involving the sharing of resources, knowledge, and capabilities" (p. 169). Power imbalances have been frequently identified in social alliances and may restrict their potential, especially when it results in partner resources not being recognized or utilized (Berger, Cunningham, & Drumwright, 2004). Thus, power balance is a critical condition in social alliances when corporations seek to impose a strategy on the social initiative.

Corporate social responsibility (CSR). There have been numerous efforts to define CSR since the 1950s (e.g., Bowen, 1953). Carroll (1979) proposed a definition of CSR as the social responsibility of business encompassing "the economic, legal, ethical, and discretionary expectations that society has of organizations at a given point in time" (p. 500). Holme and Watts (2000) defined CSR as "the continuing commitment by business to behave ethically and contribute to economic development while improving the quality of life of the workforce and their families as well as of the local community and society at large" (p. 8). The first definition implies pressure to perform CSR activities, while the latter suggests volunteer participation. These definitions highlight CSR "writ large" as motivated behavior that may take many forms and would certainly apply to cross-sector collaborations in sport for social cause.

Based on the definitions of various corporate cross-sector mechanisms, we summarize that CSR activities, actions based on CSR intentions, have a long history as a relationship mechanism between business and society. It is also the case that CSR, in a general sense, is a bigger, broader, and more general concept than philanthropy, sponsorship, cause-related marketing, social alliances, and social partnerships. Therefore, we have adopted CSR as the general frame for the implementation of corporate cross-sector relationships and include socially oriented strategic philanthropy, sponsorship, cause-related marketing, brand alliances, social alliance, and partnerships as mechanisms to enact social responsibility. Thus, CSR becomes a centerpiece of our subsequent analysis of the firm.

Actors in Cross-Sector Partnerships in Sport

Rationale for CSR Based on Theories of the Firm

To understand what kind of motivations the firm (company or corporation) may have to commit to CSR activities, it is necessary to consider perspectives on the purpose of firms. Several theories have been posited, but there is no generally accepted theory of the firm since new major theories emerge every decade (Slater, 1997). Across economies at different levels of development, firms may vary in their latitude for CSR. Thus, we briefly review the key elements of the four most influential theories of the firm to understand the firm's theoretical motivations for CSR.

The neoclassical theory of the firm. The neoclassical theory assumes perfect competition, homogeneous demand, perfect information of consumers, and homogeneous firm resources with complete mobility (Slater, 1997). The firm exists to combine labor and capital to produce a final product (Slater, 1997). It also considers the firm as a perfectly rational actor to deploy inputs to achieve internal efficiency and profit maximization (Mahoney, 2005). From this perspective, the firm treats social issues as externalities separated from the core business of the firm (Bowen, 2007). The firm must not make a commitment to social activities unless they suggest a positive economic payoff. Thus, it is difficult to explain characteristics of corporate social strategy such as noneconomic managerial values, stakeholder engagement, and intangible capability development through the neoclassical theory of the firm (Bowen, 2007). While this view of the firm no longer receives support as a theory, firm activity in some sectors might aptly be described by it.

The transactions cost economics theory of the firm. The transactions cost theory assumes that "markets and firms are alternative mechanisms for coordinating transaction, and the choice of one or the other is based on the respective cost associated with the transaction" (Slater, 1997, p. 163). Slater (1997) summarized that, in this view, cost minimization of either production or transaction costs is the goal, and behavior is opportunistic. Under these objectives, there is little room to support social causes or leverage long-term CSR reputation.

The behavioral theory of the firm. Behavioral theory started from dissatisfaction with the ability of neoclassical theory of the firm to explain actual decision-making behavior within organizations. This shortcoming of neoclassical thinking is due to the assumption of perfectly rational actors within the firm (Bowen, 2007). Under the behavioral view, the firm is more interested in survival or satisfactory profit with willing compromise among conflicting interests rather than pure profit maximization (Slater, 1997). Thus, behavioral theory is somewhat better able to explain the firm's social activities at the strategic level than either neoclassical theory or transaction cost economics theory. Also, corporate social strategy researchers (e.g., Adams & Hardwick, 1998; Seifert, Morris, & Bartkus, 2003) have considered organizational slack from behavioral theory as "a pre-requisite to afford corporate social strategy" (Bowen, 2007, p. 99). Behavioral theory, however, has a limitation in that even though organizational slack can catalyze a corporate social strategy, Bowen (2007) argued that resources alone cannot initiate a corporate social strategy.

The resource-based theory of the firm. Finally, we come to the resource-based perspective. Under this theory, resources include all assets, capabilities, organizational processes, firm attributes, information, and knowledge for a firm to use to implement strategies that improve its efficiency and effectiveness (Barney, 1991). Further, resources can be divided into tangible and intangible assets. The former includes physical and financial assets, and the latter includes corporate reputation and employee's knowledge, experience and skills, and their commitment and loyalty (Branco & Rodrigues, 2006). The firm can be thought of as a unique bundle of resources and capabilities used to develop and implement strategies (Branco & Rodrigues, 2006). However, it does not include the neoclassical assumptions of perfect information, homogeneous resources, and resource mobility (Conner, 1991). Thus, the resource-based theory of the firm can examine the relationship among resources, sustained competitive advantage, and superior economic performance while allowing for resource heterogeneity and resource immobility (Bowen, 2007). Further, the resource-based theory suggests that the resources or capabilities should be valuable, rare, inimitable, and nonsubstitutable for sustainable competitive advantage (Barney, 1991). This view of resources sits well with the often-unique events, actors, and activities that sport affords. Amis, Pant, and Slack (1997) identified how a resource-based view of sport sponsorship is useful in achieving sustainable competitive advantage.

CSR and resource-based perspective of the firm. The resource-based theory of the firm provides insights into how CSR contributes to the firm's financial performance in terms of both internal and external benefits. Branco and Rodrigues (2006) explained these benefits as follows: Internally, CSR activities and disclosure of these activities are critical in creating intangible resources and capabilities for employees, who are crucial for the success of the firm. A positive CSR reputation can improve employees' motivation, morale, commitment, and loyalty to the firm, which may lead to positive financial outcomes. In addition, CSR initiatives can foster important management competencies, such as solving problems, discovering inefficiencies, and incentivizing employees. Externally, engaging in CSR activities and disclosure can create corporate reputation as an essential intangible resource. This is accomplished by providing the firm a good relationship with external stakeholders, including customers, investors, suppliers, and competitors. In conclusion, based on the thinking of Branco and Rodrigues, the resource-based perspective is considered the most appropriate theory of the firm to explain how CSR leads to the corporate financial performance both internally and externally.

NPOs/NGOs as One of the Actors in CSR Activities

Nonprofit Organizations and Nongovernmental Organizations

The roles of NGOs and NPOs are increasingly discussed in the resolution of social development problems, both academically and politically. Most of the time, the terms NGO and NPO are used interchangeably. Still, however, we find a definitional difference between NGO and NPO in the literature. For example, the United Nations defines an NGO as follows:

> A non-governmental organization (NGO) is a not-for-profit, voluntary citizens' group, which is organized on a local, national or international level to address issues in support of the public good. Task-oriented and made up of people with a common interest, NGOs perform a variety of services and humanitarian functions, bring citizens' concerns to Governments, monitor policy and programme implementation, and encourage participation of civil society stakeholders at the community level. They provide analysis and expertise, serve as early warning mechanisms and help monitor and implement international agreements. Some are organized around specific issues, such as human rights, the environment or health. (United Nations, 2009)

On the other hand, an NPO is defined as

> incorporated entities that qualify for exemption from the federal income tax under any of 26 specific subsections of the Internal Revenue Code. (Hopkins, 1987, p. 5)

> private organizations serving a public purpose, that is some cause related to the good of the society. (O'Neil, 1989, p. 2)

In practice, the term *NGO* is mostly used in international settings and by international organizations such as the World Bank to emphasize the difference between government organizations and private organizations. On the other hand, the term *NPO* has typically been utilized to express the difference between NPOs and for-profit organizations (Badelt, 1999). In fact, we define NGO and NPO here because they are one of the actor types in a strategic model of business that often cooperates with governments. Thus, while we take an international orientation, we see NGOs as defined by the "not-for-profit" term; thus, the term *NGO* is redundant as long as NPOs are understood as private and nongovernmental.

The Identity of Nonprofit Organizations and Their Reason for Being

According to Salamon and Anheier (1992) and the European Commission (1997), NPOs have common elements in their definitions: They are formal or institutionally existent, nonprofit distributing, institutionally separated from government, and free to govern themselves according to their own rules and procedures. Salamon and Anheier (1992) added a further key element of voluntary participation in their definition, and the European Commission has also argued that NPOs should produce public good (Badelt, 1999). How is it that NPOs come into being? How does the NPO behave, and how does it, or should it, select among public goods that might be produced? There are two important theories of the arising of NPOs that may be informative: the market failure and the contract failure theories.

Government failure/market failure theory. Weisbrod (1977) argued that there are hugely differing opinions regarding which public goods to produce in democratic society, but actions only tend to reflect the preferences of the median voter. This causes considerable unsatisfied demand for public goods and does not respond to a diverse population of clients and any special needs that are not met by government (Salamon & Anheier, 1998; Schmid, 2004). In these circumstances, people rely on NPOs, which can supply public goods unsecured through either the market or government (Salamon & Anheier, 1998, p. 220). Under this thinking, NPOs also adopt an ideology of philanthropy and altruism (Schmid, 2004).

Contract failure theory. Hansmann (1980, 1987) assumed that there is asymmetry in information between customers and producers. In this case, consumers lack the information to judge the quality of the goods and services, and producers have the opportunity and incentive to take advantage of customers with services that have less quality or are at a lower quantity for their profit (Salamon & Anheier, 1998; Schmid, 2004). In these circumstances, NPOs can be alternatives for trust in the quality of the goods or services because their nondistribution constraint and the prohibition on nonprofit distribution of profits to owners can be perceived as a sign of trustworthiness compared to for-profit organizations (Salamon & Anheier, 1998; Schmid, 2004). Therefore, Schmid (2004) argued that NPOs can expand their domains and increase access to resources and capital by taking advantage of the trust that the customers hold for them. These two theories suggest that the NPO role is mainly to provide goods and services not provided by the market or government or to play a "watchdog" role in the provision of goods and services. It is also reasonable to add that, in the current context, they may, especially in international partnerships, arise to include the transfer of values or "know-how" from one sector to another.

In cross-sector partnerships related to sport, NPOs may provide, oversee, or transfer products and services. In many instances, they are beneficiary sponsors. That is, they are the recipient of money or some value that comes from a sporting organization's activities to support the NPO objective. For example, as mentioned at the start of this chapter, Children's Healthcare of Atlanta has been the primary recipient of the AT&T Classic Golf proceeds. NPOs might also harness the energy or awareness of sport events or athletes to communicate a message. For example, a group called the Grassroot Soccer Foundation (GRSF) utilizes the vast youth interest in soccer in Africa to communicate about HIV and AIDS (Botcheva & Huffman, 2004). In 2009, GRSF gained Barclays Bank as a 3-year sponsor. As mentioned, while sport alone can make a contribution to societal well-being, it is also the case that it plays a supporting role for many NPOs.

Sports Organization as One of the Actors in CSR Activities

The third actor in cross-sector partnerships is the sport itself. There are many different types of sport organizations, including sport programs, activities, and organizations that put forward events, such as the International Olympic Committee (IOC), FIFA (Fédération Internationale de Football Association), NCAA (National Collegiate Athletic Association), National Association for Stock Car Auto Racing (NASCAR), PGA (Professional Golfers' Association), and YMCA (Young Men's Christian Association). Even though they are not unitary entities, the classically accepted definitions and the objectives of sport organizations provide a good starting point to understand sport organization as one of the actors in a strategic collaboration/alliance model.

Definitions of sport organization and sport program. A number of authors have defined an "organization." For example, Rollinson (2002) defined an organization as "a social entity brought into existence and sustained in an ongoing way by humans to serve some purpose, from which it follows that human activities in that entity are normally structured and coordinated towards achieving some purpose" (p. 4). Based on Daft (1989, 2004) and Robbins (1990), Slack and Parent (2006) defined a sport organization as "a social entity involved in the sport industry; it is goal-directed, with a consciously structured activity system and a relatively identifiable boundary" (p. 5).

Myers (1999) defined a program as "any organized or purposeful activity or set of activities delivered to a designated target group, consisting of a class, a pamphlet or booklet, a poster, a video, a prescribed regimen, or a combination of interventions" (p. 10). Following from this, Chelladurai

(2005) discussed the definition of a sport program by illustrating that a youth sports program promoting sports participation among teenagers may be composed of several activities, including scheduled daily or weekly instructional, competitive, or recreational sessions. Accordingly, a program is repeated on a continuing basis, whereas a project is a one-time event (Chelladurai, 2005). The term *program* is more frequently used in the context of public groups and NPOs than in the business context (Chelladurai, 2005). The activities of a sport organization, a sport program, or a one-time sport project may be part of a cross-sector relationship.

Objectives of sport organizations. Objectives of sport organizations vary according to their classification. Although Chelladurai (2005) summarized five characteristics important in classifying the sport—profit orientation, source of funding, prime beneficiary, employee–customer interface, and volunteer participation. The most influential and inclusive characteristic is profit orientation. Therefore, we explore objectives of sport organizations based on for-profit sport organizations and nonprofit sport organizations. When we review missions and objectives that each sport organization promotes, the most important common goal among nonprofit sport organizations such as the IOC, FIFA, International Paralympic Committee, and Commonwealth Games Federation is to contribute to building and promoting a peaceful world and better future through the unifying, educational, cultural, and humanitarian value of sports. On the other hand, objectives of for-profit organizations such as the PGA, English Premier League, and NBA (National Basketball Association) are more diverse and focus on increasing interest in their sports, games, or competitions; enhancing their images and brands at all levels of society and business; and generating commercial value for their long-term success by satisfying their fans and sponsors.

Compared to for-profit sport organizations, nonprofit sport organizations have a stronger tendency to achieve goals and play roles in contributing to society by utilizing educational, cultural, and social values of sport. Having said this, it is also the case that for-profit sport organizations are rapidly developing CSR initiatives (Babiak & Wolfe, 2009). In parallel to for-profit companies, for-profit sports see their first obligation as being to their owners, but also like for-profit firms, they are motivated to engage in CSR activities.

At least two additional roles found in cross-sector partnerships should be mentioned: the role government may play and the role that society representatives may play. In-depth analysis of these roles is beyond the scope of this chapter, but experience in other sectors suggests that these forces can be facilitative or not, well organized or not, and critical or not when it comes to proposed cross-sector partnerships.

Expected Outcomes for Cross-Sector Partners

We summarize the sought outcomes of cross-sector sport-related CSR in Figure 2.1. Business can expect reduced risk from working with society to solve problems as well as enhanced reputation (Warner, 2004). NPOs gain financial support for their initiatives as well as a volunteer and contributor base (Berger et al., 1999; Samu & Wymer, 2001; Selsky & Parker, 2005). Sport organizations vary widely in their expected outcomes, but central to most sport organizations are a continued interest in the sport as well as a positive image and reputation from CSR. In addition to the outcomes for firms, nonprofits, and sport, Figure 2.1 briefly summarizes the outcomes for society, including social networks, collective identity, healthy environments, well-being, and human capital development (Lawson, 2005). Review of these outcomes as possible CSR measures is addressed in more depth in a subsequent section. While it is recognized that two actors (e.g., sport organization and government or NPO and government) may come

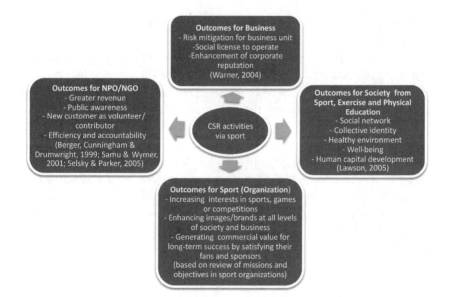

Figure 2.1   Expected outcomes for cross-sector partners' CSR activities via sport.

together in a cross-sector partnership, our interest is mainly in the more complex relationship in which a for-profit and a nonprofit come together to seek social good via sport. Further, from a transformative research perspective, our question is, How might "win-win-win-win" relationships be developed if we were better able to account for the contribution of sport to society in its various forms?

Measuring the Social Contributions of Sports via CSR Activities

Having discussed the major actors and their objectives in cross-sector partnerships and having established CSR as the central motivation for for-profit groups and as a central understanding as a social movement for other partners, we now turn to a discussion of measurement of CSR activities. We begin by considering the contribution of sport simply. As mentioned, the activities of sport are thought to contribute to society before their use as a message platform or a social intervention.

Social Contribution of Sport

Numerous policy articles claimed that sport contributes to society in terms of social inclusion and the development of social capital. For example, in a review article, Bailey (2005) identified the five areas of physical health, cognitive and academic development, mental health, crime reduction, and reduction of truancy and disaffection as areas in which sport makes contributions to society. However, there is little research that examined these contributions empirically.

Delaney and Keaney (2005) analyzed the relationship between the extent of sporting participation and the level of social capital across Europe to see how sport contributes to community bonds and active citizenship. They measured "social capital" in terms of social trust, political and institutional trust, democratic participation, and social participation. On the other hand, they measured "participation in sport" in terms of probabilities of membership in sport organizations and probabilities of being involved in sport organizations as a player as well as probabilities of volunteering in sport organizations. They found that "there are very strong correlations between a nation's level of sports membership and the levels of social trust and well being, although the correlation with trust in institutions is much weaker, which indicates that countries with higher levels of membership in sports groups among citizens also have higher levels of social trust" (Delaney & Keaney, 2005, p. 32). Also, they found that "individuals who are involved in sports organizations, both as members and players, are slightly more likely to vote, contact a politician and sign a petition than both non-members and the average citizen" (Delaney & Keaney, 2005, p. 32). Subsequently, to isolate the effects of sport from other factors such as age, income, and education, they performed several multiple regression analyses. They found that a very small effect of sports club membership on political engagement is positive and statistically significant after controlling for the other factors mentioned. Further, they found that sport has a statistically significant and substantial effect on the frequency of social meeting with friends, a statistically significant effect on trust in civil institutions but an insignificant effect on trust in other people. Naturally, some might question the causal direction of these relationships; still, sport is correlated with positive social outcomes.

Tonts (2005) examined the links between sport and social capital in rural regions in a series of face-to-face interviews and surveys that were sent to 50% of the households in the region. The interviews gathered information on the role of sport in social life; the networks associated with sport, participation, and volunteering; and the links between sport and other realms of rural life, such as economic development; the questionnaire gathered data on perceptions of community, levels of participation in sport, and the social role of sport in rural life. Tonts concluded that sport is an important arena for the creation and maintenance of social capital through participation, social interaction, and engagement.

In a more focused study, Seippel (2006) examined how social capital in relation to participation in voluntary sport organizations and other voluntary organizations has implications for various kinds of social trust: generalized trust and political commitments. He categorized a random sample of the Norwegian population as "member of sport organization only," "member of sport and other voluntary organization," and "member of other voluntary organization." He measured the intensity of social capital as the dependent variable and conducted regression analysis with group variables as independent variables. He concluded that being a member of a voluntary sport organization involves social capital that is conducive to generalized trust and political commitment. However, he noted that the effect of sport organizations is stronger when members also belong to other voluntary organizations.

In a final example of the basic contribution of sport, Jarvie (2003) examined the relationship between sport and the concept of communitarianism via three case studies in Scotland. He examined the issues of community identity, stakeholding in sport, and the mutual ownership of sports clubs. In his findings, he argued that "it is unrealistic to expect sport to be totally responsible for sustaining a sense of community or citizenship or even reinforce notions of social capital, however, sports projects and the place of sport within both imagined and active senses of Scottish communities can make a valuable contribution"(Jarvie, 2003, p. 139).

From this discussion, one can see that sport's contribution to society can take many forms. There is, however, growing use of sport as a communications vehicle. In this sense, the already positive values of sport are utilized in communication and action. One can think of this approach not as the societal contribution *of* sport but societal contributions *via* sport. Thus, we turn to societal contribution via sport.

Societal Contribution "via" Sport

In this section, we consider how sport contributes via cross-sector partnerships. As mentioned, Botcheva and Huffman (2004) evaluated the impact of the HIV/AIDS education program of the GRSF on student knowledge, self-efficacy beliefs, attitude, and perceptions of social support in Bulawayo, Zimbabwe. Data were collected from two groups of students: participants and nonparticipants in the program from four different schools. They found that the 2-week education program produced significant positive change in student knowledge about HIV/AIDS and attitudes and perception of social support but no significant changes in self-efficacy and control over disease (Botcheva & Huffman, 2004).

Mathare Youth Sport Association (MYSA) is an example of social development via sport participation. It was started by Bob Munro, a Canadian United Nations environmental development officer, in 1987 with the vision to use sport for environmental improvement. It now has over 14,000 participants through partnerships with such organizations as FIFA, the Norwegian government, and private sector supporters (MYSA Kenya, 2009). Munro (2005) summarized the achievements of MYSA as production of new role models to encourage and inspire the youth in poor and rural communities.

Go Sisters is a Zambian program designed to empower girls and young women through sport by combining education and sport, creating a platform for life skills, leadership development, poverty reduction, and HIV/AIDS education (UK Sport, 2009). It acts in partnership with NPOs and sport organizations, including Commonwealth Games of Canada (CGC) and the EduSport Foundation. The aims of Go Sisters are to improve health and fitness, improve the chance that girls will stay in school or return, decrease the exposure to HIV/AIDS, strengthen self-esteem and knowledge of rights, and provide role models. There has been little systematic effectiveness measurement of programs like those just described. Coalter (2007) argued that how we evaluate programs raises significant questions since they address the fundamental economic, cultural, and health issues. Also, Pollard and Court (2005) drew attention to the role NGOs/NPOs may play in improving the standard of evaluating procedures and improving effectiveness in programs of this type.

In summary, there has been support for the potential of sport to contribute to social development directly and indirectly, but for all the initiatives undertaken the evidence is sparse. There has been little agreement on how to approach the evaluation of outcomes. More standardized evidence about the benefits of participation in social contribution via sport is required to persuade each actor into partnerships, justify their roles, and work more effectively.

New Framework for Measurement of Social Contributions of Sport via CSR Activities

What to Measure

Lawson (2005) identified five areas in which sport, exercise, and physical education (SEPE) can contribute to sustainable and integrated social and economic development: (a) social networks, (b) collective identities, (c) health-enhancing environments, (d) well-being, and (e) human capital development. His thinking in these areas is summarized here. He argues first that SEPE can generate and strengthen social networks among participants, their families, residents of the community, and professions. Consequently, strong social networks produce social trust, norms of reciprocity, coordination and collaboration, and animate democracy and sustainable development of civil society (Lawson, 2005). Second, he states that SEPE can be designed to contribute to the development of collective identities by bridging intergroup differences, facilitating solidarity and integration. Third, Lawson reasons that SEPE can enhance and create healthy environments, which are vital to development initiatives. Fourth, SEPE can improve well-being, which includes health, nurturing relationships, opportunities for identity development, harmonious relations, and reduction of social exclusion. Fifth, SEPE can contribute to human capital development, which is focused on the knowledge, skills, attitude, competence, capacity, and citizenship of individuals and groups.

Selsky and Parker (2005) supported this new framework of social contribution of sport, stating that "in the collaborative partnerships involving business, government and civil society actors (NPOs/NGOs), organizations jointly address challenges such as economic development, education, health care, poverty alleviation, community capacity building, and environmental sustainability" (p. 850). Therefore, we support these five dimensions—social networks, collective identities, health-enhancing environments, well-being, and human capital development—as core measurement for the outcomes of CSR via sport. Naturally, any program with specific aims such as HIV awareness will have specific communication measurement. The objective with this measurement framework is to consider core measurement of the contribution of sports to society to begin to form a benchmark of sport contribution.

How to Measure

Survey research. Survey research of cross-sector partnership outcomes would be an obvious starting point. With the caution of Jarvie (2003) in mind, we seek to measure those areas central and general to sport as well as those furthered by sport in programs that vary in duration. Thus, we start with focus on only individual well-being, social capital, and healthy environments, thus capturing contributions to persons, relationships, and contexts. Many existing measures are available to capture these constructs. In considering past measures that might be directly useful or adaptable to assessing the contribution of sport to social and economic development, several criteria are outlined here. First, the measures should be flexible in terms of the application to a variety of sports and exercise programs, a wide range of developmental and cultural backgrounds, and a number of different audiences (participants and nonparticipants, community members, organizers, viewers or attendees). Second, the measures selected should be relatively global or summative rather than particular. Third, the measures should be easily understood and as much as possible easily translated into other languages.

A measurement tool considering the areas of social capital, individual well-being, and healthy environments is advanced as core, but there is also a need to catalogue more particular measures and at the minimum offer a survey of them and potentially to develop modules that might be added to the core measures. Examples of particular areas of contribution and measurement include poverty reduction, education expansion, gender equality, environmental sustainability, and disease understanding (Beutler, 2008).

Contingent valuation method (CVM). CVM focused on individual willingness-to-pay (WTP) measures constitutes common empirical methods to value public goods such as water or air quality and national parks in environmental economics (Haab & McConnell, 2002). It has been used in benefit-cost analysis of governmental projects for the past several decades, and it has gained greater acceptance in the policy and economics literature (Haab & McConnell, 2002). Since sport is perceived to generate public goods such as civic pride and community spirit, sport economists have begun to apply CVM to the evaluation of sport facilities and professional sports teams. Johnson, Groothuis, and Whitehead (2001) used CVM to measure the civic pride value of the NHL (National Hockey League) Pittsburgh Penguins. Similarly, Johnson, Mondello, and Whitehead (2007) used CVM to estimate the value of public goods of civic pride and community spirit produced by the NFL Jacksonville Jaguars.

Another aspect of CVM using a WTP measure is that it can provide persuasive evidence about the social contribution values of sport. For example, when respondents are asked about their WTP for a sport value, their answers are considered in terms of a unit of currency. This is why they have been used for benefit-cost tests for the past several decades. Policy makers and government officials can put a financial value on a difficult-to-measure construct. Therefore, we suggest the measurement concept of WTP and CVM as one approach for measuring the five dimensions of CSR via sport.

Why Is Measurement Important?

As social problems have grown while governmental budgets have shrunk, many functions previously performed by governments have been moving to the private or nonprofit sector, and as noted, expectations for corporations to contribute to the resolution of social problems are increasing as well (Austin, 2003). This trend is motivated at the individual as well as group levels. For example, the 1999 Cone/Roper *Cause Related Trends Report* noted that more than 70% of American consumers would be likely to change brands or retailers to one associated with a good cause given the same price and quality, and that 90% of workers at companies with a good cause program felt proud of their company's values (Cone, Inc.,

& Roper Starch Worldwide, 1999). Weiser and Zadek (2000) found that over 25,000 consumers in 23 countries expected companies to contribute to society beyond being profitable and law abiding. Thus, we can easily assume that corporate social contributions through CSR activities via sport can enhance competitive advantages for corporations both in direct forms including sales, target market, distribution, and revenue, and in indirect forms such as reputation, trust, respect, and learning (Steckel & Simons, 1992; Millar, Choi, & Chen, 2004; London, Rondinelli, & O'Neill, 2005). More strategically, Warner (2004) noted four types of outcomes for corporate reputation: "1) reduced risks to marketing, sales and share price associated with perceived poor management of social impacts, 2) evidence to stakeholders of the effective implementation of company policy on sustainability and corporate citizenship, 3) reduced risk of negative public reaction and 4) increased attractiveness of the company to prospective employees" (p. 27).

There have been, however, many challenges in measuring corporate CSR outcomes. In 1985, Ullmann identified lack of theory and inappropriate definitions of key terms in the causal relationship between CSR and financial performance as problematic to measurement. More than 100 studies have been conducted and published since then; yet, the lack of a theoretical foundation has been the repeated reason for failure in explaining the relationship between CSR and corporate financial performance (Aragon-Correa & Sharma, 2003; McWilliams & Siegel, 2001; Rowley & Berman, 2000; Schaltegger & Synnestvedt, 2002). Another challenge is that CSR can have less-obvious impacts or invisible values. Lankoski (2007) suggested that firm image with customers, goodwill with regulators, employee health and motivation, and attitude of local populations hold monetary values that are difficult to establish. Last, the uncertain long-term nature of CSR outcomes may be calculated only in terms of probabilities. Therefore, simple "before-and-after" comparisons are not sufficient to reveal all impacts of CSR.

To address these challenges, Lankoski (2007) argued that corporate responsibility (CR) activities influence economic performance of the corporation via one or more of three outputs: learning, reputation, and CR outcomes (Figure 2.2). Learning is generated through the acquisition, distribution, or interpretation of new information, and it causes a change in the range of potential behaviors for the organization (Huber, 1991). It can be divided into two categories: regular learning and innovative learning. The former is generated through existing knowledge or available extraorganizational capabilities, and the latter is generated through

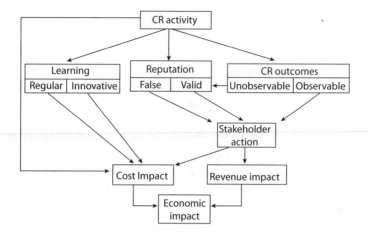

Figure 2.2 The causal chain from CR activities to economic performance. (From Lankoski, L., 2007. Corporate responsibility activities and economic performance. *Business Strategy and the Environment, 17,* 536–547. With permission of Wiley-Blackwell.)

completely new knowledge or capabilities—both forms of learning result in cost reduction (Lankoski, 2007). *Reputation* refers to "the image that stakeholders have of the firm and its corporate responsibility outcomes" (Lankoski, 2007, p. 558). Reputation and CR outcomes are argued to be separate. Reputation may be either false or valid because reputation is in the eyes of stakeholders (Lankoski, 2007). While false reputation may exist independently of actual CR outcomes, valid reputation is always linked to CR outcomes, which in turn result in revenue impact through stakeholder actions as shown in Figure 2.2.

Most important, CR outcomes refer to "improvements in the social or environmental impacts of the firm" and can be observable or unobservable (Lankoski, 2007, p. 538). Observable CR outcomes are experienced or perceived by the stakeholders' interaction with the firm, while unobservable CR outcomes are not directly experienced (Lankoski, 2007). The former results in stakeholder action directly, and the latter results in stakeholder actions only through reputation. Therefore, it is important for the current discussion that measurement of CR outcomes can make CR more observable and support corporate reputation. More observable CR outcomes and more valid reputation result in improved economic impact through cost reduction and revenue impact. For example, revenue impact may come from the positive environment afforded community members at the site of product production. Trudel and Cotte

(2009) argued from empirical investigation that "consumers are willing to pay substantially more for ethically produced goods than unethically produced goods" (p. 67).

In these ways, CSR activities via sport can become verified sustainable resources for corporations to utilize for their competitive advantage. Lankoski's causal chain from responsible corporate behavior to economic performance supports the potential of sport as an asset for firms as well as a path to sustainable development of society in terms of social networks, collective identity, healthy environment, well-being, and human capital development. Further, strong measurement of sport's contribution to society allows firms to see the contribution possible in cross-sector partnerships.

As described, measurement of CSR activities makes CSR more observable. More observable CSR outcomes can result in more stakeholder actions. In particular, consumer behavior outcomes can be readily influenced because consumers can receive information and knowledge on CSR outcomes directly through their interaction with the corporation (Lankoski, 2007). In fact, the expectation that CSR activities can influence consumers by differentiating products and services has already been found in the sponsorship context (Becker-Olsen, Cudmore, & Hill, 2006). Becker-Olsen et al. (2006) argued, however, that "consumers are unlikely to blindly accept corporate social initiatives as sincere actions and thus may or may not reward the firm" (p. 46). Further, research suggested that "consumers punish corporations that are perceived as insincere in their social involvement" (Becker-Olsen et al., 2006, p.46; Sen & Bhattacharya, 2001). Therefore, measurement of CSR outcomes is critical since it has the potential to enhance understanding of the societal contribution and thus sincerity of CSR to consumers.

In summary, the objective of this chapter has been to bring together divergent literatures to paint a broad outline of how sport can contribute to society. Our transformative agenda also has sought to show how better measurement of these intangibles should lead to wider participation of corporate social responsibilities programs involving sport. Clearly, this framework could be applied to all sorts of social projects, not simply sport. There are several limitations to the chapter, beginning with the fact that in bringing together diverse areas, depth in each was not possible. Nonetheless, we believe this to be a starting point for those keen to make a contribution to research that can at the same time address social challenges and support corporate objectives.

References

Adams, M., & Hardwick, P. (1998). An analysis of corporate donations: United Kingdom evidence. *Journal of Management Studies, 35,* 641–654.

Amis, J., Pant, N., & Slack, T. (1997). Achieving a sustainable competitive advantage: A resource-based view of sport sponsorship. *Journal of Sport Management, 11*(1), 80–96.

Andreasen, A. R., & Drumwright, M. E. (2001). Alliances and ethics in social marketing. In A. R. Andreasen (Ed.), *Ethics in social marketing* (pp. 95–124). Washington, DC: Georgetown University Press.

Aragon-Correa, J., & Sharma, S. (2003). A contingent resources-based view of proactive corporate environmental strategy. *Academy of Management Review, 28,* 71–88.

Association for Business Sponsorship of the Arts (ABSA). (1997). *ABSA sponsorship manual* (special edition for CEREC/EHG Eds.). London: Author.

Austin, J. E. (2000). Strategic collaboration between nonprofits and business. *Nonprofit and Voluntary Sector Quarterly, 29*(1), 69–97.

Austin, J. E. (2003). Marketing's role in cross-sector collaboration. *Journal of Nonprofit and Public Sector Marketing, 11*(1), 23–39.

Babiak, K., & Wolfe, R. (2009). Determinants of corporate social responsibility in professional sport: Internal and external factors. *Journal of Sport Management, 23,* 717–742.

Badelt, C. (1999). *The role of NPOs in policies to combat social exclusion* (Social Protection Discussion Paper Series 9912). Washington, DC: Social Protection Advisory Service, The World Bank.

Bailey, R. (2005). Evaluating the relationship between physical education, sport and social inclusion. *Educational Review, 57*(1), 71–90.

Barney, J. (1991). Firm resources and sustained competitive advantage. *Journal of Management, 17*(1), 99–120.

Becker-Olsen, K. L., Cudmore, B. A., & Hill, R. P. (2006). The impact of perceived corporate social responsibility on consumer behavior. *Journal of Business Research, 59,* 46–53.

Berger, I. E., Cunningham, P. H., & Drumwright, M. E. (1999). Social alliances: Company/nonprofit collaboration. *Social Marketing Quarterly, 3,* 49–53.

Berger, I. E., Cunningham, P. H., & Drumwright, M. E. (2004). Social alliance: Company/nonprofit collaboration. *California Management Review, 47*(1), 58–90.

Beutler, I. (2008). Sport serving development and peace: Achieving the goals of the United Nations through sport. *Sport in Society, 11,* 359–369.

Botcheva, L., & Huffman, L. (2004). *HIV/AIDS education program: An intervention in Zimbabwe.* The Children's Health Council. Retrieved August 16, 2009, from http://www.grassrootsoccer.org/docs/PRO%20CHC%20eval.pdf

Bowen, F. (2007). Corporate social strategy: Competing views from two theories of the firm. *Journal of Business Ethics, 75,* 97–113.

Bowen, H. R. (1953). *Social responsibilities of the businessman.* New York: Harper & Row.

Branco, M. C., & Rodrigues, L. L. (2006). Corporate social responsibility and resource-based perspectives. *Journal of Business Ethics, 69,* 111–132.

Brehm, V. M. (2001). Promoting effective North-South NGO partnerships: A comparative study of 10 European NGOs. *The International NGO Training and Research Center Occasional Papers Series, 35,* 1–75.

Carroll, A. B. (1979). A three-dimensional conceptual model of corporate performance. *Academy of Management Review, 4,* 497–505.

Chelladurai, P. (2005). *Managing organization for sport and physical activity* (2nd ed.). Scottsdale, AZ: Holcomb Hathaway.

Coalter, F. (2007). *A wider social role for sport.* New York: Routledge.

Cone, Inc., & Roper Starch Worldwide, (1999*). Cause related trends report: The evolution of cause branding.* Boston: Cone, Inc.; New York: Roper Starch Worldwide.

Conner, K. R. (1991). A historical comparison of resource-based theory and five schools of thought within industrial organization economics: Do we have a new theory of the firm? *Journal of Management, 17*(1), 121–154.

Cornwell, T. B. (2008). State of the art and science in sponsorship-linked marketing. *Journal of Advertising, 37*(3), 41–55.

Daft, R. L. (1989). *Organization theory and design* (3rd ed.). St. Paul, MN: West.

Daft, R. L. (2004). *Organization theory and design* (8th ed.). St. Paul, MN: West.

Delaney, L., & Keaney, E. (2005). *Sport and social capital in the United Kingdom: Statistical evidence from national and international survey data.* Dublin: Economic and Social Research Institute and Institute for Public Policy Research, 32. Retrieved January 20, 2009, from http://www.ippr.org.uk/uploadedFiles/research/projects/Arts_and_Culture/sport%20and%20social%20capital.pdf

Dickinson, S., & Barker, A. (2007). Evaluations of branding alliances between non-profit and commercial brand partners: The transfer of affect. *International Journal of Nonprofit and Voluntary Sector Marketing, 12,* 75–89.

Drumwright, M. E., & Murphy, P. E. (2001). Corporate social marketing. In P. N. Bloom & G. Gundlach (Eds.). *Handbook of marketing and society* (pp. 162–183). Thousand Oaks, CA: Sage.

European Commission. (1997). *Promoting the role of voluntary organizations and foundations in Europe.* Luxembourg: Author.

Haab, T. C., & McConnell, K. E. (2002). *Valuing environmental and natural resources: The econometrics of non-market valuation.* Northampton, MA: Elgar.

Hansmann, H. (1980). The role of nonprofit enterprise. *Yale Law Journal, 89,* 839–901.

Hansmann, H. (1987). Economic theories of nonprofit organizations. In W. W. Powell (Ed.), *The nonprofit sector: A research handbook* (pp. 27–42). New Haven, CT: Yale University Press.

Holme, R., & Watts, P. (2000). *Corporate social responsibility: Making good business sense.* Geneva: World Business Council for Sustainable Development.

Hopkins, B. (1987). *The law of tax-exempt organizations.* New York: Wiley.

Huber, G. P. (1991). Organizational learning: The contributing processes and the literatures. *Organization Science, 2*(1), 88–115.

International Events Group. (2000). Year one of IRL title builds traffic, awareness for northern light. *IEG Sponsorship Report, 19*(23), 1–3.

Jarvie, G. (2003). Communitarianism, sport and social capital. *International Review for the Sociology of Sport, 38*, 139.

Johnson, B. K., Groothuis, P. A., & Whitehead, J. C. (2001). The value of public goods generated by a major league sport team: The CVM approach. *Journal of Sport Economics, 2*, 6–21.

Johnson, B. K., Mondello, M., & Whitehead, J. (2007). The value of public goods generated by a national football league team. *Journal of Sport Management, 21*, 123–136.

JPMorgan Chase and Co. (2009). *JPMorgan Chase and Co. corporate change.* Retrieved August 16, 2009, from http://www.jpmorganchasecc.com/theseries.php

Lankoski, L. (2007). Corporate responsibility activities and economic performance: A theory of why and how they are connected. *Business Strategy and the Environment, 17*, 536–547.

Lawson, H. A. (2005). Empowering people, facilitating community development, and contributing sustainable developments: The social work of sport, exercise, and physical education programs. *Sport, Education and Society, 10*(1), 135–160.

Levin, I. P., & Levin, A. M. (2000). Modeling the role of brand alliances in the assimilation of product evaluations. *Journal of Consumer Psychology, 9*, 43–52.

London, T., Rondinelli, D. A., & O'Neill, H. (2005). Strange bedfellows: Alliances between corporations and nonprofits. In O. Shenkar & J. Reuer (Eds.), *Handbook of strategic alliances* (pp. 353–366). Thousand Oaks, CA: Sage.

Mahoney, J. T. (2005). *Economic foundations of strategy.* Thousand Oaks, CA: Sage.

McWilliams, A., & Siegel, D. (2001). Corporate social responsibility: A theory of the firm perspective. *Academy of Management Review, 26*, 117–127.

Mick, D. G. (2006). Presidential address: Meaning and mattering through transformative consumer research. In C. Pechmann & L. L. Price (Eds.), *Advances in consumer research* (Vol. 33, pp. 1–4). Duluth, MN: Association for Consumer Research.

Millar, C. C. J. M., Choi, C. J., & Chen, S. (2004). Global strategic partnerships between MNEs and NGOs: Drivers of change and ethical issues. *Business and Society Review, 109*, 395–414.

Munro, B. (2005, November). *Role models: Is anything more important for future development?* Role models retreat, Laureus Sport for Good Foundation, Pretoria, South Africa.

Myers, A. M. (1999). *Program evaluation for sport directors.* Champaign, IL: Human Kinetics.

MYSA Kenya. (2009). *Mathare Youth Sport Association.* Retrieved November 27, 2009, from http://www.mysakenya.org

O'Neil, M. (1989). *The third America: The emergence of the nonprofit sector in the United States.* San Francisco: Jossey-Bass.

PGA TOUR. (2009). *PGA TOUR., Inc.* Retrieved August 16, 2009, from http://www.pgatour.com/tournaments/r022/charity.html

Pollard, A., & Court, J. (2005). *How civil society organizations use evidence to influence policy processes: A literature review* (Working paper 249). London: Overseas Development Institute.

Rao, A. R., Qu, L., & Ruekert, R. W. (1999). Signaling unobservable product quality through a brand ally. *Journal of Marketing Research, 36,* 258–268.

Robbins, S. P. (1990). *Organization theory: Structure, design and applications* (3rd ed.). Englewood Cliffs, NJ: Prentice Hall.

Rollinson, D. (2002). *Organizational behavior and analysis: An integrated approach* (2nd ed.). Harlow, UK: Financial Times Prentice Hall.

Rowley, T., & Berman, S. (2000). A brand new brand of corporate social performance. *Business and Society, 39,* 397–418.

Salamon, L. M., & Anheier, H. K. (1992). In search of the nonprofit sector I: The question of definitions. *International Journal of Voluntary and Nonprofit Organizations, 3,* 125–151.

Salamon, L. M., & Anheier, H. K. (1998). Social origins of civil society: Explaining the nonprofit sector cross-nationally. *International Journal of Voluntary and Nonprofit Organizations, 9,* 213–248.

Samu, S., & Wymer, W. W., Jr. (2001). Nonprofit-business alliance model: Formation and outcomes. *Journal of Nonprofit and Public Sector Marketing, 9*(1), 45–61.

Schaltegger, S., & Synnestvedt, T. (2002). The link between green and economic success: Environmental management as the crucial trigger between environmental and economic performance. *Journal of Environmental Management, 65,* 339–346.

Schmid, H. (2004). The role of nonprofit human service organizations in providing social services. *Administration in Social Work, 28*(3), 1–21.

Seifert, B., Morris, S. A., & Bartkus, B. R. (2003). Comparing big givers and small givers: Financial correlates of corporate philanthropy. *Journal of Business Ethics, 45,* 195–211.

Seippel, O. (2006). Sport and social capital. *Acta Sociologica, 49,* 169–183.

Seitanidi, M. M. (1999). *Strategic socio-sponsorship proposal selection: A survey on the practices of the mobile telecommunication networks industry in Greece.* Dundee City, UK: School of Management, University of Abertay Dundee.

Seitanidi, M. M., & Ryan, A. (2007). A critical review of forms of corporate community involvement: From philanthropy to partnerships. *International Journal of Nonprofit and Voluntary Sector Marketing, 12,* 247–266.

Selsky, J. W., & Parker, B. (2005). Cross-sector partnerships to address social issues: Challenges to theory and practice. *Journal of Management, 31*, 849–873.

Sen, S., & Bhattacharya, C. B. (2001). Does doing good always lead to doing better? Consumer reactions to corporate social responsibility. *Journal of Marketing Research, 38*, 225–243.

Slack, T., & Parent, M. M. (2006). *Understanding sport organizations: The application of organization theory.* Windsor, Canada: Human Kinetics.

Slater, S. F. (1997). Developing a customer value-based theory of the firm. *Journal of the Academy of Marketing Science, 25*, 162–167.

Steckel, R., & Simons, R. (1992). *Doing best by doing good: How to use public purpose partnerships to boost corporate profits and benefit your community.* New York: Dutton.

Tonts, M. (2005). Competitive sport and social capital in rural Australia. *Journal of Rural Studies, 21*, 137–149.

Tour of Britain. (2009). *The Tour of Britain.* Retrieved July 16, 2009, from http://www.tourofbritain.co.uk/_ns_history

Trudel, R., & Cotte, J. (2009). Does it pay to be good? *MIT Sloan Management Review, 50*(2), 60–68.

UK Sport. (2009). *UK Sport.* Retrieved November, 27, 2009, from http://www.uksport.gov.uk/pages/go_sisters/

Ullmann, A. (1985). Data in search of a theory: A critical examination of the relationships among social performance, social disclosure, and economic performance of U.S. firms. *Academy of Management Review, 10*, 540–557.

United Nations. (2009). *NGOs and the United Nations Department of Public Information: Some questions and answers.* Retrieved July 16, 2009, from http://www.un.org/dpi/ngosection/brochure.htm

United Nations Children's Emergency Fund (UNICEF). (2009). *Unite for children.* Retrieved July 16, 2009, from http://www.unicef.org/sports/usa_45317.html

Varadarajan, P. R., & Menon, A. (1988). Cause-related marketing: A co-alignment of marketing strategy and corporate philanthropy. *Journal of Marketing, 52*, 58–74.

Waddock, S. (1988). Building successful partnerships. *Sloan Management Review Summer, 17*, 17–23.

Warner, M. (2004). Building blocks for partnerships. In M. Warner & R. Sullivan (Eds.), *Putting partnerships to work* (pp. 24–33). Sheffield, UK: Greenleaf.

Washburn, J. H., Till, B. D., & Priluck, R. (2004). Brand alliance and customer-based brand equity effects. *Psychology and Marketing, 21*, 487–508.

Weisbrod, B. A. (1977). *The voluntary nonprofit sector: An economic analysis.* Lexington: Heath.

Weiser, J., & Zadek, S. (2000). *Conversations with disbelievers: Persuading companies to address social challenges.* New York: Ford Foundation.

3

The Psychology of Fandom
Understanding the Etiology, Motives, and Implications of Fanship

Edward R. Hirt and Joshua J. Clarkson

Introduction

Time and again, we hear stories of and even witness firsthand the phenomenon of fandom. We know of those whose emotions rise and fall with the performance of their team. We know of those who forgo clothing in cold weather, withstand monsoon rains, and simmer in the summertime heat for their teams. We know of those competing in multiple fantasy leagues; in cyberspace, they follow every move of their team with faithful devotion. We also know of those who live their lives uninformed and unaware of the world of sports around them and yet still find their way into stadiums worldwide. These examples illustrate only a sample of the diverse yet complex range of behaviors exhibited by those we choose to label *fans*. For the most part, these complexities represent mere peculiarities that add intrigue to the experience of sports. For others, such as ourselves, these complexities spark fundamental questions about the psychological motives underlying fandom—and the market strategies intended to satisfy them.

Not surprisingly, then, any attempt to describe the psychology of the sports fan is a complex, multilayered process. In light of this complexity, we have elected to focus this chapter on the fundamental aspects of fandom. We first discuss the label of sports fan and the definitional issues that process incurs. In this section, we also highlight the various methods employed by researchers to index fanship. Next, we discuss the broader etiology of fanship before outlining the different motivations underlying sports fanship. Here, we highlight both the benefits and costs derived by the sports fan through identification with a favorite team or favorite player. We then introduce a new taxonomy of the fundamental needs by which these various motivations for fanship can be categorized. Last, we present several implications of this taxonomy for improving market strategies designed to both entice new fans and escalate commitment from incumbent fans.

Defining and Measuring Sports Fanship

The concept of sports fanship has a broad and rich tradition. Fanship has its roots in the more general construct of group identification. Early psychologists such as Freud (1949) and Kagan (1958) argued that identification described a process by which people include attributes or characteristics of the group as part of themselves. As a result, a notable consequence of group identification is that the individual may "react to events occurring to the group as if they occurred to him" (Kagan, 1958, p. 298). More recently, researchers in the tradition of social identity (Tajfel, 1981) and self-categorization theories (Turner, 1984) have advanced the view that group identification constitutes a condition under which the actions of a group are a central component of one's social identity. One's categorization as a member of a group is important and significant to the individual. Certainly, one of the defining elements of sports fanship is that the fan identifies strongly with a favorite team and responds to the performance of the team as if team success were a personal success and team failure a personal failure (Hirt, Zillmann, Erickson, & Kennedy, 1992). Indeed, the concept of identification is central to the working definition for fanship espoused by Wann and Branscombe (1993), who described fanship as the extent to which fans feel a psychological connection to a team and view team performances as self-relevant.

Of course, there are many ways one could define fanship. Core to this definitional issue, however, is considering the dimensions of this definition that allow for differentiation among individuals. Can the definition, for instance, separate the fair-weather fan from the faithful? One dimension that would seem to delineate this spectrum of true fan to nonfan is knowledge—that is, relevant information of the sport, a given team, specific players, or the like. While on the surface this dimension appears to be a pivotal factor in identifying sports fans, most definitions of sports fanship (including our own) do not consider knowledge as a central dimension and instead largely focus on differences in emotional commitment. However, this emphasis on emotion over knowledge is understandable, at least to some extent, given that fans at all levels of knowledge greatly differ from one another in the strength and intensity of their identification with their team.

Beyond the specific dimensions that constitute a fan, it is important to consider how we categorize or label fans. In our everyday vernacular, we tend to demarcate fans in terms of qualitative labels or categories such as casual fans, fair-weather fans, and diehard fans. Researchers, however, tend to treat sports fanship more as a hierarchy than as a set of discrete categories. In particular, the focus tends to be on the variations among fans in terms of the relative importance that their identity as a fan has within the pantheon of other social identities that comprise their overall sense of self. For some individuals, their primary social identity may be their sports team affiliation (e.g., I am, first and foremost, a New York Yankees fan or a University of North Carolina basketball fan); for others, their sports team affiliation is given less priority (i.e., I am not only a Red Sox fan but also a staunch Democrat, a devout Jew, and a full professor).

Given these issues concerning both the dimensions and categories that constitute fanship, the challenge for sports marketing researchers has been to develop measures that accurately assess and quantify a given fan's degree of identification. Within the sports science literature, three measures have received substantial use and have become widely accepted indices of sports fanship. The Psychological Commitment to Team (PCT) scale (Mahony, Madrigal, & Howard, 2000) and the Connection to Team Scale (CTS; Trail & James, 2001) are popular among sports marketing and sports management professionals. The PCT consists of 14 Likert scale items and is specifically designed to segment sports fans based on loyalty. The CTS contains only three items and has been particularly useful when examining identification with newly formed (e.g., expansion) teams (cf. Wann, 2006). Arguably the most extensively used scale within the sports psychology literature is the Sport Spectator Identification Scale (SSIS; Wann & Branscombe, 1993). The SSIS is comprised of seven Likert scale items and has received the most extensive amount of psychometric validation. This measure assesses the self-reported importance of one's team fanship, how closely one follows the team, and how much one's fanship is displayed and known by others.

Interestingly, an implicit assumption of each of these measures—and an assumption shared by researchers and sports marketers more generally—is that allegiances have a great deal of permanence and stability over time. Anecdotally, we see this stability with individuals who have been lifelong fans of particular teams and players (e.g., Green Bay Packers football fans who pass on their tickets to family members as though they were a birthright). Furthermore, test-retest reliability data using the aforementioned measures support that assumption (cf. Wann & Branscombe, 1993).

However, despite the fact that team identification appears to be a stable construct, the broader construct of social identification has been shown to be dynamic and malleable (cf. Spears, Doosje, & Ellemers, 1999). This malleability is also witnessed in the realm of sports. One's degree of identification with a team, for instance, may wax and wane over the years or even across a season depending on team potential or performance. Nonetheless, the more critical question is whether we can strategically shift fans' identification through sports marketing efforts and campaigns. Indeed, the possibility that levels of fanship can be modified serves as the basis for sports marketing in general. We argue that a more thorough understanding of the factors that contribute to fanship can inform sports marketers to devise more effective strategies to increase team identification. An essential premise underlying our analysis is that decisions about sports marketing strategies and promotions can benefit from a consideration and appreciation of the fundamental needs and motives that are satisfied by sports fans' allegiance to a particular team.

Etiology of Sports Fanship

Given the ubiquity of and profound interest in sports fanship, an important question that has permeated the literatures on sports psychology and sports marketing concerns the specific factors that encourage individuals to identify with a particular team. In other words, what transforms people into fans? Considerable investigation into this question has illuminated a broad variety of means by which people become sports fans. Researchers have shown, for instance, that family, peers, and community play prominent roles in the development of fanship (Wann, Melnick, Russell, & Pease, 2001). Furthermore, identifications form for reasons of geography (e.g., the hometown team), allegiances held by significant others (e.g., teams supported by family members and friends), and school attendance (e.g., to support one's alma mater).

However, these are but a small sampling of the vast array of factors that promote individuals to become fans. Other factors include liking for specific players (e.g., people often identify with sports franchises, like the Cleveland Cavaliers or the LA Galaxy, simply because of the popularity of a single player, like LeBron James or David Beckham, respectively), a team's strategy of play (e.g., people became fans of the 1970s Pittsburgh Steelers because of their notorious Steel curtain defense), or mere exposure/accessibility (e.g., many viewers become fans of the Chicago Cubs and Atlanta Braves due to greater television coverage on their respective superstations). As an illustration of this point, Wann, Tucker, and Schrader (1996) asked sports fans to list the reasons that they originally identified with their favorite team. Their data revealed over 40 distinct categories of reasons (not 40 different reasons, but 40 different categories). Furthermore, over 90% of those reasons were listed by fewer than 10% of respondents, suggesting that people attribute their fanship to an immense variety of sources.

Given the idiosyncratic nature of the etiology of sports fanship evidenced by these data, we believe that a more fruitful approach is to consider the broader, overarching motivations that underlie the appeal of sports fanship and sports spectatorship. This approach has a long history within the fields of communication and media research (cf. Goldstein, 1989; Raney & Bryant, 2006), and we find it especially relevant to the question of fan etiology given the wide array of factors that underlie why people watch sports and develop identifications with sports teams. Understanding the fundamental motives behind the appeal of sports fanship, then, should offer a taxonomy of core needs by which the voluminous antecedents of fanship can be summarized.

Motives Underlying Sports Fanship

Entertainment

Arguably the most basic and well-investigated motive at the core of sports fanship is that of entertainment (Gantz, 1981; Gantz & Wenner, 1991, 1995; Krohn, Clarke, Preston, McDonald, & Preston, 1998; Wann, 1995; Wenner & Gantz, 1998). More than any other reason, fans report that they watch contests involving their favorite team with the expectation of being entertained. The enjoyment and emotional satisfaction fans anticipate experiencing as they cheer on their favorite team to a hopeful victory is undeniably a primary driving force behind the appeal of sports consumption.

The disposition theory of sports spectatorship (Bryant & Raney, 2000; Zillmann, Bryant, & Sapolsky, 1989; Zillmann & Paulus, 1993) states that a fan's affiliation with a team can be represented along a continuum of affect, ranging from intense liking through indifference to intense disliking.

One's ultimate enjoyment of a sporting event, then, is a function of the outcome of the contest relative to the strength and valence of one's dispositions toward the competitors (Raney, 2006). Maximal enjoyment occurs when one's favored team defeats a disliked opponent. Indeed, fans know that rivalry games between traditional foes, such as Ohio State-Michigan, USC-Notre Dame, and Army-Navy in college football, are games by which these teams evaluate the success of their entire season. Fans of the victors of these games enjoy the bragging rights over their rival that a victory accrues them for the rest of the year. Conversely, the ultimate disappointment or negative enjoyment is experienced following the loss of a loved team to its hated rival (Zillmann & Paulus, 1993).

One of the most fascinating aspects of the disposition theory is how fans react to individual plays through the course of the game or contest. Given fans' vested interest in seeing their favorite team win, it comes as no surprise that sports fans' perceptions of plays are strongly skewed in favor of their team. Numerous studies have demonstrated that fans display selective perception and biased interpretation of events that transpire during a game, such as calls by officials or umpires (Hastorf & Cantril, 1954), and decry the "hostile media biases" against their team displayed by television announcers, reporters, and sports writers (Lau & Russell, 1980; Vallone, Ross, & Lepper, 1985).

Beyond this prevalent paranoia among sports viewers and consumers, we also witness a perverse emotion exhibited by sports fans known as *schadenfreude*. This German term refers to taking pleasure in the misfortune of others. That is, not only do sports fans relish in their own team's success, they also enjoy with intense pleasure situations in which their own team's rival takes a beating (particularly when it is at the hands of their favorite team). Anecdotally, we see this emotion displayed routinely in the community around Indiana University. A popular bumper sticker that appears prominently on numerous cars reads: "My favorite teams are Indiana and whoever is playing Purdue." Indeed, the hatred and ill-will that sports fans feel toward disliked competitors, opponents, or rivals is quite striking.

Eustress

Several studies indicate that another contributing motivation to the appeal of sports fanship is the increased arousal and excitement experienced during viewing. Many fans revel not only in the "thrill of victory" (Gantz,

1981) but also in the uncertainty and suspense associated with competitive sports (i.e., "the thrill of the experience"). Fans, for instance, report getting "psyched" or "pumped up" (Wann, 1995) prior to games or contests involving their favorite team. Interestingly, this so-called eustress motivation has been argued by some researchers to be driven by a chronic understimulation experienced by many individuals in their daily lives.

This hypothesis on the need for stimulation represents a specific example of what we view to be a broader class of mood management concerns from which the eustress motive seems to derive. For instance, Dolf Zillmann and colleagues (Biswas, Riffe, & Zillmann, 1994; Knobloch & Zillmann, 2002; Zillmann & Bryant, 1985) have repeatedly shown that people intentionally select media that will make them feel an intended emotion. Following this logic, sports fans should strategically select events that evoke desirable emotional reactions in them, such as arousal; doing so fulfills their mood management goals.

However, the intriguing aspect of sporting events is that the outcome itself is unknown, and sports fans realize that the desired outcome is often in doubt. For most nonfans, this facet of sports might lead to distress and irritation, and such individuals might shy away from choosing sporting events (or only witness events for which the outcome is less uncertain) as their means of satisfying their mood management needs. For the sports fan, on the other hand, the unscripted, suspenseful nature of sporting events makes them particularly appealing and enhances their enjoyment (DePalma & Raney, 2003). Close, hotly contested matches evoke feelings of investment and satisfaction—feelings that are *independent* of the final outcome. Thus, it seems as if the sports fan has a profound respect and admiration for intense competition, and exposure to events that are involving is sufficient to result in a highly favorable response.

Indeed, beyond simply rooting for one's favored team, sports fans display a pervasive appreciation for the philosophy that, on any given day, anyone can win. One of the most appealing features of sports is that David can beat Goliath—that is, the dominant team on paper does not always win. This perspective is clearly illustrated by the widespread appeal of the annual NCAA (National Collegiate Athletic Association) men's college basketball tournament. Deemed March madness, the tournament draws tremendous interest from viewers and gamblers (of all levels of expertise) who play tournament pools. Every year, it seems, a "Cinderella" team emerges from the field and captures the imagination (and attention) of sports spectators everywhere. These underdogs cause viewers to jump on their bandwagon and root for them as they continue in their improbable attempt to knock off perennial powerhouses (cf. Kim et al., 2008; Vandello, Goldschmied, & Richards, 2007). The uncertainty of the underdog even leads fans who fill out their tournament pools to agonize over their selections as they attempt to pick the inevitable upsets that routinely occur throughout the tournament (McCrea & Hirt, 2009).

Because increased arousal and excitement facilitates fanship, it is important for researchers to identify markers that signal stimulation. One such marker that has received considerable attention is the perceived violence contained in the action of a sporting event. Bryant, Comisky, and Zillmann (1981) compared the appeal of violent and nonviolent plays from professional American football games and found that sports fans' enjoyment increased with the degree of violence in the play. Similar results have been obtained with regard to enjoyment of hockey games (DeNeui & Sachau, 1996); in one study, the number of penalty minutes assessed in the game correlated more strongly with reported enjoyment than which team won the game. Indeed, sports broadcasters seem to recognize this fact, as evidenced by the consistent replaying of the biggest hits or most ferocious tackles for viewers. Even the commentary provided by announcers can further accentuate the intensity and drama surrounding rough, aggressive play (Comisky, Bryant, & Zillmann, 1977; Sullivan, 1991). In particular, highlighting the teams or players as enemies in describing the action elevated ratings of how enjoyable, exciting, involving, and interesting the game or match is perceived.

Finally, it is interesting to consider the physiological effects of the reported appeal by sports fans of the arousal and excitement associated with sports spectatorship. Many may wonder, for instance, whether it is in fact positive to put oneself through such stress (win or lose). There is a good amount of evidence within social psychology to suggest that people are poor at forecasting the potential affective consequences of events in their lives (Gilbert, Pinel, Wilson, Blumberg, & Wheatley, 1998; Wilson & Gilbert, 2003). Thus, there is little reason to assume sports fans will accurately predict, let alone realize, how they might react to or be affected by viewing sporting events. Anecdotally, it seems that many sports fans often exhibit a perplexing, ambivalent reaction as they watch suspenseful sporting events (e.g., uttering responses like "I can't watch" prior to critical plays). These sorts of reactions are reminiscent of the reactions that many viewers have to other media, such as horror movies. At one level, these sports fans may wonder why they put themselves through such misery. Clearly, the relief and euphoria experienced by sports fans after a close, suspenseful win would seem to make the stress worthwhile. Furthermore, research by Bernhardt, Dabbs, Fielden, and Lutter (1998) has illustrated clear physiological effects that occur after sports fans watch their team win: Male fans of the winning team show increases in mean testosterone levels, a response closely tied to expressions of dominance (Mazur, 1985). The flip side, however, is that male fans of the losing team displayed decreases in testosterone level, illustrating a potential cost associated with watching one's favorite team lose. Nonetheless, evidence of these physiological changes after team victories versus defeats suggests that the stress and excitement associated with sports spectatorship may have a broader range of consequences than previously assumed.

Escape

A distinct but related motive to those of entertainment and eustress is the fact that sports spectatorship affords sports fans the opportunity to escape the stresses of daily life. Few would argue that we live in an increasingly stressful and anxiety-provoking time. In such high-pressure lifestyles, people often look to various media content to help them take their mind off of the pressure. For many, sports fanship serves as a cathartic release in which fans can lose themselves in the events on the playing field, alleviating the monotony and boredom of everyday life (Gantz, 1981; Gantz & Wenner, 1991, 1995; Wenner & Gantz, 1998). Indeed, many wives lament the fact that they lose their husbands as they religiously watch the weekly NFL (National Football League) games for entire Sundays.

Of course, in these venues, fans are typically not simply passive observers. Fans rabidly cheer, yell, and shout for their team while watching the action. They heckle and boo the opposition and express their displeasure at the referees and officials when calls go against their team. In addition to merely evidencing their allegiance to their team, these actions have been argued to allow fans a release of their pent-up emotions and frustrations. As Smith (1988) noted, "While engrossed in the sporting event a fan's mood may fluctuate, but any pain is temporary and minor compared to the relief of gaining a respite from a wearisome existence" (p. 58).

Despite these benefits, there are some notable downsides to the escape behaviors of sports fans. As we all know, fans can get out of hand; fights erupting in parking lots, riots in the stands (or outside stadiums), even debris tossed onto playing fields, at opposing players, or at officials all exemplify negative behaviors attributed to escapism. Consequently, these sorts of behaviors are not solely instigated by the despondent fans of losing teams; fans of victorious teams set fires, vandalize, and loot businesses during celebrations.

To understand such antisocial behavior, researchers should keep in mind that sports spectatorship is often associated with other escape behaviors that may impair the judgment of sports fans, such as excessive drinking or the use of recreational drugs (Steele & Southwick, 1985). In addition, the fact that escapism is often a product of identification with a large fan base affords the sports fan conditions of relative anonymity and deindividuation (Zimbardo, 1970). When sports fans are made to feel "just like one of the crowd," individuals feel less accountable for their actions and will often lose their inhibitions against acting in an aggressive or antisocial manner (especially if others in the crowd initiate such behavior). Finally, although most sports fans believe that escape through watching violent or aggressive games lowers their own level of aggression, a large body of research in social psychology indicates just the opposite (Branscombe & Wann, 1992; Goldstein & Arms, 1971; Russell, 1981). If anything, watching aggressive or violent action primes aggressive thinking and interpretation of subsequent events, which results in a greater likelihood of aggressive behavior when someone is angry or frustrated (Berkowitz, 1993). Thus, while sports spectatorship may serve as an effective means by which sports fans can escape the stresses of everyday life, it may come at some danger and cost to themselves and those around them.

Aesthetics

Individuals are also motivated to be involved in sports from the sheer aesthetic appreciation of the skill, grace, and beauty of the athletes themselves (Krohn et al., 1998; Smith, 1988; Wann, 1995). The awe and delight inspired by watching a perfectly executed gymnastic or ice skating routine by Olympians underscores the role that this motive plays in encouraging and sustaining sports fanship. Although many scholars tend to pigeonhole this motive to certain individuals (e.g., women as opposed to men) or to certain sports in which competitions are largely evaluated on standardized, aesthetic criteria (e.g., gymnastics, figure skating, diving, skateboarding, surfing), research showed that fans of both genders and of all sports report that aesthetics has an important role in their fanship in the form of a broad appreciation for the beauty and style of the play involved in athletics (Wann & Wilson, 1999). For instance, fans will always marvel at the extraordinary athleticism displayed in mainstream sports, such as

Julius "the Doctor" Erving and Michael Jordan dunking from the free throw line or Barry Sanders and Adrian Peterson making defenders miss tackles by acrobatic moves and quick acceleration through the holes in the defense. Indeed, ESPN and other sports broadcasting networks routinely televise highlight reels of exceptional plays (diving catches, acrobatic one-hand grabs, sick crossover dribbles, and amazing cutbacks) in their play-of-the-day countdowns for the simple reason that audiences appreciate the aestheticism inherent in athletics.

Although work on this motive is less developed than others, the research that has been done focused on the facets of play that inspire such aesthetic appeal. In other words, to what are we—as fans—drawn? This is not a question unique to sports; clearly, any domain in which aesthetic enjoyment has a role in people's involvement must understand this question. However, the specific facets that make people appreciate a bicycle kick in soccer, a triple axel in ice skating, an aerial in surfing, or a knuckleball in baseball offer a unique analysis to the domain of sports. In this regard, Zillmann et al. (1989) found that fans express significant appreciation for the novelty, riskiness, and unexpectedness of the play. Fans report greater enjoyment of novel and uncommon plays, particularly ones that involve a greater risk of failure. When such plays prove to be successful, fans are elated. In general, fans are drawn to sporting events during which they feel that they "might see something they've never seen before." Thus, it would seem that the aestheticism of sports is driven by a fan's desire to witness something novel, something unexpected, and something dangerous.

Self-Esteem

Another key motivation underlying sports fanship concerns the potential benefits to one's self-esteem. We know that people have a profound need to feel that they have value (Baumeister, Heatherton, & Tice, 1993; Maslow, 1968; Rogers, 1961; Rosenberg, 1979), and considerable evidence illustrates the importance of self-esteem in how effectively people manage their everyday lives (Leary & Baumeister, 2000; Taylor & Brown, 1988). People with high self-esteem, for instance, try harder and are more successful than their counterparts with low self-esteem (McFarlin & Blascovich, 1981). Moreover, we know that people seek to maintain a positive sense of self-worth (Tesser, 1991). Indeed, a great deal of research, including much of our own work, has been devoted to showing the myriad ways people try to maintain self-esteem in the face of different challenges and threats (cf. Crocker & Park, 2004).

Cialdini and colleagues have discussed how people seek to satisfy their self-esteem needs not only by direct means (in the form of their own accomplishments) but also by indirect means (in the form of the accomplishments of others). This latter strategy is referred to as *basking in reflected glory* (often referred to by its acronym, BIRG or BIRGing), and BIRGing is often best exemplified in fans who feel intense pride in the accomplishments of their favorite sports team. For instance, Cialdini et al. (1976) had researchers survey fans of Arizona State University football about the team's recent performances. They found that after wins, fans used the pronoun "we" to describe the outcome of the game (e.g., "We beat Stanford, 31–14"), but used the pronoun "they" (or other third-person pronouns) after losses (e.g., "They lost that one, 28–21"). Note that fans are distancing themselves from the team after losses, displaying what Snyder, Lassegard, and Ford (1986) called *cutting off reflected failure* (CORF or CORFing). But, BIRGing goes beyond linguistics. In another study, Cialdini and colleagues examined the extent to which Arizona State students wore school-identifying apparel on the Mondays following college football games. Indeed, they observed that students were far more likely to wear school-identifying apparel on the days following team wins as opposed to team losses. Based on these results, Cialdini et al. (1976) argued that fans were proclaiming their association to the team following successful performances as a means of basking in reflected glory of the team's accomplishments.

We see many examples of fans BIRGing following their team success. The community pride exhibited by fans after winning championships is certainly evidenced by the increased sales of team merchandise and paraphernalia. Moreover, people are proud to identify themselves with their community ("I'm a Kansas Jayhawks fan") and use these products and logos to visibly display their association with the team to others (Oliver, 1999). Interestingly, success boosts not only the likelihood for fans to bask in reflected glory but also the tendency to derogate their team's rival (Cialdini & Richardson, 1980). That is, fans have been shown to rate the quality of various aspects of their university (e.g., academic programs, athletic programs, educational resources, social and cultural environment, and graduate placement) more favorably than that of rival institutions. This result coincides with research on social identity theory. This work shows that people have a profound tendency to value and praise groups to which they belong or with which they are affiliated (their "in-groups") while derogating and distancing themselves from groups to which they do not belong or with which they are not affiliated (their "out-groups"). Tajfel and Turner (1979) viewed this tendency to show in-group favoritism and out-group derogation as reflective of the fact that we often derive self-esteem from our group memberships—memberships that would include team affiliations.

Furthermore, Hirt et al. (1992) directly examined the effects of a team's winning and losing on the mood and self-esteem of its fans. Fans of the Indiana University and University of Wisconsin men's basketball teams watched live broadcasts of away basketball games as part of a research study. After the game, fans' mood and self-esteem were assessed. Not surprisingly, fans' mood and self-esteem were elevated after a win but depressed after a loss. Fans were then introduced to a series of different performance tasks and asked to estimate how well they could do at these tasks if asked to perform them. Interestingly, fans were optimistic about their ability to successfully perform these tasks after wins, whereas fans' predictions about their performance were far more pessimistic after losses. Moreover, the effects were most striking for fans who were highly identified with the team. The transference of team success to personal success (and team failure as personal failure) offers striking evidence for the link between people's fanship and their feelings of self-worth.

Companionship

An undeniable facet of sports fanship is that fans typically view or attend sporting events with others (family members, friends, others at the local sports bar). We all know fans who routinely tailgate before weekend football games or host Super Bowl parties. Watching sporting events with others provides fans with the opportunity to socialize and spend time with others who share their affiliation (Dietz-Uhler, Harrick, End, & Jacquemotte, 2000). Indeed, many sociologists argue that viewing sports programming with others provides a broader and more compelling set of opportunities for communication and information sharing than most other forms of media content (Wenner & Gantz, 1998).

Melnick (1993) discussed the unique communicative experience between sports fans that he called the *sports encounter*. Fans (whether they are lifelong friends or complete strangers) share a body of common knowledge in terms of teams, players, and even the sport in general. They also share a commitment to and an enthusiasm for the game. They even share and abide by a common set of assumptions about the appropriate moments during which conversation can take place (e.g., talk only when there are breaks in play). In addition, sports fans share their emotions with their companions in a manner that is unprecedented in other social encounters. Many sociologists comment that watching or participating in sports is one of the few outlets in which men in particular demonstrably share their emotions with other men (cf. Zillmann et al., 1989). Beyond these shared experiences, however, sports encounters afford one of the few conversational topics (unlike politics or religion) that allow for friendly disagreements. Sports fans can and often do endlessly debate with one another about all manner of mutable behaviors, whether a player's decision to call a time-out with none remaining, a coach's decision to leave an ace pitcher in the game, or an owner's decision to spend millions of dollars on a temperamental free agent. These friendly disagreements even extend to the unknowable: Who was the greatest Olympian of all time? Who would win a fight between Muhammad Ali and Rocky Marciano? What if steroids were better regulated? Of course, it is not the content of these conversations we find so intriguing (although that is not to say that we have not engaged in them), but rather the fact that we allow ourselves—as a culture—to openly engage in these debates or disagreements as part of common social discourse.

In short, then, there are few other ties that express the same similar degree of camaraderie and emotionality (outside one's family) than shared alliances in sports. Based on the research reviewed, it is hard not to argue that the bonds of fanship are comparable to the bonds between people from the armed services, various religious groups and social organizations, and the same alma mater. Regardless of where the bonds of fanship fit socially, it seems clear that sports fans derive a profound sense of camaraderie and companionship from sharing their fanship with others in a manner that is somewhat unique in contemporary society.

Group Affiliation

A final but critically important motive that permeates sports fanship is the sense of group affiliation it provides. We are social beings who have a need to feel a sense of connectedness or "belongingness" with others. Traditional psychological theories have long argued that once our basic needs (hunger, thirst, sex) are met, people strive for higher-order needs in the form of love and belongingness (Maslow, 1968). More recently, researchers have shown that this fundamental need leads people to form and maintain strong, stable connections with others (Baumeister & Leary, 1995).

One way that we can connect ourselves to others is to share something in common. People who share the same alma mater or hometown feel a common bond with each other, as do owners of the same product or brand (Belk, 1988; Kleine, Kleine, & Allen, 1995). Given that people like those who are similar to themselves (Byrne, 1971; Byrne & Nelson, 1965), anything that creates a bond between ourselves and others can facilitate liking (Jones & Pittman, 1982). Moreover, for those who are able to satisfy these belongingness needs, there appear to be significant advantages for both psychological and physical health. People who feel connected get sick less (DeLongis, Folkman, & Lazarus, 1988) and have a more positive sense of well-being (McAdams & Bryant, 1987). Those who do not feel connected experience a sense of loneliness and disconnectedness from others, resulting in poorer overall health and psychological adjustment (Argyle, 1987; Tambor & Leary, 1993). Fans have access to a broad community of similar others that often develops into a sense of pride in their common bond with those who share their same allegiance.

Although identifying commonalties with others has clear benefits—benefits largely accessible from the fan base afforded to any fan—people are also motivated to identify differences between themselves and others. Brewer's (2003) optimal distinctiveness theory posits that people must balance the need for inclusiveness and belongingness with the need for distinctiveness. In other words, we do not like to feel as though we are clones of everyone else, yet at the same time we do not like to feel too different from those around us (cf. Markus & Kunda, 1986). Sports fanship, like other forms of group affiliation, fulfills our desire to balance these two different needs (Wann, 2006). A great deal of research in social identity has revealed that individuals are motivated to view their own in-groups (groups to which they belong) as distinct from out-groups (Ashforth & Mael, 1989; Branscombe, Ellemers, Spears, & Doosje, 1999). These concerns have been argued to motivate sports fans not only to perceive themselves as part of something special or unique but also to believe that fans of their team are qualitatively different from fans of other teams (Wann & Branscombe, 1995).

Beyond the opportunity to satisfy identification needs, however, the affiliation motive of fanship allows the fan the opportunity to connect to something beyond ourselves. Intriguing research shows that this broader connection, if made, allows people to transcend their innate fear of death (cf. Solomon, Greenberg, & Pyszczynski, 1991). Dechesne, Greenberg, Arndt, and Schimel (2000), for instance, demonstrated that when the salience of one's mortality is increased, sports fans identify more strongly with their sports teams. In other words, when confronted with the inevitability of their own death, fans clung to their team allegiances, arguably in an attempt to grasp hold of something that would extend beyond their own existence.

The Fundamentals of Fandom

Of the multitude of reasons people have for their fanship (Wann et al., 1996), we reviewed a selection of the more prominent motives in the previous section. We believe that these motives can be subsumed under a broader taxonomy of core needs that people often turn to sports to satisfy, thus transforming them into fans. These core needs reflect a consolidation of prior research that has identified these needs as fundamental for all human beings and has illustrated how these needs can be satisfied through a variety of means. As depicted in Table 3.1, this taxonomy consists of three central needs: validation, pleasure, and arousal:

- *Validation* refers to the need to confirm or substantiate oneself and can be satisfied, for instance, by claiming the succes of Manchester United as your own. We believe fans seek validation not only through the ways in which they view themselves directly but also indirectly through the ways in which they view their family, friends, and group allegiances. This need for validation thus subsumes the self-esteem, companionship, and group affiliation motives discussed. Validation can come through actual interaction—or even perceived association—with others (e.g., as a Florida Gator fan, I have shared experiences with other Florida Gator fans across the country). Leary's sociometer hypothesis (Leary, Tambor, Terdal, & Downs, 1995) argues that our self-esteem is best construed as a barometer of how connected we feel to others in our social world. Thus, by aligning themselves with their team, fellow fans, and its rich

TABLE 3.1 Core Needs of Fanship

Need	Selected Examples of Motives Subsumed Under These Needs
Validation	Self-esteem
	Companionship
	Group affiliation
Pleasure	Entertainment
	Aesthetics
Arousal	Escape
	Eustress

history and legacy, fans are able to feel a part of something special and unique, serving to validate their self-worth, sense of belongingness, and optimal distinctiveness as well as provide a means by which they can transcend feelings of loneliness, isolation, and even existential fears of mortality and death. Fanship satisfies this fundamental need for validation by serving as an avenue by which one can bolster one's sense of low self-worth (after experiencing some challenge or threat to our self-esteem or an event like 9-11 that arouses mortality concerns in the general populace) as well as a mechanism to sustain one's sense of high self-worth when things go well.

- *Pleasure* refers to the hedonistic need to experience satisfaction or enjoyment and can be satisfied, for instance, by rooting one's team on to victory or by appreciating the technical skill and grace of a gymnast. This need for pleasure underscores the entertainment and aesthetic motives discussed. Human beings crave pleasure and gravitate toward stimuli that have produced rewarding or reinforcing outcomes in the past. Fans can derive pleasure from external factors, such as reveling in the pomp and circumstance surrounding sporting events (e.g., fireworks, cheerleaders, music, game rituals). Fans also derive pleasure from internal factors, such as one's idiosyncratic criteria for what is deemed novel, unexpected, or risky (and thus more inherently pleasing) in an athlete's performance. Of paramount importance, though, this need for pleasure highlights the fact that sports fans garner a tremendous amount of enjoyment simply from the experience of athletic competition.

- *Arousal* refers to the desire for stimulation and excitement and can be satisfied, for instance, by watching a daredevil skateboarder launch over the Great Wall of China. Fans satisfy their need for arousal by seeking out events and shared experiences that elicit stimulation, thereby alleviating the boredom and monotony of their everyday lives. In this way, the need for arousal subsumes the eustress and escape motives discussed. However, the physiological aspect of this need leads to both constructive (i.e., heightened loyalty, enthusiastic support for one's team) and destructive (i.e., rioting, taunting, derogating opposition and opponent) behaviors in fans. Yet, the desire for stimulation remains an important—and arguably unique—facet of fanship.

Strategic Implications

This taxonomy offers clear implications to those interested in developing strategies targeted to fans. We first address specific strategies that could be derived from this taxonomy. We then identify situations in which these various strategies may be most effective.

What Strategies Do These Specific Needs Inform?

Validation

The key elements of fanship that a need for validation informs surround the identity that fans accrue from their team allegiances. In many ways, sports team affiliations can be construed as brands, and as such, sports marketing efforts must focus on the creation and articulation of the features of that brand. For instance, what defines a specific group of fans, such as Cubs fans, and distinguishes them from fans of other teams? Strategies to create a distinctly positive in-group identity for the fans of a particular team, something that offers fans something unique relative to fans of other teams (out-groups) can simultaneously satisfy the belongingness and self-esteem motives of the individual as well as optimal distinctiveness needs to differentiate oneself. Indeed, we see teams attempt to create the sense of identity among their fans in a variety of ways (e.g., by having fans all wear the same team colors and logos, act out rituals or sing fight songs in unison at games, etc.). Often, these campaigns are used to try to motivate fans to support capital projects for new stadia or arenas or efforts to come out and "pack the house" for special events. These efforts reinforce the idea that fans are part of something larger than themselves, linking them to a history and tradition that extends beyond the past and present into the future. Obviously, the best ways to accomplish these efforts will vary depending on such factors as (a) the longevity and past success of the franchise; (b) the changes that occur to the team due to coaching changes, free agency pickups, scandals; or (c) even franchise relocations, necessitating a revision of a past identity or even the reinvention of a new identity. Nonetheless, these approaches all share a common focus on the creation and accentuation of a shared positive identity among fans, validating their common allegiance to the team.

Pleasure

The key elements of fanship that the need for pleasure informs are the sheer enjoyment and entertainment value fans derive from watching their favorite team play. Clearly, the most notable facet of entertainment based on disposition theory is the success of the team: Fans will jump on the bandwagon and come out in droves to see a winning team, so efforts to encourage fans to join in the fun of supporting a successful team throughout the season or during the playoffs is relatively straightforward. We know that people are profoundly influenced by and conform to the behavior of others, and campaigns that simply display the fact that many others are attending and enjoying particular sporting events provide "social proof" (Cialdini, 2000) that fanship is the right thing to do. However, beyond simply wins and losses, there are many avenues available for strategists to illustrate the unique entertainment opportunities of sports fanship. Creating a fun and entertaining atmosphere at the game (e.g., cheerleaders, upbeat music, halftime shows, etc.) is an obvious investment to generate entertainment. Also, fan involvement serves to heighten fan enjoyment and increase team allegiance and thus should be maximized if possible. Minor league franchises have been successful, for instance, in their efforts to accentuate the entertainment value for the whole family by basing their season on game day themes. These themes are often predictable and offer a host of interactive activities, such as giveaways, prizes, and contests throughout the game. Photos with players or team mascots have been used to add to the enjoyment of kids, who at some parks are even permitted to enter the field and run the bases following the game. Similarly, franchises with outstanding players often highlight the ability or the determination of the athletes that sports fans appreciate and admire, as well as advertise the possibility that fans may see something they have never seen before. Aesthetically pleasing arenas and stadia in which every seat is a good seat to view the action contributes to enjoyment. Efforts to reconnect with the past by commemorating outstanding former players or wearing retro uniforms also allow fans to relive past glories and nostalgic memories that make fanship something uniquely enjoyable and appealing.

Arousal
The key elements of fanship that the need for arousal informs are the unique stimulating and energizing aspects of sports fanship. Fanship affords a means to alleviate the routine of everyday life in a unique and enticing way: Fans experience game time as a chance to let loose, to feel adrenaline (e.g., get pumped up), and to lose themselves in the excitement of the action on the playing field. Fans display their allegiance by wearing team-identifying apparel, wearing costumes, or even painting their face or body to help get into the appropriate frame of mind for the game. Efforts to emphasize the escape and release aspects that sports fanship provides will successfully highlight the ways fanship satisfies the need for arousal.

In addition, we cannot deny the emotional exhilaration that sports fans feel during sporting events themselves. The unscripted nature of the action provides mounting tension and uncertainty regarding the final outcome. Fans relish nail-biting, competitive matches that keep them on the edge of their seats (after all, "It's never over 'til it's over!" right?). Anyone who can recall the aftermath of March Madness upsets like the 1993 North Carolina State victory in the title game over a heavily favored University of Houston (Phi Slamma Jamma) team with exuberant North Carolina State coach Jim Valvano running onto the court after an improbable buzzer beater can attest to the emotions evoked by such events among viewers as well as spectators and players. Indeed, these facets of sports spectatorship are regularly pitched to fans by ads that encourage them to "catch all the action." Furthermore, specific aspects of play are highlighted to draw fans, aspects that appeal directly to this need for arousal. The violence and aggressiveness of play in several sports (e.g., the hard hits and bone-crushing tackles in football, the jaw-rattling checks in hockey, the fiery crashes in auto races) are often promoted with pride to elicit excitement and emphasize the stimulating aspects of sporting events. Indeed, we believe that any of a broad range of features of sports—the physical, the sensual, the controversial, the unexpected—all serve to illustrate the myriad ways strategists can engage fans through their need for arousal.

When Should These Strategies Be Most Effective?

We believe that one of the most beneficial aspects of this taxonomy of basic needs is that it provides a framework to inform and guide sports marketing efforts to draw in new fans and to sustain and enhance the allegiance of incumbent fans. Indeed, psychological research has consistently pointed out that the importance of different needs varies as a function of time and context (Baumeister & Leary, 1995; Brewer, 2003; Maslow, 1968). Thus, it is critical to consider the parameters that might affect the relative priority and salience of these needs for fans of different teams to optimize the effectiveness of sports marketing efforts. For instance, in the aftermath of 9-11, a resumption of Major League Baseball in the days immediately following the tragedy was deemed crucial for fans' psyches as it served to satisfy our need for validation and to allow a return to normalcy, epitomized by the "grand old game." In other situations, fans' need for entertainment or arousal may take precedence, and strategies to accentuate these facets of sports fanship will be most effective. A comprehensive list of these different parameters is certainly beyond the scope of the present chapter.

However, in this final section, we briefly discuss a few key parameters that we feel deserve attention.

Value of Needs Should Vary With the Specific Sport

The relative importance of needs clearly varies with the specific sport under consideration. A sport like figure skating or gymnastics, in which we know that aesthetics are highly valued, is one in which the need for pleasure should be highlighted. Conversely, sports like football, hockey, and boxing, whose appeal may reside primarily in terms of the eustress of violent and aggressive play, would be ones in which the need for arousal is paramount. Thus, it would be valuable for sports marketers to determine the primary motives and needs satisfied by particular sports to most effectively develop campaign strategies. This is not to say that one cannot acknowledge or even cultivate additional need served by fanship to those sports; indeed, efforts to do so might broaden the appeal of that sport to a larger constituent of the population. However, to sustain and enhance the allegiance of fans of a sport, efforts to highlight the fundamental needs met by that particular sport would seem to be most advisable.

Value of Needs Should Vary With Level of Fanship

Indeed, another variable that should affect the relative importance or value of particular needs is an individual's level of fanship. New fans might be drawn to a particular sport (like mixed martial arts [MMA]) to satisfy their need for arousal and stimulation, whereas incumbent fans might have developed an entirely different appreciation of the aesthetics of the sport and find that it satisfies their need for pleasure. In such cases, sports marketers may want to promote the arousal aspects of the sport to attract new fans but highlight the pleasure (aesthetics, enjoyment) aspects of the sport to sustain or enhance the allegiance and devotion of current fans.

Value of Needs Should Vary With Team Success

One would also expect that the relative importance of particular needs would depend on the level of success of the team or franchise. Losing teams or franchises in the midst of rebuilding may need to devote efforts to enhance the validation needs served by fanship. Efforts to stress the loyalty and identity of the existing fan base of the team may enable the team to better weather poor performance or scandals. Conversely, efforts to illustrate the pleasure needs satisfied by joining the bandwagon of a successful team may entice new fans to the team.

Conclusion

Fandom is an intriguing field of study, and it is clear from this analysis that the motives that underlie sports fanship are broad and pervasive. Sports fanship satisfies a variety of different motives for individuals, justifying the growing numbers of people who turn to sports as a means to address what we believe are a handful of fundamental core needs. A consideration of these needs not only can provide a richer and more thorough appreciation of the appeal of sports fanship but also can serve to inform efforts on the part of sports marketers to develop campaigns that capitalize on the particular needs that fans garner from their allegiance. We hope that researchers and practitioners alike can build on this analysis to further understand the psychological makeup of fans, to design more effective strategies to attract new fans, and to sustain and deepen the identification and allegiance of current fans.

References

Argyle, M. (1987). *The psychology of happiness*. London: Methuen.

Ashforth, B. E., & Mael, F. (1989). Social identity theory and the organization. *Academy of Management Review, 14*, 20–39.

Baumeister, R. F., Heatherton, T., & Tice, D. (1993). When ego threats lead to self-regulation failure: Negative consequences of high self-esteem. *Journal of Personality and Social Psychology, 64*, 141–156.

Baumeister, R. F., & Leary, M. (1995). The need to belong: Desire for interpersonal attachments as a fundamental human motivation. *Psychological Review, 117*, 497–529.

Belk, W. (1988). Possessions and the extended self. *Journal of Consumer Research, 15*, 139–168.

Berkowitz, L. (1993). *Aggression*. New York: McGraw-Hill.

Bernhardt, P. C, Dabbs, J. M., Fielden, J. A., & Lutter, C. D. (1998). Testosterone changes during vicarious experiences of winning and losing among fans at sporting events. *Physiology and Behaviors, 18*, 263–268.

Biswas, R., Riffe, D., & Zillmann, D. (1994). Mood influence on the appeal of badness. *Journalism Quarterly, 71*, 689–696.

Branscombe, N., Ellemers, N., Spears, R., & Doosje, B. (1999). The context and content of social identity threat. In N. Ellemers, R. Spears, & B. Doosje (Eds.), *Social identity* (pp. 35–58). Oxford, UK: Blackwell.

Branscombe, N., & Wann, D. L. (1992). Role of identification with a group, arousal, categorization processes, and self-esteem in sports spectator aggression. *Human Relations, 45*, 1013–1033.

Brewer, M. B. (2003). Optimal distinctiveness, social identity, and the self. In M. R. Leary & J. P. Tangney (Eds.), *Handbook of self and identity* (pp. 480–491). New York: Guilford.

Bryant, J., Comisky, P. W., & Zillmann, D. (1981). The appeal of rough-and-tumble play in televised professional football. *Communication Quarterly, 29*, 256–262.

Bryant, J., & Raney, A. A. (2000). Sports on the screen. In D. Zillmann & P. Vorderer (Eds.), *Meida entertainment: The psychology of its appeal* (pp. 153–174). Mahwah, NJ: Erlbaum.

Byrne, D. (1971). *The attraction paradigm*. New York: Academic Press.

Byrne, D., & Nelson, D. (1965). Attraction as a linear function of proportion of positive reinforcements. *Journal of Personality and Social Psychology, 1*, 659–663.

Cialdini, R. B. (2000). *Influence: Science and practice* (4th ed.). Boston: Allyn & Bacon.

Cialdini, R. B., Borden, R. J., Thorne, A., Walker, M. R., Freeman, S., & Sloan, L. R. (1976). Basking in reflected glory: Three (football) field studies. *Journal of Personality and Social Psychology, 34*, 366–375.

Cialdini, R. B., & Richardson, K. (1980). Two indirect tactics of image management: Basking and blasting. *Journal of Personality and Social Psychology, 39*, 406–415.

Comisky, P., Bryant, J., & Zillmann, D. (1977). Commentary as a substitute for action. *Journal of Communication, 27*, 150–153.

Crocker, J., & Park, L. (2004). The costly pursuit of self-esteem. *Psychological Bulletin, 130*, 392–414.

Dechesne, M., Greenberg, J., Arndt, J., & Schimel, J. (2000). Terror management and the vicissitudes of sports fan affiliation: The effects of mortality salience on optimism and fan identification. *European Journal of Social Psychology, 30*, 813–835.

DeLongis, A., Folkman, S., & Lazarus, R. (1988). The impact of daily stress on health and mood: Psychological and social resources as mediators. *Journal of Personality and Social Psychology, 54*, 486–495.

DeNeui, D. L., & Sachau, D. A. (1996). Spectator enjoyment of aggression in intercollegiate hockey games. *Journal of Sport and Social Issues, 21*, 69–77.

DePalma, A., & Raney, A. A. (2003, May). *The effect of viewing varying levels of aggressive sports programming on enjoyment, mood, and perceived violence*. Paper presented at the annual meeting of the International Communication Association, San Diego, CA.

Dietz-Uhler, B., Harrick, E. A., End, C., & Jacquemotte, L. (2000). Sex differences in sport fan behavior and reasons for being a sport fan. *Journal of Sport Behavior, 23*, 219–231.

Freud, S. (1949). *Group psychology and the analysis of the ego*. London: Hogarth.

Gantz, W. (1981). An exploration of viewing motives and behaviors associated with television sports. *Journal of Broadcasting, 25*, 263–275.

Gantz, W., & Wenner, L. A. (1991). Men, women, and sports: Audience experiences and effects. *Journal of Broadcasting and Electronic Media, 35,* 233–243.

Gantz, W., & Wenner, L. A. (1995). Fanship and the television sports viewing experience. *Sociology of Sport Journal, 12,* 56–74.

Gilbert, D. T., Pinel, E. C., Wilson, T. D., Blumberg, S. J., & Wheatley, T. P. (1998). Immune neglect: A source of durability bias in affective forecasting. *Journal of Personality and Social Psychology, 75,* 617–638.

Goldstein, J. H. (1989). *Sports, games, and play: Social and psychological viewpoints* (2nd ed.). Hillsdale, NJ: Erlbaum.

Goldstein, J. H., & Arms, R. L. (1971). Effects of observing athletic contests on hostility. *Sociometry, 34,* 83–90.

Hastorf, A. H., & Cantril, H. (1954). They saw a game: A case study. *Journal of Abnormal and Social Psychology, 49,* 129–134.

Hirt, E. R., Zillmann, D., Erickson, G., & Kennedy, C. (1992). Costs and benefits of allegiance: Changes in fans' self-ascribed competencies after team victory versus defeat. *Journal of Personality and Social Psychology, 63,* 724–738.

Jones, E. E., & Pittman. T. S. (1982). Toward a general theory of strategic self-presentation. In J. Suls (Ed.), *Psychological perspectives on the self* (pp. 231–262). Hillsdale, NJ: Erlbaum.

Kagan, J. (1958). The concept of identification. *Psychological Review, 65,* 296–305.

Kim, J. H., Allison, S. T., Eylon, D., Goethals, G. R., Markus, M. J., Hindle, S. M., & McGuire, H. A. (2008). Rooting for (and then abandoning) the underdog. *Journal of Applied Social Psychology, 38,* 2550–2573.

Kleine, S. S., Kleine, E. E., III, & Allen, C. T. (1995). How is a possession "me" or "not me"? Characterizing types and an antecedent of material possession attachment. *Journal of Consumer Research, 3,* 327–343.

Knobloch, S., & Zillmann, D. (2002). Mood management via the digital jukebox. *Journal of Communication, 52,* 351–366.

Krohn, F. B., Clarke, M., Preston, E., McDonald, M., & Preston, B. (1998). Psychological and sociological influences on attendance at small college sporting events. *College Student Journal, 32,* 277–288.

Lau, R. R., & Russell, D. (1980). Attributions in the sports pages. *Journal of Personality and Social Psychology, 39,* 29–38.

Leary, M. R., & Baumeister, R. (2000). The nature and function of self-esteem: Sociometer theory. In M. Zanna (Ed.), *Advances in experimental social psychology* (Vol. 32, pp. 1–63). San Diego, CA: Academic Press.

Leary, M. R., Tambor, E. S., Terdal, S. K., & Downs, D. L. (1995). Self-esteem as an interpersonal monitor: The sociometer hypothesis. *Journal of Personality and Social Psychology, 68,* 518–530.

Mahony, D. F., Madrigal, R., & Howard, D. (2000). Using the Psychological Commitment to Team (PCT) scale to segment sports consumers based on loyalty. *Sports Marketing Quarterly, 9,* 15–25.

Markus, H., & Kunda, Z. (1986). Stability and malleability of the self-concept. *Journal of Personality and Social Psychology, 51,* 858–866.

Maslow, A. H. (1968). *Toward a psychology of being.* New York: Van Nostrand.

Mazur, A. (1985). A biosocial model of status in face-to-face primate groups. *Social Forces, 64,* 377–402.

McAdams, D. P., & Bryant, F. B. (1987). Intimacy motivation and subjective mental health in a nationwide sample. *Journal of Personality, 55,* 395–413.

McCrea, S. M., & Hirt, E. R. (2009). Match madness: Probability matching in the prediction of a sporting event. *Journal of Applied Social Psychology, 39,* 2809–2839.

McFarlin, D. B., & Blascovich, J. (1981). Effects of self-esteem and performance feedback on future affective preferences and cognitive expectations. *Journal of Personality and Social Psychology, 40,* 521–531.

Melnick, M. J. (1993). Searching for sociability in the stands: A theory of sports spectating. *Journal of Sport Management, 7,* 44–60.

Oliver, R. L. (1999). Whence consumer loyalty? *Journal of Marketing, 63,* 33–44.

Raney, A. A. (2006). Why we watch and enjoy mediated sports. In A. A. Raney & J. Bryant (Eds.), *Handbook of sports and media* (pp. 313–329). Mahwah, NJ: Erlbaum.

Raney, A. A., & Bryant, J. (2006). *Handbook of sports and media.* Mahwah, NJ: Erlbaum.

Rogers, C. R. (1961). *On becoming a person.* Boston: Houghton Mifflin.

Rosenberg, M. (1979). *Conceiving the self.* New York: Basic Books.

Russell, G. W. (1981). Spectator moods at an aggressive sports event. *Journal of Sport Psychology, 3,* 217–227.

Smith, G. J. (1988). The noble sports fan. *Journal of Sport and Social Issues, 12,* 54–65.

Snyder, C. R., Lassegard, M., & Ford, C. (1986). Distancing after group success and failure: Basking in reflected glory and cutting off reflected failure. *Journal of Personality and Social Psychology, 51,* 382–388.

Solomon, S., Greenberg, J., & Pyszczynski, T. (1991). A terror management theory of social behavior: The psychological function of self-esteem and cultural worldviews. In M. Zanna (Ed.), *Advances in experimental social psychology* (Vol. 24, pp. 91–159). San Diego, CA: Academic Press.

Spears, R., Doosje, B., & Ellemers, N. (1999). Commitment and the context of social perception. In N. Ellemers, R. Spears, & B. Doosje (Eds.), *Social identity* (pp. 59–83). Oxford, UK: Blackwell.

Steele, C. M., & Southwick, L. (1985). Alcohol and social behavior I: The psychology of drunken excess. *Journal of Personality and Social Psychology, 48,* 18–34.

Sullivan, D. B. (1991). Commentary and viewer perception of player hostility: Adding punch to televised sport. *Journal of Broadcasting and Electronic Media, 35,* 487–504.

Tajfel, H. (1981). *Human groups and social categories.* Cambridge, UK: Cambridge University Press.

Tajfel, H., & Turner, J. (1979). An integrative theory of intergroup conflict. In W. G. Austin & S. Worchel (Eds.), *The social psychology of intergroup relations* (pp. 33–47). Monterey, CA: Brooks-Cole.

Tambor, E. S., & Leary, M. (1993). *Perceived exclusion as a common factor in social anxiety, loneliness, jealousy, depression, and low self-esteem.* Unpublished manuscript.

Taylor, S. E., & Brown, D. (1988). Illusion and well-being: A social psychological perspective on mental health. *Psychological Bulletin, 103,* 193–210.

Tesser, A. (1991). Emotion in social comparison processes. In J. Suls & T. A. Wills (Eds.), *Social comparison* (pp. 115–145). Hillsdale, NJ: Erlbaum.

Trail, G. T., & James, J. D. (2001). An analysis of the sports fan motivation scale. *Journal of Sport Behavior, 24,* 107–127.

Turner, J. C. (1984). Social identification and psychological group formation. In H. Tajfel (Ed.), *The social dimension: European developments on social psychology* (Vol. 2, pp. 518–538). Cambridge, UK: Cambridge University Press.

Vallone, R. P., Ross, L., & Lepper, M. R. (1985). The hostile media phenomenon: Biased perceptions and perceptions of media bias in coverage of the Bierut massacre. *Journal of Personality and Social Psychology, 49,* 577–585.

Vandello, J. A., Goldschmied, N. P., & Richards, D. A. (2007). The appeal of the underdog. *Personality and Social Psychology Bulletin, 33,* 1603–1616.

Wann, D. L. (1995). Preliminary validation of the Sports Fan Motivation Scale. *Journal of Sport and Social Issues, 19,* 377–396.

Wann, D. L. (2006). The causes and consequences of sports team identification. In A. A. Raney & J. Bryant (Eds.), *Handbook of sports and media* (pp. 331–352). Mahwah, NJ: Erlbaum.

Wann, D. L., & Branscombe, N. (1993). Sports fans: Measuring degree of identification with the team. *International Journal of Sport Psychology, 24,* 1–17.

Wann, D. L., & Branscombe, N. (1995). Influence of identification with a sports team on objective knowledge and subjective beliefs. *International Journal of Sport Psychology, 26,* 551–567.

Wann, D. L., Melnick, M. J., Russell, G. W., & Pease, D. G. (2001). *Sports fans: The psychology and social impact of spectators.* New York: Routledge Press.

Wann, D. L., Tucker, K. B., & Schrader, M. P. (1996). An exploratory examination of the factors influencing the origination, continuation, and cessation of identification with sports teams. *Perceptual and Motor Skills, 82,* 995–1001.

Wann, D. L., & Wilson, A. M. (1999). The relationship between aesthetic fan motivation and preferences for aggressive and nonaggressive sports. *Perceptual and Motor Skills, 89,* 931–934.

Wenner, L. A., & Gantz, W. (1998). Watching sports on television: Audience experience, gender, fanship, and marriage. In L. A. Wenner (Ed.), *Mediasport* (pp. 233–251). London: Routledge.

Wilson, T. D., & Gilbert, D. T. (2003). Affective forecasting. In M. P. Zanna (Ed.), *Advances in experimental social psychology* (Vol. 35, pp. 345–411). San Diego, CA: Academic Press.

Zillmann, D., & Bryant, J. (1985). *Selective exposure to communication*. Hillsdale, NJ: Erlbaum.

Zillmann, D., Bryant, J., & Sapolsky, N. (1989). Enjoyment from sports spectatorship. In J. Goldstein (Ed.), *Sports, games, and play* (pp. 241–278). Hillsdale, NJ: Erlbaum.

Zillmann, D., & Paulus, P. B. (1993). Spectators: Reactions to sports events and effect on athletic performance. In R. N. Singer, M. Murphey, & L. K. Tennant (Eds.), *Handbook of research on sports psychology* (pp. 600–619). New York: Macmillan.

Zimbardo, P. G. (1970). The human choice: Individuation, reason, and order versus deindividuation, impulse, and chaos. In W. J. Arnold & D. Levine (Eds.), *Nebraska symposium on motivation* (Vol. 17, pp. 237–307). Lincoln: University of Nebraska Press.

4

Spectator Rage
An Overview

Scott A. Jones, Stephen J. Grove,
and Gregory M. Pickett

Introduction

The influence of customer-to-customer interactions on perceptions of a service encounter has received considerable attention from a number of marketing researchers (Arnould & Price, 1993; Bitner, Booms, & Mohr, 1994; Grove & Fisk, 1997; Harris & Reynolds, 2004; Huang, 2008). When such interactions are of an unpleasant nature, such incidents may assume the form of customer rage (Kalamas, Laroche, & Makdessian, 2008). While customer rage may occur in a wide variety of industries, incidents of rage in spectator sport seemingly receive a great deal of notoriety and scrutiny. However, while customer rage has been examined within a number of disciplines, it has received minimal attention by the marketers of sport (Hunt, Bristol, & Bashaw, 1999). This omission is somewhat perplexing given the importance of live sporting events within the larger sport industry.

The live sporting event is often referred to as the primary product of the sport industry (Mullin, Hardy, & Sutton, 2000). This description underscores the importance of the event as a precursor for all other sport-related products. For example, licensing agreements, broadcast rights, and sponsorships are all contingent on the event itself. With this in mind, any circumstance that undermines the attractiveness of sporting contests may have adverse consequences for any of a number of stakeholders associated with the event. Further, the potential adverse impact of rage behavior may be particularly damaging for spectator sport since repeat patronage (typically in the form of season ticket sales) and extended contractual agreements (sponsor relations and media partnerships) are often the subject of considerable media attention.

Complicating the relationship between rage at a sporting event and efforts to prevent it is the fact that many of the factors that may promote rage are prompted by the sport marketers' desire to provide the optimum experience for spectators attending such events and the quest to maximize revenue opportunities. The following discussion introduces a number of factors that may help to foster spectator rage at sporting events. Further, we offer comments noting how such factors may be influenced by marketing activities. Of particular interest throughout the discussion is how concerns over spectator rage may conflict with the goals of providing a fun and exciting atmosphere for spectators.

Defining Rage and Spectators

In the discussion that follows, the term *spectator* is used to identify consumers who attend live sporting events. The term *spectator*, then, distinguishes between those that attend the live sporting event from those consuming the contest through other mediums, such as radio, television, or the Internet. The term *rage* is also used throughout our discussion to refer to violent and uncontrolled anger. We suggest rage in this context is synonymous with the concept of aggression, described as verbal or physical behavior intended to control or harm another person (Coakley, 1998). Under this conceptualization, spectator rage may include a range of behaviors, such as taunting opposing players, coaches, or officials; physical acts such as throwing objects on the field of play or at other spectators; obscene gestures; or the destruction of the physical setting. It should be emphasized that this conceptualization incorporates both physical and nonphysical behavior. Some examples of spectator rage that reflect this conceptualization include the following:

- A fight involving players during a professional basketball contest between the Indiana Pacers and Detroit Pistons spilled into the stands when a fan threw a beverage at one of the players (Associated Press, 2004).
- Italian soccer authorities postponed an entire round of games and closed down stadiums that did not satisfy safety regulations in the wake of spectator clashes with stadium security personnel (Sports Network, 2007).
- A Boston Red Sox fan at Fenway Park threw beer into the face of an outfielder of arch rival New York Yankees, Gary Sheffield, prompting him to take a swing at the perpetrator (Edes, 2005).

While incidents of spectator rage may appear more common today than ever before, it is worth noting that it is not a new phenomenon. Many historians attribute the start of the Nika riots in the sixth century to a rivalry between supporters of the Blue and Green chariot-racing teams in Constantinople (Encyclopedia Britannica, n.d.). Further, incidents of spectator rage have been persistent over time. Some historians note only two periods in British history have been relatively free of soccer-related violence: the interwar years and the decade following World War II. Finally, while the subsequent discussion focuses primarily on professional and collegiate sport, it bears noting that incidents of spectator rage have plagued all levels of organized sport, including youth events.

Spectator Disposition

Prior to discussing influences that may predispose sport spectators to aggressive behavior, it is important to recognize a number of factors that may prompt hostile behavior across a variety of service contexts. Indeed, there are numerous circumstances that may provoke a spectator (or any consumer for that matter) to engage in rage behavior. Among them, for instance, are a number of physiological conditions, including low levels of serum cholesterol (Spitz & Hillbrand, 1994) or serotonin (Brown, Goodwin, & Bunney, 1982). In addition, individuals with passive-aggressive personalities or Type A personalities may be more likely to commit acts of aggression (Holmes & Will, 1985; Stone, 1993). Last, temporary conditions that spectators bring with them or that emerge at a sporting event may affect their likelihood to rage. For example, moods may influence one's consumption experience (Gardner, 1985; Knowles, Grove, & Pickett, 1993), and obviously, spectators who are in a poor mood or develop one at the sport venue are likely candidates for rage behavior.

More specific to spectator sport, those attending live sporting events may be prone to rage due to various psychological and sociological influences. Consider, for example, the phenomenon of identification. Identification is described as the process of maintaining a positive, self-defining relationship with others one deems attractive (Kelman, 1958, 1961). Ardent sport fans may view their favorite team or athlete as an extension of the self (End, Dietz-Uhler, Harrick, & Jacquemotte, 2002; Kahle, Duncan, Dalakas, & Aiken, 2001), resulting in an orientation of the self in which individuals define themselves in terms of their group membership and gain a sense of identity from the affiliation (Harris & Ogbonna, 2008).

This connection may lead spectators to perceive threats to their favorite team, such as the fans of an opponent or officials responsible for supervising the contest, as a personal threat. In such instances, actions of opposing fans or a poor ruling by a game official may cause other fans to respond with aggressive reactions as a defense strategy in an effort to restore self-esteem (Branscombe & Wann, 1992, 1994).

The perceived significance of a given sporting event may also increase the likelihood of rage. Given the strong psychological connection between many spectators and "their" team or favorite athlete, similarly strong reactions may result particularly when the outcome of a contest is of heightened importance. Sport rivalries involving local teams like college football's Alabama Crimson Tide and Auburn Tigers, teams with a long history of competition such as the New York Yankees and Boston Red Sox, or events involving national rivals such as the India and Pakistan cricket teams may be particularly vulnerable to such behavior. Obviously, such events are also coveted by organizers and media interests. Media partners, facility operators, and host communities may benefit from the passion spectators hold for such rival contests and consequently may benefit through increased interest in such events from potential sponsors and advertisers, greater attendance, related sales, and the like. In this respect, such constituents may derive financial benefit by adding "more fuel to the fire" among those who closely follow the participants in such rivalries.

A sporting event may also have increased significance for some spectators based on gambling interests. Wagering money on the outcome of a sporting event is likely to increase the importance of the outcome for some, resulting in a propensity to engage in rage behavior (Parke & Griffiths, 2004). Despite such concerns, many sport entities have relaxed policies that in the past restricted the formation of relationships with gambling interests (McKelvey, 2004).

Spectators may also be influenced by several sociological factors. For instance, some fans may presume their role of spectator at a sporting event is, in part, to create a hostile atmosphere for the opponent of the team or athlete they support (Pratt & Cardador, 2006). An extreme example of this are those spectators who have been described as "hooligans"—fanatical fans who have a lengthy history of hostile behavior and violence at European soccer events (Hughson, 1998; Spaaij, 2008). In this regard, it is possible that spectator rage may be a learned response imparted via socialization as acceptable behavior in the context of live sporting events (Bandura, 1973, 1986). Contributing to this phenomenon may also be the branding efforts of sport marketers. Venues and stadiums designed to host sporting events are frequently promoted with nicknames such as "Death Valley," "The Pit," or "The Swamp," and the establishment of such associations may encourage the acceptance of aggression as a means of fulfilling the role of spectator. It is also important to note that such branding may also serve to differentiate the licensed products of a sport entity from others, making that intellectual property more valuable.

In addition, as described by Bredemeier, Shields, and Horn (1985), some spectators may neglect the norms prescribed for acceptable social behavior in lieu of a more egocentric perspective. Behavior considered inappropriate in most contexts may be viewed as acceptable and required as part of the role assigned to a true fan. Contributing to this phenomenon are group dynamics that are present at many sporting events. For example, holding all else constant, consequences for aberrant spectator actions are recognized to be less in large groups than when acting alone (Guerin, 1994, 1998). In short, spectators attending a sporting event may perceive that the crowd provides a degree of anonymity protecting them from the normal repercussions of hostile behavior (Wann, Hayes, McLean, & Pullen, 2003; Wann, Peterson, Cothran, & Dykes, 1999). This is perhaps most evident when the target of the hostility is an athlete or official on the field.

Ancillary Factors

A number of factors that may help to promote rage behavior may be a function of conditions inside the venue or stadium serving as host of a sporting event. One such factor receiving considerable scrutiny in recent years is the proximity of spectators to the athletic contest. Consider the incident described involving the violence that erupted during a National Basketball Association contest between the Indiana Pacers and Detroit Pistons. The proximity of the spectators to the game action may have created a strong sense of involvement and the opportunity for direct, physical interaction between the spectators and the players. Close proximity to the athletes and teams may also be viewed as one of the primary benefits associated with attending the live sporting event as opposed to consuming the event through other means. Further, those seats closest to the game action also command premium prices and, consequently, are important sources of revenue for the marketers of live sporting events.

Spectators attending a sporting event are also often seated close to one another, affording the opportunity for substantial verbal and physical interaction between spectators. The crowded conditions found in many stadiums may also serve to stoke reactions of hostility (Hui & Bateson, 1991; Stokolos, 1972). Discomfort and dissatisfaction may increase as the number of people in a service setting grows (Eroglu & Machleit, 1990; Machleit, Eroglu, & Mantel, 2000). Large crowds are, however, part of a sport marketer's goal of maximizing the number of seats available within a sport venue and filling those seats with paying spectators. A crowded stadium increases the likelihood of one spectator bumping into another or accidentally spilling food or a beverage—either of which may prompt an aggressive response. Similarly, a large crowd likely increases the chance that spectators will encounter a variety of queues at a sporting event. Lines frequently form at entry and exit gates, in concession areas, and in restrooms. Such queues, and the wait time resulting from delays in service, may increase anxiety and stress, thereby increasing the probability of hostile behavior (Grove & Fisk, 1997; Kumar, Kalwani, & Dada, 1997). As it relates to the sport marketer's desire to have a full stadium for a sporting event, as noted by Lovelock (1994), maximum capacity may not necessarily be optimum capacity in terms of the patrons' consumptive experience. Complicating matters is the fact that many sporting events are also played outdoors and are subject to weather conditions that may exacerbate circumstances. A number of researchers have noted that uncomfortably hot temperatures may lead to aggressive and hostile behavior (e.g., Anderson, 2001; Anderson & DeNeve, 1992). Temperature extremes, delays, cramped seating, and the like—separate or in combination—may cause irritability that can ignite into rage.

It should also be noted that sporting events are usually attended by spectators supporting the opposing teams or athletes involved in the competition. In such instances, the ideal outcome of the contest may vary depending on the team or individual a spectator supports, and interactions among those in attendance may reflect this conflict of objectives. Live sporting events often involve indirect interaction between spectators and those participating in the game itself such as players, coaches, and officials. Indeed, the interaction between spectators and game participants is often a fundamental component of the spectator sport experience. As described by Shank (2002), "In the case of an athletic event, there is no separation between the athlete, the entertainment, and the fan" (p. 234). However, these circumstances provide both the opportunity and the potential catalyst for rage expression.

Noise is often encouraged in a sports arena to enhance the spectator experience and to serve as an intimidation factor for opponents of the home team. It is common for arenas to play loud music during intermissions and, increasingly, while a game is in progress. In addition, the lyrics of some songs broadcast in arenas have been appropriately criticized for glamorizing hostility (Elmore, 2004). Further, promotional tactics such as handing out devices to fans that are used to create noise or in-stadium messages imploring spectators to "make some noise" are frequently featured as an important part of the spectator experience. From the perspective of sport marketers, such game day promotions may also serve as important inventory for sponsor activation. It is important, however, that such noise has been found in some contexts to promote hostile or aggressive behavior (Geen & McCown, 1984).

Alcohol is perhaps the factor most often thought to promote spectator rage. Unfortunately for those concerned with the adverse impact of such behavior, the consumption of alcohol is in many respects an inherent part of the spectator experience. The consumption of alcohol is frequently part of pregame rituals such as "tailgating" as well as postgame celebrations or commiserations. According to one study, roughly 10% of males exiting a professional baseball game are legally drunk (O'Brien & Hersch, 1998). Alcohol has been shown in a number of studies to increase the likelihood of aggressive behavior (e.g., Bushman & Cooper, 1990), and there is some evidence that the mere exposure to alcohol-based advertising may evoke aggressive tendencies (Bartholow & Heinz, 2006). Alcohol, however, is also an important source of revenue for venues where it is sold inside the stadium, and for many spectators the absence of alcohol may substantially diminish the enjoyment of attending sporting events.

In summary, the preceding discussion points to a number of ancillary factors that may prompt spectators to engage in aggressive behavior. It should be emphasized that these factors often operate in combination to create a consumptive environment conducive for acts of rage. For example, a crowded stadium filled with spectators witnessing a heated rivalry combined with loud noises and excessive alcohol consumption may interact to create an increasingly volatile atmosphere that is ripe for spectator rage.

Discussion

Customer rage is one of many forms of aberrant customer behavior. In the form of spectator rage, it is a complex and potentially disruptive response that patrons exhibit as a reaction to extreme irritation or frustration created by a variety of interactive elements present at many sporting events. It is important to recognize that some of the features discussed throughout this chapter that may serve to foster the likelihood of spectator rage behavior may be addressed by those responsible for the marketing of sporting events, while others may not. In addition, as mentioned throughout the preceding discussion, other features may also be critical elements for enhancing the spectator experience or act as important sources of revenue for sport organizations.

As a way of diminishing the potential impact of various factors that prompt rage, various marketing communication efforts may be initiated to remind spectators of those behaviors considered appropriate and inappropriate. For example, the National Football League has attempted to define appropriate behavior for fans through the publication of a "Fan Code of Conduct" (McCarthy, 2008). This guide notifies spectators of unacceptable behavior, including excessive intoxication, disruptive behavior, foul language, obscene gestures, game interference, and the verbal harassment of opposing team supporters. Teams may also list actionable offenses on the backside of game tickets required for entry as well as other promotional materials sent to those purchasing tickets in advance of the event. Similarly, a Florida youth baseball organization has been referred to as a model for educating parents and spectators through the production of a video on how to be a good sports parent, a handbook describing sportsmanship, and the requirement for parents to sign a sportsmanship pledge (Cary, Dotinga, & Comarow, 2004). These and similar campaigns may be best described as attempts to alter the perceived role assumed by many spectators—to serve as an exemplar for appropriate behavior in lieu of the hostile role assumed by many spectators.

In addition, some sport organizations have incorporated technology such as monitoring systems (e.g., closed-circuit cameras) to ensure effective coverage of potential trouble locations. Such systems have aided numerous professional teams attempting to identify disruptive spectators and are now mandatory for all Greek and Italian professional soccer stadiums (Gatopolous, 2007; Sanminiatelli, 2007).

Other actions by sport venues attempt to reduce the influence of alcohol as a potential factor in spectator rage. The National Collegiate Athletic Association (NCAA) prohibits the sale of alcoholic beverages in on-campus athletic facilities; the National Football League terminates alcohol sales at the start of the final quarter of play, while Major League Baseball terminates alcohol sales after the completion of the seventh inning. In more aggressive action, the New York Jets and New England Patriots with cooperation from the New Jersey Sports and Exposition Authority (facility owners) agreed to ban the sale of alcohol inside the stadium for an entire game involving the two teams. Marketers may also create different seating options for fan seg-mentation (i.e., students, opposing fans, etc.). A feature common in many European soccer stadiums is special fencing and security around sections designated for spectators supporting an opponent of the home team. Other teams offer family sections inside the stadium that are free from alcohol sales, exposure to alcohol, and foul, suggestive or vulgar language. Venues may also be designed to reduce the potential adverse impact of queuing encountered by spectators. Concession waits might seem shorter if sport venues offered fans closed-circuit viewing of the action they are missing. Increasingly, teams are offering creative concession options such as single-item purchase lines or special queues for popular items. Making the wait as comfortable as possible, such as incorporating fans or air conditioners in queuing areas, may alleviate some concerns.

Another factor that may influence the likelihood of spectator rage is the presence (or absence) of authority figures such as law enforcement, stadium staff, and the like (Pfohl, 1994). When present, such figures may reduce the probability of hostility by acting as a reminder of the ramifications of inap-propriate behavior. Further, significant others (e.g., spouse, child, etc.) may perform a similar social control function informally that inhibits the like-lihood of spectator hostility due to the scorn, embarrassment, or rejection that might ensue from those cherished others (Goode, 2007).

In action related to curbing fan rage, sport organizing bodies have sub-jected teams to significant financial penalties for failing to enforce secu-rity policies. In 2005, the international governing body for soccer (FIFA, Fédération Internationale de Football Association) fined three national football clubs "for lack of proper security arrangements for that match" (CNN.com, 2005). Similarly, the Southeastern Conference (SEC) fined the University of Arkansas $5,000 when spectators stormed the court to cel-ebrate a victory by the men's basketball team (Associated Press, 2005b). The Italian Soccer Federation, with the backing of the Italian government, passed several "zero-tolerance" rules intended to curb fan violence at soc-cer matches. A soccer match will be abandoned if anything is thrown on the field, and the team whose fans perpetuated the act will be penalized with an automatic 3–0 loss (Associated Press, 2005a).

Summary

As the discussion illustrates, spectator rage is a complex and often multifaceted phenomenon. Efforts to develop strategies to reduce the incidence of rage behavior may be both impractical or directly conflict with other goals associated with the marketing of sporting events. Sport organizations are faced with difficult decisions about what can be done to control the potential for rage expression and what should be done to control spectators' behavior while preserving the essence of the fan experience. We have attempted to highlight some of the issues in live sports in an effort to enhance our comprehension of spectator rage. In the context of spectator sport, organizations must recognize that inappropriate hostile behaviors may diminish the consumption experience in which the organizations have invested so heavily to create for many fans and have an adverse impact on future patronage. It is perhaps wise to conduct an audit of the mechanisms in place to deal with fan rage and critically assess if they are adequate. Improvements that may be necessary need to be evaluated in terms of their costs versus potential benefits. It is unlikely that spectator rage will simply "go away," but there is the possibility that systematically addressing the phenomenon can reduce its occurrence or impact.

References

Anderson, C. A. (2001). Heat and violence. *Current Directions in Psychological Science, 10,* 33–38.

Anderson, C. A., & DeNeve, K. M. (1992). Temperature, aggression and the negative escape model. *Psychological Bulletin, 111*(2), 347–351.

Arnould, E. J., & Price, L. J. (1993). River magic: Extraordinary experience and the extended service encounter. *Journal of Consumer Research, 20,* 24–46.

Associated Press. (2004, November 19). Carlisle: I was fighting for my life out there. http://www.espn.com/nba/recap/_/id/241119008/indiana-pacers-vs.-detroit-pistons

Associated Press. (2005a, April 14). Italy imposes new anti-violence measures for soccer games. http://www.nbcsports.msnbc.com/id/74891201/

Associated Press. (2005b, February 21). SEC fines Arkansas $5,000 for fans' jubilation. http://www.msnbc/msn.com/id/11467687/

Bandura, A. (1973). *Social learning theory.* Englewood Cliffs, NJ: Prentice-Hall.

Bandura, A. (1986). *Social foundations of thought and action.* Englewood Cliffs, NJ: Prentice-Hall.

Bartholow, B. D., & Heinz, A. (2006). Alcohol aggression without consumption. *Psychological Science, 17*(1), 30–37.

Bitner, M. J., Booms, B. H., & Mohr, L. L. (1994). Critical service encounters: The employee's viewpoint. *Journal of Marketing, 58*(4), 95–106.

Branscombe, N. R., & Wann, D. L. (1992). Role of identification with a group, arousal, categorization processes and self-esteem in sports spectators aggression. *Human Relations, 45,* 1013–1033.

Branscombe, N. R., & Wann, D. L. (1994). Collective self-esteem consequences of outgroup derogation when a valued social identity is on trial. *European Journal of Social Psychology, 24,* 641–657.

Bredemeier, B. J., Shields, D. L., & Horn, J. C. (1985). Values and violence in sports today. *Psychology Today, 19,* 22–31.

Brown, G. L., Goodwin, F. K., & Bunney, W. E. (1982). Human aggression and suicide: Their relationship to neuropsychiatric diagnoses and serotonin metabolism. In B. T. Ho, J. Schoolar, & E. Usdin (Eds.), *Serotonin in biological psychiatry* (pp. 287–307). New York: Raven Press.

Bushman, B. J., & Cooper, H. M. (1990). Effects of alcohol on human aggression: An integrative research review. *Psychological Bulletin, 107,* 341–354.

Cary, P., Dotinga, R., & Comarow, R. (2004). Rescuing children's games from crazed coaches and parents. *U.S. News and World Report, 136*(20), 44–52.

CNN.com. (2005). FIFA fine Swiss after fans protest. Retrieved September 26 from http://www.topics.edition.cnn.com/topics/fifa-unitedkingdom

Coakley, J. J. (1998). *Sport in society: Issues and controversies* (6th ed.). St. Louis, MO: Times Mirror/Mosby.

Edes, G. (2005, April 15). Sheffield says he got hit in face. *Boston Globe,* 1.

Elmore, C. (2004, November 28). An image problem. *The Palm Beach Post,* 1.

Encyclopedia Britannica. (2009). Nika insurrection. Retrieved October 1 from http://www.britannica.com/EBchecked/topic/415179/Nika-insurrection

End, C. M., Dietz-Uhler, B., Harrick, E. A., & Jacquemotte, L. (2002). Identifying with winners: A re-examination of sport fans' tendency to BIRG. *Journal of Applied Social Psychology, 32,* 1017–1130.

Eroglu, S. A., & Machleit, K. (1990). An empirical study of retail crowding. *Journal of Retailing, 66,* 201–221.

Gardner, M. P. (1985). Mood states and consumer behavior: A critical review. *Journal of Consumer Research, 12,* 281–300.

Gatopoulos, D. (2007, April 12). Security cameras promised for Greek soccer stadiums. *Associated Press Worldstream,* 1.

Geen, R. G., & McCown, E. J. (1984). Effects of noise and attack on aggression and physiological arousal. *Motivation and Emotion, 8,* 231–241.

Goode, E. (2007). *Deviant behavior* (8th ed.). Englewood Cliffs, NJ: Prentice-Hall.

Grove, S. J., & Fisk, R. P. (1997). The impact of other customers on service encounters: A critical incident examination of "getting along." *Journal of Retailing, 73*(1), 63–85.

Guerin, B. (1994). *Analyzing social behavior: Behavior analysis and the social sciences.* Reno, NV: Context Press.

Guerin, B. (1998). Religious behaviors as strategies for organizing groups of people: A social contingency analysis. *Behavior Analyst, 21*(1), 53–72.

Harris, L. C., & Ogbonna, E. (2008). The dynamics underlying service firm-customer relationships: Insights from a study of English premier soccer fans. *Journal of Services Research, 10*, 302–399.

Harris, L. C., & Reynolds, K. L. (2004). Jay customer behavior: An exploration of types and motives in the hospitality industry. *Journal of Services Marketing, 18*, 339–357.

Holmes, D. A., & Will, M. J. (1985). Expression of interpersonal aggression by angered and nonangered persons with type A and type B behavior patterns. *Journal of Personality and Social Psychology, 48*, 723–727.

Huang, W. (2008). The impact of other-customer failure on service satisfaction. *International Journal of Service Industry Management, 19*, 521–536.

Hughson, J. (1998). Among the thugs. *International Review of the Sociology of Sport, 33*(1), 33–47.

Hui, M. K., & Bateson, J. E. G. (1991). Perceived control and the effects of crowding and consumer choice on the service experience. *Journal of Consumer Research, 18*(September), 174–184.

Hunt, K. H., Bristol, T., & Bashaw, R. E. (1999). A conceptual approach to classifying sports fans. *Journal of Services Marketing, 13*, 439–452.

Kahle, L., Duncan, M., Dalakas, V., & Aiken, D. (2001). The social values of fans for men's and women's university basketball. *Sport Marketing Quarterly, 10*, 156–162.

Kalamas, M., Laroche, M., & Makdessian, L. (2008). Reaching the boiling point: Consumers' negative reactions to firm-attributed service failures. *Journal of Business Research, 61*, 813–824.

Kelman, H. C. (1958). Compliance, identification and internalization: Three processes of attitude change. *Journal of Conflict Resolution, 2*, 51–60.

Kelman, H. C. (1961). Processes of opinion change. *Public Opinion Quarterly, 25*, 57–78.

Knowles, P. A., Grove, S. J., & Pickett, G. M. (1993). Mood and the service customer. *Journal of Services Marketing, 7*(4), 41–52.

Kumar, P., Kalwani, M., & Dada, M. (1997). The impact of waiting time guarantees on customers' waiting experiences. *Marketing Science, 16*, 295–314.

Lovelock, C. H. (1994). *Product plus.* New York: McGraw-Hill.

Machleit, K. A., Eroglu, S. A., & Mantel, S. P. (2000). Retail crowding and shopping satisfaction: What modifies this relationship? *Journal of Consumer Psychology, 9*(1), 29–42.

McCarthy, M. (2008, August 6). NFL policy cracks down on unruly fans. http://www.usatoday.com/sports/football/nfl/2009-11-18-1a-cover-nfl-fans_N.htm

McKelvey, S. M. (2004). The growth in marketing alliances between US professional sport and legalised gambling entities: Are we putting sport consumers at risk? *Sport Management Review, 7*(2), 193–210.

Mullin, B., Hardy, S., & Sutton, W. (2000). *Sport marketing* (2nd ed.). Windsor, Ontario, Canada: Human Kinetics.

O'Brien, R., & Hersch, H. (1998). Go figure. *Sports Illustrated, 88*(22), 22.

Parke, A., & Griffiths, M. (2004). Aggressive behaviour in slot machine gamblers: A preliminary observational study. *Psychological Reports, 95*(1), 109–114.

Pfohl, S. J. (1994). *Images of deviance and social control.* New York: McGraw-Hill.

Pratt, M. G., & Cardador, M. T. (2006). Identification management and its bases: Bridging management and marketing perspectives through a focus on affiliation dimensions. *Journal of the Academy of Marketing Science, 34,* 174–184.

Sanminiatelli, M. (2007, February 5). Fans could be barred from Italian soccer stadiums if security not improved. *Associated Press Financial Wire, 2.*

Shank, M. D. (2002). *Sports marketing: A strategic perspective.* Upper Saddle River, NJ: Prentice-Hall.

Spaaij, R. (2008). Men like us, boys like them: Violence, masculinity, and collective identity in football hooliganism. *Journal of Sport and Social Issues, 32,* 369–392.

Spitz, R. T., & Hillbrand, M. (1994). Serum cholesterol levels and aggressive tendencies. *Psychological Reports, 74,* 622.

Sports Network. (2007, February 3). Series: A play suspended after fan violence on Friday.

Stokolos, D. (1972). On the distinction between density and crowding: Some implications for future research. *Psychological Review, 79,* 275–278.

Stone, M. H. (1993). *Abnormalities of personality: Within and beyond the realm of treatment.* New York: Norton.

Wann, D. L., Hayes, G., McLean, B., & Pullen, P. (2003). Sport team identification and willingness to consider anonymous acts of hostile aggression. *Aggressive Behavior, 29,* 406–413.

Wann, D. L., Peterson, R. R., Cothran, C., & Dykes, M. (1999). Sport fan aggression and anonymity: The importance of team identification. *Social Behavior and Personality: An International Journal, 27,* 597–602.

Section II

Building Relationships With Consumers Through Sports

Relationships and relationship marketing have become recognized as critical strategies in effectively reaching consumers. The chapters in this section look seriously at this topic.

Scammon, Fuller, Karniouchina, and Masters conducted a Web-based survey of skiers and snowboarders to show the relative impact of many consumer-behavior-oriented variables, including motivations to ski or snowboard, risky behaviors, sources of learning, and informal "rules of thumb" on and off the snow. The snowboarders and skiers maintain different motivations, attitudes, and behaviors related to their sport. The different ways of segmenting users may suggest different strategies for ski areas, event venues, leisure marketers, and retailers, each of whom can leverage this consumer behavior knowledge.

Kennett-Hensel, Lacey, and Biggers propose a framework that explains how corporate social responsibility initiatives contribute to the success of NBA teams through better fan relationships. Andrews shares a chapter that links together micro and macro issues surrounding youth sports participation in the United States in a multitier ecological framework from the perspective of a young person's developmental environment.

Kurpis and Bozman integrate research on social values and embed research on Hoopfest, a unique basketball sporting event. Understanding various aspects and properties of social values as they influence sports can help sports marketers to foster sport subcultures and to ensure viability of the promoted sport. Burton, Tripodi, Owen, and Kahle discuss using hospitality to leverage sponsorship investments through relationships. Hospitality is an underresearched but important tool in establishing relationships that characterize sports marketing.

5

Sport-Related Subculture as a Useful Basis of Market Segmentation
Insights for Ski Area Managers

Debra L. Scammon, Dan A. Fuller,
Ekaterina V. Karniouchina, and Tamara Masters

Introduction

Sports and recreation are critical components of the modern lifestyle. Love of adventure, the superstar cultural appeal of professional athletes, and concerns about obesity and other health conditions related to a sedentary lifestyle are among the many factors that contribute to the ever increasing popularity of sports. Growing affluence around the world and the accessibility and relative affordability of travel have boosted revenues of recreational sports destinations, such as ski resorts. The ski resort industry is a major player in recreation; in the United States alone, in 2002 ski resorts directly employed over 70,000 people and reported revenues exceeding $1.8 billion (Bunting, Wagner, & Jones, 2005). Beyond the direct contribution of the ski resort industry to the economy, there is also a trickle-down effect to other sectors, including construction, travel and hospitality, and sports equipment manufacturing. Despite the size of the industry, its economic viability faces challenging conditions.

Challenges to the Industry

Winter sports resorts increasingly face environmental pressures. Climate change may shorten or increase the variability of an already limited winter revenue season. The ski season is normally short, on average less than 5 months a year, but with the effects of global warming, the season has become less predictable. Although sensitive to regional snow conditions, nationwide skier *days*[1] continue to climb, albeit slowly. Additionally there are demands on resorts for a "greener" footprint. Many ski areas have invested in snowmaking capacity as a safety net against the risk of low natural snow accumulations. However, snowmaking consumes significant water and energy resources. Faced with competing priorities, resorts are investing in next-generation water recycling and sophisticated snowmaking equipment. Increasingly, managers must consider the economic impact of rapid climate changes.

The market for recreation is highly competitive. Ski resorts face intra-industry competition (e.g., with other ski resorts) as well as inter-industry competition (e.g. with other sports and recreational activities). To deal with these pressures, winter sports resorts have started experimenting with new business models. Many resorts have responded by purchasing the latest technologies such as high-speed detachable chairlifts, increasing snow-grooming capacities, and expanding restaurant facilities and other guest amenities. These investments come at a high cost and resorts are pursuing a number of strategies to increase revenues and manage business risk. Some corporate models are based on a regionally diversified portfolio of ski areas. Others couple real estate development with resort operations to subsidize capital expenditures. Many resorts are morphing into all-season destinations by developing infrastructure for summer activities such as zip rides, golf, and hiking and mountain bike trails. Smaller ski resorts are competing by finding specific market niches and catering to distinct segments such as park and pipe enthusiasts or local participants. Others differentiate themselves through community outreach programs, services, and promotions; training programs; or competitions specifically geared toward the local winter sports enthusiasts and their families.

Changes in consumer demand have influenced and continue to impact the ski resort industry. Consumer demand is affected by economic conditions, social factors, individual consumer characteristics and preferences, and available alternatives. Significant loss of wealth and adjustment to new macroeconomic and global equilibria brought about by the economic recession of 2008–2009 may cause consumers to permanently alter recreational patterns in unforeseen ways. In addition, the challenges engendered by the retiring baby boom generation suggest significant changes in

---

[1] A skier day is roughly defined as one person utilizing a lift ticket for any portion of a day of operation.

the demographics of the customer base for ski resorts. Alternative recreational activities vie in a more and more competitive market for consumers' attention and dollars.

Evolution in Sports and Implications for Consumer Demand

From the 1978–1979 to the 2005–2006 seasons, total U.S. skier days are estimated to have increased by about 17% (*Kottke*, 2006). It is difficult to characterize this as other than slow growth. Anecdotal evidence suggests that over the last decade, increases in skier days have largely been due to the growth in popularity of snowboarding. Originally banned from lift-serviced areas, snowboarding was widely regarded as a counterculture alternative to alpine skiing. Snowboarding was developed to embody movement patterns similar to surfing and skateboarding. This appealed to a younger more adventuresome consumer segment which could take advantage of the relatively fast learning curve. As the popularity of snowboarding spread, ski areas recognized the revenue potential and began accommodating the sport, later designing areas that included elements such as tables, rails, jumps, and half pipes which enable snowboarders to perform tricks and jumps. Today, these areas are variously known as park and pipe or terrain parks. The required technical skill is called freestyle. The cross fertilization between skateboarding and snowboarding as well as the introduction of the X Games fueled the growth and sophistication of these specialized terrain parks such that today most ski resorts have at least one, and in many cases, multiple park and pipe areas. Once the domain of snowboards, alpine skis were adapted to terrain parks through a technology called twin tips. Today, users of these facilities include snowboarders as well as skiers.

The rate of equipment innovation has accelerated with the introduction of different snowboards. Boards that specialize in carving quickly followed the basic board. Alpine skis were redesigned to explore the benefits of added width, shape, and shorter lengths. Ultra-short skis such as Blades and Big Feet enjoyed a brief period of popularity. Besides the already mentioned twin-tips technology, new adaptations to alpine skis include "reverse cambering" purportedly advantageous in deep snow. Innovation in equipment has also extended to telemark enthusiasts, a fringe population with a small presence at most ski areas. The implication for ski areas is that their potential customer base is increasingly heterogeneous in their choice of recreational technology, skills, interests, and attitudes. A few ski areas have modified the majority of their services to appeal more to snowboarders and have become de facto boarder-only areas (e.g., Mountain High in Southern California) (Makens, 2001). A handful of resorts still cater exclusively to skiers. As of the beginning of the 2007–2008 season, only Taos Ski Valley (New Mexico), Mad River Glen (Vermont), Alta (Utah), and Deer Valley (Utah) had a skier only policy (*Snowboarding*, 2009).

The transition by ski resorts to accommodate evolving consumer segments not envisioned 20 years ago has been challenging. Nationwide, it is estimated that snowboarders account for 31% of total skier days (*Kottke*, 2008). Differences in technology, expectations, and culture have generated rivalries among consumer segments that have not always been friendly. Segmentation is likely to be an ongoing process given the pace of technological change in the last decade. In this chapter, we explore the differences in needs and wants between distinct customer segments defined by sports subcultures. Ski resort managers would benefit from a deeper understanding of their customer segments, including their cultural identities, motivations and frustrations, and behaviors, as well as the dynamics between segments.

Understanding Consumer Segments

Demographics

One of the most common bases for market segmentation is consumer demographics. Marketers frequently rely on variables such as age, gender, place of residence, and income to define the consumer groups to whom they target their products and services. The ski industry is no exception. For example, the 2007–2008 National Ski Areas Association study (*Kottke*, 2008) reported that international visitation was 6.4% of total visits, an increase of 1% from 2007 attributed to a comparatively weak U.S. dollar. In 2001, the National Ski and Snowboard Retailers Association reported several demographic differences between the skier and snowboarder segments: 40% of skiers and 26% of snowboarders were female; 42% of skiers were 24 years of age or younger compared to 80.8% of boarders; 73% of skiers had household incomes over $50,000, while 54.6% of boarders had household incomes in this range. The snow sports population is currently more multigenerational than seen previously. Older generations are staying healthier and active longer, and participants are starting earlier; thus, a wider range of ages is found on the slopes (Chapman, 2006).

Resorts typically attempt to track guests by such characteristics, and many tailor their offerings based on demographics. For example, while lessons are routinely offered for youth and adults, larger resorts target lessons further for the youngest children as well as the geriatric enthusiast. Typically, more affluent users have the option of buying private lessons, and some areas offer higher-cost passes that allow faster access to the lift. Consumer demographics, however, may do little to help marketers truly understand their market segments. Other individual characteristics, such as motivation and personality, and variables such as lifestyle are useful in building consumer profiles that facilitate marketers' understanding of the experiences consumers are seeking. Particularly useful in the context of sports participation is an understanding of group culture.

Culture and Subculture

Culture can be formed on the basis of various common characteristics, such as national origin, lifestyles, and even consumption experiences. Thus it provides a rich perspective for understanding consumer behavior. Culture may be thought of as the personality of a society or group. A culture consists of three functional aspects: ecology (the way the group adapts to its surroundings), social structure (the way social order is maintained within the group), and ideology (the mental characteristics of the people and the ways they relate to their environment and other social groups) (Solomon, 2004). Consumers in the same culture often share similar attitudes and preferences. In the marketing literature, the word *subculture* is often used to describe ethnic or minority groups. The word is also commonly utilized by researchers to reflect groups based on age, social class, or religious affiliation. While these groupings are unarguable instances of subculture, people often construct their identities and create unique subcultural categories around their consumption choices (Schouten & McAlexander, 1995). During the past decade, the concept of brand communities has gained popularity because of its ability to help understand and influence consumer behavior (Muñiz & O'Guinn, 2001). Consumers have been found to identify with others who own and use products of the same brand. The notion of consumption communities can be used to help understand not only consumers who buy the same brand of product but also consumers who engage in the same activities, including recreation activities. Identity as a skier or snowboarder can be easily discerned by the differences in their equipment (e.g., skis, snowboards, clothing) and by differences in the on-slope actions demanded by their equipment or facilitated by their peers. The challenge to ski resort managers is both to understand existing subcultures and to keep up with the dynamics of emerging and fading subcultures. As we discuss later, one difference between skiers and snowboarders may lie in their unique approach and orientation to risk.

Risk Taking

Adventure sports and high-risk recreational activities have been growing in popularity. The X Games, sponsored by ESPN and introduced in 1995, is a multisport event, attesting to the appeal of high-risk activities to both participants and spectators or viewers. Researchers have long been interested in the psychological profiles of participants in various sports, including their risk preferences and risk-taking behaviors. Research has demonstrated a link between "sensation seeking" and participation in such high-risk activities as rock climbing, hang gliding, canoeing, kayaking, skydiving, motorcycle racing, and scuba diving (Zuckerman, 1983b). Skiing is also among those sports drawing a high proportion of sensation seekers (Zuckerman, 1983b).

In his early work, Zuckerman (1983a) found that demographics, especially gender and age, are correlated with sensation seeking. Specifically, sensation seeking tends to be higher among men than women and tends to increase from late childhood through adolescence, peaking in the early 20s. Although participation by women in snowboarding is growing, females comprised just over one quarter of snowboarders in 2006 according to the National Sporting Goods Association (Pow Productions, 2009). The average age of snowboarders is increasing, especially among females, which some have attributed to mothers taking up the sport along with their children (Pow Productions, 2009).

Over many years of research, Zuckerman developed and refined a scale that measures the personality trait he called "sensation seeking." Those who engage in "explosive" or "adrenaline" sports rate high on four related dimensions: thrill and adventure seeking (TAS), experience seeking, disinhibition, and boredom susceptibility (Zuckerman, 1983b; Zuckerman, Eysenck, & Eysenck, 1978). The TAS subscale, reflects an individual's desire to engage in risky, impulsive, and adventurous sports activities, offering the individual unique sensations (Zuckerman, 1994). Other researchers also have found that people who participate in higher-risk sports score higher on the arousal-seeking dimension. For example, Kerr (1991) measured arousal avoidance among sports enthusiasts in Australia, Britain, and Denmark and found that those who engaged regularly in risky sports, such as surfers and glider pilots, could be characterized as arousal seekers. Specifically with regard to skiing, Bouter, Knipschild, Feij, and Volovics (1988) found that those who participate in downhill skiing scored higher on the sensation-seeking scale than did a control group. Understanding the risk preferences of participants in different segments of the skier market can help resort managers deliver satisfying experiences for different user groups.

Although in its introduction, snowboarding was touted as having a lower risk of anterior cruciate ligament injury than skiing, it was widely regarded as more edgy and innovative than skiing. Simple observation of the activities in which snowboarders and twin-tip skiers engage suggests that they may be especially high on the TAS dimension. Research in the sports medicine field documents comparatively high injury rates among snowboarders. In their study Tarazi, Dvorak, and Wing (1999) reported the risk of spinal injuries for snowboarders was four times as high as that for skiers. Over three quarters (77%) of snowboarders received these serious injuries while engaging in stunts (jumping) compared to 20% of skiers. Geddes and Irish (2005) found that, while controlling for gender, snowboarders were six times more likely to sustain a spleen injury than skiers. Geddes and Irish (2005) also presented evidence suggesting that risk-taking patterns among snowboarders follow traditional gender stereotypes. They reported that the risk of splenic injury was 21.7 times greater for male snowboarders than for female snowboarders ($p = .002$).

Ronning, Gerner, and Engebretsen (2000), using a newly developed measure of distance traveled on skis or snowboards, found that snowboarders were more likely than were skiers to receive injuries requiring treatment at a hospital. Specifically, they reported injury rates per 1,000 skier days (adjusted by distance traveled) of 0.9 for telemark skiing, 1.2 for alpine skiing, and 4.0 for snowboarding. Based on behavior patterns and injury data for snowboarders, we suggest that, compared to skiers, snowboarders will rate higher on sensation seeking.

Industry Response to Risk
Although personal challenge and risk taking have always been inherent in downhill snow sports, the increasing popularity of skiing engendered by historical developments such as the ski train, rope tows, T-bars, lifts, and trail systems brought with it problems of congestion. Lifts and complex,

interconnected trail systems capable of accommodating large numbers of skiers challenged the industry with issues of social behavior (e.g., stopping, starting, merging, and granting rights-of-way). The threat of collision and unpredictable traffic patterns introduced an externality unwelcomed by enthusiasts. Although the industry haltingly moved to establish rules of conduct, in 1966 the National Ski Areas Association established "Your Responsibility Code" as a code of ethics for all skiers (National Ski Patrol, 2009). All countries with major ski industries have adopted a code of ethics, although the actual content varies country by country. The rising popularity of park and pipe (also known as freestyle), rise in personal injury rates, and serious implications of slope congestion led the National Ski Areas Association in conjunction with Burton Snowboards to introduce Smart Style, a code of progression and ethics for freestyle terrain. Despite educational campaigns and occasional enforcement efforts, adherence to these various codes of ethics has been largely voluntary, subject to personal and subcultural values and influences.

Characterizing Winter Sports Subcultures

By the 1970s, high profile destination ski areas arguably sought to characterize themselves as sophisticated, upscale, and establishment. In contrast, snowboarding has populist roots. Prior to acceptance at ski areas, participants had to hike to gain the necessary vertical to engage in the sport. According to Howe (1998), snowboarding traces its beginnings to surfing and skateboarding. Snowboarding is most popular in the Pacific West region, where it accounts for about 45% of total skier days (*Kottke*, 2008). Perhaps because of latent feelings of discrimination by snowboarders who have witnessed seemingly slow and begrudging acceptance of their sport by ski areas and traditional alpine enthusiasts or because of differences that the technology demands in participant behavior, the introduction and growth of snowboarding at ski areas has resulted in what some call a "clash of cultures."

In what has become a classic sociological exposé on snowboarding, Howe (1998) chronicled the evolution of this sport. According to her research, snowboarders and skiers belong to two different subcultures. Sports related behaviors, attitudes, clothing styles, even language differ between the two groups. Howe describes skiers as seeking "alpine pleasure" in which they feel "one with nature," enjoying the pristine qualities and serenity of an uncrowded alpine environment. In addition to enjoying the mountain environment, skiers have a tradition of socializing and eating and drinking after skiing. Snowboarders are characterized as out for the thrill of going fast, jumping, and doing stunts; turning while going down the mountain is of little interest. Howe further characterized snowboarders as rebels seeking new experiences, freedom, and independence while not looking out for others. Snowboarders have been characterized as individualistic and self-centered and according to skiers, snowboarders seek social acceptance by always "showing off" in front of each other (Howe, 1998).

These differences have implications for how the groups view one another. For example, Williams and colleagues (1994) reported that skiers view snowboarders as intruding on the pristine quality of the resort, exhibiting little respect for the natural beauty of the environment. Snowboarders, out for "the adrenalin rush" and described as "deviant," self-focused, impulsive, and spontaneous, tend to be present-oriented, focused on technical and competency-related issues. Williams et al. (1994) reported that snowboarders find skiers to be "predictable" and perhaps as a result are less concerned about their presence on the slopes than skiers are about snowboarders. Edensor and Richards (2007) presented a qualitative study that explored the tension between the two groups and concluded that there are striking differences between their underlying cultures; these differences are communicated through clothing, skillful performance, and sensual experiences.

Many sources provide vivid descriptions of cultural clashes taking place on the winter slopes, from respected academic sources (e.g., Makens, 2001) to You Tube videos depicting skier versus snowboarder challenges and fights; there is ample evidence of the discontent of the two groups over each other's behavior. While some view the expansion of the snowboarder clientele as a way to combat decreasing alpine skiing revenues, some attribute a recent decline in alpine skiing to the ruthless behavior of snowboarders and advocate confining skiers and boarders to separate resorts to prevent a further slump in alpine skiing. Makens (2001) cited striking statistics suggesting that the major perceived perils preventing people from skiing are the risks of falling down and of injury. He argued that these risks make peaceful coexistence with risk-taking snowboarders a challenge for skiers. Makens (2001) believed that the increase in snowboarders has contributed to skier retention problems, and that skier numbers are likely to deteriorate further as the snowboarder population grows. The inherent tension between these two cultures has been addressed by industry practitioners as well as by researchers. Industry sources indicate that embedded cultural differences often complicate their marketing efforts. For instance, Grapetine (2004) described the delicate situation of trying to market pain relievers to snowboarders, a culture in which pain is admired. In this culture that highly regards risk taking, injuries are often seen as a rite of passage and subsequently worn as a badge of honor.

There is evidence that the biomechanical and technical requirements of the two different recreation technologies impose additional cultural wedges, especially when on-slope congestion is an issue. Vaske, Carothers, Donnelly, and Baird (2000) noted that conflict is especially likely when the actions of one user group interfere with the goals and motivations of another group since these different goals are manifested in different norms regarding acceptable behavior. Vaske and his colleagues (2000) also suggested that conflict may be greater when traditional users (e.g., skiers) interact with those using newer technologies (e.g., snowboarders). For example, skiers, especially older skiers, complain of and are intimidated by the loud noise that snowboards make when skidding on edge. This increase in noise is due to a combination of increased pressure on a single edge and the tendency of snowboards to amplify noise because of their large surface area. Snowboarders typically ride lifts with one binding unattached, which requires them to spend time at the top of the lift reattaching the binding, potentially creating congestion. Loading and unloading is often more difficult for snowboarders, especially for beginners and novices. It is also widely noted that when skiers stop and rest in groups, they tend to organize themselves vertically down the hill, in contrast to snowboarders, who tend to spread horizontally across the hill, a practice that creates congestion. One explanation links the desire to maintain eye contact with how the group organizes itself on the hill. These and other examples of technology driven differences in the ways in which skiers and snowboarders experience their sport and navigate the hill have been a source of conflict and rivalry.

Despite the aforementioned vivid descriptions of conflicts, there appears to be some movement toward increased acceptance and mutual respect. This movement appears to be based in the desire for socialization. During our time at the ski areas, we saw anecdotal evidence of an increasing integration of skier and snowboarder populations. Families are often seen with a mix of snowboarding children and parents on skis. Park and pipe groups are often a mixture of twin tippers and snowboarders. Differences in clothing appear less pronounced than previously, and the counterculture snowboard rhetoric appears somewhat more muted than in previous years. This integration raises the question of whether the cultural rivalry between skiers and snowboarders has (or will) become less heated over time.

A Study of Skiers and Snowboarders

Purpose

In an attempt to better understand the differences in how skiers and snow-boarders approach their sport, we conducted an Internet survey. Our primary interest was in comparing skiers and snowboarders in terms of their motivations for participating in their sport, the things that contribute to them having a good day, their frustrations in participating in their sport, and the strategies they use to minimize the impacts of congestion. We were particularly interested in risk preferences, risky behaviors, and risk avoidance behaviors of the different segments of the skier market.

Skiers (of all types) and snowboarders have several things in common. First is their love of the slopes. Second, both groups are less risk averse and more adventurous than the general population. At the same time, their differences hold some important implications for ski resort management. We explore the ways in which skiers and snowboarders play together and share the common space of the ski area during play. We investigate the similarities as well as the differences between the two groups to help ski resort management better understand their clientele.

In our investigation, we uncovered a number of interesting empirical regularities. For instance, we found participants' age to be one of the most powerful predictors of on-slope behavior. Both risk-seeking propensity and participation in snowboarding and use of park and pipe facilities are related to age. We attempt to provide a better understanding of these age and risk behaviors across sports preference groups. Although our sample included individuals from a number of countries, we did not find any significant differences between participants based on their country of origin. Sport group membership had a much stronger impact on affiliation than did national culture. Thus, we concentrated on understanding differences between sport groups. Comparisons between skiers and snowboarders, and in some cases between those who use park and pipe facilities and those who do not, were the focus of our analyses.

Study Procedures

A survey instrument was designed using primarily 5-point Likert scale questions. We gathered information regarding attitudes, motivations, behavioral patterns, adherence to the Skier's Code of Responsibility, learning style, and sport participation and demographic data (National Ski

Areas Association, 2010). Once the survey was designed and posted on the Internet, we solicited participants in the United States, Canada, Europe, New Zealand, and Australia for approximately 6 weeks in the fall of 2006, primarily by posting notices on skier and boarder bulletin boards and soliciting Web marshals to send out e-mails to ski club members. Using online communities allowed us to gather a relatively large sample in a timely and efficient manner. In doing this research, we enlisted the help of opinion leaders (club presidents, blog writers, and board moderators) in soliciting participants; we found the help of such gatekeepers crucial, especially in gaining access to a skeptical snowboarder segment. Survey participants represented a number of countries: 15% of respondents were from New Zealand and Australia, 52% were from the United States and Canada, 20% were from Great Britain, with the remainder being from other countries.

Sample Description

The sample included 792 participants. The majority of the survey respondents were male (79%). About one quarter (24.2%) were between 18 and 24 years of age. Slightly over one quarter (27.1%) were 25–34 years of age, another quarter (22.9%) were 35–44 years of age, and 15.2% were between 45 and 54 years of age. Less than 5% of participants were over 55 years of age. Although it is estimated that industrywide 12.3% of skier visits occur in the age group 12 and under and 15.4% occur in the 13–17 age group, our sample included only 6% of individuals under 18 years of age. Because of the guidelines on human subjects of the institutional review board of our university, we did not solicit participation in our survey among individuals under 18 years of age.

We asked respondents to indicate the number of years they had participated and their skill level with the different technologies of skiing, snowboarding, telemark skiing, and park and pipe. Our data revealed that roughly two thirds of the sample reported experience with more than one technology. Roughly 40% of the sample reported experience with both alpine skis and snowboards, while about 18% of the sample reported experience with telemark and another technology. Of the 35% of the sample reporting experience in just one technology, snowboarding made up about 12%, with the remainder dominated by alpine ski experience only. Given that in the United States it is estimated that snowboarding accounts for around 30% of total skier days, it is likely that many of those who reported both ski and snowboard skills primarily snowboard.

Of the respondents, 96% rated their skill level as intermediate or higher in at least one technology. We also asked on what kind of terrain most of their time was spent. About one quarter of the sample characterized themselves as participants on groomed runs only. Of this, 4% reported most of their time spent on beginning terrain only, whereas 23% reported beginning-to-intermediate terrain. While 26% of the sample reported most of their time spent in off-piste or backcountry, by far the largest portion of the sample, 43%, reported that they spent their time in a mixed variety of terrain (groomed and off piste). Despite the fact that only 3% of the sample reported spending most of their time in park and pipe, 48% of the sample reported some experience with park and pipe or stunts.

A majority of the sample was likely to hold a season pass. Over half (58%) of the sample reported spending more than 21 days per season on the hill, while 17% reported 10 days or fewer. Furthermore, 70% of the sample rated their physical conditioning for snow sports as good to excellent, while 5% rated their conditioning as poor.

Analysis and Results

Goals and Motivations

Participants were asked to rate the importance to them of six motivations for engaging in their sport, where 5 = highly motivated. Among all participants, the primary motivations of winter sports participants were "thrill and adrenaline rush" ($\bar{x}$ = 4.34) followed by "acquire new or improve skills" ($\bar{x}$ = 4.31) and "enjoyment of nature" ($\bar{x}$ = 4.04). Least motivating was "competition" ($\bar{x}$ = 2.36) (see Table 5.1 for details). These results suggest that, for most participants, coming to the slopes is associated with adventure—a fact that marketers seem not to have missed. However, the close second-place finish of acquiring new or improving skills, in addition to the large portion of the sample that had experience with multiple technologies, suggests that marketers may be missing an important nuance. That is, for existing participants the satisfaction from skill acquisition may not be confined to honing skills in their current sport; it can come from a desire to try a new sport. This may contribute to the preference for a wide variety of terrain noted above. We note also that enjoyment of nature scored high, followed by mental relaxation. While we can only speculate regarding what these motivations mean to our respondents, we suspect that escape from routine, commercial, and workday environments is a key. This suggests that management should be conscious about the extent to

TABLE 5.1   Primary Motivations for All Participants[a]

Motivation	Sample Mean	Skier Mean	Snowboarder Mean	Difference in Means	Standard Error	Significance
Thrill and adrenaline rush	4.34	4.20	4.47	.28	.058	.000
Enjoy nature	4.04	4.17	3.93	.24	.064	.000
Acquire new or improve skills	4.31	4.27	4.36	−.09	.053	.099
Mental relaxation	3.80	3.89	3.71	.18	.074	.014
Socialization	3.30	3.17	3.40	−.23	.078	.003
Competition	2.36	2.23	2.46	−.23	.082	.005

[a]Scale 1 = not motivated at all to 5 = strongly motivated.

which everyday, routine, and commercial environments are present at the ski area.

There were, however, significant differences in primary motivations between skiers and snowboarders. In Table 5.1, we compared the means on each of the motivations for skiers and snowboarders. Snowboarders were significantly more motivated by the anticipation of thrills and adrenaline rush (pairwise t-test $p = .000$), social factors ($p = .003$), and competition ($p = .005$), while skiers were more likely to engage in their sport to enjoy nature ($p = .000$) and relax mentally ($p = .014$). Snowboarders were marginally more motivated than skiers by new skill acquisition (see Table 5.1 for results of pairwise comparison of means). Skiers were found to rate socialization low as a motivation compared to boarders. Park and pipe enthusiasts had the highest means for socialization ($\bar{x} = 4.04$), competition ($\bar{x} = 3.04$), and the development of new skills (data not shown).

To better understand the acquisition of new skills, we attempted to examine learning styles. The Professional Ski Instructors Association (PSIA) defines four fundamental learning styles: feelers, watchers, thinkers, and doers. We asked respondents to indicate which of four statements based on these learning styles best described their approach to acquiring a new skill. Overall, we classified 27% of the sample as feelers, 29% as watchers, 34% as thinkers, and 10% as doers. Categorizing participants into four groups (pure skiers, pure snowboarders, those who both ski and board, and park and pipers), a chi-square test of independence between participant type and learning style was rejected at the .99% level of significance. Skiers, as well as park and pipers, were significantly more likely to be thinkers, while snowboarders were significantly more likely to be doers. Those with both ski and snowboard experience were more likely to be feelers.

We also attempted to assess the importance of different sources of information when learning about behavior expected of participants. Not surprisingly, common sense was ranked highest of five possible sources, followed by information provided by ski areas and instructors. Pure skiers were more likely to learn through these information programs (p = .001) and by using common sense (p = .026) compared to snowboarders. Consistent with learning by watching others, snowboarders were also more likely than skiers to let those more skilled go first (p = .008). One possibility is a cultural norm among snowboarders of watching and appreciating the skills demonstrated by others. Another possibility is that skill plays a more important role in determining hierarchy among one's snowboarding peers. In this culture, in which socialization is a key motivation for the sport, emulation is likely and peer acceptance important.

Sense of Good Day
Table 5.2 reports how participants responded with regard to how important seven items were to them in terms of having a good day on the slopes, where 5 = extremely important. Not surprisingly, given the importance of edge-to-snow contact for winter sports, "good snow conditions" ($\bar{x}$ = 4.39) was rated as the most important factor for the sense of a good day. While ski areas are in some sense limited in their ability to ensure snow conditions, this finding underscores the importance of expenditures throughout the industry on snowmaking and snow grooming. "Feeling personal achievement (good technique, flow, etc.)" ($\bar{x}$ = 4.35) was rated as the next most important aspect of a good day. While this suggests that ski and snowboard schools and organized skill development programs can make an important contribution to guests having a positive experience at the resort, the concept of personal achievement deserves further exploration. Having and executing skill are perhaps more important than the acquisition of skill. The next most important factor was "the ski area was not busy" ($\bar{x}$ = 3.87), attesting to the importance of crowd management. "Time spent with friends" ($\bar{x}$ = 3.74) was also relatively important, suggesting that facilities and programs targeted to groups should be considered. For example, "partner ticket" offers allowing season pass holders to buy a second ticket at a discount for a friend or group-oriented programs such as group discounts on lift tickets, equipment rentals and lessons, or eating facilities and menu items that accommodate groups could enhance time shared with friends. It is worthwhile to note that, despite the desire

TABLE 5.2   Importance to Sense of Having a Good Day[a]

	Sample Mean	Skier Mean	Snowboarder Mean	Difference in Means	Standard Error	Significance
Total runs/ vertical feet	2.99	2.99	2.99	.001	.081	.994
Feeling personal achievement	4.35	4.37	4.33	−.04	.053	.465
Time spent with friends	3.74	3.63	3.86	−.23	.069	.001
Ski area was not busy	3.87	3.82	3.90	.07	.061	.239
Good snow conditions	4.39	4.29	4.47	−.18	.052	.001
Was a "bluebird" day	3.12	3.11	3.13	.03	.082	.728
Others ski/ride in control	3.17	3.36	3.02	.34	.085	.000

[a]Scale from 1 = not important at all to 5 = extremely important.

for socialization, participants expressed strong preferences for small- versus large-group experiences on the hill. In addition, comments collected often identified large groups and ski classes as significant sources of on-hill congestion. Despite the availability of devices that record number of vertical feet skied, the item of least importance to our survey participants was "total runs/vertical feet."

There were significant differences between the two sport groups with regard to the importance of these different factors as contributors to their overall sense of a good day. Snowboarders were more sensitive to general snow conditions ($p = .001$) and enjoyed spending time with friends ($p = .001$), while skiers were significantly more concerned with others being in control ($p = .000$). These findings make sense given the importance of snow conditions to the ease with which snowboarders can navigate the slopes and their general enjoyment of spending time with friends. These findings are also consistent with other research reporting that skiers frequently worry about being injured by others who go too fast for their skill and experience level (Makens, 2001).

Frustrations

Participants were asked about eight conditions that potentially reduce enjoyment on the hill, where 5 = "a lot." The results are presented in Table 5.3. Negative externalities seem to be the primary source of reduced

TABLE 5.3   Conditions That Reduce Enjoyment on the Hill[a]

	Sample Mean	Skier Mean	Snowboarder Mean	Difference in Means	Standard Error	Significance
Crowded roads, parking lots, buses	3.02	3.04	2.98	−.06	.065	.342
Waiting at a ticket window	2.63	2.63	2.63	−.001	.071	.984
Equipment logistics or problems	3.25	3.27	3.24	−.03	.074	.635
Long lift lines	3.75	3.73	3.76	.03	.059	.609
Crowded restaurants, eating areas	2.75	2.83	2.67	.151	.071	.028
Crowded runs, parks and pipes, traverses	3.71	3.70	3.72	.022	.068	.743
"Attitudes" on the hill	3.43	3.53	3.34	−.186	.073	.010
Incompetent or rude employees	3.29	3.32	3.26	−.06	.076	.403

[a]Scale from 1 = not an issue to 5 = a disaster.

enjoyment. Long lift lines ($\bar{x}$ = 3.75) and crowded runs, park and pipes, and traverses ($\bar{x}$ = 3.71) were the two dominant factors. Somewhat surprisingly given the sample averages, 21% of the sample rated crowded runs a 5, while 18% rated crowded lifts a 5 for enjoyment reduction. This suggests that there is a trade-off between high-speed, high-capacity lifts and on-run congestion that deserves careful consideration. Lack of consideration of others was also an important source of enjoyment reduction. "Attitudes" on the hill ($\bar{x}$ = 3.43) and incompetent or rude employees ($\bar{x}$ = 3.29) ranked second after on-hill congestion. The sample seemed more tolerant of crowded restaurants, waiting in ticket lines, and crowded roads and parking lots. However, equipment logistics or problems ($\bar{x}$ = 3.25) do appear to be an important source of frustration for winter sport participants, which attests to the importance of ensuring competent and efficient repair and rental facilities.

Only two of the eight factors were rated significantly differently by skiers and snowboarders. Skiers appeared to be frustrated more than snowboarders when restaurants were crowded (p = .028). They were also more sensitive to "attitudes" on the hill (p = .000).

Etiquette

We examined the strategies people use to deal with these frustrations. In particular, since crowded conditions are an important source of dissatisfaction, we focused on the ways in which snowboarders and skiers navigate a crowded lift line. Table 5.4 presents the results of a logistic regression where the dependent variable represents the odds of observing a skier or snowboarder. A positive coefficient indicates increased odds of a skier while a negative coefficient shows higher odds of observing a snowboarder. Skiers were more likely to move to different, less-crowded lifts, while snowboarders were more likely to crowd in, hoping to move up in line. This strategy by snowboarders may contribute to the attitude that skiers find objectionable. Despite the value snowboarders place on socialization, they were more likely to use the singles line even if it meant temporarily breaking away from their group.[2]

We also asked participants about their feelings with regard to interacting with others on the hill. Interestingly, when asked if they were most comfortable on the hill among others who use the same type of equipment, the sample mean was 2.6, suggesting relative disagreement with this item. There were no significant differences between skiers and snowboarders. It may be that the extent of the previously documented cultural clash has diminished somewhat over time as the presence of multiple-sport groups at ski resorts has become more common. However, the heightened sensitivity to "attitude on the hill" perceived by skiers noted here suggests that management should still be vigilant in finding ways to minimize potential culture clashes.

---

[2] In the case of logistic regressions, model significance was evaluated with the Hosmer-Lemeshow (H-L) goodness-of-fit test (Hosmer & Lemeshow, 1989). This test was used because of its appropriateness for situations in which continuous variables are categorized into several groups (i.e., our age variable). This test is also recommended for large data sets with more than 400 observations, similar to the one used in this study. The H-L test is performed by dividing the predicted probabilities into deciles (based on percentile ranks) and then computing a Pearson chi-square statistic that compares the predicted to observed frequencies. The H-L so-called lack-of-fit statistic is calculated as follows:

$$G^2_{HL} = \sum_{j=1}^{10} \frac{(O_j - E_j)^2}{E_j(1 - E_j / n_j)} \sim \chi^2_8$$

where n_j is the number of observations in the jth group, O_j is the observed number of cases in the jth group, and E_j is the expected number of cases in the jth group. Large G^2_{HL} values (with small p values associated with them) are associated with poor fit.

TABLE 5.4   Logistic Regression Skier Versus Snowboarder Based on Strategies for Waiting in Line

Strategies for Waiting in Line	B	SE	Wald	df	Significance	Exp(B)
I wait patiently in line for my turn.	.057	.076	0.561	1	.454	1.058
I use the singles line (if available), even if it means breaking up my group.	**−.152**	**.062**	**5.962**	**1**	**.015**	**0.859**
I look for opportunities to move ahead by filling empty chair seats (e.g., calling out "Single?").	−.076	.062	1.485	1	.223	0.927
I crowd in hoping to move up in line.	**−.231**	**.068**	**11.697**	**1**	**.001**	**0.793**
I move to a different, less-crowded lift.	**.187**	**.076**	**6.125**	**1**	**.013**	**1.205**
I take a break and come back later.	−.001	.068	0.000	1	.990	0.999
I take a lesson so I can go in the "instructors only" line.	.164	.091	3.226	1	.072	1.178
I anticipate busy days and go to a more expensive, but less-crowded ski area.	.043	.059	0.531	1	.466	1.044
I try not to ski/board on busy days (e.g., weekends, holidays).	−.042	.053	0.604	1	.437	0.959
Hosmer-Lemeshow goodness of fit[a]			.701			
Nagelkerke R-square			.064			

[a]Estimates above .05 are indicative of good fit; boldface items are significant at $p < .05$.

Risky Behaviors

As noted, both skiing and snowboarding are generally considered to be relatively risky sports (Bouter et al., 1988; Zuckerman, 1983b). Using Zuckerman's (1979) 10-item TAS scale, we assessed the overall attitude toward risk across the two sport groups (Table 5.5). To calculate the scale score, individuals' responses on each of the 10 items were summed. As noted, this scale has been used in a variety of studies. A general finding from such studies is that, compared to control groups, participants in more risky sports score higher on the scale. In our sample, the scale had a Cronbach (1951) alpha of .812, which exceeds the .7 cutoff level suggested by Nunnally (1978) and that is commonly used in this type of research. All

TABLE 5.5   Reliability of Zuckerman's (1978) 10-Point Thrill- and Adventure-Seeking Scale

Items	Scale Mean If Item Deleted	Scale Variance If Item Deleted	Corrected Item-Total Correlation	Cronbach's Alpha If Item Deleted	Cronbach's Alpha (Overall Scale)
I (would) like to mountain climb or boulder.	31.91	54.571	.456	.800	.812
I sometimes do things that are a little frightening.	31.08	58.930	.466	.801	
I (would) like to water ski.	31.68	53.815	.512	.793	
I (would) like to surf.	31.52	53.415	.551	.789	
I (would) like to fly an airplane.	31.63	53.881	.497	.795	
I (would) like to scuba dive.	31.54	53.342	.544	.790	
I (would) like to parachute jump.	31.92	50.944	.571	.786	
I (would) like to dive off the high board.	32.11	51.166	.607	.782	
I (would) like to sail a long distance in a small but seaworthy sailing craft.	32.27	55.952	.369	.810	
I (would) enjoy the sensation of skiing very fast down a high mountain slope.	30.67	60.177	.365	.808	

10 items improved the reliability of the scale score. Based on this scale, we found that, consistent with common beliefs, the risk propensity of snowboarders is higher than that of skiers ($p < .001$).

Looking at the individual items included in the scale, we find significant differences between skiers and snowboarders (Table 5.6). On all 10 items, snowboarders were higher than skiers, supporting our expectation that snowboarders are sensation seekers. The only item for which there was not a significant difference was "I (would) enjoy the sensation of skiing very fast down a high mountain slope." As could be expected, both skiers and snowboarders rated high on this item.

TABLE 5.6   Mean Thrill and Adventure Seeking by Snowboarders and Skiers

Thrill- and Adventure-Seeking Item	Skier Mean	Boarder Mean	t	Significance (p)
I (would) like to mountain climb.	3.05	3.42	−3.69	.000
I sometimes do things that are a little frightening.	3.95	4.19	−3.76	.000
I (would) like to water ski.	3.26	3.66	−4.02	.000
I (would) like to surf.	3.17	4.07	−9.92	.000
I (would) like to fly an airplane.	3.37	3.66	−2.98	.003
I (would) like to scuba dive.	3.47	3.73	−2.71	.007
I (would) like to parachute jump.	2.88	3.56	−6.33	.000
I (would) like to dive off the high board.	2.72	3.33	−5.96	.000
I (would) like to sail a long distance in a small but seaworthy sailing craft.	2.77	2.98	−2.07	.039
I (would) enjoy the sensation of skiing very fast down a high mountain slope.	4.43	4.52	−1.36	.174
Additive thrill- and adventure-seeking scale	33.06	36.51	41.23	.000

In Table 5.7, we report the results of a logistic regression with a binary variable taking on a value of 1 if the person was a skier to determine whether the two sports groups engaged in different aggressive and risk-associative behaviors. The regression showed that skiers were generally less aggressive and less likely to engage in behaviors that can increase risks. For instance, they were less likely to "listen to tunes" while skiing. Skiers were more likely to abide by the NSAA's "Your Responsibility Code" (National Ski Areas Association, 2010), as seen in their lower likelihood of "ducking under rope lines" and "ignoring area control signs" and higher likelihood of "observing area slow signs" and "giving extra room to beginners." They were, however, less likely to "signal their intent to go" to others using the same slopes. The regression has explanatory power of about 17% (see Table 5.7 for detailed results). These responses suggest that the two sport groups engage in different risk-taking behaviors.

Consistent with previous research, there was a strong relationship in our data between risk seeking and age. The general risk-seeking propensity in our sample declined with age. Snowboarders as a group were much younger than skiers (chi-squared analysis of age is presented in Table 5.8).

At the next stage, we analyzed whether individuals who utilized the increasingly popular park and pipe areas developed by many ski resorts

TABLE 5.7   Results of Logistic Regressions Predicting Sport Group Based on Risk-Inducing and Risk-Protective Behaviors

	Risk-Inducing/-Protective Behaviors Only as Covariates[a]					Risk-Inducing/-Protective Behaviors and Use of Park and Pipe Facilities as Covariates					Risk-Inducing/-Protective Behaviors and Age as Covariates				
	B	SE	Wald	p-value	Exp(B)	B	SE	Wald	p-value	Exp(B)	B	SE	Wald	p-value	Exp(B)
I wear a helmet when I ski/board.	.051	.047	1.193	.275	1.052	.081	.049	2.682	.101	1.084	.032	.048	0.449	.503	1.033
I listen to tunes when I ski/board.	-.325	.065	24.811	.000	0.722	-.257	.069	14.031	.000	0.774	-.222	.069	10.44	.001	0.801
At the top of a powder run, I jump ahead of others who have paused or hesitated.	-.051	.067	0.574	.449	0.951	-.011	.070	0.025	.874	0.989	-.051	.069	0.554	.457	0.950
At the top of a park, pipe, or narrow run, I signal to others my intent to go.	-.274	.072	14.587	.000	0.761	-.153	.075	4.147	.042	0.858	-.278	.073	14.39	.000	0.757
I duck under rope lines and ignore area control signs.	-.201	.077	6.788	.009	0.818	-.119	.081	2.117	.146	0.888	-.151	.079	3.591	.058	0.860
I observe "slow area" signs when I ski/board.	.176	.073	5.834	.016	1.192	.124	.077	2.613	.106	1.132	.077	.076	1.012	.315	1.080
At the top of a park, pipe, narrow, or challenging run, I let the more skilled go first.	-.097	.080	1.455	.228	0.908	-.114	.084	1.847	.174	0.892	-.057	.082	0.478	.489	0.945
I give beginners or those making unpredictable turns or maneuvers extra room.	.363	.118	9.548	.002	1.438	.316	.123	6.628	.010	1.371	.283	.120	5.572	.018	1.328
I perform stunts/use park and pipe.						-1.413	.173	67.055	.000	0.243					
Age											.399	.071	31.658	.000	1.490
Hosmer-Lemeshow goodness of fit			.65[b]					.57[b]					.27[b]		
Nagelkerke R-square			.17					.27					.22		

Note: The dependent variable takes on a value of 1 if a person is a skier and 0 otherwise. Boldface items are significant at $p < .05$.
[a] We adopt the terminology of Hosmer and Lemeshow (1989) and refer to the variables on the right side of the logistic regression equation as "covariates."
[b] Estimates above .05 are indicative of good fit.

TABLE 5.8   Age Differences in Snowboarder and Skier Populations

		Snowboarders (%)	Skiers (%)	Total (%)	Significance of Chi-Squared Test
Age	Under 18	7.9	4.0	6.0	
	18 to 24	33.3	14.5	24.2	
	25 to 34	31.0	23.0	27.1	
	35 to 44	18.1	28.0	22.9	.000
	45 to 54	8.4	22.4	15.2	
	55 to 64	1.0	7.9	4.3	
	65+	0.2	0.3	0.3	
Total	100.0%	100.0	100.0		

might also be more prone to engage in dangerous activities. We then extended the analysis by including control variables for engaging in park and pipe activities and age. As shown in Table 5.7, both variables are highly significant ($p < .01$) and increase the explanatory power of the regression. While there were no sign reversals, incorporating the factor of age caused the significant and positive coefficient of "observing slow area signs" to become insignificant while the coefficient of "giving beginners extra room" became significant. Resulting in the largest increase of explanatory power, adjusting for use of park and pipe facilities caused the significant negative coefficient of "ducking under rope lines" to become insignificant. These results indicate that age and park and pipe use are associated with aggressive and risk associative behaviors. Further analysis revealed that those who frequented park and pipe facilities were younger and more prone to breaking rules and engaging in disruptive behaviors regardless of whether they were skiers or snowboarders. That is, some of the observed cross-cultural difference appears to be generational. However, our results also point out that the subcultures are responding differently to externally imposed rules of conduct. Specifically, the variable "I signal to others my intent to go," an element found in Smart Style, but not included in the Skiers' Code of Responsibility (National Ski Areas Association, 2010), was negative and significant (meaning a higher likelihood that the person was a snowboarder). This suggests that subcultural differences in aggressive and risky behaviors may reflect, in part, different reactions to externally imposed codes of conduct.

Contribution and Managerial Implications

This study examined preferences, attitudes, and behaviors of subgroups of winter sport participants. By examining adventure-seeking propensity, motivations, frustrations, and behaviors of skiers, snowboarders, and those who frequent park and pipe areas we identified a number of differences between these sports subcultures. The findings from this study provide a number of insights for managers of ski resorts. They can also be helpful to others in the travel industry.

Cultures Matter

The finding that skiers, snowboarders, and increasingly park and pipers, represent different cultures is important. These groups approach their sports differently, and these differences can have an impact on the experience of those in the other groups. The propensity of snowboarders to engage in thrill-seeking behaviors may significantly detract from the solitude and enjoyment of nature desired by skiers. Although our data suggest the extent of the previously documented cultural clash may have diminished somewhat over time as snowboarders have gained prominence at ski areas, overall more than a quarter of our sample reported that they were most comfortable on the hill among others who used the same type of equipment. Thus, ski area management should make deliberate decisions about whether and how to segregate or integrate its different sport cultures.

One possibility is to enhance opportunities for on-hill self-selection. A study suggested that trail design and grooming both have significant impacts on the incidence of injuries at ski areas (Bergstrom & Ekeland, 2002). Trail design and grooming also have an impact on user experiences and can be used to encourage self-selection of facility use by different groups. As noted, some resorts have introduced designated areas for those interested in doing stunts and negotiating elements such as rails, tables, and jumps. Our analysis suggests that rather than focus on run-by-run differentiation, resorts might consider developing entire areas serviced by a specific lift so that they appeal to one group of users. Managers could then rate the terrain served by that lift based on its risk-reward appeal. Grooming, run development, and features that have specific subcultural appeal developed around a specific lift could facilitate enhanced self-selection. Given the historical emphasis on individuality in winter sports, we caution managers about designating areas as family friendly or user specific since this could be perceived as reducing choice and freedom. However, self-selection can be encouraged through thoughtful terrain selection and management. For example, long, comparatively flat areas that are difficult for snowboarders to navigate may, if groomed extensively, attract families and timid participants and discourage high-thrill-seeking users. Beyond the suitability of terrain for the implementation of special facilities, resorts may distinguish areas with different appeal to minimize on-hill interactions between user groups potentially in conflict. However, such a strategy is not without risk. While our survey did not specifically address the issue of participants' desire to experience the entire resort, there is a danger that actions designed to limit the number of runs, terrain, and exposure to the entire ski area might themselves be a source of dissatisfaction with the experience.

Trail design can also accommodate the natural behaviors of users. Our data, and our informal observations, suggest that snowboarders are likely to gather in groups. Areas can be designed to help reduce congestion created by such behavior. For example, park and pipe facilities could be designed with wide areas where those who wish to watch the stunts of other, more skilled participants can stop without interfering with the flow of skier traffic alongside the park and pipe area. Careful consideration should also be given to how trails used by those taking advantage of park-and-pipe facilities merge with those frequented by skiers.

It is important for resort management to be sensitive to usage patterns associated with new trends in the sports. With the increased popularity of twin-tip skis that enable skiers to do stunts and ski backward, park-and-pipe facilities are attracting these users along with snowboarders. Observing their behaviors and adapting facilities to enhance the experience of both boarders and twin tippers will help ensure these thrill seekers have sufficient play areas. As they spend more time in the areas specially designed for them, they will be less likely to use runs selected by skiers, thus enabling skiers to have the more serene experience they desire.

Risk Taking and Safety Programs

Our data reinforce the notion that a key motivation for most (if not all) participants is thrill and adrenaline. Downhill winter sports have a history of appeal for individual risk taking and management. But, the inherent social context of the sport requires at least a fundamental awareness of the social (and increasingly personal) consequences of risky actions.

Ski areas have developed and instituted fairly successful safety programs based around the 1966 Skiers' Code of Responsibility (National Ski Areas Association, 2010). While beautifully uncomplicated and brief, it is an old institution, dating back to the days of wooden alpine skis with screw-on edges and "bear-trap" bindings. The technology of winter sports has changed drastically since 1966, and with new technologies come new issues that old institutions are ill equipped to handle. As a brief analogy, consider the impact of the development of Internet file-sharing technologies on the institution of copyrights.

The industry deserves congratulations for developing the Smart Style code of ethics for the freestyle enthusiast. However, we suggest that a segmented approach to codes of ethics and safety may send the wrong signal. Our basic hypothesis suggests that subcultures have and are developing in the ski industry. Initially, subcultures were based on user differences driven by ski and snowboard technology; the emerging park and pipe subculture is based on skill as well as technology. The need for a common set of ethics arises when these subcultures interact. For example, park-and-pipe participants are adept at maneuvers such as switches, hits, grabs, and other explosive actions. Executed in congested areas, these movements create irregular and unpredictable traffic patterns that other participants unfamiliar with park and pipe may find threatening. The Smart Style code of ethics addresses activity only in the park and pipe. There is an implicit understanding that the Skiers' Code of Responsibility (National Ski Areas Association, 2010) applies outside the park and pipe. We suggest, however, that the title, Skiers' Code of Responsibility, explicitly ignores the subcultural structure of winter sports. This title perpetuates the sense of historical alienation experienced by snowboarders, and it ignores the developing reality of the freestyle subculture. We suggest that the comparative success of safety programs based on the Skiers' Code of Responsibility (National Ski Areas Association, 2010) among skiers is in part due to their subcultural affiliation with skiers.

While we leave it to industry participants to debate this issue further, we suggest that a successful code of ethics will (a) be inclusive of all participants, (b) express rules in a commonsense manner, and (c) opt for fewer rather than more rules. Serious consideration should be given to rebranding the Skiers' Code of Responsibility (National Ski Areas Association, 2010). We further suggest that ski areas undertake educational programs to promote a common set of ethics if one emerges. Finally, we urge that the common code of ethics be revisited on a regular basis to take account of new challenges raised by technological changes.

Growth Strategies

Most resorts realize that long-term sustainable growth in the industry is tied to the successful retention of entry-level participants. Educational programs play a particularly important role in this effort. While our data revealed the importance of "thrill and adrenaline" as a motivator, they also suggest that participants are curious, seek new skills, and desire a sense of personal satisfaction. We encourage thinking out of the box even though experimentation brings business risk. Ski lessons are typically targeted at skill acquisition, with progression measured by conquering increasingly difficult runs. While this undoubtedly contributes to personal satisfaction, it may neglect others and miss the importance of social interaction, voluntary or forced. For example, cultural clashes could be mitigated by explaining the links between technology and why participants undertake certain actions (e.g., why snowboarders often sit when they stop on the hill). For the younger participant, learning that one can have fun and still be responsible might go a long way in reducing intergenerational issues. For the older participant, learning about the history of the ski area, the sport, and notable aspects of the natural surroundings might be an additional source of enjoyment. Multi-day lessons with the same group of people can offer opportunities for socialization not found in single day lessons. It might even be possible to experiment with lessons of mixed users (e.g., snowboarders and skiers).

Our data suggest that different education strategies may be necessary for different user groups. By equipment type, both ski and snowboarding lessons were up slightly, but snowboarding lessons were not proportional to snowboarder participation, perhaps indicating resistance by some snowboarders to lessons. This trend is supported by our finding that snowboarders were more likely to learn by observing those with greater skill. Our analysis suggests that snowboarders, as well as other younger users, may be particularly influenced by peer role models, raising several possibilities. Areas may want to explore recognition programs in which high-skill participants are given opportunities to exhibit their skills, thus providing visual demonstrations to those less skilled. Area-sponsored contests can provide dual benefits of entertainment and education. Another possibility would be to invite particularly skilled boarders and twin tippers to participate with employed instructors as demonstration team members, giving them an incentive to encourage friends to enroll in lessons. Park and pipe areas could also be made available for a fee on days when an "expert" is available; in this "non-lesson" environment, all could learn and practice what they see the expert do as if they were friends playing together. Given that areas would participate in the selection process of the role model, there is the additional possibility of shaping the personality of the area through the selection process—a strategy of differentiation.

Our data further suggest that programs designed to help first timers, particularly those new to snowboarding, could have benefits for both snowboarders and skiers. Our data suggest that many skiers are experimenting with snowboarding and vice versa. Equipment and instruction can have an impact on the rate at which new participants become proficient at the sport. Since skiers may already have had experience taking lessons and since the acquisition of new skills is one of their top motivations, lesson programs specifically for those with experience skiing but not snowboarding should be considered. Included with instruction on technique could be the introduction of tips on etiquette for interacting with other boarders and with skiers. If safe and considerate behavior is stressed when one is first learning the sport, such behavior is more likely to be incorporated as habit.

Facilities Management

Beyond the slopes at ski areas, there are insights for both lift and food service management. "Singles-only" lines have gained popularity because they help reduce congestion in lift lines and help the user willing to "go alone" to get to the top of the hill faster. Other strategies, including "fast-track" lines for individuals willing to pay a premium to get onto lifts without standing in line are helping some ski resorts increase revenue. Resorts may also consider redirecting participants to areas serviced by lifts that are underutilized; signs indicating average waiting time on such lifts may attract participants anxious for quicker access to runs.

While waiting in the lift line has garnered much attention in the industry, our data suggest that congestion on the slope is now an equally important issue for participants. Just as too little uphill lift capacity can be a negative, our data suggest that too much lift capacity relative to ski terrain is also a negative. There are many ways to read data, but we note that total runs/vertical feet rated lowest in the sense of having a good day. Congestion on the slope impedes the sense of thrill and adrenaline that participants seem to crave. It also challenges the ability of participants to mentally relax. We suggest that the commercially successful ski area will find options that balance uphill lift capacity with on-slope congestion. While there are price discrimination possibilities, it is important to consider that such pricing schemes will only work if they do not anger the buyer.

The efficiency of food service areas is also important for ensuring that enthusiasts can enjoy both their time with friends and their time on the slopes. Resorts might consider instituting food service areas that can capitalize on the socialization motive of snowboarders by providing seating areas that accommodate groups, serving foods that can be shared (such as whole pizzas instead of pizza by the slice), and offering discounts for groups during off-peak times, thus encouraging snowboarders to avoid the busiest eating times. For those wishing to optimize their time on the slopes, grab-and-go food selections could be made available in ski-in, ski-out kiosks for faster service. Supporting attention to a "greener" environment, such facilities should incorporate plentiful trash receptacles.

Travel and Related Industries

Study findings also hold some important implications for those in the travel industry. Pizam et al. (2004) found that travel destination selection varies with the risk-taking and sensation-seeking (RSS) score of a traveler. When marketing resorts to the snowboarder and park and pipe segments, appeals that fit with the risk-taking propensity of these groups should be considered. Photos or video clips of skilled riders navigating the park and pipe, shots of the "steeps," and descriptions of the "thrills" available are likely to attract them. Conversely, depictions of the pristine environment, the solitude on the slopes, and skiers enjoying a lesson from a professional ski instructor likely will appeal more to skiers. Cross-promotional opportunities with après-ski facilities such as bars and restaurants and hotels with an ambience appropriate to each segment as well as with other resort destinations with similar allure are suggested by our analysis.

While cross-marketing opportunities have formed the core of several well-documented corporate strategies (some successful, some not), we urge caution and careful deliberation on the part of ski areas. While the financial pressures of expensive capital investments may prompt cross-marketing endeavors, our data highlight the importance of mental relaxation and enjoyment of nature as motivations for participation. The omnipresence of corporate sponsorships and promotions such as ads on lift chairs and marketing time-share properties in area restaurants may actually increase the attractiveness of other alternatives for the consumer's dollar. There may be a short-run, long-run trade-off involved in increasing the commercialization of the winter sport experience.

In addition, resort management should take note of the risk-seeking propensity of the park and pipe crowd. Marketing other extreme sports to them and expanding off-season offerings to include other adrenaline sports (e.g., mountain climbing and mountain biking) may be an effective way to diversify the offerings of the resort.

Finally, with age a significant factor in risk-taking propensity and disruptive risk-seeking behaviors associated with the snowboarder and park and pipe cultures, it will be interesting to follow the further evolutions of the sport. It will bear review in time to see what happens with the "edgy" cultures as their participants age, presumably becoming more risk averse.

References

Bergstrom, K. A., & Ekeland, A. (2002). Effect of trail design and grooming on the incidence of injuries at alpine ski areas. *British Journal of Sports Medicine, 38*, 264–268.

Bouter, L., Knipschild, P., Feij, J., & Volovics, A. (1988). Sensation seeking and injury risk in downhill skiing. *Personality and Individual Differences, 9*, 667–673.

Bunting, D., Wagner, M., & Jones, D. P. (2005). *The economic impact of ski areas represented by the Inland Northwest Ski Association.* Institute of Public Policy and Economic Analysis, Spokane, WA: Eastern Washington University.

Chapman, B. (2006). Ski demographics broaden. Retrieved August 10, 2009, from http://www.allbusiness.com/transportation-communications-electric-gas/4238842–1.html

Cronbach, L. (1951). Coefficient alpha and the internal structure of tests. *Psychometrika, 16*, 297–334.

Edensor, T., & Richards, S. (2007). Snowboarders vs. skiers: Contested choreographies of the slopes. *Leisure Studies, 26*(1), 97–114.

Geddes, R., & Irish, K. (2005). Boarder belly: Splenic injuries resulting from ski and snowboarding accidents. *Emergency Medicine Australasia, 17*, 157–162.

Grapetine, T. (2004). No pain, no pain reliever. *Marketing Research, 16*(4), 4.

Hosmer, D., & Lemeshow, S. (1989). *Applied logistic regression.* New York: Wiley.

Howe, S. (1998). *(Sick) a cultural history of snowboarding.* New York: St. Martins Griffin.

Kerr, J. H. (1991). Arousal-seeking in risk sport participants. *Personality and Individual Differences, 12*, 613–616.

Kottke National End of Season Survey 2005/06: Final Report (26th ed.). (2006). National Ski Areas Association in conjunction with RRC Associates, Inc. (July), Boulder, CO.

Kottke National End of Season Survey 2007/08: Preliminary Report. (2008). National Ski Areas Association in conjunction with RRC Associates, Inc., Boulder, CO.

Makens, J. C. (2001). A ski-industry challenge: Clashing cultures on the slopes. *Cornell Hotel and Restaurant Administration Quarterly, 42*(3), 74–79.

Muñiz, A. M., & O'Guinn, T. C. (2001). Brand community. *Journal of Consumer Research, 27,* 412–432.

National Ski and Snowboard Retailers Association. (2001). *Downhill ski participation; snowboarding participation.* Retrieved August 9, 2009, from http://www.nssra.com/2001/nssra/index.asp?centre=stat&section=skipart

National Ski Areas Association. (2010). "Your Responsibility Code" http://www.nsaa.org/nsaa/safety/know_the_code.asp

National Ski Patrol. (2009). *Your responsibility code.* Retrieved September 18, 2009, from http://www/nsp.org/slooopesafety/slope_safety.aspx

Nunnally, J. C. (1978). *Psychometric theory* (2nd ed.). New York: McGraw-Hill.

Pizam, A., Jeong, G.-H., Reichel, A., van Boemmel, H., Lusson, J. M., Steynberg, L., … Montmany, N. (2004). The relationship between risk-taking, sensation-seeking, and the tourist behavior of young adults: A cross-cultural study. *Journal of Travel Research, 42,* 251–260.

Pow Productions. (2009). *The facts.* Retrieved August 8, 2009, from http://www.powproductions.com/facts.html

Ronning, R., Gerner, T., & Engebretsen, L. (2000). Risk of injury during alpine and telemark skiing and snowboarding. *The American Journal of Sports Medicine, 28,* 506–508.

Schouten, J. W., & McAlexander, J. H. (1995). Subcultures of consumption: An ethnography of the new bikers. *Journal of Consumer Research, 22,* 43–61.

Snowboarding. (2009). Retrieved August 8, 2009, from http://snowboarding.about.com/od/snowboardresorts/i/snowboardingban.htm

Solomon, M. R. (2004). *Consumer behavior: Buying, having and being* (6th ed.). Saddle River, NJ: Pearson Prentice-Hall.

Tarazi, F., Dvorak, M., & Wing, P. C. (1999). Spinal injuries in skiers and snowboarders. *The American Journal of Sports Medicine, 27,* 177–180.

Vaske, J. J., Carothers, P., Donnelly, M. P., & Baird, B. (2000). Recreation conflict among skiers and snowboarders. *Leisure Sciences, 22,* 297–313.

Williams, P. W., Dossa, K. B., & Fulton, A. (1994). Tension on the slopes: Managing conflict between skiers and snowboarders. *Journal of Applied Recreation Research, 19,* 191–213.

Zuckerman, M. (1978). Dimensions of sensation seeking. In H. London & J. Exner (Eds.), *Dimensions of personality* (pp. 487–549), New York, Wiley.

Zuckerman, M. (1979). *Sensation seeking: Beyond the optimal level of arousal.* Hillsdale, NJ: Erlbaum.

Zuckerman, M. (1983a). *Biological bases of sensation seeking, impulsivity, and anxiety.* Hillsdale, NJ: Erlbaum.

Zuckerman, M. (1983b). Sensation seeking and sports. *Personality and Individual Differences, 4*(3), 285–293.

Zuckerman, M. (1994). *Behavioral expressions and biosocial bases of sensation seeking.* Cambridge: Cambridge University Press.

Zuckerman, M., Eysenck, S., & Eysenck, H. J. (1978). Sensation seeking in England and America: Cross-cultural, age, and sex comparisons. *Journal of Consulting and Clinical Psychology, 46*(1), 139–149.

6

The Impact of Corporate Social Responsibility on NBA Fan Relationships
A Conceptual Framework

Pamela A. Kennett-Hensel,
Russell Lacey, and Matt Biggers

> There is more to basketball than what happens on the court, and some of the NBA's most significant efforts occur off the court.
>
> **David Stern, NBA commissioner[1]**

Introduction

Corporate social responsibility (CSR) efforts are on the rise. It is estimated that U.S. organizations alone have contributed $14.5 billion in charitable giving (Giving USA Foundation, 2009), with over 91% of companies reporting formal CSR policies (HRfocus, 2007). This CSR focus is also found globally with four of five companies indicating some participation in CSR practices (HRfocus, 2007). The heightened focus on CSR is encouraging, to say the least, and indicates that many decision makers feel that maximizing profit and behaving in a socially responsible manner are not conflicting goals (Husted & Salazar, 2006).

These social responsibility initiatives cut across industries. According to *Fortune Magazine* (2009), the top five socially responsible companies, representing a diverse group of industries, are Anheuser-Busch, Marriott International, Integrys Energy Group, Walt Disney, and Herman Miller. Any given industry possesses its own motivations and demands that guide

---

[1] 2008–2009 NBA Cares Community Report, p. 4.

the level and nature of CSR efforts. This is true of the sports industry, which has been called on to make a positive contribution to society (i.e., Wilbon, 2004; Zeigler, 2007). Given the visibility and reach of sports, it has been argued that "sport, more than any other potential vehicle, contains qualities that make it a powerful force in effecting positive social contributions" (Smith & Westerbeek, 2007, p. 44).

Within this arena of sports, perhaps, nowhere is social responsibility taken more seriously than in the National Basketball Association (NBA). Through its NBA Cares program, the league, its teams, and its players have donated over $100 million and 1 million hours of service (NBA, 2009b). As explained by New Orleans Hornets owner George Shinn, "I feel like it's very important for me to reach out and help others. And I love this community and I like to be involved. I think it helps us as a business, and certainly it helps me as a human being" (Eichenhofer, 2009). The efforts of the NBA family are diverse and far reaching. They include such actions as New Orleans Hornets player Chris Paul's CP3 Foundation donating $55,000 to local charities (Martel, 2009) to players traveling to Turkey, India, and South Africa to teach youngsters about basketball through the Basketball Without Borders program (NBA, 2009b).

Like any for-profit operation, the NBA and its teams must balance CSR initiatives against other stakeholder responsibilities. These responsibilities lie internally (i.e., to players, front-office employees, and owners) and externally (i.e., to customers, community, and environment) (Mendoza, 2007) and cannot all be met if a team is not financially viable. Therefore, how does one implement a CSR plan that ultimately leaves all stakeholders better off, and how do these initiatives help a team achieve its more financially oriented objectives?

The purpose of this chapter is to propose a framework that explains how these CSR initiatives contribute to the success of NBA teams through better fan relationships. In particular, the efforts of the New Orleans Hornets are highlighted given our familiarity and work experience with this NBA franchise. Also, the Hornets represent a unique CSR case study due to the unprecedented situation facing the city of New Orleans, which is still struggling to recover from Hurricane Katrina, one of the largest natural disasters in U.S. history. The proposed framework will assist sports management in making CSR choices and in understanding how investments in CSR yield a positive return. While examined in the context of the NBA, the proposed framework is relevant for all sports organizations and can be easily modified for nonsports entities.

CSR and Factors Contributing to Its Practice

Effective CSR initiatives result from the appropriate corporate mindset. This focus is communicated through the corporate mission, integration with objectives, and support of owners and senior management. As illustrated in Figure 6.1, these issues set the tone for and are critical to a company's ability to reap CSR benefits.

Mission or Vision Statement

Mission and vision statements guide the strategic direction of an organization. Typically, mission statements identify in what business a company is engaged, while vision statements address the issue of what a company wants to become (Ferrell & Hartline, 2008). If a company wishes to be socially responsible, this should be underscored in its mission or vision statement. For instance, the mission of the NBA is "to be the most successful and respected professional sports league in the world." In addition to this broad mission, the NBA goes a step further by stating, "We understand that the popularity and visibility of our teams, players and league obligate us to demonstrate leadership in corporate social responsibility" (NBA, 2009c). The NBA has been praised for using the mission statement as a road map to guide everything it does, including placing a strong importance on CSR (Economou, 2009).

The New Orleans Hornets exhibit a similar focus through its mission of "Passion, Purpose and Pride" (New Orleans Hornets, 2009). In what has been viewed as a departure from traditional sports marketing, the Hornets have focused on community since the team's post-Katrina return to the city. Not only has this mission guided the strategic direction of the team, including a prominent role in the rebuilding and recovery of the devastated city, but it has also sent the message to the community regarding its long-term commitment to these efforts (Sauer, 2007).

Corporate Objectives

A company with a CSR-inclusive mission or vision should follow through by integrating CSR into its corporate objectives. By doing so, the focus on CSR is ensured, the company is given the opportunity to better define

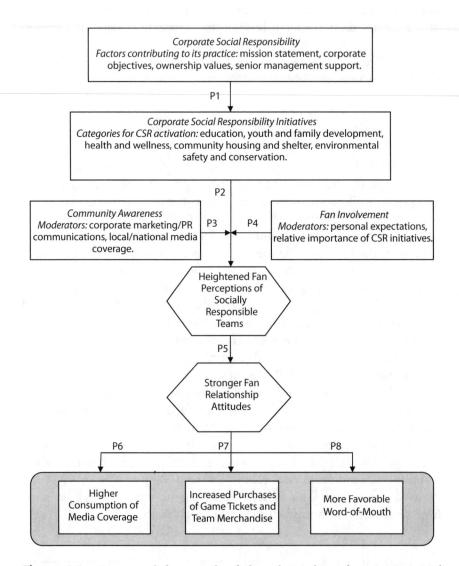

Figure 6.1 Conceptual framework of the relationship of corporate social responsibility with sports fans.

CSR as it relates to the organization, and measurable outcomes that will determine CSR success are articulated. In its broadest sense, CSR is conceived as the adoption of moral and ethical practices as they relate to the needs (i.e., environmental, social, and economic) of the entire stakeholder community (Kirdahy, 2007). In practice, cause-related marketing, corporate giving, employee volunteering, and responsible business practices are among the various ways that this definition can be realized (Berger, Cunningham, & Drumwright, 2007; Bhattacharya & Sen, 2004).

NBA teams have significant latitude when it comes to setting their own CSR objectives. The league requires some minimums and maximums on certain issues, such as player appearances as dictated by the NBA collective bargaining agreement with the players' union (see National Basketball Players Association, 2009, Article II, Section 8). There are also some mandatory league initiatives and platforms that require team participation at specified levels, but most are left to the discretion of individual teams. The NBA encourages "best practices" sharing among teams to spur CSR ideas.

The New Orleans Hornets set multifaceted CSR objectives. These annual objectives follow from the mission of the league and team and result from a planning process that assesses issues such as the success of current and past programs, stakeholder needs, and sponsorship interest in development of specific programs. Objectives are specified for CSR areas that include, but are not limited to, number of player appearances, number of player and charity ticket programs, fundraising, and external charity support. Further, objectives are set for specific initiatives. For instance, the Hornets Bookmobile program has a target number of books to distribute during the year.

Ownership and Senior Management Support

Given that the direction of the company is set by those in charge, no CSR initiative will be successful without the support of ownership and senior management. Employees should see that company owners and senior management view CSR as a priority and value employees who share this mindset. It is important to note that supporting CSR should be done not only through words but also through actions. The New Orleans Hornets owner George Shinn and the NBA commissioner, David Stern, are both staunch proponents of CSR. They talk about its importance and its integral place in their respective value systems, but their actions speak louder than words. The George Shinn Foundation supports over 18 different local charities through time and money. The Hornets owners are a visible presence at charitable events, whether visiting mothers at local hospitals or serving Christmas dinners to the elderly (New Orleans Hornets, 2009). Commissioner Stern has exhibited similar CSR behaviors, such as participating in the Hoops for Home program during the 2009 All-Star game in New Orleans.

Harvard Business School professor John Quelch suggested younger, lower-level managers, particularly those of the millennial generation, are more concerned about CSR initiatives and would like to be empowered to pursue these activities (White, 2008). Transformational leadership such as that seen with the NBA and Hornets empowers others in the organization to engage in CSR activities and attracts CSR-oriented individuals as employees. Researchers have found that any behaviors that could be perceived as discretionary are best cultivated through transformational leaders (Rowold & Rohmann, 2009).

Types of CSR Initiatives

If the correct foundation for CSR is in place, the company must then focus on implementation issues. The following relationship, as outlined in Figure 6.1, is proposed:

> P1: The combined presence of a CSR-oriented mission or vision statement and corporate objectives with ownership or senior management support will result in activation of CSR initiatives.

Activation of CSR initiatives requires choosing causes to support and how to demonstrate this support. In the economically challenging business world of today, managers are encouraged to adopt a strategic focus when it comes to CSR and to look beyond a purely altruistic approach (Husted & Salazar, 2006; Warhurst, 2008). The ability to align social and economic goals is paramount (Berger et al., 2007; Husted & Salazar, 2006; Porter & Kramer, 2002). Unfortunately, it is not unusual for companies to struggle with this, resulting in programs that are unfocused and diffused (Porter & Kramer, 2002).

Categories of CSR Causes

Many categorization systems for charitable causes exist (see National Center for Charitable Statistics, 2009, for a good overview). Companies are encouraged first to identify categories of causes that will serve as the focus of their CSR initiatives. One issue to consider is the relationship between the brand or company and the cause. Do the two have to be a natural fit (e.g., Home Depot and Habitat for Humanity)? Lafferty (2007) concluded that the fit between the company and the cause is not critical. Becker-Olsen, Cudmore, and Hill (2006) concluded that fit alone is not the main determinant of consumer behavior. Beyond fit, a more relevant consideration might be the importance or meaningfulness of the cause to various stakeholders (Lichenstein, Drumwright, & Braig, 2004).

Based on the interest and needs of its stakeholders, the NBA has chosen to focus on three categories of causes: education, youth and family development, and health and wellness. The Hornets actively support these same categories of causes through a variety of activities. In addition, the team places a strong emphasis on community housing and shelter services and environmental safety and conservation. These two additional causes are of particular importance to the New Orleans market as a result of Hurricane Katrina.

CSR Implementation Causes and Initiatives[2]

Once categories have been selected, specific causes and initiatives must be identified and implemented. Resources (e.g., monetary, nonmonetary, and human) necessary to employ these initiatives should also be identified as part of the implementation strategy. A schedule should be developed to ensure that CSR efforts are ongoing throughout the season and year and individual efforts are coordinated.

For instance, the New Orleans Hornets organize all holiday season efforts under the Season of Giving initiative. This Season of Giving includes Toys for Tots toy drives, senior citizen holiday parties, homeless shelter shoe donations, and family "adoptions." Similarly, the Hornets coordinate the Player Community Ticket Program in which players purchase and distribute game tickets to children via nonprofit organizations. During the 2008–2009 NBA season, 6,300 home game tickets were distributed, giving underprivileged children the opportunity to sit in players' sections such as CP3's Leaders, Ju Ju Bees, Mo's Maniacs, and Bop's Biddy Ballers. The criteria for ticket donation are set by each player. For instance, some may choose

---

2 All NBA CSR initiative information in this section came from the NBA and its NBA Cares program Web site unless otherwise noted. All New Orleans Hornets CSR information in this section came from the New Orleans Hornets Web site unless otherwise noted. www.nba.com, www.nba.com/nba_cares/, www.nba.com/hornets/index_main.html

to reward students for good grades or attendance, while others choose to focus on those meeting healthy lifestyle benchmarks. While multiple categories of causes are addressed through Season of Giving and the Player Community Ticket Program, coordination of these efforts is necessary.

Education Initiatives

One way in which the NBA implements its commitment to education is through the Read to Achieve program. This global literacy campaign is designed to cultivate a love of reading in children and involves recruitment of adults to participate in reading aloud and shared readings. Launched in 2000, this program is estimated to reach 50 million children a year and is considered the largest educational outreach initiative in professional sports. It is supported by all arms of the NBA family, including current and retired players, the WNBA (Women's National Basketball Association), minor and development leagues, employees, and the NBA Officials Association.

The New Orleans Hornets are supportive of the Read to Achieve initiative and have customized their involvement to fit the needs of their stakeholders. Monthly Read to Achieve events are hosted at local elementary schools. At each event is the Hornets/Best Western Bookmobile, a retired school bus that has been transformed into a library on wheels with over 2,000 publications on board. Students, with the assistance of Hornets players and personnel, board the bus and choose a free book. They are then treated to a read-aloud event. This initiative has particular meaning for children in the New Orleans metropolitan area, many of whom lost everything (including all of their books) during Hurricane Katrina. Over the first two NBA seasons following the return of the Hornets to New Orleans post-Katrina, more than 50,000 books were distributed. According to the Hornets, "The bookmobile has become much more than a vehicle for book donation. It has been a visible statement that the Hornets don't just play basketball—they ensure long-term educational success in our community."

Further, the Hornets are involved in many other educational programs, such as the Leadership Summit held at Xavier University, the Chevron MVP program, the Emerge program in conjunction with the Salvation Army Greater New Orleans Area Command, and an incentive program built around the Louisiana Educational Assessment Program (LEAP) test. At the start of the 2009 school year, the team "adopted" Edward P. Harney Elementary School, a New Orleans Recovery District school, and has pledged to assist them through multiple initiatives. All of these education initiatives encourage and reward attendance and successful performance and spark dialogues about issues that have an impact on the lives of these children.

Youth and Family Development

The NBA family demonstrates its dedication to youth and family development through many initiatives. The intent is to champion such issues as fitness, nutrition, healthy lifestyle choices, sportsmanship, and teamwork to both children and their families. These initiatives include the Jr. NBA/Jr. WNBA Program. This program encompasses free basketball clinics and leagues and has touched over 2 million individuals. A similar program, Basketball Without Borders, promotes these values in African, Asian, and Latin American countries. As part of this initiative, the New Orleans Hornets host Summer Hoops Clinics for Louisiana children ages 7 to 14.

Health and Wellness

While the theme of health and wellness is found in many NBA initiatives, specific efforts are directed toward this as well. For instance, the NBA is involved in Nothing But Nets, which sends malaria nets to families in Africa. Also, it partners with Kaboom in an effort to build playgrounds and with the Partnership for a Drug-Free America.

The New Orleans Hornets host fitness events for local schoolchildren, encouraging them to "Bee Fit." Children who are struggling with illness are touched through the league and team involvement in the Make-A-Wish Foundation, which grants wishes of terminally and chronically ill children.

Community Housing and Shelter

In response to the devastation of Hurricane Katrina, community housing and shelter initiatives have taken on particular importance for the New Orleans Hornets and their stakeholders. In an effort to respond, Hoops for Homes was created with the objective of rebuilding shattered homes and hearts. As the New Orleans recovery has evolved, so has this program with the help of partners such as the New Orleans Area Habitat for Humanity and the Salvation Army. A current focus of this initiative is assisting displaced teachers to rebuild their homes so that the education of area children does not suffer.

Environmental Safety and Conservation

Although not an official team color, the New Orleans Hornets are "green" and post-Katrina have been involved in many environmental and conservation issues. These efforts are collectively organized under the Hornets Planet Rebound program, which has the overall objective to educate various stakeholders on the importance of being environmentally responsible. This program is composed of three pillars: energy efficiency, preserving coastal wetlands, and community beautification. Specific events, such as Energy Efficient Night presented by Chevron and planting trees and marsh grass in Bayou Savage National Wildlife Refuge to replace what Hurricane Katrina had destroyed, have been designed in support of Hornets Planet Rebound. The Hornets office also has become environmentally friendly through recycling efforts and removal of fax machines and Styrofoam™. The NBA supports similar issues through the NBA Green Week. Several of the Hornets Planet Rebound efforts are timed to coincide with this league-wide event.

CSR Perceptions

For organizations implementing CSR initiatives, two questions must be addressed: How do these CSR initiatives have an impact on consumers (i.e., fans), and how does an organization leverage efforts to maximize this impact? If CSR is viewed as an investment, the return on this investment is of paramount concern, and the process underlying this return must be understood. As posited in Figure 6.1, an organization that implements CSR initiatives will see heightened fan perceptions, which in turn will lead to stronger fan relationship attitudes. Awareness of CSR initiatives and fan involvement moderate the impact of CSR.

Heightened Fan Perceptions of Social Responsibility

By undertaking CSR initiatives, organizations will be viewed as socially responsible. "Brands are now judged on what they do, not say" (Clarke, 2003). While an organization may claim be to socially responsible, actually behaving in a socially responsible manner is critical. The issue of actual behavior becomes important due to the skepticism that many consumers attach to CSR (Porter & Kramer, 2006; Vlachos, Tsamakos, Vrechopoulos, & Avramidis, 2009). Webb and Mohr (1998) attributed some of this skepticism to the fact that CSR is integrated into advertising campaigns, and consumers have an inherent level of mistrust in advertising. Bronn and

Vrioni (2001) contended that CSR promotion does not correspond to behavior in many instances.

As fans of the New Orleans Hornets see the many CSR initiatives of the team in action, their perceptions are positively influenced regarding the level of the social responsibility of the Hornets organization to its stakeholder community.

P2: The implementation of CSR initiatives will result in heightened fan perceptions of socially responsible teams.

Influence of Community Awareness of CSR Initiatives

While undertaking CSR activities is laudable, not all stakeholders will benefit if there is no awareness of these activities. Bhattacharya and Sen (2004) identified awareness as the key prerequisite to a successful CSR effort and explained that without this awareness no attitudinal or behavioral response from consumers will be realized. Historically, awareness of CSR activities was deemed low (e.g., Boulstridge & Carrigan, 2000; Sen, Bhattacharya, & Korschun, 2006), but more recent studies found improvement in awareness levels and efforts (e.g., Birth, Illia, Lurati, & Zamparini, 2008; Lewis, 2008).

Generating awareness is the responsibility of the organization; thus, the NBA and the New Orleans Hornets identify generating CSR awareness as a marketing communications and public relations (PR) goal. However, care must be taken not to overpromote CSR efforts, which in turn can fuel skepticism, be seen as self-serving, or be perceived as a PR stunt. Companies too often become distracted by the PR benefits of CSR and lose sight of its true purpose: to create social value (Porter & Kramer, 2002). Concerns regarding these pitfalls are lessened when an organization, such as the New Orleans Hornets, has already built up goodwill in the community over time.

To promote its activities, the New Orleans Hornets undertakes external PR to local and national media through press releases and by contacting the media before the event to encourage coverage. The team is conscious and strategic on how they position media opportunities. They must be seen as intriguing so that the media will cover them. This includes the activity choice itself, who is representing the Hornets (e.g., if players or ownership are involved, the CSR activity is much more likely to get covered), and that it is viewed as novel (i.e., either a new event or a new twist on an ongoing project).

In addition to the external media, the Hornets also maximize their controlled media assets to raise the visibility of CSR activities. These assets include the team Web site, e-mail, TV and radio game broadcasts, in-arena messaging, and team magazine. While distribution may be smaller than some external media, these media are more likely to reach the most engaged customers, such as season ticket holders and other fans of the organization, and help chronicle and reinforce the organization. A final strategy employed by the Hornets is to use community CSR partners as the voice to tell the story. For example, sometimes it is more powerful for the Red Cross or the Salvation Army to say what a great job the Hornets are doing in the community than if the Hornets say it themselves.

Given that fans are unlikely to view a team as socially responsible unless they are aware of the CSR efforts of the team, awareness will moderate the relationship between CSR initiatives and fan perceptions of socially responsible teams.

P3: The relationship between CSR initiatives and fan perceptions is moderated by community awareness.

Influence of Fan Involvement

Another moderator of the relationship between CSR initiatives and fan perceptions of socially responsible teams is fan involvement. Fan involvement is conceptualized as an individual-level construct and includes personal expectations and relative importance of CSR initiatives. In general, consumers' expectations regarding CSR efforts are increasing (Becker-Olsen et al., 2006). However, individually, consumers range from unresponsive to highly responsive when it comes to CSR activities and socially responsible consumption (Mohr, Webb, & Harris, 2001; Webb, Mohr, & Harris, 2008). Simply put, some individuals value CSR behavior more highly than others, are attuned to companies' CSR records, and align their behaviors in support of socially responsible companies.

Personal importance of CSR initiatives also must be considered. For example, fans who firsthand witnessed the devastation wrought by Hurricane Katrina might consider the Hornets support of rebuilding charities such as the organization's Hoops for Homes program in partnership with Habitat for Humanity more relevant. A cause favorably viewed by the target market will more likely result in success (Barone, Miyazaki, & Taylor, 2000).

Other researchers have explored the role of CSR-based identification and its contribution to high-level needs, such as self-definition and enhancement (i.e., Lichenstein et al., 2004; Sen et al., 2006). Even when formal membership does not exist, individuals who perceive themselves as a member of an organization (in this case, a fan of the Hornets) will feel ownership in the CSR efforts of the organization (Sen & Bhattacharya, 2001).

P4: The relationship between CSR initiatives and fan perceptions is moderated by fan involvement.

Stronger Fan Relationship Attitudes

Organizations that *are* socially responsible, and *are perceived* as socially responsible by stakeholders, should reap attitudinal benefits (e.g., Bhattacharya & Sen, 2004; Du, Bhattacharya, & Sen, 2007; Lee, Park, Moon, Yang, & Kim, 2009; Pivato, Misani, & Tencati, 2008). With a focus on relationship building, modern marketers are concerned with developing longer-term, mutually beneficial relationships (Garbarino & Johnson, 1999). As illustrated by Morgan and Hunt (1994), a successful relationship requires commitment and trust between the parties involved. The notion of consumer trust has been shown to be the linchpin of CSR effectiveness (Vlachos et al., 2009) and results in a consumer believing that a firm is reliable, stands by its word, fulfills its promise, and is sincere (Anderson & Narus, 1990). Similarly, a consumer who is committed desires to continue the relationship (Moorman, Zaltman, & Desphande, 1992).

CSR initiatives enhance this commitment and trust through the display of shared values (Doney & Cannon, 1997; Lichenstein et al., 2004; Morgan & Hunt, 1994). Through a process called "consumer-company identification" (see Bhattacharya & Sen, 2003), consumers connect with CSR-oriented companies. If a Hornets fan volunteers his or her time to help children learn to read and sees the Hornets players, coaches, and administration doing the same, the individuals have similar values sets, and a tighter bond is forged. In a broader sense, if one values "doing good," one will gravitate toward organizations that share this value.

P5: Heightened fan perceptions of socially responsible teams will result in stronger fan relationship attitudes.

Fan Relationship Strength Behaviors

The measurable outcomes of CSR have received significant attention. Companies benefit in many ways, including enhanced national visibility, greater awareness, image reinforcement, sales increases, repeat purchases, and improvement in overall financial performance (Curtis, 2006; Du et al., 2007; Orlitzky, Schmidt, & Rynes, 2003; Varadarajan & Menon, 1988). For some organizations, returns on CSR are not always immediately seen and require a more strategic, longer-term perspective (e.g., Brammer & Millington, 2008; Wang, Choi, & Li, 2005). For the NBA and the New Orleans Hornets, the significant resources invested in CSR cultivate strong fan attitudes that manifest in stronger fan relationships. In terms of behaviors, fan relationship strength is measured by media consumption, game ticket and team merchandise purchases, and favorable word of mouth. Universally, these are key mechanisms through which sports fans show support (Mason, 1999).

Higher Consumption of Media Coverage

Commitment, as applied to sports fans, must incorporate their fanaticism about and attachment to the team. Engaged sports fans tend to track the team's performance (Meenaghan, 2001; Shani & Sandler, 1998). Truly committed fans "continue their interest in the event or a team to the point that parts of every day are devoted to either the team or the sport itself" (Trail & James, 2001, p. 109). The more one identifies with a sports team, the more likely one is to consume related media (Phua, 2008), with sports fans showing higher media usage statistics than the general public (European Interactive Advertising Association [EIAA], 2008). Subsequently, one would expect true NBA and New Orleans Hornets fans to follow the team through the various media (e.g., print, electronic, broadcast) available to them.

P6: Strong fan relationship attitudes will lead to higher consumption of media coverage.

Increased Purchases of Game Tickets and Team Merchandise

These same committed fans will support the team through purchasing behavior. Increases in ticket sales will be seen, but a ceiling effect can occur in professional sports due to limited supply. Team merchandise sales also will increase as a result of stronger fan relationship attitudes. Many individuals show their identification with a team through their dress and possessions.

After the Hornets returned to New Orleans post-Katrina, residents began to embrace the team. Ticket sales and sales of Hornets merchandise increased dramatically. During the 2008–2009 season, the Hornets sold 98.7% of available tickets, ranking eighth on the 2009 NBA attendance report (ESPN, 2009). In the league, the team currently ranks 6th of 30 on the list of most popular merchandise sales, with Chris Paul's jersey listed as the third most popular league-wide (NBA, 2009a). Interestingly, post-Katrina, the Hornets logo has evolved to include the fleur-de-lis, a symbol associated worldwide with New Orleans and one that has become popular among individuals with ties to the city.

P7: Strong fan relationship attitudes will lead to increased purchases of game tickets and team merchandise.

Favorable Word of Mouth

The critical role favorable word of mouth plays in supporting new customer acquisition is well understood (e.g., Anderson, 1998; Zeithaml, Berry, & Parasuraman, 1996). The New Orleans Hornets desire to establish an engaged fan base in part because "buzz" about the team is generated. As fan commitment increases, individuals show a greater propensity for positive word-of-mouth communication (Brown, Barry, Dacin, & Gunst, 2005; Hagenbuch, Wiese, Dose, & Bruce, 2008; Harrison-Walker, 2001). Often, when this strong psychological attachment or bond exists, a consumer will become an advocate for the team (Du et al., 2007; Fullerton, 2005). The influence and reach of word of mouth continue to grow, fueled by increasingly rapid dissemination of online communications, including e-mail, social networks, blogs, video- and photo-sharing sites, and message boards. For instance, Swarm City, the official social network of the New Orleans Hornets, allows fans to connect and discuss all things Hornets.

P8: Strong fan relationship attitudes will lead to more favorable word of mouth.

Discussion and Managerial Implications

CSR and relationship marketing have emerged as core marketing concepts. *Relationship marketing* refers to marketing activities directed toward creating, nurturing, and enhancing sustainable and mutually beneficial relationships. CSR is realized by adopting moral and ethical practices that leave all stakeholders better off; ideally, corporate social initiatives are altruistic and principled endeavors. As signals of the company's values, CSR provides a source for building and maintaining relationships for all stakeholders. In recognition of the respective importance of CSR and relationship marketing, scholars continue to devote a great deal of attention to improving marketers' understanding of these concepts.

The primary objective of this chapter is to explain how CSR initiatives contribute to the success of NBA teams via enhanced fan relationships. We lay the groundwork for how these two concepts are linked by exploring the potential benefits of CSR on building and reinforcing fan relationships. In doing so, this chapter provides a broader view of CSR as a contributor to enhanced fan relationship attitudes and manifesting behaviors and should be particularly helpful to sports marketers responsible for building mutually beneficial and sustainable networks of relationships with their customers.

The conceptual framework is supported by a balance of marketing literature review and real-world examples, with the latter primarily comprised of our experience with the New Orleans Hornets. In the sports industry, the NBA has demonstrated its deep commitment to social responsibility. As shown in Figure 6.1, the conceptual framework illustrates how CSR investments contribute to NBA fan relationship building by providing a linkage between fans' perceptions regarding their awareness for the CSR contributions of a particular team and the quality of their relationship with the team. Strengthened bonds between individual fans and the sports team are forged by their mutual appreciation for preserving and improving the well-being of society.

The common thread to the variety of CSR initiatives is that social welfare is served through the deployment of organization resources. Managers may activate CSR via a broad array of corporate social initiatives, ranging from corporate philanthropy and cause-related marketing to corporate community involvement, employee volunteerism, and socially responsible business practices. NBA teams frequently lend their support to high-profile nonprofit organizations (e.g., Red Cross, Special Olympics, Boys and Girls Clubs of America, etc.), sometimes resulting in formal alliances, such as the New Orleans Hornets' Hoops for Homes program in partnership with Habitat for Humanity and the Salvation Army.

In addition to working with independent nonprofit organizations, sports teams also create and financially support their own league-wide initiatives (e.g., the Read to Achieve program of NBA Cares). Finally, sports teams may create or emphasize their own local corporate social initiatives. Typical community outreach activities held by sports teams involve "grassroots" combinations of education, recreation, and fitness programs. Given the special challenges in New Orleans, the Hornets place added emphasis on community housing and shelter services and environmental safety and conservation.

Choosing among the myriad CSR options should be viewed as a strategic decision led by the team's principals. This process should be guided by carefully formulated selection criteria, beginning with the fundamental question of how consistent or closely aligned is the proposed CSR activity with the team's corporate mission or vision statement. Managers must carefully guard against sponsoring a CSR initiative that fans interpret to be a disguised PR stunt. One way for managers to avoid this pitfall is to create social value first before drawing attention to the organization's good deeds. Otherwise, the risk of marketing communications that promote the team's good deeds may be construed by its fans as exploitive or self-serving.

Sports marketers are chiefly responsible for raising fan awareness levels regarding their organization's CSR performances. Without awareness, fans are unlikely to be familiar with the team's CSR initiatives unless the initiatives have a direct impact on them. However, in the case of the New Orleans Hornets, CSR activities frequently undertaken are primarily geared to help economically disadvantaged individuals. In such cases, CSR activities are reaching individuals who are less likely to overlap or interface with the team's ticket and merchandise purchasing fan base.

CSR clearly presents special marketing challenges for maximizing fan awareness while minimizing any associated fan skepticism about the organization's philanthropic efforts. Extant research suggests that managers should not presume that fan perceptions will be favorably affected though CSR initiatives alone. Indeed, CSR awareness is erroneously assumed to be established, which leads to exaggerating the impact of CSR on customers' beliefs, attitudes, and behaviors (Sen et al., 2006). Ultimately, whether the corporate social initiatives are recognized by the team's fans depends on the level of community awareness of these activities. Through the sports team's visible sponsorship and activation of CSR initiatives, fans can more easily link the team with CSR to maximize impact.

By capturing the moderating effects of community awareness of CSR activities, the conceptual framework captures the critical combination of good deeds and supporting marketing communications. The posited model also recognizes the moderating impact that individual fan involvement characteristics have on their CSR perceptions. Some fans have a predisposition for gaining greater awareness of CSR initiatives. In particular, individuals differ in how much they appreciate and are willing to align their attitudes and behaviors in support of socially responsible companies.

Socially responsible sports teams use CSR initiatives to connect with fans, resulting in a stronger bond between the team and the fans. As fans' perceptions regarding the team's social responsibility are raised, their CSR beliefs have a positive impact on their fan relationship attitudes toward the team. Similar to the multidimensional construct of relationship quality (see Palmatier, Dant, Grewal, & Evans, 2006), fan relationship attitudes capture the different but related facets of a relationship, such as commitment and trust building. When fans hold higher CSR perceptions, a stronger emotional attachment and more trusting relationship emerges.

The framework encapsulates the multidimensional view of relational behaviors. Moreover, the model's final group of propositions shows the broader value and downstream relationship benefits of CSR. In the domain of sports marketing, as fan relationship attitudes are strengthened, higher levels of purchasing behaviors through ticket sales and team merchandise sales will result. Even though the teams' CSR activities are unlikely to directly impact most fans who purchase season tickets, individual game tickets, and team merchandise, many of them are more likely to support the team through their purchases, in part because they believe the team is a good corporate citizen.

Relationship building through CSR benefits the Hornets in other ways, including media consumption and positive word of mouth. CSR is a contributing factor to enhancing fan relationships because of its posited influence on media consumption behaviors. Through enhanced fan relationship attitudes, fans are more likely to follow the team via a variety of media outlets. Similarly, stronger relationship attitudes will enhance favorable word of mouth generated by its supportive fan base. Social media have further elevated the already crucial role of word of mouth to relationship building.

Future Research Opportunities

This chapter presents a conceptual framework for how CSR initiatives have an impact on NBA fan relationships. Generalizations of this work can be transferred to other contexts outside the NBA and beyond professional sports. Future researchers are encouraged to test the eight proposed relationships. The model has relevance, and should be tested, across type and level of sports. Further, it can be adapted to nonsports contexts.

We hope that other researchers will continue to build and refine this conceptual framework. For example, more robust CSR-relationship marketing models may be extended to include other types of consumer relationship-based behaviors (e.g., higher tolerance for product or service failures, decreased sensitivity to price increases, higher customer lifetime values, etc.). Another possibility for framework expansion is to study how other stakeholder CSR benefits (e.g., higher employee satisfaction and retention) contribute to consumer attitudes and behaviors.

Researchers are also encouraged to examine the time frame in which these relationships materialize. If CSR is indeed a strategic, long-term investment, how long will it take an organization to reap these returns on investment? Further, if CSR investments are discontinued, what will be the outcome? During difficult economic times, it is easy to see why a company may reduce its CSR efforts, but will this move alienate certain stakeholders who have come to expect companies to be socially responsible and make patronage decisions based on this? Further, there are long-term societal implications if companies choose to reduce CSR. Society has come to rely on corporate monies and involvement.

References

Anderson, E. W. (1998). Customer satisfaction and word-of-mouth. *Journal of Service Research, 1*(1), 5–17.

Anderson, J. C., & Narus, J. A. (1990). A model of distributor firm and manufacturer firm working partnerships. *Journal of Marketing, 54*(January), 42–58.

Barone, M. J., Miyazaki, A., & Taylor, K. A. (2000). The influence of cause-related marketing on consumer choice: Does one good turn deserve another? *Journal of the Academy of Marketing Science, 28*, 248–262.

Becker-Olsen, K. L., Cudmore, B. A., & Hill, R. P. (2006). The impact of perceived corporate social responsibility on consumer behavior. *Journal of Business Research, 59*(1), 46–53.

Berger, I. E., Cunningham, P. H., & Drumwright, M. E. (2007). Mainstreaming corporate social responsibility: Developing markets for virtue. *California Management Review, 49*(4), 132–157.

Bhattacharya, C. B., & Sen, S. (2003). Consumer-company identification: A framework for understanding consumers' relationships with companies. *Journal of Marketing, 67*(April), 76–88.

Bhattacharya, C. B., & Sen, S. (2004). Doing better at doing good: When, why, and how consumers respond to corporate social initiatives. *California Management Review, 47*(1), 9–24.

Birth, G., Illia, L., Lurati, F., & Zamparini. A. (2008). Communicating CSR: Practices among Switzerland's top 300 companies. *Corporate Communications: An International Journal, 13*, 182–196.

Boulstridge, E., & Carrigan, M. (2000). Do consumers really care about corporate responsibility? Highlighting the attitude-behavior gap. *Journal of Communication Management, 4*, 355–368.

Brammer, S., & Millington, A. (2008). Does it pay to be different? An analysis of the relationship between corporate social and financial performance. *Strategic Management Journal, 29*, 1325–1343.

Bronn, P. S., & Vrioni, A. B. (2001). Corporate social responsibility and cause related marketing: An overview. *International Journal of Advertising, 20*, 207–222.   .

Brown, T. J., Barry, T. E., Dacin, P. A., & Gunst, R. F. (2005). Spreading the word: Antecedents of consumers' positive word-of-mouth intentions and behaviors in a retailing context. *Journal of the Academy of Marketing Science, 33*, 123–138.

Clarke, B. (2003, December 11). Brands are now judged on what they do, not say. *Marketing*, p. 18.

Curtis, J. (2006, September 13). Why don't they trust you with CSR? *Marketing*, pp. 30–31.

Doney, P. M., & Cannon, J. P. (1997). An examination of the nature of trust in buyer-seller relationships. *Journal of Marketing, 61*(April), 35–51.

Du, S., Bhattacharya, C. B., & Sen, S. (2007). Convergence of interests—cultivating consumer trust through corporate social initiatives. *Advances in Consumer Research, 34*, 687.

Economou, G. (2009, April 6). Mission statement can provide roadmap to company's success. *Sports Business Journal*. Retrieved from http://sportsbusinessjournal.com/article/62164

EIAA. (2008, February 6). *EIAA: Sport and the shift to interactive media*. Retrieved from http://noticias.info/Asp/aspCommunicados.asp?nid=361273

Eichenhofer, J. (2009, May 12). Hornets believe: Shinn makes annual birthday visit to newborns. *New Orleans Hornets*. Retrieved from nba.com/hornets/community/Hornets_Believe_Shin_Makes_A-312779–15404.html

ESPN. (2009). *NBA attendance report*. Retrieved from http://espn.go.com/nba/attendance

Ferrell, O. C., & Hartline, M. (2008). *Marketing strategy*. Mason, OH: Southwestern-Cengage Learning.

Fortune Magazine. (2009, March 16). World's most admired companies: Best and worst in social responsibility. *Fortune Magazine*. Retrieved from http://money.cnn.com/magazines/fortune/mostadmired/2009/best_worst/best4.html

Fullerton, G. (2005). The impact of brand commitment on loyalty to retail service brands. *Canadian Journal of Administrative Sciences, 22*(2), 97–110.

Garbarino, E., & Johnson, M. S. (1999). The different roles of satisfaction, trust, and commitment in customer relationships. *Journal of Marketing, 63*(April), 70–87.

Giving USA Foundation. (2009, June 10). *U.S. charitable giving estimated to be $307.65 billion in 2008.* Press release.

Hagenbuch, D. J., Wiese, M. D., Dose, J. J., & Bruce, M. L. (2008). Understanding satisfied and affectively committed clients' lack of referral intent. *Services Marketing Quarterly, 29*(3), 24–74.

Harrison-Walker, L. J. (2001). The measurement of word-of-mouth communication and an investigation of service quality and customer commitment as potential antecedents. *Journal of Service Research, 4*(1), 60–76.

HRfocus News Brief. (2007, June). Corporate social responsibility practices are on the rise. *HRFOCUS,* p. 9.

Husted, B. W., & Salazar, J. J. (2006). Taking Friedman seriously: Maximizing profits and social performance. *Journal of Management Studies, 43*(1), 75–91.

Kirdahy, M. (2007, November 27). Responsibility pays. *Forbes.* Retrieved from http://www.forbes.com/2007/11/12/corporate-philanthropy-projects-lead-citizen-cx_mk_1112donors.html

Lafferty, B. A. (2007). The relevance of fit in a cause-brand alliance when consumers evaluate corporate credibility. *Journal of Business Research, 60,* 447–453.

Lee, H., Park, T., Moon, H. K., Yang, Y., & Kim, C. (2009). Corporate philanthropy, attitude towards corporations, and purchase intentions: A South Korea Study. *Journal of Business Research, 62,* 939–946.

Lewis, S. E. (2008). *Corporate social responsibility (CSR): Consumer awareness and use of Internet to research claims has grown.* Retrieved from http://social-corporate-responsibility.suite101.com/article.cfm/corporate_social responsibility_csr

Lichenstein, D. R., Drumwright, M. E., & Braig, B. M. (2004). The effect of corporate social responsibility on customer donations to corporate-supported nonprofits. *Journal of Marketing, 68*(4), 16–32.

Martel, B. (2009, July 29). Chris Paul headed back to China as basketball ambassador. *The Times Picayune.* Retrieved from http://www.nola.com/hornets/index.ssf/2009/07/chris_paul_headed_back_to_chin.html

Mason, D. S. (1999). What is the sports product and who buys it? The marketing of professional sports leagues. *European Journal of Marketing, 33,* 402–419.

Meenaghan, T. (2001). Understanding sponsorship effects. *Psychology and Marketing, 18*(2), 95–122.

Mendoza, M. (2007). Breakthroughs in corporate social responsibility in the Philippines. In *Best practices in Asian corporate governance* (pp. 129–125). Tokyo: Asian Productivity Organization.

Mohr, L. A., Webb, D. J., & Harris, K. E. (2001). Do consumers expect companies to be socially responsible? The impact of corporate social responsibility on buying behavior. *The Journal of Consumer Affairs, 35*(1), 45–72.

Moorman, C., Zaltman, G., & Desphande, R. (1992). Relationships between providers and users of marketing research: The dynamics of trust within and between organizations. *Journal of Marketing Research, 29*, 314–329.

Morgan, R. M., & Hunt, S. D. (1994). The commitment-trust theory of relationship marketing. *Journal of Marketing, 58*(July), 20–38.

National Basketball Association (NBA). (2009a, April 30). *Bryant reclaims place as NBA's most-sold jersey.* Press release. Retrieved from nba.com/2009/news/04/30/jersey.leaders.2009/index

National Basketball Association (NBA). (2009b). NBA cares. Retrieved from http://www.nba.com/nba_cares/

National Basketball Association (NBA). (2009c). National Basketball Association Mission and Values Statement. Retrieved from http://www. nba.com/careers/mission_statement_article.html

National Basketball Players Association (NBA). (2009). *Collective bargaining agreement.* Retrieved from nbpa.com/cba/2005

National Center for Charitable Statistics. (2009). *Nonprofit organization and program classifications.* Retrieved from urban.org/classification/index.cfm

New Orleans Hornets. (2009). Retrieved from http://www.nba.com/hornets/index_main.html

Orlitzky, M., Schmidt, F. L., & Rynes, S. L. (2003). Corporate social and financial performance: A meta-analysis. *Organization Studies, 24*, 403–441.

Palmatier, R. W., Dant, R. P., Grewal, D., & Evans, K. R. (2006). Factors influencing the effectiveness of relationship marketing: A meta-analysis. *Journal of Marketing, 70*(4), 136–153.

Phua, J. (2008, May 21). *Consumption of sports team-related media: Its influence on sports fan identity salience and self-esteem.* Paper presented at the annual meeting of the International Communication Association, Montreal, Quebec, Canada.

Pivato, S., Misani, N., & Tencati, A. (2008). The impact of corporate social responsibility on consumer trust: The case of organic food. *Business Ethics: A European Review, 17*(1), 3–12.

Porter, M. E., & Kramer, M. R. (2002). The competitive advantage of corporate philanthropy. *Harvard Business Review, 80*(12), 56–69.

Porter, M. E., & Kramer, M. R. (2006). Strategy and society: The link between competitive advantage and corporate social responsibility. *Harvard Business Review, 84*(12), 78–92.

Rowold, J., & Rohmann, A. (2009). Relationships between leadership styles and followers' emotional experience and effectiveness in the voluntary sector. *Nonprofit and Voluntary Sector Quarterly, 38*, 270–286.

Sauer, P. J. (2007, October 39). The big easy sell. *Conde Nast Portfolio.Com.* Retrieved from http://www.portfolio.com/culture-lifestyle/culture-inc/sports/2007/10/30/NBA-Hornets-Help-New-Orleans-revival

Sen, S., & Bhattacharya, C. B. (2001). Does doing good always lead to doing better? Consumer reactions to corporate social responsibility. *Journal of Marketing Research*, 38(May), 225–244.

Sen, S., Bhattacharya, C. B., & Korschun, D. (2006). The role of corporate social responsibility in strengthening multiple stakeholder relationships: A field experiment. *Journal of the Academy of Marketing Science*, 34(2), 158–166.

Shani, D., & Sandler, D. M. (1998). Ambush marketing: Is confusion to blame for the flickering of the flame? *Psychology and Marketing*, 15, 367–383.

Smith, A. C. T., & Westerbeek, H. W. (2007). Sport as a vehicle for deploying corporate social responsibility. *Journal of Corporate Citizenship*, 25(Spring), 43–54.

Trail, G. T., & James, J. D. (2001). The motivation scale for sport consumption: Assessment of the scale's psychometric properties. *Journal of Sport Behavior*, 24(1), 108–127.

Varadarajan, P. R., & Menon, A. (1988). Cause-related marketing: A coalignment of marketing strategy and corporate philanthropy. *Journal of Marketing*, 52(4), 58–74.

Vlachos, P. A., Tsamakos, A., Vrechopoulos, A. P., & Avramidis, P. K. (2009). Corporate social responsibility: Attributions, loyalty, and the mediating role of trust. *Journal of the Academy of Marketing Science*, 37(2), 170–180.

Wang, H., Choi, J., & Li, J. (2005). Too little or too much? Reexamining the relationship between corporate giving and corporate financial performance. *The Academy of Management Proceedings*, G1–G6.

Warhurst, A. (2008, December 9). The future of corporate philanthropy. *Business Week Online*, p. 16. Accessed through EBSCO full text; direct link is http://www.businessweek.com/globalbiz/content/dec2008/gb2008128_757524.htm

Webb, D. J., & Mohr, L. A. (1998). A typology of consumer responses to cause-related marketing: From skeptics to socially concerned. *Public Policy Marketing*, 17, 226–238.

Webb, D. J., Mohr, L. A., & Harris, K. E. (2008). A re-examination of socially responsible consumption and its measurement. *Journal of Business Research*, 61(2), 91–98.

White, E. (2008). Wooing customers with social good efforts. *Wall Street Journal Online*. Retrieved from http://www.online.wsj.com/article/SB122816696112070087.html

Wilbon, M. (2004, November 25). Hip-hop culture contributes to NBA's bad rap. *Washington Post*, p. D01.

Zeigler, E. F. (2007). Sport management must show social concern as it develops tenable theory. *Journal of Sport Management*, 21, 297–318.

Zeithaml, V. A., Berry, L. L., & Parasuraman, A. (1996). The behavioral consequences of service quality. *Journal of Marketing*, 60(2), 31–46.

7

And a Child Athlete Will Save Us
Marketing Psychosocial and Physical Benefits of Sport to Children, Adolescents, Coaches, and Parents

Steven J. Andrews

Golf is a good walk spoiled.

Mark Twain

Mark Twain was being funny, but as was typical of him, this particular quotation came stuffed with irony wrapped in a lightly breaded shell of truth. It might reflect an outcome-based outlook on a sports activity that seems to spoil the enjoyment process. Or perhaps more subtly, it reflects the self-fulfilling prophecy of a self-defeating outcome-based perspective on a sporting contest. Perhaps if Mark Twain expected good outcomes going into the activity and perhaps if Twain could count on positive support and positive evaluation from the innermost people in his social circles, he might not have found the good walk to be so tainted after all? Under those circumstances, perhaps Twain might look forward to making that walk again, and again, and again. It would do wonders for Twain's health, and if more of us in the United States were like this new, more positive Twain, it would do wonders for American society as a whole.

This chapter links both the broadest and the narrowest issues relating to youth sports participation in America within a multitier ecological framework of a young person's developmental environment (Bronfenbrenner, 1977). Then, from a marketing perspective, I piece together some clues from various disciplines within the social science domain regarding how to encourage every kid in America to spend more time engaging in organized physical activity—that is, youth sports. Given the recent global economic crisis and in particular given some of the serious economic challenges related to health care that the United States will face as it moves deeper into the 21st century, in some senses sports participation is no longer just about leisure. It may well be the best option for building a more psychologically well-rounded society in addition to a physically healthier one. America desperately needs strong minds and strong bodies moving forward. Maybe the answer is right in our own backyards, street corners, and playgrounds.

Physical Fitness: Societal Challenges

A decade into the 21st century, the richest country in world history is weighed down by many challenges and threats. Not the least of these issues is a weight problem that has ballooned exponentially since the 1970s. By some measures, two thirds of all adults in the United States are overweight. More recently, the problem is manifesting itself in American children. Since the 1970s, the number of kids aged 6–19 in the United States who are overweight or obese has almost tripled to about 16% of the population. Current trends project that nearly half of all children could be overweight or obese heading into the second decade of the century (Kirka, 2006). Given that most overweight and obese children become overweight and obese adults, the current problem could ignite a host of potential health problems that could overwhelm many aspects of the U.S. economy.

Excessive weight is linked to many chronic diseases: type 2 diabetes, many types of cancers, congestive heart failure, and diseases related to high cholesterol are just a few of the most common health problems linked to excessive overconsumption of food. These weight-related health issues are already overwhelming health care and prescription drug costs in the United States, and they are threatening to put even more pressure on them in the near future. Farrey (2008) cited predictions that by 2015 health care costs could consume an astronomical 20% of the entire U.S. gross domestic product. Obese children incur health care costs at three times the rate of non-obese children. As a greater percentage of adults face these chronic illnesses, American productivity in the workplace could suffer massive declines. Even worse, the labor market could shrink much faster than it can be replenished. Collectively, chronic diseases associated with overeating already account for the majority of the deaths in the United States, and if current trends continue, their contribution to U.S. mortality will skyrocket.

The most basic cause of weight gain that can lead to obesity is that a person consumes more calories than he or she expends. Calorie intake is one half of the equation, and the other half of the equation, low energy expenditure (i.e. "burning off excess calories"), is a bigger problem (Tokmakidis, Kasambalis, & Christodoulos, 2006). Therefore, lack of physical activity is a central component of weight gain and is consequently a central component of a mounting economic and social catastrophe.

Farrey (2008) reported that the turn of the century saw a 3% overall decline in physical activity in American high school students, accelerating rapidly from freshman year to senior year. The problem stands to get worse in the coming years as less than 8% of schools from elementary to high school report that kids get the minimum amount of time recommended for physical activity. With parents working longer hours and more families living in urban population centers with decreased access to parks and open areas, most opportunities for kids to engage in physical activity occur through structured programs such as school programs and community-based after-school programs. In particular, participation in sports programs is the most common avenue for exposure to structured physical activity available to American youth.

Declining Sports Participation: Broad Issues

The decline in youth sport participation in the United States begins in earnest for adolescents starting at age 11 and progresses rapidly through high school. Evidence suggests that physical activity through sports programs or exercise programs is the most effective means of stemming weight problems in young people, which in turn increases the likelihood that they will develop into much happier and much more effective adults (Larson, 2000). So, simply stated, a potentially powerful solution to this rapidly accelerating problem is to create more opportunities and to encourage more kids to participate in physical activity, particularly through sports programs. Unfortunately, sports and physical activity requirements are being increasingly reduced for children as school budgets rapidly shrink across the country. Given the gravity of the issue, this is a problem that marketers should feel compelled to take up in conjunction with policy makers and along with concerned parents and citizens. This chapter examines through a social science lens some potential strategies to reverse the decline of sports participation by American youth in the 21st century. I blend ideas from several social science domains in search of some fruitful clues marketers might find advantageous in putting together a comprehensive social marketing initiative.

Farrey (2008) lamented the current state of American sports at the international level. Only a glance below the surface of some seemingly typical results in the 2004 and 2008 Olympics reveals clues that the American system for producing champions is on the decline this decade. For example, the United States won 110 medals in the 2008 Beijing Summer Olympic games, 10 more than second-place China. On the surface, that seems exemplary; however, China won 51 gold medals to 36 for the United States. The United States won the overall medal count by virtue of dominating the silver and bronze medal stand. Deeper examination of these numbers is more troubling: Australia in the 2004 Olympics won eight more medals per million people than the United States. The Australian system is particularly interesting for its almost platonic efficiency. Children are given tests at an early age to determine their muscle fiber composition, and based on these results they are strongly encouraged to pursue sports in which they are most likely to succeed. Clearly, these numbers strongly suggest that the United States is not fulfilling its potential in sports at the highest levels of competition in spite of enjoying vastly superior resources compared to other countries that are performing better.

The problem, said Farrey (2008), started not at the top of the sports talent food chain but at the bottom, at the grassroots level. The essential grassroots issue is that the environment that kids enter when participating in sports is too outcome oriented, that is, too focused on early success and achievement. Too often, kids do not get to just "play around," socialize with their friends and peers, and have fun like kids want to do even in a sports context. Instead, kids are pressured to develop into "stars" too soon, and those participants who fall behind get "weeded out" and end up with few if any options for participation opportunities. The more promising kids end up getting more attention, but the problem is that there are too few adequate resources in the form of either good facilities or good coaches to support them. Furthermore, in this system the late bloomers often get ignored. Because the United States is the only wealthy country without a "federal feeder system" to support its promising young international sports stars, America instead relies heavily on its grassroots sports participation system as a surrogate training ground, infecting it with the credo "faster, higher, and stronger."

The end result in the big picture is that both the "regular kids" who might just want to play sports for fun and the more promising young athletes get shortchanged. This problem is systemic. Smith, Kilgo, and Jenkins (1999) called it "society's number one syndrome." The media fuels it with shows like ESPN SportsCenter that show nothing but amazing highlights and outcome-oriented information 24 hours a day and local newspaper clips that only put kids' names in the paper when they win something. As such, some kids, some parents, and many coaches thrust into mentor roles without adequate training also unwittingly contribute to the problem. Eventually, this toxic "win-or-go-home" attitude filters down from the national ethos into the attitudes of those people closest to the children, shrouding the experience in stress and negativity and over time pushing the kids away completely to other activities that are more sedentary, such as computer games or just "hanging out." Farrey (2008) noted that from 1990 to 2005, the number of kids participating in basketball declined 15%, softball participation declined 50%, and baseball participation dipped over 20%; only soccer participation increased 5% during this time period.

Farrey's (2008) depiction of the problems with grassroots sports participation for youth in America is at what Bronfenbrenner (1977) termed the macrosystem level of the environment in which humans (children and adolescents in this case) develop. For purposes of brevity, I also include Bronfenbrenner's (1977) ecosystem concepts together with the macrosystem in this chapter. The macrosystem is the "blueprint" for society at the cultural level. The macrosystem can exist formally, such as in the case of laws and policies, and it can exist informally, as in the case of customs or norms. The macrosystem to which we refer here also includes government at every level, not just national. It also includes the media channels that marketers would use to execute marketing strategies.

The problems Farrey (2008) brought to light in terms of grassroots youth sports in America are due to both broad policy-based issues and societal customs and norms. Consistent with the definition of a macrosystem, these problems exist in similar form from town to town across the entire country. It should be pointed out here that in reality lots of other factors at the macrosystem level are important, most notably socioeconomic status, race, and other demographic characteristics. The complexity of those specific issues is beyond the scope of this discussion at this time. Whenever possible, I examine the issues that are common to both genders, occasionally pointing out the most salient gender differences with respect to youth and sports participation.

Increasing Sports Participation: Social Group Dynamics

Having considered sports participation issues from the broadest (i.e., macrosystem) developmental level, it makes sense now to look at these issues with sports participation at the more proximal developmental levels to the child athlete. This is most important because the solutions to the problems at all developmental levels, from the broader levels down to the most intimate developmental environment of the individual, will most likely manifest themselves within the psyche of the individual child in the context of his or her most salient social groups. These developmental levels include the mesosystem and microsystem. Bronfenbrenner (1977) defined the mesosystem as that level of an individual's developmental environment that includes interpersonal relationships with social groups that are most prevalent and most influential; in the case of a young person participating in sports, this includes parents, coaches, and friends or peers. The microsystem is the most proximal level of an individual's developmental environment, to include the individual's own internal psychophysiological environment.

Hansen, Larson, and Dworkin (2003) provided self-reports from adolescents regarding what they purported to learn from participating in organized activities such as sports at both the interpersonal and personal levels. Interpersonally, activities such as sports participation provide opportunities to develop teamwork and leadership skills. These kids learn to work together to achieve goals and to navigate through difficulties and challenges together in the process. Holt, Tink, Mandigo, and Fox (2008) pointed out that sports participation does not directly teach these skills but rather offers the participant opportunities to express them and develop them naturally. This learning is more individualized because the lessons come from the actions and initiative of the performers rather than passively from a teacher or lecturer.

Furthermore, Hansen et al. (2003) noted that adolescents believe that sports participation helps them to develop and enhance relationships with adults such as coaches and parents. It is here that there is some risk to sports participation, however, due to the possibilities that competing agendas and differing perspectives between the social groups and the children inject stress and negative experiences into the process. In fact, in contrast to other activities such as fine arts, community organizations, and vocational clubs, kids participating in sports reported higher instances of negative interactions with coaches and parents. Because these social relationships are so important to a young person's development in sports participation, it is useful to discuss in greater detail the specific roles each social group plays in creating the healthiest developmental environment possible in the context of sports participation.

Sports Participation: Relationship Dynamics With Coaches, Parents, and Peers

There is ample evidence that a positive relationship between the players and the coach enhances the development of the athlete both personally and interpersonally, improves play, and increases motivation for further participation. Holt et al. (2008) detailed life skill learning from 12 soccer players and their coach for an entire season. The authors observed that the coach had an impact on the players at the macrosystem level of development, through team policies and overall coaching philosophy, as well as at the mesosystem level of development through the ongoing person-to-person relationship. The athletes reported more favorable reactions to strict yet fair policies on things such as missed practices or misbehavior on the part of the athletes in addition to demands that the athletes be accountable for their attitudes and be supportive of their teammates. In a rare published example of such a system, Smith et al. (1999), in a chapter titled "The Carolina Way," outlined the exact macrosystem-level policies Smith used for 36 years on the way to winning more college basketball games than any Division I-level coach in history on his retirement. The system was structured and based on equal treatment of every athlete regardless of the status the athlete held on the team. The most famous examples of this were stories about Michael Jordan, just like any other player, having to carry luggage for his older teammates or having to miss starting a game because he was late for a team meal.

Furthermore, at the interpersonal level Holt et al. (2008) reported reactions from the soccer players that a "good coach" offers neither gratuitous praise nor baseless criticism. Praise for specific good behavior and performance is received best by the athlete, and specific corrective feedback is most well received by the athlete when mistakes are made. In general, a well-received coach maintains a positive, fun, humorous atmosphere with the athletes while demanding sportsmanship and good play. Another study that tracked soccer players for 1 year (Ullrich-French & Smith, 2009) reported that athletes whose coaches were more supportive and less controlling and manipulative in their behavior exhibited greater internal motivation to perform and to keep playing in the future.

I should point out that the Hoyle study (Hoyle & Leff, 1997) and the study by Ullrich-French and Smith (2009) were case studies involving intense observations and in-depth interviews of just a few kids. As it turns out, both of these studies involved soccer players as the small group of kids. However, there is an abundance of anecdotal as well as experimental evidence that I will discuss that corroborates the conclusions these authors made, and these conclusions apply to a broader range of kids and sports contexts.

Anecdotally, when great athletes praise their coaches they usually discuss how the coach challenged them to improve as players while demanding that they respect their teammates, coaches, and opponents and understand that they are no better than anybody else as people despite their athletic gifts. Martens (2004) echoed this view in his description of a mandate of "person first, athlete second" for coaching young people. Martens (2004) noted that John Wooden, arguably the greatest college basketball coach in history and certainly the most successful in terms of national championships, advocated a policy of "25% praise and 75% corrective instruction" for communicating with the athletes during practice. Any form of criticism or punishment was reserved for extreme last-resort measures only.

Another important and highly complex social group with enormous influence on youth participation in sports is parents. Parental influence on child development in the domain of sports participation exists along two dimensions (Barnes, Reifman, Farrell, & Dintcheff, 2000): parental support and parental control. The support dimension includes categories such as nurturing, love, cohesion, and acceptance. The parental control dimension includes punishment, discipline, monitoring, and supervision. Research generally suggests that a positive relationship between parents and their kids participating in sports fuels the kids' motivation to keep playing.

Hoyle and Leff (1997) cited comprehensive research linking parental support to children enjoying playing sports more and feeling better about themselves and their performance regardless of outcomes. Numerous studies (Keegan, Harwood, Spray, & Lavallee, 2008; Ullrich-French & Smith, 2006, 2009) showed that parental support behaviors increased the child's self-esteem and lowered stress related to the sports activity. In addition, kids who reported satisfaction with parental support when participating in sports reported higher levels of perceived competence in skill-related activity, higher overall relationship quality with their parents, and lower stress levels. Scanlon and Lewthwaite (1986) conducted a field study of adolescent wrestlers regarding factors that most contributed to their fun and enjoyment with wrestling. Results of this study indicated that the perception of greater parental satisfaction with their performance, reduced parental pressure, and increased parental support explained about 38% of the variance related to fun and enjoyment.

To put it bluntly, parents can be a dual-edged sword when it comes to their children and sports. Holt et al. (2008) alluded to the strong potential for sports participation to have detrimental effects on children's development, considerably more than in activities such as fine arts or other types of organized activities that offer similar psychosocial benefits as sports. Sports are highly emotional activities, particularly for spectators (Madrigal, 1995) and likely even more so for spectators who feel they have a lot at stake in the outcome of the event. Parents obviously mean well, but there is a fine line that parents sometimes cross when it comes to serving as their child's mentor or even as their coach in the context of sports.

Taken together, parents and coaches wield considerable influence over a child athlete's developmental environment in the context of sports participation through macrolevel policies and through interpersonal dynamics at the mesosystem level. Overwhelmingly, kids themselves reported that parents and coaches who create a positive, supportive, low-stress environment create a psychological environment in which kids are happier and much more internally motivated to naturally express and develop initiative, emotion control, leadership skills, and desire to make sports a part of life for potentially their entire lives.

Another important constituency at the mesosystem level of a child's developmental environment is peers. This social group is not as well understood in terms of the specific nature of their influence on youth sports participation. For example, there are no studies that compare and contrast the influence of peers who are and who are not also part of the same program as the child athlete. At this point, most studies (Keegan et al., 2008; Ullrich-French & Smith, 2006, 2009) list general factors such as "peer acceptance," "peer support," and "positive friendship quality" as significant contributors to the child athlete's enjoyment of sports and internal drive to keep participating. But, these factors are not well defined in terms of the specific psychosocial benefits they offer the child athlete.

Daniels and Leaper (2006) examined the link between long-term sports participation, peer acceptance, and self-esteem among both adolescent girls and boys. They found that, for both boys and girls, positive peer acceptance mediated the relationship between enhanced self-esteem and increased sports participation. Another study (Ullrich-French & Smith, 2009) showed quantitatively that the effects of positive relationships with all three social groups in the child athlete's developmental environment (parents, coaches, and peers) are additive such that the benefits conferred exponentially increase enjoyment levels and the likelihood of continued participation. In general, this is a good start, and common sense certainly suggests that if the supportive influence of coaches and parents makes a difference in a child athlete's success and enjoyment of sports participation that a supportive peer environment should do the same. Still, more studies about the nature of the peer relationship to the child athlete specifically and more generally about the additive nature of all of these key social group dynamics are needed to best understand how to market youth sports participation to all relevant constituencies.

Increasing Sports Participation: Individual Dynamics

Let me now turn inward to the most proximal level, the microsystem level, of the developmental environment of a young person engaging in sports activities and examine more closely how the benefits of sports participation discussed previously can have an impact on an individual mentally as well as physically. Recall that adolescents reported (Hansen et al., 2003) believing that sports participation affords them benefits on both interpersonal and personal levels. Adolescents interpret the benefits of sport participation at the personal level as developing initiative, character development, identity exploration, and emotional learning. In general, these qualities are developed though sports participation by working through challenges, learning to set short-term and long-term goals, time management, and problem solving. Of particular interest to researchers (Larson, 2000) is the rare opportunity an activity like sport offers a young person in 21st-century America to develop initiative.

The activities that take up the most time for typical children and adolescents are sitting in class and spending time socially with friends. While these activities are crucial for a young person's development, by themselves Larson (2000) claimed that they offer incomplete opportunities for kids to develop initiative. According to Larson, the structure of the formal education system in modern society at the secondary level more often than not deprives children of intrinsic motivation. Sitting in class taking notes or taking an exam challenges kids to concentrate, but this education structure tends to be passive in nature, neither requiring nor encouraging high levels of intrinsic motivation in the young student. Larson cited ample evidence that students in middle grades through high school admit to high levels of boredom and lack of engagement in classroom settings.

On the other hand, time spent with friends is a form of unstructured leisure. This kind of activity stimulates a great deal of intrinsic motivation but rarely does it stimulate high levels of concentration.

Although sports participation takes up a relatively small percentage of a kid's daily life, it offers adolescents in modern Western society a rare opportunity to combine intrinsic motivation with deep attention and concentration. These two components combined are key elements, in Larson's (2000) opinion, of positive psychological development. In modern society, few activities give this rare combination of benefits to a developing child's mind, to include fine arts (e.g., marching band) and some organized civic organizations (e.g., junior achievement). Remembering the broader health-related issues with which the current discussion is directly related, it also bears reminding that sports participation offers crucial long-term physical fitness benefits that these other activities typically do not.

To this point, I have chronicled some broad issues and societal health-related challenges that America faces that are linked to a decline in physical activity in young people. One prominent mechanism that is fueling this decline in physical activity is declining participation in grassroots-level organized youth sports. We have looked at some cultural and policy issues that might be contributing to the problem. On our way to figuring out some potential strategies toward reversing the trend, we have just examined some important elements of the most influential social relationships to child athletes in the context of sports participation.

I now discuss some specific psychological mechanisms that a substantial amount of research seems to indicate might trigger the positive benefits necessary to enact meaningful behavioral change at the societal level. Again, it is important to keep in mind that sweeping societal changes must begin deep inside the mind of a single individual, and such a change is manifested through the individual's most salient social relationships. Finally, I hope that through institutional support from some much-needed policy changes along with full-scale social marketing initiatives throughout the country, those scary health-related trends outlined at the beginning of the chapter might hastily begin to reverse.

Social Facilitation and Self-Preserving Psychological Mechanism: Core Psychophysiological Elements of Increased Sports Participation

Recall that each of the major social groups for a typical grassroots child athlete (parents, coaches, and peers) plays a somewhat unique yet pivotal role in creating a positive, supportive developmental environment for a young person engaging in sports activities. This section of the discussion integrates two streams of theoretical research on key psychological and psychophysiological variables—social facilitation and self-efficacy—which are fundamental mediators between mesosystem-level (e.g., important social relationships) factors related to a positive developmental environment and the desired behavioral outcome: increased or continued sports participation. As the research discussed makes clear, another reason to place a premium on a supportive developmental environment is that on top of all the developmental challenges and potential developmental rewards mentioned (i.e., intrinsic motivation, goal setting, and problem solving, to name a few), the skills required to excel in sports are many and complex. Although it is important to maintain the positive mental states that encourage kids to keep playing, at some point it is also critical that the child athletes acquire a satisfactory level of mastery of the sport-specific physical skills.

Researchers have considered the nature of skill performance, and factors involved in performance enhancement, on a theoretical level for a long time. Strauss (2002) gave a comprehensive review of the phenomenon known as "social facilitation," the core premise of which dates to 1898 when early researchers first noticed that people performed motor tasks better in the presence of an audience than they did when the audience was not present. Studies throughout the 20th century showed similar effects for people riding a bike, walking, taking dictation, and various school-related tasks such as math, concentration and memory tasks, and other activities that did not involve competition. Thus, social facilitation has been studied and shown to be valid for both cognitive and physical skills, although most recent studies have examined the phenomenon in the realm of physical tasks such as sport performance.

Strauss (2002) divided the research on social facilitation into two theoretical camps: the activation theories camp and the attention theories camp. These camps offer separate ideas with respect to the potential biological mechanisms behind the performance enhancement phenomenon. In general, the most researched and therefore the most accepted of the two theoretical camps is the activation theories camp, pioneered by Zajonc's (1965) generalized drive theory: People are more physiologically aroused in the "mere presence" of others; therefore, performance in the skills that they have already mastered will improve but not performance of novel skills. In contrast, attention theories offer a cognitive-resource-based explanation: Complex tasks involve greater amounts of cognitive effort and attention; therefore, in the presence of others, people are too distracted to allot the required cognitive resources, so performance on more difficult tasks suffers.

Building on the generalized drive theory by Zajonc (1965), Strauss (2002) reviewed more nuanced versions of social facilitation activation theories that suggest that performance enhancement or degradation stems from a serious account of the performer's environment. Specifically, it might not be enough for the audience just to be present, as Zajonc suggested. Several different approaches within this branch of activation theories (evaluation approaches, alertness approaches, and the challenge vs. threat approach) all consider the performer's awareness of and uncertainty regarding the potential for either negative or positive evaluation of the performance. These approaches blend together the psychophysiology of the performer with the anticipated behavior of the audience. In other words, the performer's beliefs regarding the evaluative intentions of the audience could play a significant role in affecting performance.

Worringham and Messick's (1983) study is an example of a study that used the evaluative approach to social facilitation activation that set out to disprove that the "mere presence" of an audience is enough to produce social facilitation effects and to establish a baseline for a good rigorous study design when studying the phenomenon in the realm of sports. The study examined the performance of track runners in three conditions: running alone with no audience present, running with an audience present but with their backs turned, and running with an audience present and facing the runners. The results showed that runners performed better in front of an audience only when the audience members were facing the runners and looking "evaluative." When the audience had their backs to the runners, performance did not improve any more than when no audience was present.

Technological advances have recently paved the way for more concrete physiological studies within the activation theories camp of social facilitation research. Blascovich and his colleagues conducted a series of studies that measured distinct physiological reactions—labeled "challenge" and "threat" in several contexts—for example, in response to a cognitive task (Blascovich, Mendes, Hunter, & Salomon, 1999) and in response to people in the immediate environment (Blascovich, Mendes, Hunter, Lickel, & Kowai-Bell, 2001). The distinctions in the physiological responses were not inherently perceptible by the performers. The distinctive physiological responses involved different patterns of heart rate and mean arteriole pressure (e.g., blood pressure). The physiological reactions were theorized to symbolize the individual's assessment of whether he or she had the resources to match the perceived demand of the task at hand. The challenge physiological patterns emerged when the individual did believe that he or she had the resources to match the demand, and the threat patterns emerged when he or she did not.

The research by Blascovich and his colleagues (Blascovich et al., 1999, 2001; Tomaka, Blascovich, Kelsey, & Leitten, 1993) was not conducted in the sports domain, but the studies point to some interesting notions that merit further investigation in the context of sports performance. For one thing, these studies confirmed that the individual, even if not aware of it, is making a detailed assessment of the environment and responding in distinct ways physiologically based on the outcome of the assessment. In terms of social facilitation, this observation implies that individuals do indeed assess their "audience"; therefore, it is possible that performance enhancement or degradation could be linked to the performer's perceptions of audience intentions.

The research on social facilitation up to this point, particularly in the activation theories camp, points to a strong indication that the presence of an evaluative audience may indeed make a difference in terms of performance in some cases. The physiological evidence also points to the fact that not only the audience intentions but also the athlete's perceptions of audience intentions along with athlete perceptions about his or her ability to respond to task demands are important psychological components to consider in a sports participation context. Essentially, social facilitation theory by itself may not be adequate to explain differential performance in sports.

At this point, it is worth noting that a major challenge in terms of measuring social facilitation effects in sports is that there is tremendous variability across the entire sports domain in terms of the types of skills required to be successful (Strauss, 2002). Some sport skills are more quantitative in nature, such as running. Measuring performance is generally more straightforward for these types of tasks. Others are more qualitative, such as gymnastics. The largest category is the third category of sports skills, which consist of a hybrid set of quantitative and qualitative aspects, such as those involved in tennis, basketball, and wrestling. Success in these hybrid activities can be measured in terms of skill acquisition and mastery as well as in more quantitative terms with respect to rankings and winning and losing games and tournaments. The difficulty with categorizing sports skills underscores how hard it is to associate social facilitation effects only with measured skill enhancement. It is likely that achieving meaningful understanding of the effects of an audience on sports performance may require a more complex examination of how the presence of an audience and the athlete's perceptions of audience intentions have an impact on performance.

Bond and Titus (1983) confirmed this notion with a meta-analysis of 241 studies on social facilitation effects, some of them in the sports domain. They found that social facilitation only explained at most 3% of the variance in skill performance. Taking cues from more recent studies such as the Blascovich studies (Blascovich et al., 1999, 2001) to gain a stronger understanding of the most salient factors that contribute to sports performance, it is important to consider psychological variables that work in concert with physical performance variables. These more concrete psychophysiological studies strongly suggested that the presence of a supportive evaluative audience in sports may certainly make a difference, but this particularly occurs when another important factor is considered: the self-preserving psychological functioning of the performer.

Abundant evidence links improved sports performance (and therefore presumably increased participation) with enhanced self-protective psychological strategies such as self-esteem (or self-confidence) and self-efficacy. Self-esteem is a more general evaluation of overall self-competence, whereas self-efficacy refers to perceptions of one's ability to meet the demands of a specific task that is immediately at hand. For purposes of this discussion, both of these constructs exert similar influence on improved sports performance and continued participation in sports. The link works in the other direction as well: Improved performance enhances self-esteem and self-efficacy, which overwhelmingly seems to point to greater enjoyment of and more long-lasting participation in sports.

While discussing the links between an individual's psychological states and sports performance, it is also important to keep in mind the importance of positive relationships with the key social groups for child athletes: coaches, parents, and friends. Dwyer, Allison, and Makin (1998) developed a self-report measure for self-efficacy in sports participation for adolescents. The measure divided factors that adolescents believed to predict sports participation into two dimensions: external factors and internal factors. Key external factors included support from friends and family, which for an adolescent are the people most likely to comprise the "audience" at a sporting event. Furthermore, the three highest-loading internal factors involved "feeling discomfort," "feeling stressed," and "not feeling in the mood." Two other high-loading internal factors were "not having fun" and "feeling self-conscious."

Richman and Shaffer (2000) examined the effects of sports participation on self-esteem in precollege females. Female participation in sports on a scale similar to males is a fairly recent cultural trend in the United States, stimulated by the passage of Title IX in the 1970s. Richman and Shaffer found that aspects of self-esteem that seemed to relate most to sports for girls included physical competence, body image, and gender-typed traits such as androgyny (i.e., having both masculine and feminine behavioral characteristics). In all cases, sports participation afforded tremendous improvements in self-perception of these qualities.

Ryska (2002) examined in a bit more detail the link between global feelings of self-worth and sports performance. This study found that enhanced feelings of self-worth improved sports performance both for young athletes who naturally had lower self-confidence and for young athletes who naturally had a higher general opinion of themselves. While performance improved for both groups, it improved significantly more so for young athletes who were naturally lower in self-confidence. Interestingly, both high- and low-confidence young athletes reported having lower perceived control of performance outcomes when they were being evaluated by an audience. Ryska noted that the primary difference in a sports context between performers with low and high self-confidence was in the nature of expected outcomes. Performers with high self-confidence naturally expected better outcomes than performers with low self-confidence. Ryska concluded, therefore, citing evidence from the psychology literature (e.g., Bandura, 1986), that managing how athletes perceive outcome expectations may be a key component toward enhancing general feelings of self-worth. This may in turn lead to significant improvements in performance for those who may naturally suffer from low self-confidence.

Self-efficacy has been shown to correlate strongly with positive effort and performance in sports (Hattie, Marsh, Neill, & Richards, 1997). Self-efficacy has also been strongly linked to the social facilitation phenomenon. In the discussion section of their article, Geisler and Leith (1997) cited evidence inferring that the nature of the audience, not the size, may be more influential to performance. Audience intimacy with the performers influenced performers' feelings about how the audience would react to their performance. Shermer (2000) provided an interesting description of social facilitation effects in sports performance, in terms of what is going on psychologically for the performer, that correlates strongly with the work of Blascovich et al. (1999):

Competition provides the promise of positive (and the threat of negative) reinforcement, stimulates an increase in physiological activity and arousal, and
locks the athlete into a self-generating feedback loop between performance
expectations and outcomes. (p. 3)

Shermer (2000) corroborated in a sense what Ryska (2002) was refer-
ring to about managing outcome expectations as a way of exerting positive
influence on a person's self-protective psychological mechanisms like self-
efficacy. While Ryska emphasized that audience members such as coaches
and parents should understand their role in managing athletes' outcome
expectations in the context of a sports performance, Shermer emphasized
that the athletes, with a little practice, can also learn to manage these
expectations themselves.

Finally, one study (Sanna, 1992) actually defined social facilitation
effects on sports performance by the meditational influence of internal
psychological variables. Furthermore, this study provided further evidence for the influence that the audience has on defining outcome expectations for the athlete. Sanna (1992) found that, regardless of the task
difficulty, subjects who expected either positive evaluations or successful
performance outcomes exhibited performance enhancement relative to
controls. The author hinted that encouraging the athletes ignited a chain
reaction of positive expectations that led to positive outcome expectancies
that in turn led to better performance.

To reiterate, child athletes at the grassroots levels of youth sport have three
principal audience constituents: coaches, parents, and peers. In a broad sense,
we have seen that a "positive environment" will increase the likelihood that
a child athlete will enjoy sports and continue to play. The evidence regarding social facilitation and self-protective psychological mechanism suggests
that this positive environment manifests itself when the child athlete expects
that the audience will offer positive and encouraging feedback of his or her
performance. This expectation of positive feedback from the audience may
in turn influence the child athlete to develop his or her positive outcome
expectations. This produces an additive effect that can have a strong impact
on the likelihood that the young person will continue to participate in sports
well into adulthood (and it is hoped for an entire lifetime).

Turning the Tides: Theory-Based Marketing Suggestions

I close this discussion by offering some theory-based suggestions for full-
scale social marketing initiatives in conjunction with policy initiatives

and fundamental changes in social norms related to physical activity. Together, these should enhance the health of American society by enhancing participation in organized youth sports. Social marketing utilizes the full complement of basic marketing principles (Lefebvre & Flora, 1988)—a consumer orientation, market research, targeted messages, and feedback and control mechanisms to make incremental improvements in the execution. The main distinction with social marketing campaigns is that the "product" marketed is typically an idea or a concept. The truth campaign against Big Tobacco is a long-standing and successful example of such a campaign that benefits from substantial national awareness. While social marketing can be effective, including a specific test case based on the subject matter covered in this chapter (Wong et al., 2004), one clear limitation of social marketing efforts is that they are only sustainable in conjunction with wholesale policy efforts at every level of government (Lefebvre & Flora, 1988).

This chapter examined some of the core elements of what leads young American kids toward increased sports participation within an ecological framework of a child's developmental environment (Bronfenbrenner, 1977). Our recommendation is that any serious marketing initiatives designed to encourage behavior change must be comprehensive in that they address the issue at all ecological levels in an integrated and coordinated fashion, taking account of how each developmental level has an impact on the others. Furthermore, serious marketing initiatives must accurately and specifically address the most relevant constituencies in the optimum manner to produce the desired results.

In the case of a young person participating in sports, a successful initiative must benefit from the support of macrosystem-level policies that are optimally designed to create the right environment.

Farrey (2008) cited a case study example of the Hyde Leadership Public School in Washington, D.C. This school considers sports as "cocurricular" along with other traditional disciplines. Coaches give grades based on attitude, effort, and demonstrations of accepting accountability. As Farrey noted, these are the kinds of qualities that great chief executive officers of great companies such as Jack Welch of General Electric desperately crave in their personnel. Presumably, the current economic crisis in the United States and around the world highlights that these kinds of characteristics are no longer sufficiently part of the basic fabric of many of the fundamental elements of the U.S. economic system. As mentioned (Larson, 2000), these are exactly the kinds of personality characteristics that sports, if done properly, can develop in young people. This is just the kind of boost to the educational system the research clearly showed would offer enormous benefits to American society that go far beyond just physical fitness.

Instituting this kind of a learning system at the national level would require specific training for coaches and teachers. In support of the policy efforts, marketing efforts can help define expectations for successful coaching—kids demonstrating these specific attitude and behavioral qualities associated with positive youth development as opposed to just focusing on tangible outcomes such as winning. To borrow a well-known sports-related marketing phrase, "just do it" would constitute a far more fruitful educational policy ethic instead of the all-too-pervasive "just get it done." Perhaps Nike would permit the rather substantial expansion of the scope of that phrase beyond selling athletic apparel into selling a comprehensive national ethos.

Along similar lines, sports television such as ESPN could run regular features on coaches who are identified as highly successful in the mold of John Wooden and Dean Smith, coaches who embody the macrosystem-level policy skills and the mesosystem-level relationship skills that studies showed are most beneficial to child athletes. At the grassroots level, coaches can take weekend seminars on leadership and how to set up the incentives. The marketing message to the coaches at the grassroots level needs to be "the child's success is your success." The encouraging thing about what the research reviewed (Farrey, 2008; Hansen et al., 2003; Holt et al., 2008) implies about building a successful macrosystem coaching framework and about teaching coaches proper leadership skills from a policy standpoint is that they do not require a lot of initiative on the part of policy makers beyond enforcing the policies. The very nature of the sports learning process that kids experience suggests that if the sports environment is properly constructed and properly incentivized, the participants will be internally motivated to persevere through all the hard work themselves (Larson, 2000).

Furthermore, as we have seen, the child athlete's most relevant social groups in the context of sports participation are coaches, parents, and peers. Martens (2004) and Farrey (2008) both cited field research that highlighted a potential disconnect between kids and parents (and many coaches) when it comes to what is most sought from participating in sports. Most kids will not list winning in the top five reasons why they enjoy sports. The challenge, the social benefits, and just simple fun are often the top reasons that kids will give for enjoying sports. Kids are by nature "process-oriented" thinkers. Adults, on the other hand, especially adults in modern Western society, live in an outcome-oriented world where victory is measured in tangible ways, such as "profits." According to Martens (2004) and Farrey (2008), most parents and coaches, when asked to list the main reasons kids enjoy sports, will list outcomes like winning and pleasing their adult mentors as among the top reasons.

Marketing is likely not the panacea for the disconnect, but a full-scale national awareness campaign, with the help of entities like ESPN on one level and policy initiatives and local grassroots efforts at another level, could help bridge the "incentive gap" between most adult mentors and kids when it comes to sports. The message to parents and coaches needs to educate them on what their kids actually want (e.g., fun, support, and low stress), and that if kids receive these things from their adult mentors, they are more likely to play better and to keep playing longer. If kids play better and keep playing longer, then their odds of outcome success increase substantially. Furthermore, parents and coaches need to be reminded of the potentially tremendous long-term benefits that sports participation offers in terms of physical health. This benefit is something that other activities such as fine arts and organized clubs cannot offer. Although sports are risky, and in terms of the relationship dynamic between adults and children it can be complicated and even potentially disastrous, the potential rewards make it very much worth the risk.

Perhaps consumer culture theory (Arnould & Thompson, 2005) may provide insight into bridging macrolevel policies with effective marketing to social groups and specific target individuals such as child athletes. Consumer culture theory analyzes the nature of an individual's life within a culture. The theory encompasses both social science and public policy perspectives and since the 1980s has examined how marketing messages can have an impact on people concurrently as self-interested individuals and as part of a collective society. While broad policies in conjunction with broad marketing message strategies are an essential foundation toward communicating effectively to the individual as part of a collective whole, the most effective way to extend the broad strategy into the immediate lives of child athletes is by distributing marketing messages that reach them within their smaller and extremely influential social groups. In the consumer product realm, it has always been generally accepted that word-of-mouth communications are the most effective form of marketing. Concrete evidence continues to accumulate to support this commonly held belief (Bone, 1995; Brown & Reingen, 1987; Hogan, Lemon, & Libai, 2004). Brown and Reingen (1987) cited a wealth of evidence that strong social ties are the more effective form of advertising in some important contexts; source influence and "purchase likelihood" are two important examples pertaining to the current discussion. Another study (Hogan et al., 2004) also noted that, for more complicated decisions, word-of-mouth discussion is relied on even more heavily than normal.

Essentially, parents and peers must be properly educated on the special roles that they play in the enjoyment and potential success of the child athlete. As we have seen, if these social elements are constructed properly, this will likely trigger more positive self-protective psychological mechanisms within the child athlete, which will then lead to the development of some useful life skills, better skill performance, more enjoyment of the activity, stronger relationships with adults and mentors, and of course increased participation in the activities. Parents especially must be informed that increased participation will lead to better physical health, which will in turn take tremendous pressure off of what could be a devastating economic health-related crisis for the United States in the coming generations. However, it is important that the parents not pressure the athlete in any way to perform. For both the audience, such as parents, and the athlete to work together to promote sports participation, the messages to each constituency must be framed differently to align incentives.

Principles of message framing (Rothman & Salovey, 1997) are useful for this kind of education-based promotion strategy. Messages can be framed as either potential gains or potential losses. Rothman and Salovey (1997) showed that for health-related pursuits such as sports participation, it is best to frame the message in terms of what there is to gain by participation. Given that adults tend to be outcome-oriented, message-framing techniques can help reframe what the proper outcomes worth pursuing should be: attitude, effort, accountability, and fun. These are processes in the minds of kids, but if they are framed as outcomes in the minds of adults, that framing creates the possibility of aligning the incentives of both the audience and the performer. In addition, sports participation should be framed as an experience during which the audience expects to encourage the performers to achieve the previously stated outcomes and performers expect to be evaluated in a positive manner and to have fun pursuing the proper outcomes. If successfully executed, these subtly different messages should encourage audience and athlete alike to focus on the same things: enjoy sports more, succeed more, and play more.

Finally, communications to the child athletes must go beyond just those regarding "fun" and social benefits. They must educate the athlete on the myriad developmental skills that kids themselves say they expect to learn from sports (Hansen et al., 2003; Larson, 2000). Furthermore, based on the social facilitation and self-esteem linkages evident in the literature, it would also be useful for these messages to prime the child athlete to expect positive evaluations of their performance and positive outcomes. As we have seen, it is hoped that this will put athletes in a physiological state in which they expect a "challenge" but not a "threat" (Blascovich et al., 1999), and they expect that they will be able to meet the challenge successfully.

In closing, I guess we can ponder what Mark Twain might have said about golf if he, along with his parents and his closest friends, had been the recipient of these kinds of marketing initiatives as a young boy. It is hard to speculate, but given Twain's penchant for irony, it is likely that we as a culture would not have had the benefit of this particular quote. A phrase like "golf is a good walk" would not have been nearly as humorous, but ideally that would have been Twain's opinion on the subject—and so be it. The stakes are high in America and other modern Western societies seeing similar trends in terms of steep declines in youth participation in physical activity. Ironically, it is time for every kid to start having a lot more "serious fun."

References

Arnould, E .J., & Thompson, C. J. (2005). Consumer culture theory (CCT): Twenty years of research. *Journal of Consumer Research, 31*, 868–882.

Bandura, A. (1986). *Social foundations of thought and action: A social cognitive theory*. Englewood, Cliffs, NJ: Prentice-Hall.

Barnes, G. M., Reifman, A. S., Farrell, M. P., & Dintcheff. B. A. (2000). The effects of parenting on the development of adolescent alcohol misuse: A six-wave latent growth model. *Journal of Family and Marriage, 62*, 175–186.

Blascovich, J., Mendes, W. B., Hunter, S. B., Lickel, B., & Kowai-Bell, N. (2001). Perceiver threat in social interactions with stigmatized others. *Journal of Personality and Social Psychology, 80*, 253–267.

Blascovich, J., Mendes, W. B., Hunter, S. B., & Salomon, K. (1999). Social "facilitation" as challenge and threat. *Journal of Personality and Social Psychology, 77*, 68–77.

Bond, C. F., & Titus, L. J. (1983). Social facilitation: A meta-analysis of 241 studies. *Psychological Bulletin, 94*, 265–292.

Bone, P. F. (1995). Word-of-mouth effects on short-term and long-term product judgments. *Journal of Business Research, 32*, 213–223.

Bronfenbrenner, U. (1977, July). Toward an experimental ecology of human development. *American Psychologist*, pp. 513–531.

Brown, J. J., & Reingen, P. H. (1987). Social ties and word-of-mouth referral behavior. *Journal of Consumer Research, 14,* 350–362.

Daniels, E., & Leaper, C. (2006). A longitudinal investigation of sport participation, peer acceptance, and self-esteem among adolescent girls and boys. *Sex Roles, 55,* 875–880.

Dwyer, J. J., Allison, K. R., & Makin, S. (1998). Internal structure of a measure of self-efficacy in physical activity among high school students. *Social Science and Medicine, 46,* 1175–1182.

Farrey, T. (2008). *Game on: The all-American race to make champions out of our children.* New York: ESPN.

Geisler, G. W., & Leith, L. M. (1997). The effects of self-esteem, self-efficacy, and audience presence on soccer penalty shot performance. *Journal of Sport Behavior, 20,* 322.

Hansen, D. M., Larson, R. W., & Dworkin, J. B. (2003). What adolescents learn in organized youth activities: A survey of self-reported developmental experiences. *Journal of Research on Adolescents, 13,* 25–55.

Hattie, J., Marsh, H. W., Neill, J. T., & Richards, G. E. (1997). Adventure education and outward bound: Out-of-class experiences that make a lasting difference. *Review of Educational Research, 67,* 43–87.

Hogan, J. E., Lemon, K. N., & Libai, B. (2004, September). Quantifying the ripple: Word-of-mouth advertising effectiveness. *Journal of Advertising Research,* pp. 271–280.

Holt, N. L., Tink, L. N., Mandigo, J. L., & Fox, K. R. (2008). Do youth learn life skills through their involvement in high school sport? A case study. *Canadian Journal of Education, 31,* 281–304.

Hoyle, R. H., & Leff, S. S. (1997). The role of parental involvement in youth sport participation and performance. *Adolescence. 32*(125), 233.

Keegan, R. J., Harwood, C. G., Spray, C. M., & Lavallee, D. E. (2008). A qualitative investigation exploring the motivational climate in early career sports participants: Coach, parent, and peer influences on sport motivation. *Psychology of Sport and Exercise, 10,* 361–372.

Kirka, D. (2006, March 6). Study: Obesity in kids to increase sharply. *Opelika-Auburn News,* 8.

Larson, R. W. (2000). Toward a psychology of positive youth development. *American Psychologist, 55,* 170–183.

Lefebvre, R. C., & Flora, J. A. (1988). Social marketing and public health intervention. *Health Education Quarterly, 15,* 299–315.

Madrigal, R. M. (1995). Cognitive and affective determinants of fan satisfaction. *Journal of Leisure Research, 27,* 205.

Martens, R. (2004). *Successful coaching* (3rd ed.). Champaign, IL: Human Kinetics.

Richman, E. L., & Shaffer, D. R. (2000). "If you let me play sports": How might sport participation influence the self-esteem in adolescent females? *Psychology of Women Quarterly, 24,* 189–199.

Rothman, A. J., & Salovey, P. (1997). Shaping perceptions to motivate healthy behavior: The role of message framing. *Psychological Bulletin, 121,* 3–19.

Ryska, T. A. (2002). Effects of situational self-handicapping and state self-confidence on the physical performance of young participants. *Psychological Record, 52,* 461.

Sanna, L. J. (1992). Self-efficacy theory: Implications for social facilitation and social loafing. *Journal of Personality and Social Psychology, 62,* 774–786.

Scanlon, T. K., & Lewthwaite, R. (1986). Social psychological aspects of competition for male youth sport participants: Predictors of enjoyment. *Journal of Sport and Exercise Psychology, 8,* 1–11.

Shermer, M. (2000). Psyched up, psyched out: Science tries to determine whether sport psychology actually works. *Building the Elite Athlete: Scientific American Presents, 38*–44.

Smith, D. E., Kilgo, J., & Jenkins, S. (1999). *A coach's life.* New York: Random House.

Strauss, B. (2002). Social facilitation in motor tasks: A review of research and theory. *Psychology of Sport and Exercise, 33,* 237–256.

Tokmakidis, S. P., Kasambalis, A., & Christodoulos, A. D. (2006). Fitness levels of Greek primary school children in relationship to overweight and obesity. *European Journal of Pediatrics, 165,* 867–874.

Tomaka, J., Blascovich, J., Kelsey, R. M., & Leitten, C. L. (1993). Subjective, physiological, and behavioral effects of threat and challenge appraisal. *Journal of Personality and Social Psychology, 65,* 248–260.

Ullrich-French, S., & Smith, A. L. (2006). Perceptions of relationships with parents and peers in youth sport: Independent and combined prediction of motivational outcomes. *Psychology of Sport and Exercise, 7,* 193–214.

Ullrich-French, S., & Smith, A. L. (2009). Social and motivational predictors of continued youth sport participation. *Psychology of Sport and Exercise, 10,* 87–95.

Wong, F., Huhman, M., Heitzler, C., Asbury, L., Bretthauer-Mueller, R., McCarthy, S., & Londe, P. (2004). VERB—A social marketing campaign to increase physical activity among youth. *Public Health Research, Practice, and Policy, 1,* 1–7.

Worringham, C. J., & Messick, D. M. (1983). Social facilitation of running: An unobtrusive study. *Journal of Social Psychology, 121,* 23–29.

Zajonc, R. B. 1965. Social facilitation. *Science, 149,* 269–274.

8

The Motivations Associated With Attendance and Participation in an Amateur Sporting Event

Lada Helen V. Kurpis and Carl S. Bozman

Introduction

Motives are the driving force, the reasons behind our behavior. In a most basic sense, the study of motivation is the study of action (Eccles & Wigfield, 2002). The importance of studying sport-related motivations for marketing of amateur sporting events cannot be overstated. Understanding why individuals and communities choose to engage in sport-related activities is a prerequisite to designing an amateur athletic event that will fully engage all constituents through relating to their motivations. Sport motivation knowledge, among other things, enables marketers to tailor their communications to specific segments of sport consumers, design sporting events with desirable characteristics, foster sport subcultures, and as a long-term outcome, ensure viability of the promoted sport.

A promising avenue of sport motivation research involves studying the properties of social values. Rokeach (1973) defined a value as an enduring belief that a specific mode of conduct or end state of existence is personally or socially preferred. A number of social psychologists (Eccles & Wigfield, 2002; Feather, 1990; Verplanken & Holland, 2002) suggested treating social values as motivational constructs. This theoretical perspective interprets social values either as abstract, higher-order goals that motivate people to engage in goal-reaching behavior (Feather, 1990; Rohan, 2000; Rokeach, 1973) or as forces guiding actions (Lewin, 1952; Verplanken & Holland, 2002).

Amateur sporting events provide many opportunities for sport participants and spectators to fulfill a broad variety of sport-related values. Almost anyone can choose either to participate in or to watch an amateur sporting event. A desire to fulfill a value of accomplishment might prompt an amateur athlete to sign up for a 10-K race, while a willingness to affirm a warm relationship with a friend might encourage someone else to watch the event.

Amateur sporting events play an important role even in promoting healthy lifestyles and fitness. In a national survey by the Sporting Goods Manufacturers Association (SGMA), 55% of the respondents (62% male and 50% female) participated in sport-related activities during 2007 (Ryan, 2008). Despite an overall growth in sport participation, a significant drop-off in team sport engagement was observed among adults. When survey respondents were asked what factors would increase adult team sport participation, several issues were identified. Three of the top five categories are directly affected by the organizations and communities that sponsor amateur sporting events: spousal/family member participation, better access to facilities, and more organized activities.

As stated, from the perspective of sport marketers, sporting event organizers, and sport commissioners, a better understanding of the psychological motivations associated with amateur sporting events would provide the prospect for more effective communications with participants and spectators and the ability to better anticipate and satisfy consumer needs and, as a consequence, successfully build long-term relationships with both consumers and host communities. Perhaps even more important, such an understanding would allow identification of ways in which amateur sporting events can be used to exert an energizing and motivational influence on the population whose sport participation will be critically important to the future physical health of the nation.

This chapter provides an overview of extant sport marketing research on motivations for sport participation and spectatorship. The case for treating social values as motivational constructs is presented and thereafter related to the consumption of amateur sporting events. Findings from a longitudinal study of a large amateur basketball tournament are then discussed to demonstrate both the utility of using social values to discern the motivations of event participants and spectators and to show how such an understanding, coupled with articulated community needs, led to a successful strategic reorientation of the tournament. The concluding section discusses the outcomes of the strategic reorientation and sets directions for further research.

Sport Consumption Motivations

Sport marketing research clearly recognizes the importance of consumer motivations in sport participation and attendance (e.g., Rohm, Milne,

& McDonald, 2006; Wann, Grieve, Zapalac, & Pease, 2008). Models of sport consumption behavior often differentiate between groups of sport consumers based on motive distinctions. Sloan (1989) and Roberts (2001) provided comprehensive reviews of several motivation theories applied to sport-related consumption. Suffice it to say, sport consumption models based on these theories utilize an extremely broad variety of motives to explain sport fan and sport participant behavior.

For instance, Melnick (1993) focused entirely on sport spectators' motivation for social interaction, while Trail, Fink, and Anderson (2000) predicted sport fan behavior using nine different motives: vicarious achievement, acquisition of knowledge, aesthetics, social interaction, drama/excitement, escape, family, physical attractiveness of participants, and the physical skills of participants. James and Ross (2004) made a distinction between fans of three collegiate nonrevenue sports using a classification of nine motives: entertainment, skill, drama, team effort, achievement, social interaction, family, team affiliation, and empathy. Wann et al. (2008) found significant differences among fan motivational profiles for alternative sports across eight types of motives: escape, economic, eustress, self-esteem, group affiliation, entertainment, family, and aesthetics. For example, the aesthetic motivation was particularly prominent in individual sports and in nonaggressive sports, while economic, eustress, group affiliation, and entertainment motivations were more prevalent for team sports. Kahle, Kambara, and Rose's (1996) model, based on Kelman's (1974) functional theory of attitudinal influence, predicted attendance at college football from motives of self-expression through identification with the team, compliance/camaraderie (yielding to group influence), or internalization. Kahle et al. (1996) distinguished between internalization as a strong and enduring motivation versus compliance and identification, which are more situational and transitory in nature.

Theoretical perspectives have also focused on the motivational properties of sport spectators' moment-to-moment experiences. Sporting events have been found to differ from other forms of entertainment, such as the theater, in that sport performances are often characterized by tension and uncertainty about the outcome (Deighton, 1992; Madrigal & Dalakas, 2008). Conceptually, these models are related to the construct of "flow," described as the feeling of being lost in the moment (Csikszentmihalyi, 1991). The last author defined *flow* as "the state of mind when consciousness is harmoniously ordered, and they [people] want to pursue whatever they are doing for its own sake" (Csikszentmihalyi, 1991, p. 6). Suspense, characterized by changing emotions of hope and fear, in conjunction with uncertainty, constitutes the experience of many sport spectators. Madrigal, Bee, and LaBarge (2005; cf. Madrigal & Dalakas, 2008) found that experience of suspense was related to the enjoyment of sport consumers: Viewers' enjoyment of a competition was greater in response to a high-suspense competition in which their preferred competitor lost than for those who viewed a competition in which their preferred athlete lost in a low-suspense competition. The conceptualization of flow in sport consumption was further developed by Madrigal (2006) in his work on the Sporting Event Consumption Scale (FANDIM scale). The FANDIM scale consists of two higher-order factors: autotelism and appreciation. The autotelism dimension is comprised of the factors of flow (state of being immersed in the moment, absorbing the experience), fantasy (imagining behaviors and their consequences), and evaluation (evaluating athletes' actual performance). The appreciation factor, in its turn, consists of aesthetics (focus on the aesthetic appeal of the sporting event), personalities (focus on the personalities of individual athletes), and physical attraction (focus on the physical appeal of individual athletes).

A similar variety in motivation classifications is easily discerned in the models predicting sport participation. Laverie (1998) provided an overview of the motivations that have been utilized in existing research to predict amateur sport participation. These include, but are not limited to, enjoyment and social interaction, positive affect, competition, health and fitness, a sense of achievement, and personal satisfaction.

Although some classifications of sport participation motives strive to be comprehensive and derive classifications of motives from theory, others choose to focus on arbitrarily selected subsets of motives. For example, McDonald, Milne, and Hong's (2002) model explained sport participation based on 13 motivations derived from Maslow's (1970) hierarchy of needs: achievement, competition, social facilitation, physical fitness, skill mastery, physical risk, affiliation, aesthetics, aggression, value development, self-esteem, self-actualization, and stress release. In contrast, a study by Recours, Souville, and Griffet (2004) focused on just four motivational factors to predict amateur sport participation: competition, exhibitionism, sociability, and "playing to the limit" (presumably, conceptually related to the flow experience described by Csikszentmihalyi, 1991).

This brief examination of sport spectatorship and participation motivation research reveals that, despite significant overlap in the motive classifications, there is little consensus on either the motives that should be included in such a study or the methodology most useful in determining how particular motives have an impact on sport consumption activities. A focus on one (often subjectively determined) set of variables has been criticized on the grounds that other variables may have been overlooked that could have better contributed to explaining sport-related behaviors (Gray-Lee & Granzin, 1996). The lack of consistency in methodology also inhibits comparing findings across various studies. Should a universally applicable classification of sport consumption motivations ever be developed, sport marketers could benefit from applying it to explore similarities and differences between motivations for attending different sports (e.g., Robinson & Trail, 2005). In addition, studies on sport motivations have been criticized for the lack of sufficient theoretical foundation (Frederick, Morrison, & Manning, 1996). McDonald et al. (2002) called for integration of existing knowledge about sport consumption motivations on the grounds that "quantifiable research on these motivations is fragmented and inconclusive," and "there is little consensus on the boundaries … of [sport motivation theories]" (p. 101).

The observed variety in existing classifications of motives used in sport consumption research is probably not too surprising considering that it reflects the multitude of competing motivation theories, most of which can be applied to the study of sport consumption. Roberts (2001) counted at least 32 distinct theories of motivation that can be applied to explain sport-related behaviors. Such a diversity in theoretical perspective, although nourishing the field of sport behavior inquiry, might easily confuse sport marketing practitioners, such as sporting event organizers, sport commissioners, or advertising professionals, who would benefit from a simple and universally applicable methodology for studying motivations of event participants and spectators. A more systematic approach to the study of sport consumption motivations could enhance knowledge accumulation in the field by enabling sport marketing researchers to build on the findings of past studies.

It must be reiterated that the marketing of amateur sporting events to potential participants, spectators, and the broader set of constituents in a hosting community differs from marketing of professional, or revenue, sports. The sporting events of the latter kind focus on entertainment value as well as on the element of mastery on the part of sport participants, that is: "Sporting events represent a unique form of consumer entertainment that emphasizes the skill of the actors which are, in this case, athletes or teams" (Madrigal & Dalakas, 2008, p. 859). In contrast, amateur sporting events have much less of a "skill" component and much more of a social component. In most cases, there is no insurmountable mastery barrier between participants and spectators, and sport consumers may easily move between these two categories. Event organizers often need to increase the size of one group but not the other. For instance, increase in the number of spectators, but not in the number of participants, is desirable due to logistic constraints on increased participation (Green, 2001; Kurpis, Bozman, & Kahle, 2010). This characteristic of amateur sport events makes it particularly important for sport researchers to use a common method for discerning the motivations of participants and spectators so that event organizers can influence the relative composition of these two groups.

Motivational Properties of Social Values

Social values provide a theoretically compelling alternative to the current methodological medley in sport motivation research. A frequently cited definition by Rokeach (1973) states that a social value is an "enduring belief that a specific mode of conduct or end-state of existence is personally or socially preferable to an opposite or converse mode of conduct or end state of existence" (p. 5). The perspective that values are motivational constructs is widely shared by contemporary motivation researchers (e.g., Eccles & Wigfield, 2002; Feather, 1982, 1992, 1995; Verplanken & Holland, 2002). Feather (1992, 1995) considered values to be a special class of motives affecting behaviors through valences attached to choice alternatives. Verplanken and Holland (2002) did not equate values and motives but stressed that living up to a value "fulfills a particular, highly abstract goal" (p. 434). They further clarified their interpretation of values as "cognitions that may define a situation (e.g., as one in which honesty is needed), elicit goals (e.g., benevolence), and guide action (e.g., tell one's spouse that one made a mistake)" (Verplanken & Holland, 2002, p. 435). In this interpretation, values are not synonymous with goals but activate value-relevant goals by reinterpreting a situation in terms of value relevancy.

Values hold a unique and fundamental place in the system of social science constructs. Values are relatively stable but gradually changing abstract cognitions that result from a person's interaction with society and the person's adaptation to an ever-changing environment (Kahle, 1983). These learned ways of thinking summarize an individual's past experiences (Feather, 1982) and have a normative or prescriptive quality (Feather, 1982; Rokeach, 1973) as well as the property of transcending objects and situations (Rokeach, 1973). As a consequence, values are important to consumer behavior researchers because they have been shown to influence attitudes and behaviors over time (Homer & Kahle, 1988), and as demonstrated in means-end chain research, value fulfillment is often a fundamental reason for a consumer's choice of a particular product (e.g., Gutman, 1982).

In terms of sport consumption research methodology, the social values approach provides the inherent advantage of well-developed and validated value inventories (e.g., Kahle, 1983; Rokeach, 1973; Schwartz & Bilsky, 1987, 1990). Such inventories provide a comprehensive but finite number of values that can be administered to respondents in their entirety, thus enhancing the comparability of findings from different studies and across domains.

The use of social values theory and methods is particularly relevant to the study of sporting events in light of findings that sport subcultures are distinguishable by their sets of "identifiable beliefs, values, and means of symbolic expression" (Green, 2001, p. 3). From a managerial standpoint, the sport marketing literature suggests that notable marketing benefits in sporting event design and management can be derived by incorporating insights from the study of sport subculture values and identities (Green, 2001; Green & Chalip, 1998). Even though social values have been successfully used to explain sport consumption in the past (e.g., Florenthal & Shoham, 2000; Kahle, Duncan, Dalakas, & Aiken, 2001; Shoham & Kahle, 1996), their utilization in sport marketing research remains relatively limited. This reluctance to use the social values construct in sport marketing research might be attributable, in part, to the challenge of explaining the frequently observed inconsistency in value-behavior relationships (Feather, 1992; Verplanken & Holland, 2002).

Kahle and Xie (2008) noted that not all consumer decisions directly relate to values, although "an understanding of a person's values will help researchers to understand a person's relation to a particular brand or product above and beyond what can be learned only from other demographic and lifestyle information" (p. 575). Recent developments in expectancy-value theory provide an opportunity to further the explanation of the value-behavior relationships in sport consumption research. For instance, Feather (1982, 1992, 1995) proposed a model grounded in expectancy-value theory in which the perceived likelihood of an outcome and outcome attractiveness have an impact on choices. In this theoretical account, values affect decision making by influencing the attractiveness of those choice options that are relevant to those values. Specifically, Feather (1995) stated: "Values exert their effects ... by way of valences that become attached to objects and events within a person's psychological environment following the activation of those values that the person holds to be important for self" (p. 1136). Feather (1995) demonstrated that the attractiveness of choice options was, in fact, positively correlated with related values. Feather's (1982, 1992, 1995) model is consistent with the self-efficacy paradigm (Bandura, 1997) in that it theorizes that behaviors depend on a person's expectations about whether he or she can perform a task to the required standard. In a more recent extension of this model, Verplanken and Holland (2002) proposed that the more specific values are central to a person's self-identity, the more they are likely to affect this person's behavior. Verplanken and Holland (2002) distinguish between the concepts of "value centrality" (i.e., defining oneself in terms of a particular social value) and "value importance" (i.e., certain values might be deemed important because of the perceived social norms). Verplanken and Holland showed that the weight given to value-relevant product attribute information increased and value-congruent behavior was observed whenever task-related values were central to a person's sense of self and were cognitively activated.

These findings are relevant to amateur sporting events for several reasons. First, sport marketing research indicates that sport subcultures are characterized by a set of shared values and beliefs, and that interactions with a sport subculture (e.g., by participating in or attending a sporting event) shape and then enable the expression of the sport-related identity of a consumer (e.g., Green, 2001; Kahle et al., 1996). Thus, conducting an amateur sporting event serves to increase the cognitive accessibility of sport-related values (e.g., sense of accomplishment, excitement). By fostering a sense of sport-related community and enhancing sport consumers' self-identification with a particular sport, amateur sporting events also make sport-related values more central to consumers' self-identity. As social value accessibility and centrality increase, sport consumers become more likely to behave in ways that lead to value fulfillment. These considerations suggest the following propositions regarding the role of social values in amateur sporting events:

1. Social values that are central to self-identities of the participants in a particular sport subculture can be identified.
2. The participants and spectators in a sporting event might differ in terms of values that are central to their self-identities. This difference can be discerned and used to predict their actual event consumption behavior.
3. Referencing the central values held by a particular sport subculture in marketing communications has a potential to increase the impact of such communications (e.g., increased participation or spectatorship).
4. The mere act of highlighting a specific sport subculture through amateur sporting events might increase the accessibility and centrality of

the sport-related values and facilitate the transmission of the sport sub-culture's values across generations of sport consumers.

5. The transmission of a sport subculture's values to young people is necessary to ensure the long-term viability of a sport (e.g., by creating new lifetime participants or spectators).

6. Future investigations regarding the motivational properties of social values in sporting events promise significant benefits for sport marketing theory and practice.

Participant and Spectator Social Values

The proposition that social values can be used to discriminate participant from spectator behavior was examined at the largest three-on-three basketball tournament in the world. Hoopfest is an annual competition held every summer in Spokane, Washington. The 3-day event boasts over 25,000 players and 175,000 spectators. More than 400 basketball courts in the downtown core are needed to accommodate all the amateur contests. A random sample of 51 sites at 37 times was selected from these courts. Three different teams of interviewers administered a survey and gathered a total of 416 paper questionnaires.

We incorporated the list-of-values (LOV) methodology (Kahle, 1983) to distinguish between the social values of Hoopfest participants and spectators (Kurpis et al., 2010). The LOV methodology has been used successfully in the past to explain sport-related consumption (Beatty, Kahle, Homer, & Misra, 1985; Florenthal & Shoham, 2000; Kahle et al., 2001). The LOV included in the survey consisted of nine social values: a sense of belonging, excitement, warm relationships with others, self-fulfillment, being well respected, fun and enjoyment, security, self-respect, and a sense of accomplishment. Survey respondents self-identified as either participants or spectators.

We would like to stress that amateur sporting events differ from the majority of revenue-producing sporting events in that often there is no insurmountable mastery barrier between the event participants and spectators. Given adequate motivation, a spectator of a Hoopfest might easily become a participant next year. In contrast, in most revenue-producing sporting event situations, spectators cannot shift to participants' roles, no matter how involved they might be with a particular team or a sport. This property of amateur sporting events makes them a promising research setting for exploration of the effects of social values on sport consumption behavior.

We reasoned that when a person can freely choose whether to become either a participant or a spectator in an amateur sport tournament, then the relative weight he or she gives to each social value and the valence of related outcome assessments will determine the effect on his or her behavior. For example, knowing that participation in the sport tournament could lead to a physical injury, individuals who place a high value on security might perceive this possible outcome as especially negative and opt to watch the event instead. In a similar fashion, people who value excitement more heavily should have a greater propensity to become a participant because competition in the tournament allows them to experience a higher degree of excitement than simply watching the event.

Homer and Kahle (1988) identified three dimensions of LOV values: external values, consisting of the sense of belonging, warm relationships with others, security, and being well respected; internal values, consisting of self-fulfillment, a sense of accomplishment, and self-respect; and a fun/excitement value dimension, reflecting respondents' hedonistic orientation. We used this mapping of LOV values onto underlying dimensions to assess the influence of values on a respondent's propensity to participate (as opposed to become a spectator) of Hoopfest.

A logistic regression was used to examine the relationship between the LOV value ratings and tournament participation or spectatorship status of the respondents. The results of the study are presented in Table 8.1. The LOV ratings, taken together, were significant as predictors of tournament participation or spectatorship. A sense of accomplishment and the value of excitement were both positively related to tournament participation (internal and fun/excitement value dimensions), while warm relationships with others and security (from the external values dimension) were positively related to tournament spectatorship (Kurpis et al., 2010).

Inclusion of demographic variables in the analysis further increased the precision of the model. A logistic regression based on respondents' age and LOV ratings correctly classified 81.1% of the spectators and 58.6% of active participants, explaining 24.1% of the variance (older age was negatively related with tournament participation). The inclusion of gender as a predictor resulted in a model that correctly classified 79.2% of the spectators and 65.4% of active participants, which explained 30.2% of the variance. Female respondents were more likely to be tournament spectators than participants. Income made no significant contribution to the ability of the model to distinguish between the event participants and spectators when it was included in the analysis.

TABLE 8.1   Logistic Regression: List of Values

LOV Values	B	SE	Wald	df	p	Odds Ratio
Internal Values						
Sense of accomplishment	0.315	0.153	4.235	1	0.04	1.371
Self-fulfillment	−0.039	0.110	0.125	1	ns	0.962
Self-respect	0.036	0.156	0.052	1	ns	1.036
External Values						
Warm relationships	−0.232	0.114	4.120	1	0.042	0.793
Security	−0.264	0.117	5.117	1	0.024	0.768
Being well respected	−0.095	0.135	0.496	1	ns	0.909
Sense of belonging	−0.010	0.091	0.013	1	ns	0.990
Fun/Excitement Values						
Excitement	0.236	0.100	5.605	1	0.018	1.266
Fun and enjoyment	0.165	0.146	1.277	1	ns	1.180

Note: Data from Kurpis, L. H. V., Bozman, C. S., & Kahle, L. R., (2010). *International Journal of Sport Marketing and Management, 7*(3/4), 190–201.

These findings are consistent with the results from other studies. For instance, Beatty et al. (1985) found that spectators, rather than participants, are more likely to be guided by select external values (security and sense of belonging). Although participation in a community-based amateur competition may pose relatively minor risks for players, certain dangers do still exist. The social risk (e.g., of public embarrassment) or the previously mentioned physical risk of injury could cause those people who place a high value on security to be averse to tournament participation. In contrast, being a spectator in such a tournament is a significantly less risky way to fulfill external values by being there for other people (e.g., socializing with friends and family). Although amateur sporting events are rarely graced by the presence of star athletes, masterful performance is not what ultimately attracts spectators to these events. Instead, amateur sporting events provide spectators with an opportunity to support people who they care about, have a sense of camaraderie, and enjoy a festive community-building atmosphere.

Sports are competitive and achievement-oriented activities by definition. The value of achievement, however, is fulfilled by winning as well as through testing one's ability to persevere in the face of failure (McDonald et al., 2002). Participants, as opposed to spectators of a sport tournament, are in a much better position to fulfill an achievement value. When contest participants win or affirm their physical fitness, endurance, and competitive spirit in active participation, they are much more likely to meet needs associated with the internal values of self-respect, a sense of accomplishment, and self-fulfillment.

Research on social values has striking managerial implications for sport event marketers and managers as a consequence. It can provide a better understanding of participant and spectator motivations and allow the event coordinators to exert much more effective control over all elements of a tournament, such as program design and event social dynamics. Understanding a specific value's centrality to spectators' and participants' social identities would permit organizers to distinctly target either group. The last managerial application might become an important benefit if, for example, tournament organizers wish to attract more spectators while maintaining the current level of competitor participation due to the physical limitations associated with event facilities. To achieve this objective, sport marketers might, for instance, focus communications aimed at potential spectators on the "community-centered" nature of the event and the "relationship-centric" benefits of attending the tournament. While both participants' and spectators' support contributes to the success of amateur athletic events, there may certainly be circumstances for which an increase in one group is more desirable than another.

The long-term sustainability of any amateur athletic event will also depend on the degree or centrality of specific sport-related values within a community. Sport marketers can use a better understanding of social values to design events with features and characteristics that serve the purpose of keeping a sport subculture vibrant and growing by creating conditions that enhance relevant value cognitive accessibility and the centrality to self within a target population. It becomes particularly important to ensure that such values are broadly held and easily accessible among the youth. Providing regular opportunities for children to be in contact with a sport while ensuring that they are socialized into the sport subculture will be critical to sport sustainability. In other words, understanding which social values appeal most to participants and spectators helps ensure that event organizers can create athletic experiences that better suit the needs of all constituents and thereby perpetuate the viability of an event.

Strategic Redesign of Hoopfest

Why should a community support an amateur sport tournament? Economic development is the most commonly stated reason (Andersson, Rustad, & Solberg, 2004; Crompton, 1995; Preuss, Seguin, & O'Reilly, 2007; Rueda-Cantuche & Ramirez-Hurtado, 2007). Spectators and participants from outside the local population contribute to the economy of a region whenever they spend money that would have otherwise been saved or spent elsewhere. Urban core revival, tourism benefits, the creation of a sporting legacy, local entertainment, and quality-of-life issues are other rationales often offered either independently or in combination to justify the sponsorship of a sporting event to a community (Turco, 1998; Wilson, 2006). Although a variety of such arguments can be and are made, little doubt exists that the success of most amateur sporting events depends on broad-based community support. Besides attendance at the event, forms of community support range from providing space and equipment to far more obvious public financial commitments.

Hoopfest management relied on the understanding of its participant and spectator social values, in conjunction with traditional business process improvement tools, to expand local economic benefits and assuage related concerns within the business community. This approach has been applied to strategic redesign of the Hoopfest amateur basketball tournament (Bozman, Kurpis, & Frye, 2010). By 1998, after 8 years of continuous growth, ensuring a quality player experience had become increasingly difficult for the event organizers even though there was still some opportunity for additional participant growth. Spectators had also been found to spend relatively more money than players on purchases other than food and lodging (the average spectator spent $101.90 vs. $77.73 per player). These circumstances, taken together, inspired a thorough revision of the event strategy and compelled the Hoopfest organizers to target spectator rather than participant growth.

The objective of achieving growth in spectator numbers predetermined Hoopfest's managerial focus on "augmenting" the sporting event (Green, 2001), which, on a practical level, translated into ensuring spectators' satisfaction with the event experience. The process of strategic redesign started with a customer survey conducted during Hoopfest 1998 and organized around the known areas of concern for the event organizers. For instance, several merchants in Spokane had complained about holding the basketball tournament downtown. They felt that the street congestion associated with the competition made it extremely difficult for regular customers to patronize their stores. These merchants proposed moving Hoopfest to the suburbs. This site location seemed less than desirable to Hoopfest managers, who believed that the downtown location of the tournament, next to Riverfront Park, was an important element of the success of the event.

Management first identified how people perceived parking availability and the importance of the Hoopfest downtown site location. It turned out that high parking utilization rates did not affect the willingness and ability of people to come downtown and shop. Those attendees who shopped during Hoopfest preferred the downtown site location over the suburban alternatives. The economic impact of the event was then used to reassure downtown merchants of the beneficial aspects of the tournament as well as negotiate a permanent site location. Hoopfest now occupies much of the downtown area with little objection on the part of downtown merchants.

Bozman et al. (2010) documented the effects of a Hoopfest strategic reorientation over a period of time. Although both participants and spectators are expected to share some psychological characteristics, they clearly differed in terms of endorsement of a number of social values. Discernment of these distinctions between participants and spectators of an amateur sporting event helped Hoopfest better serve the needs of each group by designing a superior event and creating more effective promotions. As Rohm et al. (2006) pointed out: "Understanding consumers' underlying motivations for sports or fitness participation points to both the opportunity and challenge for marketers in developing effective ... market segmentation practices that are based on consumer typologies" (p. 29). Indeed, understanding consumer motivations is essential for building a relationship marketing strategy and tailoring various aspects of a sporting event to the specific needs of participants and spectators.

Concerts in the park and an expanded food court were combined with safety and convenience initiatives to make attending Hoopfest even more attractive to spectators. These enhancements were designed to change the image of the event in peoples' minds from primarily a sports competition into a sport festival or basketball celebration. Other spectator-oriented activities that Hoopfest organizers added included shooting contests and games such as the Safeco Last Second Shot, a 3-point contest, AT&T Hoopshoot, the Kalispel Tribe Monster Shot Contest, U.S. Bank Plinko, the U.S. Air Force Slam Dunk completion, an Alaska Air/Horizon Air Slide, and a Toyota Shoot-off for three new Toyota trucks. Furthermore, a variety of new athletic product demonstrations and themed guest appearances were incorporated (e.g., the Seattle Seahawks cheerleaders promoted balanced diet and fitness). Autograph sessions with professional and collegiate basketball players also competed with a center court sponsored by Nike that featured some of the nation's most talented basketball players. Overall, a number of activities deemed appropriate to fostering and promoting the amateur basketball sport subculture were implemented into the event design.

From a measurable and practical perspective, this Hoopfest shift to a festival orientation had the desired consequences. The number of spectators per Hoopfest participant increased from 4.83 per player to 7.24 per player in less than 8 years. Spectators almost doubled to 175,000 people even though the number of players increased by less than a third. The most recent economic impact study also demonstrated that the expenditures of attendees from outside the Spokane region more than doubled. This was due to a larger proportion of spectators coming from outside the community, 52% versus 43%, as well as the relatively higher per capita spectator level of spending. The aggregate out-of-area expense for these individuals was $20,831,450 versus the previous total of $9,930,541. The discrepancy between spectator and player expenditures was even more noticeable. Spectators spent almost 30% more than players every day they attended the tournament.

The study did not account for economic activities that may or may not have taken place in the absence of Hoopfest. The beneficial social effects of Hoopfest were also not quantified. The fact remains, however, that many residents of the Spokane community felt it was a better place to live because of Hoopfest. The impact of sporting events is not limited to economic effects but extends to the tourism attractiveness, physical environment, strengthening of traditions and values of a region, increased local pride, increased national and international recognition, and a heightened sense of community for a host location (Andersson et al., 2004; Chalip, 2006).

Leveraging Social Values in Amateur Sports

There is certainly a relationship between a willingness of a community to host a sporting event and the thoughts and feelings of residents who reside in the area even though it would be inappropriate to compare individual motivations for participating in or viewing an amateur sporting event with the composite motivations of all the people within a community. Sport event organizers, however, need to anticipate the needs of those with whom they interact (e.g., sport commissioners and community leaders) to better ensure their support. Without question, they would benefit from the guidance of sport marketing researchers who understand the dynamics and the full potential of amateur sporting events.

As we stated, economic development is the most frequently cited reason for local communities to sponsor sporting events (e.g., Andersson et al., 2004; Crompton, 1995; Getz, 1997; Preuss et al., 2007; Rueda-Cantuche & Ramirez-Hurtado, 2007). However, the positive social impact of sporting events deserves an equally thorough consideration (e.g., Chalip, 2006; Green, 2001, Green & Chalip, 1998; Preuss, 2007). The social effects of amateur sporting events, because of their profound and lasting nature, may be at least as important as the economic benefits delivered by those events (Chalip, 2006). Several anthropological studies (Green & Chalip, 1998; Handelman, 1990; Kemp, 1999) have shown a transcendental impact of sporting events: a sense of something immensely important going on and a heightened sense of community. This aspect of a sporting event is termed *liminal* in the literature. It is this energy, excitement, and sense of community evoked by an amateur sport tournament that makes it so attractive to host and attend (Chalip, 2006).

Event liminality is not an outcome achieved without effort or guaranteed simply by scheduling a sport competition. To the contrary, it requires event organizers to consciously plan a value creation process focused on sport consumer desires (Bramwell, 1997; Chalip, 2006). A relatively recent trend in sport event organization is augmentation of the main sporting event with add-on activities and services to broaden the demographic and psychographic appeal of the activity (Green, 2001). Many of the most successful strategies involve bundling sporting events with other features at the host destination (Chalip & McGuirty, 2004). Event augmentation enhances liminality by increasing the celebratory and interactive opportunities for all attendees.

Green and Chalip (1998) identified two key elements in the creation of the event liminality: a sense of celebration and a sense of social camaraderie. It is not hard to see how these two elements correspond to LOV values. A sense of celebration can be traced to the values of excitement and enjoyment, while camaraderie maps directly onto the values of sense of belonging and warm relationships with others. Chalip (2006) suggested at least five strategies to foster liminality at sporting events: enabling sociability (e.g., designing venue and off-venue facilities, particularly seating areas, where people can socialize); creating event-related social events (e.g., Green, 2001, cited that the week leading up to Preakness, a Triple

Crown horse race, is now packed with social activities, parades, parties, and concerts); facilitating informal social opportunities (e.g., live street events, creating popular places to meet others); producing ancillary events (e.g., sport-related art events); and theming (the use of event colors, symbols, and decorations throughout the hosting locale).

Augmentation of sport events through educational activities also serves an important purpose in socializing new generations of sport fans and participants into the subculture of a specific sport, contributing to the long-run sustainability of that sport. Social values are prominent constructs in the emerging research stream that examines the social leverage of sporting events. Green (2001) stressed that the subculture associated with each sport is characterized by its own distinct set of values, beliefs, and symbolic modes of expression. Her research suggested that the adoption of the values and beliefs associated with a particular sport subculture affects the centrality of that subculture in a person's self-identity.

The foregoing discussion suggests the importance of childhood-oriented sport activities. Early socialization into the sport subculture increases sport value relevance as well as the ease with which value-related cognitions are activated in the future. The consequences of failing to involve young people at an early age, as either participants or spectators, would not bode well for specific sport demand and related corollary outcomes (e.g., personal health, work force productivity, infrastructure development, or subsidy via sponsorship). Creating sport enthusiasts for life must become an integral objective of amateur sport event planning to ensure the sport's long-term viability.

Discussion and Future Research

What is Hoopfest doing to improve the largest basketball tournament in the world when both participants and spectators already express high levels of satisfaction? Whatever directions for further development the management considers will have to avoid significant growth in the absolute number of either participants or spectators. As of today, the tournament already faces both a lodging constraint (recruiting out-of-town participants and spectators necessitates that they have a place to stay) as well as an extraordinarily high penetration in the local community (more people attend Hoopfest than reside in the city of Spokane). Recognition of these constraints has led the Hoopfest management to concentrate on a new stage in the evolution of this sport festival.

Hoopfest organizers chose to focus on leveraging the social effects of the tournament to develop the local basketball-centered community and ensure the long-term viability of the sport festival. To do this, they decided to target childhood-oriented basketball activities. Sport engagement at a young age, as we have argued previously, enhances commitment to sport participation through the promotion of sport-related social values. The consequences of failing to involve young people at an early age, as either participants or spectators, does not bode well for long-term viability and related corollary outcomes of a specific sport (e.g., personal health, workforce productivity, infrastructure development, and business subsidy via sport sponsorship). The prospect for such youth sport engagement in the Spokane area had become somewhat problematic because of the budget cuts to a number of athletic programs in public elementary schools (e.g., elimination of interschool basketball competition). Hoopfest has chosen to help fill this void and expanded its focus to organize and run the region's premier basketball league for young men and women. The Amateur Athletic Union (AAU) provides young boys and girls with an extraordinary opportunity to develop their basketball skill as well as to compete at a high level. Hoopfest also decided to manage the Midnight Basketball Association (MBA) in conjunction with the Spokane school district. The MBA was organized as an intervention for at-risk youth, provides a safe place for character development, and helps prepare young people for personal success.

Hoopfest continues to leverage its large and loyal participant and spectator base by supporting other basketball-related charitable causes throughout the year. Since its inception in 1990, this nonprofit organization has donated over $1 million to the Special Olympics and a number of local sport entities. Included in these charitable donations is an outdoor basketball court construction program. Twenty public basketball courts have either been extensively renovated or built with Hoopfest assistance. Most of these courts are located within the city of Spokane's public parks. Both the courts and the basketball backboards prominently display the Hoopfest logo and color scheme.

By promoting the acquisition of social values related to its tournament, Hoopfest has almost certainly enhanced the future prospects for basketball in the region. The relationship between the sport-related values that young people acquire and their subsequent propensity to play in or watch that sporting event is both positive and significant. To date, this choice of strategic direction has been successful, and the prospects for Hoopfest's future look bright.

Hoopfest organizers, as well as many other professional and volunteer managers of amateur sporting events, have and will continue to benefit from a relatively recent stream of theoretical and empirical marketing research focused on the specific issues associated with designing and promoting amateur sporting events.

Uncovering amateur sport participants and spectators' motivations is an objective of utmost importance, and social values research represents an attractive methodology for this type of inquiry. As we have shown, the participants and spectators of amateur sporting events may often be guided by different sets of social values. Future research should therefore focus on exploring the sport-related social values as well as on understanding the differences between amateur and professional sport participants and spectators. The processes of acquiring social values and identifying the factors that contribute to the centrality of the specific values to the sense of self represent other important and viable avenues for further scientific inquiry. Likewise, more empirical research is needed to better understand the value endorsement patterns characteristic of particular sports.

Other questions that need to be answered include identification of the most effective methods of cognitive activation of sport-related values through marketing communications. Which marketing strategies might ensure sport viability by achieving a "participation-for-life" behavioral outcome? To answer this and other related questions focused on the impact of social values on behaviors of amateur sporting event attendees, sport marketers have to study them within the broader context of the social dynamics and the unique aspects of the sport subcultures specific to amateur, as opposed to professional, sports.

Knowledge of amateur sport-related motivations will have the most positive, transformative impact if it is actively shared with the general public. For instance, sport marketing scientists need to do a better job of communicating their findings regarding all aspects of social benefits that can be leveraged by local communities in addition to the positive economic impact of hosting an amateur sporting event. Among other things, sport marketing practitioners need to be familiarized with the concepts of sport subculture, the advantages provided by conducting the "augmented" sporting events, as well as the diverse benefits derived from better understanding of social values of event attendees.

Marketing of amateur, as opposed to professional, sporting events represents a promising area of scientific exploration. This domain of inquiry ultimately belongs to the area of transformative consumer behavior research by indicating ways to promote healthier lifestyles and create more socially vibrant communities.

References

Andersson, T. D., Rustad, A., & Solberg, H. A. (2004). Local residents' monetary evaluation of sports events. *Managing Leisure, 9*(July): 145–158.

Bandura, A. (1997). *Self-efficacy: The exercise of control.* New York: Freeman.

Beatty, S. E., Kahle, L. R., Homer, P., & Misra, S. (1985). Alternative measurement approaches to consumer values: The list of values and the Rokeach value survey. *Psychology and Marketing, 2*, 181–200.

Bozman, C. S., Kurpis, L. V., & Frye, C. (2010). Hoopfest: Using longitudinal economic impact data to assess the success of a strategic reorientation. *Sport Management Review, 13*(1), 65–81.

Bramwell, B. (1997). Strategic planning before and after a mega-event. *Tourism Management, 18*, 167–176.

Chalip, L. (2006). Towards social leverage of sport events. *Journal of Sport and Tourism, 11*(2), 109–127.

Chalip, L., & McGuirty, J. (2004). Bundling sport events with the host destination. *Journal of Sport Tourism, 9*(3), 267–282.

Crompton, J. L. (1995). Economic impact analysis of sport facilities and events: Eleven sources of misapplication. *Journal of Sport Management, 9*, 14–35.

Csikszentmihalyi, M. (1991). *Flow: The psychology of optimal experience.* New York: Harper Perennial.

Deighton, J. (1992). The consumption of performance. *Journal of Consumer Research, 19*, 362–372.

Eccles, J. S., & Wigfield, A. (2002). Motivational beliefs, values, and goals. *Annual Review of Psychology, 53*, 109–132.

Feather, N. T. (1982). Human values and the prediction of action: An expectancy-values analysis. In N. T. Feather (Ed.), *Expectations and actions: Expectancy-value models in psychology* (pp. 263–289). Hillsdale, NJ: Erlbaum.

Feather, N. T. (1990). Bridging the gap between values and actions: Recent applications of the expectancy-value model. In E. T. Higgins & R. M. Sorrentino (Eds.), *Handbook of motivation and cognition: Foundations of social behavior* (Vol. 2, pp. 151–192). New York: Guilford Press.

Feather, N. T. (1992). Values, valences, expectations, and actions. *Journal of Social Issues, 48*(2), 109–124.

Feather, N. T. (1995). Values, valences, and choice: The influence of values on the perceived attractiveness and choice of alternatives. *Journal of Personality and Social Psychology, 68*, 1135–1151.

Florenthal, B., & Shoham, A. (2000). Value differences between risky sport participants and nonparticipants. *Sport Marketing Quarterly, 9*(1), 26–33.

Frederick, C. M., Morrison, C. S., & Manning, T. (1996). Motivation to participate, exercise affect, and outcome behavior toward physical activity. *Perceptual and Motor Skills, 82,* 691–701.

Getz, D. (1997). *Event management and event tourism.* New York: Cognizant Communication.

Gray-Lee, J. W., & Granzin, K. L. (1996). Understanding participation in exercise and sport: An extended application of personal investment theory. *Journal of Sport Behavior, 20,* 37–53.

Green, B. C. (2001). Leveraging subculture and identity to promote sport events. *Sport Management Review, 4,* 1–19.

Green, B. C., & Chalip, L. (1998). Sport tourism as the celebration of subculture. *Annals of Tourism Research, 25,* 275–291.

Gutman, J. (1982). A means-end chain model based on consumer categorization processes. *Journal of Marketing, 46*(2), 60–72.

Handelman, D. (1990). *Models and mirrors: Towards an anthropology of public events.* New York: Cambridge University Press.

Homer, P. M., & Kahle, L. R. (1988). A structural equation analysis of the value-attitude-behavior hierarchy. *Journal of Personality and Social Psychology, 54,* 638–646.

James, J. D., & Ross, S. D. (2004). Comparing sport consumer motivations across multiple sports. *Sport Marketing Quarterly, 13*(1), 17–25.

Kahle, L. R. (1983). *Social values and social change: Adaptation to life in America.* New York: Praeger.

Kahle, L. R., Duncan, M., Dalakas, V., & Aiken, D. (2001). The social values of fans for men's versus women's university basketball. *Sport Marketing Quarterly, 10*(2), 156–162.

Kahle, L. R., Kambara, K. M., & Rose, G. M. (1996). A functional model of fan attendance: Motivations for college football. *Sport Marketing Quarterly, 5*(4), 51–60.

Kahle, L. R., & Xie, G.-X. (2008). Social values in consumer psychology. In C. Haugvedt, P. Herr, & F. Kardes (Eds.), *Handbook of consumer psychology* (pp. 575–585). Mahwah, NJ: Erlbaum.

Kelman, H. C. (1974). Further thoughts on the processes of compliance, identification, and internalization. In J. T. Tedeschi (Ed.), *Perspectives on social power* (pp. 125–171). Chicago: Aldine.

Kemp, S. F. (1999). Sled dog racing; the celebration of cooperation in a competitive sport. *Ethnology, 38,* 81–95.

Kurpis, L. H. V., Bozman, C. S., & Kahle, L. R. (2010). Distinguishing between amateur sport participants and spectators: The list of values approach. *International Journal of Sport Marketing and Management, 7*(3/4), 190–201.

Laverie, D. A. (1998). Motivations for ongoing participation in a fitness activity. *Leisure Sciences, 20,* 277–302.

Lewin, K. (1952). Constructs in field theory [1944]. In D. Cartwright (Ed.), *Field theory in social science: Selected theoretical papers by Kurt Lewin* (pp. 30–42). London: Tawistock.

Madrigal, R. (2006). Measuring the multidimensional nature of sporting event performance consumption. *Journal of Leisure Research, 38,* 267–292.

Madrigal, R., Bee, C., & LaBarge, M. (2005). *The thrill of victory and agony of defeat: An affective sequence describing the experience of suspense* (Working paper). Eugene, OR: R. Madrigal.

Madrigal, R., & Dalakas, V. (2008). Consumer psychology of sport: More than just a game. In C. P. Haugtvedt, P. M. Herr, & F. R. Kardes (Eds.), *Handbook of consumer psychology* (pp. 857–876). New York: Erlbaum.

Maslow, A. H. (1970). *Motivation and personality.* New York: Harper & Row.

McDonald, M. A., Milne, G. R., & Hong, J. B. (2002). Motivational factors for evaluating sport spectator and participant markets. *Sport Marketing Quarterly, 11*(2), 100–113.

Melnick, M. J. (1993). Searching for sociability in the stands: A theory of sports spectating, *Journal of Sport Management, 7,* 44–60.

Preuss, H. (2007). The conceptualization and measurement of mega sport event legacies. *Journal of Sport and Tourism, 12*(3–4), 207–227.

Preuss, H., Seguin, B., & O'Reilly, N. (2007). Profiling major sport event visitors: The 2002 Commonwealth Games. *Journal of Sport and Tourism, 12*(1), 5–23.

Recours, R. A., Souville, M., & Griffet, J. (2004). Expressed motives for informal and club association-based sport participation. *Journal of Leisure Research, 36*(1), 1–22.

Roberts, G. C. (2001). Understanding the dynamics of motivation in physical activity: The influence of achievement goals on motivational processes. In G. C. Roberts (Ed.), *Advances in motivation in sport and exercise* (pp. 1–51). Champaign, IL: Human Kinetics.

Robinson, M. J., & Trail, G. T. (2005). Relationships among spectator gender, motives, points of attachment, and sport preference. *Journal of Sport Management, 19,* 58–80.

Rohan, M. J. (2000). A rose by any name? The values construct. *Personality and Social Psychology Review, 3,* 255–277.

Rohm, A. J., Milne, G. R., & McDonald, M. A. (2006). A mixed-method approach for developing market segmentation typologies in the sports industry. *Sport Marketing Quarterly, 15*(1), 29–39.

Rokeach, M. J. (1973). *The nature of human values.* New York: Free Press.

Rueda-Cantuche, J. M., & Ramirez-Hurtado, J. M. (2007). A simple-to-use procedure to evaluate the social and economic impacts of sporting events on local communities. *International Journal of Sport Management and Marketing, 2,* 510–525.

Ryan, T. J. (2008). SGMA SURVEY: Americans delusional regarding their health. *SGB, 41*(7), 12.

Schwartz, S. H., & Bilsky, W. (1987). Toward a psychological structure of human values. *Journal of Personality and Social Psychology, 53,* 550–562.

Schwartz, S. H., & Bilsky, W. (1990). Toward a theory of the universal content and structure of values: Extensions and cross-cultural replications. *Journal of Personality and Social Psychology, 58*, 878–891.

Shoham, A., & Kahle, L. R. (1996). Spectators, viewers, readers: Communication and consumption communities in sport marketing. *Sport Marketing Quarterly, 5*(1), 11–19.

Sloan, L. R. (1989). The motives of sports fans. In J. H. Goldstein (Ed.), *Sports, games and play: Social and psychological viewpoints* (pp. 175–240). Hillsdale, NJ: Erlbaum.

Trail, G. T., Fink, J. S., & Anderson, D. F. (2000). A theoretical model of sport spectator consumption behavior. *International Journal of Sport Management, 1*, 154–180.

Turco, D. M. (1998). Traveling and turnovers measuring the economic impact of a street marketing tournament. *The Journal of Sport Tourism, 5*(1), 7–14.

Verplanken, B., & Holland, R. W. (2002). Motivated decision-making: Effects of activation and self-centrality of values on choices and behavior. *Journal of Personality and Social Psychology, 82*, 434–447.

Wann, D. L., Grieve, F. G., Zapalac, R., & Pease, D. G. (2008). Motivational profiles of sport fans of different sports. *Sport Marketing Quarterly, 17*(1), 6–19.

Wilson, R. (2006). The economic impact of local sport events: Significant, limited, or otherwise? A case study of four swimming events. *Managing Leisure, 11*(January), 57–70.

Section III

Providing Service to Consumers Through Sports and Event Sponsorship

Sporting events are supposed to provide a service experience to consumers. Reynolds presents a meaningful analysis of the controversial topic of the Bowl Championship Series rankings, which are intended to provide a service to football fans. Reynolds employs an R-methodology to ascertain the series rankings. He presents a strong case for how college football could handle the coronation of its champion in a manner that improves fan perceptions and sense of fairness and service.

Riedmueller develops an alternative, theory-driven approach to evaluating the service quality of sporting events called the PROSPORT model. The chapter cogently illustrates how marketing theories can be applied to sports in general and especially to the illustration of quality at professional sporting events. Finney, Lacey, and Close describe how the Tour de Georgia cycling race teaches about effective use of events and sponsorships to reach fans.

9

Hospitality
A Key Sponsorship Service in Sports Marketing

Rick Burton, John Tripodi, Scott Owen,
and Lynn R. Kahle

Introduction

In her work *Sports Marketing* (1994), Brooks presented a definition for hospitality in a chapter titled "Putting a Sports Sponsorship Plan Together": *"When the prime objective of a sponsorship program is to provide hospitality to distributors, employees, trade contacts or decision makers, monitoring the effects the hospitality program has on these publics can provide direct feedback on whether or not the program has had the desired effect"* (italics as original). Irwin, Sutton, and McCarthy (2002) discussed this notion further in the work *Sport Promotion and Sales Management* by writing about "incentivizing sport consumers" and suggested interpersonal facilitation is one of the "unique features of the sport product" (p. 47) because attendance at a sporting event generally takes place in a public setting and "satisfaction [is] greatly influenced by interaction with other people" (Mullin, Hardy, & Sutton, 2000, p. 220). Melnick (1993) discussed this social behavior and suggested sport venues are an excellent arena for engagement among strangers or people who may only know each other casually because the sporting event facilitates a common viewing experience and allows for noncommittal socialization. The service activity described, also known as "customer entertainment" or "auxiliary social functions" (Irwin et al., 2002), has its roots in interpersonal facilitation and usually represents a provision sold by the property organization (e.g., the International Olympic Committee) to a sponsor (e.g., Coca-Cola) for the purpose of providing social entertainment to the sponsor's personally selected guests in proximity to a desired sponsored event (e.g., Beijing 2008 Olympic Games).

The growing use of hospitality to leverage sponsorship investments is now thought by some sponsorship experts to differentiate sponsors from each other and, in some cases, to make the difference in measuring return on sponsorship investment (based on the value of business conducted during hospitality activities) and even sponsorship renewal. In Beijing, International Olympic Committee (IOC) sponsor Johnson & Johnson expressed displeasure with the nature of public access to their hospitality building on the Olympic Green. Months later, Johnson & Johnson chose not to renew their quadrennial sponsorship of the Olympics.

Ultimately, the concept of corporate hospitality is not new and might trace its roots to ancient Greece, where sponsors were afforded specific privileges (Burton, Quester, & Farrelly, 1998), including private access to the athletes. Today, when an Olympic sponsorship can cost US$70 million prior to activation, corporate hospitality is more important than ever. Hospitality at sporting events incorporates elements of services marketing, relationship marketing, participation marketing, and experiential marketing, usually in a tightly controlled sponsorship environment.

In the previous literature about hospitality, the discussion has not connected the concept of place-based privilege or restricted-access ticketing. In essence, as sport has grown as a spectator-based activity over the years, sports marketers have learned that, as with real estate, location matters. Thus, the best seats, be they behind the dugouts, on the 50-yard line, in the corners of a hockey rink, or behind the bench or goal, are often seen by discerning fans as better locations (than the upper grandstand) from which to watch the game. Added to this continuum of good, better, best has been the creation of "skyboxes" or luxury suites for the wealthiest fans. Burton (1999) detailed that in building the Houston Astrodome in 1965, Judge Roy Hofheinz introduced the phrase *skyboxes* to describe a special kind of luxury treatment in which amenities such as a private toilet, liquor bar, or padded seats would be available. These private boxes quickly became ideal opportunities, similar to business meetings on a golf course, for conducting business, hosting key clients, or "talking sports."

These hospitality gatherings have traditionally offered sponsors the chance to "wine and dine" key customers, discuss business with vendors, motivate senior or junior employees, reward employees or distributors for performances in sales incentive contests, and facilitate media relations for publicity purposes. In past years, this sponsorship function might have taken place in a modest tent erected near the sponsored event. But according to Roberts (2002), "More than ever before, demands are being placed on the providers of corporate hospitality at sports events to deliver a total entertainment package" (p. 40). In addition, existing rights holders at a facility (i.e., Stadium Australia) may find that they are prohibited from their normal hospitality rights if they are seen as ambush competitors to official sponsors of an event like the Olympics.

One activity that hospitality facilitates is sports talk (Kahle, Elton, & Kambara, 1997), which often aids relationship building. People with little in common can agree on the topic of sports as a vehicle to define roles, explore common values and interests, and establish interaction patterns. People can even be drawn into a consumption community based on sports that will create an environment of enhanced cooperation (Shoham & Kahle, 1996). The sports guise may open opportunities for communication and business interaction that would otherwise be closed or difficult to achieve in traditional business settings. For example, an invitation to spend 4 hours with a salesperson may sound less attractive than an invitation to spend 4 hours at a sporting event, even if the 4 hours at the sporting event involve an accompanying salesperson and presentation. Hospitality often facilitates sports talk as a mechanism to launch into business talk once the shared values have been established.

In addition, as Kolah (2001b) found, "It is often the case that the best tickets or packages to an event are only available to sponsors" (p. 23); thus, hospitality packages represent an enhanced way of providing client and supplier entertainment while tying into the sports sponsorship. Irwin and Sutton (1995) detailed 40 sport sponsorship inventory criteria (predicted by corporate sponsorship objective dimension) and listed hospitality accommodations as the first item. In addition, in their inventory matrix, hospitality accommodations were checked off under the "status enhancement" dimension (Irwin et al., 2002). Hospitality may not be worth as much in a sponsorship agreement as category exclusivity, title sponsorship, or media guarantees, but hospitality accommodations are critical to the sponsorship sale because of the tickets provided, the special restricted-access gathering areas for a sponsor's guests, the food and beverage activities, and the likelihood that celebrities (from either the participant or management side) will visit the hospitality area at some point during the day's or evening's proceedings and welcome the sponsor's guests.

Roberts (2002) has gone so far as to suggest that "corporate entertaining at sports events has become established as a must-do element of so many companies' marketing strategies [and that] the guests themselves have become increasingly sophisticated and somewhat more choosy" (p. 40) about whose hospitality function to attend. In addition, anecdotal evidence suggests that once a sports fan has been the beneficiary of corporate hospitality, he or she is likely to seek this more cherished lifestyle at the stadium but may ultimately become less and less excited by the actual hospitality. These individuals take the hospitality for granted (Roberts, 2002). Perhaps, in some ways, guests admitted to hospitality functions become, in their importance, a form of idealized target customer, much like an athlete, who participates and consumes differently from traditional fans.

Hospitality is a function of service marketing. Brooks (1994) wrote about identity theory and participation marketing. She suggested that four factors exist in influencing the decision to adopt an active lifestyle pursuit. Although her work was formulated with athletes in mind, the four dimensions (participation objectives, learning environment, accessibility, and sport exercise identity) may lend themselves to a discussion of customers who are targeted for hospitality privileges. Simon Gillespie of Sports World Travel noted,

> I am sure that attitudes have changed in the last five years or so, but corporate hospitality has become ingrained in the business cycle in terms of budget and acceptance. It is successful because people feel it has worked. However, some senior executives need things to be a little more stimulating than the standard package [to encourage them to attend an event]. They are becoming very demanding. (Roberts, 2002, p. 40)

There is also qualitative evidence to suggest elitist executives are now demanding to know who will be in a private hospitality suite and declining to attend in some cases if they feel the guests will not offer business value.

Hospitality's Internal and External Purposes

Companies use corporate hospitality for both internal and external purposes. Internal use generally focuses on providing entertainment to a company's workforce as a reward or to motivate departmental staff to increase productivity levels. For example, aiming to inspire its workforce, Coca-Cola implemented its Go for the Gold Ambassadors employee reward program at the 2008 Beijing Olympic Games. Winners included an employee who helped formulate the company's strategy for addressing health and well-being concerns about beverages; a manager who helped develop Coke Light Plus, which is a version of Diet Coke sold in some markets; and another employee who won for his work on a climate change program. Winners received five-star hotel accommodation, sight-seeing tours, and prime seating to take in the Olympic action (Wang & McKay, 2008). The same holds for North American sport championships such as the Super Bowl (National Football League [NFL]), World Series (Major League Baseball), Daytona 500 (National Association for Stock Car Auto Racing [NASCAR]), Indianapolis 500 (Indy Racing League [IRL]), the Stanley Cup (National Hockey League [NHL]), and the Finals of the National Basketball Association (NBA) and the equivalent high-profile sporting events in Australia. The dual benefit of providing an internal corporate hospitality program is that it rewards employees for their efforts with a nonregular experience funded by the company, which in turn generates increased employee loyalty as a result of appreciation for the event experience.

Corporate hospitality for external purposes is predominantly focused on *relationship marketing,* by which firms set out to entertain customers or clients to solidify and enhance business relationships. Relationship marketing is "a business strategy which proactively builds a preference for an organisation with its individual customers, channel partners, and employees, driving increased performance and sustainable business results" (cited from Newell and Roger's 2002 book, *Loyalty.com: Customer Relationship Management in the New Era of Internet Marketing*). For example, the suppliers of a firm may be "wined and dined" with the objective to purchase future raw materials at a better price, while the firm's distributors may be invited to foster better trading terms or motivate them to "push" the firm's products in the marketplace. In both cases, underlying the entertainment component of corporate hospitality is a business-related transaction (or potential future benefit to the company) that has taken place in a relaxed environment.

In both situations (internal and external audience focus), it is imperative that a process to measure costs and attainment of corporate or departmental objectives is implemented, monitored, and evaluated. Whether utilized as a stand-alone investment or as part of a sponsorship mix, corporate hospitality must deliver an appropriate return on investment (ROI) for companies to justify the expenditure vis-à-vis other marketing activities. The return from corporate hospitality may take the form of improving relationships with customers or clients, closing a business deal, courting new business, and motivating staff. Implementing some form of evaluation or measurement system for corporate hospitality (e.g., feedback surveys) has been lacking—predominantly due to its inherent relationship marketing function, which historically has facilitated nonquantifiable outcomes. However, a study jointly conducted by the American Productivity and Quality Center and the Carlson Marketing Group, titled *Improving Growth and Profits Through Relationship Marketing* (2002), has highlighted the need to increase the accountability of relationship marketing initiatives. The study concluded that companies employing comprehensive evaluation systems generate more effective relationship marketing outcomes in the future.

Functional Theory Motives in Hospitality

Kelman (1958, 1961, 1974) has proposed a functional model of attitudes that can help illuminate the area of hospitality at sporting events (Kahle, Kambara, & Rose, 1996). Kelman proposed that attitudes can serve three different functions. The most superficial function of attitudes he called *compliance*, which consists of following the obvious rewards and punishments associated with a certain situation. *Identification*, the midlevel motive, involves the referent power of groups. People want to attach themselves to admired groups. The most deeply felt motives have to do with what Kelman termed *internalization*, which encompasses the core of a person's essence.

Kahle et al. (1996) found support for Kelman's theory in the realm of attending sporting events, although their research showed that the two more superficial levels (compliance and identification) included both a public or external component and a private or internal component. These results imply that sports consumers are primarily motivated by a desire for a unique, self-expressive experience; camaraderie (a desire for group affiliation); and internalization (an overall attachment to and love of the game). Antecedents of seeking a unique, self-expressive experience include identification with winning and the desire for a self-defining experience, while antecedents of camaraderie include obligation and compliance. Although their dependent variable was attendance at a sporting event, attendance at sporting event hospitality may well have similar core psychological motivations and add greatly to the self-expressive or self-defining experience.

Each of Kelman's stages incorporates a different macrotheory of psychology (Bee & Kahle, 2006). Kelman maintained that the conditions that stimulate and allow change for attitudes, motivated by compliance, depend on the principles of behaviorism (Kahle, Beatty, & Kennedy, 1987; Skinner,

TABLE 9.1   Audience, Their Motives, and Corporate Goals in Sports Hospitality

Audience:	External (clients)			Internal (employees)		
Motives:	Compl.	ID	Internal	Compl.	ID	Internal
Goals:						
Participation						
Learning						
Accessibility						
Identity						

Note: Compl., compliance; ID, identification; Internal, internalization (following Kelman, 1958). Goals follow Brooks (1994).

1974; Watson, 1913). Neopsychoanalytic theories are relevant at the identification level (Erikson, 1968). The relevant macrotheory is humanistic psychology for internalization (Kahle, 1996; Kahle, Beatty, & Homer, 1986; Rogers, 1961).

To understand how to use hospitality effectively, we need to consider the data included in Table 9.1. How the influence attempt is carried out is influenced by the nature of the target of influence.

Targets are usually internal (employees) or external (clients or potential clients). Either target can have people with motives that emphasize compliance, identification, or internalization. Once the target and motives have been defined, the next step is to establish the behavioral goals of the hospitality event. The four topics mentioned by Brooks (1994) provide a useful list of behavioral goals: participation, learning, accessibility, and identity.

Consider the case in which the target is a client, the client's motive for participation in the hospitality event is compliance, and the company's goal is to increase learning about the company's product line. This set of circumstances would imply that the change should emphasize rewarding the client for being exposed to learning opportunities at the hospitality event by emphasizing the pleasurable elements of the experience. For example, a table displaying appetizers may be placed under a banner extolling some product virtue.

In contrast, imagine a case in which the target is an employee motivated by internalization, and the goal is to instill pride in participation in company activities. The hospitality should be structured in such a way that the information provided clarifies how the nature of a good target employee fully participates in company activities. For example, the enthusiastic participation in a successful sales campaign is equated with attending a sports hospitality opportunity.

Australian Examples of Hospitality Strategy

To acknowledge the worldwide trend of sponsorship use of hospitality, we seek to describe Australian corporate entertaining firsthand in richer detail because strategic hospitality has been sophisticated in Australia. Corporate hospitality, fueled in part by the significant growth of corporate sponsorship, has turned into a multimillion-dollar industry. The majority of corporate hospitality expenditures emphasize high-profile sporting events. Corporate entertaining has evolved from its infamous reputation of "a good excuse to get drunk with colleagues" to a business practice that needs to achieve specific sales and marketing objectives. Producing a tangible ROI is paramount given the cost of providing corporate hospitality.

The expenditures on corporate hospitality vary in accordance with the status of an event—the more elite an event, the higher the cost of the corporate hospitality provision. At the elite end are *hallmark* events that are defined as "special events, of limited duration, of significant scale, attended by large crowds whose attention is focused on a distinct theme" (Nicholls, Laskey, & Roslow, 1992, p. 215). In this category, Australian events such as the Australian Formula One Grand Prix, rugby union's Bledisloe Cup, Australian Football League's Grand Final, horse racing's Melbourne Cup, and the Australian Open tennis tournament are considered illustrative. In the United States, similar events include the Super Bowl, NCAA (National Collegiate Athletic Association) Final Four, NBA Finals, or the World Series. Australia has also been noted for staging unique once-only events such as the Sydney Olympic Games (2000), the Rugby World Cup (2003), and Commonwealth Games (2006).

The investment required to secure corporate hospitality facilities at Australia's major sporting venues and events is expensive. Accessing a chalet at the 2009 Australian Open tennis event can cost a company AU$46,000 (the gold corporate package costs AU$5,990 per eight-seat box), while obtaining access to the Pit Lane for the best view of the 2009 Australian Formula One Grand Prix at Albert Park costs AU$3,995 per head. Moreover, a company will need to outlay a minimum of AU$100,000 on an annual basis for the access rights to a box at Australia's two largest stadiums, the Melbourne Cricket Ground (MCG) and the ANZ Stadium (formerly known as Stadium Australia and Etihod Stadium), respectively. Corporate hospitality providers argue that such costs are justified given that high-profile sporting events provide an opportunity for recipients to indulge in an unforgettable experience of live sporting action from the comfort of VIP-style facilities.

The growth of corporate hospitality has certainly not gone unnoticed by venue owners and operators. The potential incremental revenue generated via a noncore sporting product component such as corporate hospitality has led to the increase of the importance of corporate seating when devising architecture for a new stadium. As a result, lavish corporate boxes and suites, with food catering from steak, halibut, meat pies, and chips to oysters and Peking duck, have been built increasingly into the menu for the corporate executives willing to pay the associated price tag to utilize the facilities for business purposes.

Stadiums in the sports-loving city of Melbourne, perpetually voted the sports capital of the world and home to the majority of Australia's hallmark events, such as the Australian Formula One Grand Prix, Melbourne Cup horse race, Australian Open tennis, the Australian Masters golf tournament, the Australian Football League grand final, the 2006 Commonwealth Games, and the 1956 Olympic Games, have long catered to corporate Australia. Since 1854 when the MCG hosted its first cricket match, corporate hospitality facilities of major stadiums have evolved with the advent of new technologies and a parallel increase in pricing structures. At the Etihod Stadium, individuals and firms could purchase one of a thousand luxury seats with a video screen for AU$5,000 each, while an investment of AU$7,000 would secure a seat in the corporate box.

The corporate hospitality component of sponsorship does not have to take place at the actual event location itself. For example, Kolah (2001a) reported that IBM hired a cruise liner containing 740 cabins equipped to entertain nearly 1,000 passengers as part of its corporate hospitality strategy to leverage its sponsorship of the Sydney 2000 Olympics.

The 4-day Melbourne Cup Carnival horse racing, which includes the internationally renowned Melbourne Cup horse race, is one of Australia's corporate hospitality showpieces. The extravagant nature of corporate entertaining that takes place at the carnival arguably renders the horse racing to peripheral importance. The objective for many is just to be invited or seen at a marquee during the 4-day carnival. Tripodi, coauthor of this chapter and former corporate executive, attended numerous Melbourne Cup Carnival marquees as both an invited guest and host. In his opinion, little business discussion occurs during the carnival as the predominant activity is one of improving and cementing relationships with existing and potential business partners by "getting pissed with them."

Corporate entertaining at the carnival originates from the Victoria Racing Club (VRC) introducing corporate hospitality packages in 1983 in which eight tents were pitched behind the main grandstand. Since 1983, the carnival has evolved into a corporate showcase in which companies compete for guests' admiration by building the most lavish and extravagant marquees. The bulk of these fully themed marquees are located in the "Birdcage" area, where media celebrities and business leaders seem more interested in wining and dining than in seeing the winning horses. According to the VRC corporate marketing manager, Brendan Ford, tents and marquees used during the 1980s were quite elaborate. However, the arrival of new corporate players in the 1990s, such as car manufacturer Saab, fashion house Louis Vuitton, and champagne maker Moet & Chandon, have taken corporate hospitality at the carnival to another level (Robinson, 2002).

As sponsors will testify, corporate entertaining at the carnival is not cheap. For example, in 2009 it cost just over AU$3,200 per head to secure a spot in the corporate suite in the Hill Stand, while marquee entertaining could cost up to AU$1,100 per head. The popularity of corporate entertainment at the Melbourne Cup Carnival is evident, and competition to secure a presence at the carnival is fierce. For a company to be able to access tent space, it must either be a member of the VRC or a horse race sponsor.

Corporate Hospitality Conflict

Generally, corporate hospitality is undertaken as a stand-alone investment or as part of a sponsorship package. The former is exemplified by a company purchasing an annual corporate box "package" at a multipurpose sporting arena for the purpose of entertaining internal and external stakeholders. The latter usage of corporate hospitality pertains to a company leveraging its official sponsorship of a particular event or sports property; however, sometimes these two reasons to use corporate hospitality conflict, especially when strategies to curb ambush marketing are implemented.

Ambush marketing occurs when a company attempts to associate with a particular sports property without purchasing the official rights to it. Thus, ambush marketers have a negative effect on brand-building efforts of official sponsors by nullifying the impact of their authorized associations (Tripodi, 2001), and at the very least, it creates confusion in the consumer's mind, which may deny the sponsor valuable recognition for its investment

(Tripodi & Sutherland, 2000). A prominent example of corporate hospitality conflict occurred at the Sydney 2000 Olympic Games. Many companies, including Qantas, Australia Post, and the Nine Network, which held rights to corporate boxes at the main arena of the Sydney 2000 Olympics, Stadium Australia (now ANZ Stadium), were told by Olympic organizers that they could not access their regular corporate facilities at the stadium because they were considered to be competitors to official Olympic sponsors. This request was reasonable given the copious amount of money that sponsors spent on securing official Olympic rights. One clever individual, the late billionaire businessman Kerry Packer, found a way around the system despite his Nine Network being refused corporate hospitality access as it was a direct competitor to official Olympic broadcaster the Seven Network. Packer still managed to enjoy the Olympic experience in the confines of a Stadium Australia corporate box, which he bought for personal, not business, purposes (Ross, 2000).

Conclusions

We have reviewed a number of significant aspects of hospitality. Sponsorship has received a great deal of attention, but the literature has not thoroughly covered the tactical marketing component known as corporate hospitality. We have described and explored this service known as corporate hospitality in a sports context. Hospitality can be directed at internal and external corporate audiences. Goals of hospitality include participation, learning, accessibility, and identity. Important motives necessary to understand for effective use of hospitality are derived from Kelman's functional approach to attitudes. Critical motives of compliance, identification, and internalization characterize hospitality consumers. Australia provides several compelling examples of hospitality strategy. Ambush marketing and other activities can create conflict surrounding hospitality.

Given the importance and expense of hospitality, it warrants increased attention both theoretically and empirically. Reasons for whether, when, and how to employ hospitality often lack sophistication commensurate with the physical resources at stake. This is notable since contemporary sponsors who are provided hospitality benefits as part of a larger package of assets now increasingly expect collaborative and proactive opportunities to enhance their business (Farrelly, Quester, & Burton, 2006). No inherent obstacle prevents intricate inquiry into the effective use of hospitality. We hope marketers everywhere will examine the purposes and effectiveness of sports and special event hospitality programs.

References

American Productivity & Quality Center. (2002). *Improving growth and profits through relationship marketing.* Houston, TX: Author.

Bee, C. C., & Kahle, L. R. (2006). Relationship marketing in sports: A functional approach. *Sport Marketing Quarterly, 15,* 101–110.

Brooks, C. (1994). *Sports marketing: Competitive business strategies for sports.* Englewood Cliffs, NJ: Prentice-Hall.

Burton, R. (1999, Dec. 19). From Hearst to Stern: The shaping of an industry over a century. *New York Times,* p. 52.

Burton, R., Quester, P., & Farrelly, F. (1998). Organizational power games. *Marketing Management, 7*(1), 26–36.

Erikson, E. H. (1968). *Identity: Youth and crisis.* New York: Norton.

Farrelly, F., Quester, P., & Burton, R. (2006). Changes in sponsorship value: Competencies and capabilities of successful sponsorship relationships. *Industrial Marketing Management, 35,* 1016–1026.

Irwin, R. L., & Sutton, W. A. (1995). Creating the ideal sponsorship arrangement. *Proceedings from the Bi-Annual AMS World Marketing Congress.* Melbourne, Australia: AMS.

Irwin, R. L., Sutton, W. A., & McCarthy, L. M. (2002). *Sport promotion and sales management.* Champaign, IL: Human Kinetics.

Kahle, L. R. (1996). Social values and consumer behavior: Research from the list of values. In C. Seligman, J. M. Olson, & M. P. Zanna (Eds.), *The psychology of values: The Ontario symposium* (Vol. 8, pp. 135–151). Mahwah, NJ: Erlbaum.

Kahle, L. R., Beatty, S. E., & Homer, P. (1986). Alternative measurement approaches to consumer values: The list of values (LOV) and values and life style (VALS). *Journal of Consumer Research, 13*(December), 405–409.

Kahle, L. R., Beatty, S. E., & Kennedy, P. (1987). Comment on classically conditioning human consumers. In P. Anderson & M. Wallendorf (Eds.), *Advances in consumer research* (14). Ann Arbor, MI: Association for Consumer Research.

Kahle, L. R., Elton, M. P., & Kambara, K. M. (1997). Sports talk and the development of marketing relationships. *Sport Marketing Quarterly, 6*(2), 35–40.

Kahle, L. R., Kambara, K. M., & Rose, G. M. (1996). A functional model of fan attendance motivations for college football. *Sport Marketing Quarterly, 5*(December), 51–60.

Kelman, H. C. (1958). Compliance, identification, and internalization: Three processes of attitude change. *Journal of Conflict Resolution, 2,* 51–60.

Kelman, H. C. (1961). Processes of opinion change. *Public Opinion Quarterly, 25,* 57–78.

Kelman, H. C. (1974). Further thoughts on the processes of compliance, identification, and internalization. In J. T. Tedeschi (Ed.), *Perspectives on social power* (pp. 125–171). Chicago: Aldine.

Kolah, A. (2001a). *How to develop an effective hospitality programme.* London: SportBusiness Group.

Kolah, A. (2001b). *How to develop an effective sponsorship programme.* London: SportBusiness Group.

Melnick, M. J. (1993). Searching for sociability in the stands: A theory of sport spectating. *Journal of Sport Management, 7,* 44–60.

Mullin, B. J., Hardy, S., & Sutton, W. A. (2000). *Sport Marketing* (2nd ed.). Champaign, IL: Human Kinetics.

Newell, F., & Rogers, M. (2002). *Loyalty.com.* New York: McGraw-Hill.

Nicholls, J. A. F., Laskey, H. A., & Roslow, S. (1992). A comparison of audiences at selected hallmark events in the United States. *International Journal of Advertising, 11,* 215–225.

Roberts, K. (2002, August). Taking hospitality for granted. *SportBusiness International,* p. 40.

Robinson, F. (2002). Camping out. In *The Sunday Age "The Field" Spring Racing Handbook 2002.*

Rogers, C. R. (1961). *On becoming a person.* Boston: Houghton Mifflin.

Ross, E. (2000). The spoils of office. *Business Review Weekly, 20*(April), 20.

Shoham, A., & Kahle, L. R. (1996). Spectators, viewers, readers: Communication and consumption communities in sport marketing. *Sport Marketing Quarterly, 5*(March), 11–19.

Skinner, B. F. (1974). *About behaviorism.* New York: Knopf.

Tripodi, J. A. (2001). Sponsorship—A confirmed weapon in the promotional armoury. *International Journal of Sports Marketing and Sponsorship, 3*(1), 95–116.

Tripodi, J. A., & Sutherland, M. (2000). Ambush marketing—An Olympic event. *The Journal of Brand Management, 7,* 412–422.

Wang, S., & McKay, B. (2008, August 20). The rewards of Olympic hospitality. *Wall Street Journal,* p. B1.

Watson, J. (1913). Psychology as a behaviorist views it. *Psychological Bulletin, 20,* 158–177.

10

Assessing the Existential Validity of the Bowl Championship Series Rankings

Thomas J. Reynolds

Introduction

The preoccupation of the *number 1-ness* in America is perhaps best evidenced in the competitive arena of athletics. Starting as preschoolers, America's youth are conditioned that there must be a champion for the athletic season to be complete. From a cultural perspective, championships are simply seen as the universal goals to which we all should strive. Winning the championship defines a successful season.

This fundamental orientation toward athletics continues to strengthen the older the child becomes. Along with the trophies, the media emphasize and reinforce this explicit assumption that, if we compete, there *must* be one crowned as champion. Over the course of time, this all-American cultural perspective simply becomes the collective, unstated basis of our latent, unquestioned belief that we must formally identify a champion for each competitive sport each year.

As the amateur competition moves to the collegiate level, we see tournament champions, conference champions, and, yes, national champions. The scores of collegiate sports complete their season with the single determination of a national champion, which is typically the result of a postseason tournament of regional or conference champions. Again, the American sports consumer psyche demands a champion, and part of the mission of competitive athletic administration is to provide the mechanism, or structure, to determine *the* champion.

In most sports, the determination of a national champion involves selecting participants and a competitive venue that, when fully played out, will yield one winner—one champion. Think about the flip side of this for a moment: Requiring that there *must* be one winner necessarily means that every other participant *must* be a nonwinner. (It might well be said that the reality of this last perspective defeats much of the true essence of sports.)

This template for postseason tournament play, directed toward crowning a single champion, functions well across any sport, individual or team, for which there can be multiple competitions played within a relatively short time period. Unfortunately, the high-profile, high-economic-value sport that does not fit this mold is major college football (National Collegiate Athletic Association [NCAA] Division I). Because of a unique combination of the extremely physical demands and the time required to rest after competition, along with the critical strategic aspect that requires the development and practice of an opponent-specific game plan, big-time college football does not lend itself easily to tournament play. Thus, we have a conundrum in declaring a national champion, which has resulted in a monopolistic economic opportunity taken advantage of by those member conferences controlling the selection of teams for the major postseason bowls, the Bowl Championship Series (BCS).

Ostensibly, the birth of the BCS was driven by the idea to provide a computational methodology for pairing the top two college football teams in a championship game at season end. The BCS formulation is comprised of a combination of expert opinion and computer algorithms that yields an overall ranking of teams that would serve to determine the two top teams as well as the other teams to play in the highly lucrative BCS-designated bowls. The very existence of the BCS is predicated on the fundamental assumption that the rankings they produce are valid; that is, they accurately represent some "true order" of the level of potential performance of each team. This true order, of course, is not known, but how valid the rankings are at any point in time can be assessed by measuring how well a given set of ranks predicts wins and losses in subsequent games. This concept of predictive or criterion validity (Cronbach, 1970, p. 122) provides an empirical framework for evaluating the existential validity of the BCS rankings by providing an estimate of its relative contribution to representing the "true order" represented by wins and losses. In particular, one such ranking method, which is significantly less complicated and more commonsensical than the current BCS formulation, serves as a benchmark level to assess the incremental predictive validity contribution provided by the BCS system. This conceptually straightforward approach to developing team rankings, termed the R methodology, is based only on a team's on-field performance factoring in the quality of the opponents they defeat.

By comparing the increase in predictive validity of the BCS system to the R methodology, we can assess the existential validity of the BCS ranking methodology, that is, whether the increase is significant enough to justify its existence.

Background

In the 1930s, the fathers of college football realized some postseason recognition was deserved, and this took the form of a few bowl games, pitting outstanding teams from different geographic areas against one another. Given the limited travel schedule of most teams until the 1960s, these bowl games permitted questions to be answered regarding which regional "championship" teams were the best. These bowl games became the centerpiece of the New Year's media programming and were greatly anticipated and universally enjoyed by all involved: players, attending fans, and television viewers alike. The results of these bowl games were then digested by experts, who produced an ordering of teams to yield a number 1 team, the national champion. And, because there were two separate polls, coaches and media, two teams on occasion could lay claim to the mythical national championship.

Over the years, bowl games continued to experience great success. As a result, the economic forces that drive the decision making of community leaders began to serve as the basis of organizing new bowl games, with the hope of sharing in the media attention (which should read as dollars) for their respective cities. Fast-forward three quarters of a century to today: We see a rise from a single-digit number of bowl games to over 30. The reality is that the economics do not support many of the bowls, resulting in some bowls in which the teams actually have to guarantee ticket sales and sponsorships to participate. In fact, simply having a record of six wins (i.e., essentially average) is all that is required to play in a postseason bowl game.

The proliferation of bowl games has significantly reduced their importance, essentially resulting in a multitude of mediocre teams playing in half-full stadiums to provide low-rated filler entertainment for the multichannel media environment. Are all bowl games really special? Maybe perhaps a dozen or so are, but certainly not anywhere near the more than 30 today. The marketing problem, then, may be defined as making the bowl scheme a more financially viable business (not to mention fairer). To address this economic issue, one must first ask: What role do bowl games offer toward producing a national champion? Should one bowl game determine the national champion? This, of course, is the current underlying assumption of the BCS. But, why then play the other bowl games, which have no direct impact on determining who ultimately will be named *the* national champion? Perhaps therein lies the answer to the marketing problem of providing additional interest to the secondary bowls while providing a framework to crown the national champion.

This unsatisfied need for crowning one definitive national champion resulted in a significant business opportunity, which was recognized by the six major football conferences (Atlantic Coast, Big East, Big 12, PAC-10, Big 10, and Southeastern Conference) as a source of additional revenue that they could receive on an ongoing basis. In 1998, these conferences organized to design the BCS system to control the selection of teams to the four major postseason bowls (Rose, Sugar, Orange, and Fiesta) under the auspices of guaranteeing that the top two teams of college football, determined by their tripartite rating system, combining expert opinion and computer rankings, would play every year in a national champion-ship game. It is important that the BCS had the self-serving proviso that each conference would have at least one team participating, thus guar-anteeing a big payday for each. In regard to the self-serving nature of the BCS conferences automatically being included in the premier bowl games, it has been posited that the reason it is not subject to Sherman antitrust litigation is the ranking "service" it provides for the public (Carroll, 2004).[1]

Currently, the BCS ranking methodology, which has been revised mul-tiple times since its inception to address perceived inequities, is calculated by averaging the ranks obtained from three sources: the Harris Interactive poll (subjective), *USA Today* poll (subjective), and a summary of the six objective computer polls (Anderson & Hester, Richard Billingsley, Colley Matrix, Kenneth Massey, Jeff Sagarin, and Peter Wolfe).

---

[1] After a threatened antitrust lawsuit in 2003 by the president of Tulane University, a non-BCS conference school, in 2004 five other second-tier conferences coincidentally were included with the original six in the BCS with specific stipulations including (a) that one of the five new mem-ber conference champions would appear annually in a BCS bowl; (b) a guaranteed payout of 9% per year would be split among the five new members, beginning with the 2006 season; and (c) a provision as to how an additional team in one of the five nonfounder conferences could qualify to participate in a BCS bowl based on their end of season ranking using the BCS ranking system. (For a complete history of the BCS, see History tab at http://www.bcsfootball.org)

R Methodology: An Unbiased, Performance-Only Benchmark

A benchmark solution to produce a ranking of teams should be conceptually simple to understand and implement and be basically a function of the performance of each team on the field, as opposed to being based on subjective rankings (which are potentially prone to several types of bias) and proprietary computational algorithms, which in combination precisely define the current tripartite BCS rating system. A conceptually simple, methodologically transparent measure based only on on-field performance, then, may be defined as a function of the number of games a team won and by what margin (50%), combined with the quality of the respective competitor the team beat (50%). There is no subjectivity to this performance-only approach to determine team rankings or any other consideration of secondary statistics or variables, such as home field advantage. This benchmark R methodology to quantify team performance may be considered a best estimate of a team's potential because this formulation does not explicitly penalize a team for the games it lost, except by virtue of the fact that there was a missed opportunity to gain wins (see Appendix for details).

Thus, a simple equation that will yield an overall quality rating R_i for each team i, developed from games against Division I-A opponents, is

$$R_i = .5W_{i(1)} + .333W_{i(2)} + .167W_{i(3)} \qquad (10.1)$$

where $W_{i(1)}$ is a summary value reflecting the percentage of team wins, including a conservative adjustment for margin of victory, which is also applied to $W_{i(2)}$ and $W_{i(3)}$ in quantifying the quality of the opponent beaten by a combination of implied victories over the direct j teams they beat (first order) and the indirect k teams j beat (second order), respectively.

Thus, there are three components used to compute the inferential quality of the performance ranking of a given football team: a weighted-by-victory-margin percentage of teams they beat $W_{(1)}$s (50%), the performance-weighted quality of the teams they defeated $W_{(2)}$s (33.3%), and the performance-weighted quality of the teams their defeated opponents beat $W_{(3)}$s (16.7%) (see Appendix for a detailed specification of the R methodology). The standardization Z of the three components of Equation 10.1 is computed to put the measures on the same scale so the weights will reflect their predetermined contribution to a summary measure that provides the basis for generating the rankings for all the teams.

$$Z_{Ri} = .5Z_{Wi(1)} + .333Z_{Wi(2)} + .167Z_{Wi(3)} \qquad\qquad (10.2)$$

Using this method, teams can then be rank ordered by their Z_{Rs}, or overall ratings, beginning after roughly the seventh or eighth week of the season when the first BCS ranking appears. (As is readily apparent from this "best estimate" team performance measure, teams that win against quality opponents score higher.)

Predictive Validity of BCS and R Method Benchmark

The existential validity of the BCS tripartite rating system can be assessed by quantifying the increase in predictive validity it provides from the benchmark statistical methodology that is only based on the strength of the wins of a team in combination with the quality of their performance against the opponents they beat. All of the data from the inception of the BCS (1998 to 2009 seasons) were used to assess the increase in validity in two ways: (a) predicting regular season game outcomes based on the top-ranked teams of the prior week (15 initially, growing to 25 teams in later years) for both the BCS and the R benchmark methodologies, respectively, and (b) using the end-of-season top-ranked teams for the BCS to select bowl games to determine the predictability of both models. The summary data for both methods of assessing predictive validity are presented in Table 10.1.

In terms of the (a) regular season predictions for all 12 years of the BCS, both models predict nearly identically, in the 76–78% range, with the R methodology in fact predicting slightly better. In terms of the bowl game predictions involving (b) the top BCS ranked teams (15 initially expanded to 25 teams in 2003), both models predict nearly identically again (57–58%), although at a somewhat lower level due to the fact that these pairs of teams are more equally matched: They all must have at least six wins to play in a postseason bowl game. Again, the R methodology predicts slightly better for Division I bowl games. And, for the major BCS bowls, the R methodology correctly predicts 59.61% of the 52 games played since the inception of the BCS, as compared to the BCS ranking predictions of 55.77%.

Clearly, this historical analysis reveals that there is no increase whatsoever in predictive validity for the BCS combination of subjective and objective rating systems over the conceptually simple, transparent benchmark alternative of the R methodology. Thus, one can make the statement that the existential validity of the BCS system, that is, the additional contribution it makes to produce a meaningful set of ranks, is zero, which

TABLE 10.1   Predictive Validity of BCS and R Method Rankings, 1998–2008

	Regular Season BCS Ranked[a] vs. R Ranked[a]				All Bowl Games BCS Ranked[a] Teams Only			Only BCS Bowl Games		
	BCS (%)	Games	R (%)	Games	BCS (%)	Games	R (%)	BCS (%)	Games	R (%)
1998	83.8	74	84.9	73	66.7	9	44.4	75	4	25
1999	80.0	55	82.1	56	70.0	10	50.0	75	4	50
2000	76.4	55	76.3	59	80.0	10	70.0	75	4	75
2001	69.7	66	75.7	70	70.0	10	70.0	50	4	50
2002	76.8	69	78.7	75	45.4	11	54.5	50	4	75
2003	77.2	101	80.0	105	60.0	15	73.3	50	4	25
2004	77.1	118	76.8	112	71.4	14	71.4	100	4	75
2005	77.1	105	76.7	111	53.3	15	60.0	50	4	100
2006	78.2	124	81.7	126	70.6	17	64.7	60	5	60
2007	73.3	116	70.6	119	46.7	15	53.3	40	5	40
2008	73.0	111	78.8	118	26.7	15	33.3	40	5	60
2009	78.3	129	78.6	131	26.7	15	33.3	20	5	80
Total 1998–2009	76.66	1123	78.18	1155	57.05	156	58.33	55.77	52	59.61

[a]Top 15 for 1998–2002 and top 25 for 2003–2009.

means that the rating system cannot be considered a procompetitive benefit justifying the existence of the BCS; therefore, it should be subject to antitrust litigation.

Suggested Research and Strategic Options

Given that the BCS rating system has no existential validity, a determination of which statistical rating system should become the standard to provide rankings should be undertaken. The R methodology predictive validity data presented here can serve as the initial benchmark for assessing the relative contribution of competing systems. Critical to this evaluation, however, is the requirement that all of these potential ranking methods be totally transparent. Many such statistical prediction methodologies have been proposed for producing optimal rank orders of this type (see West & Lamsal, 2008, for an excellent review of these alternative methods). These authors noted that one of the statistical models they reviewed predicted as many as 58.7% of bowl games (Trono, 1988) and a second as high as 76.2% of future games (Pardee, 1999), which at this point in time suggests that they are no better than the R methodology prediction data presented here. It is important that this evaluation of these competing models should not be retrodictive in nature; that is, the models should not have been developed using the same data that will be the basis of the evaluation. And it is worth noting that because the R methodology was only developed to serve as a benchmark and never optimized in any way, this approach could serve as a basis for future statistical extensions.

Three options emerge to provide an unbiased methodology to determine which team is crowned number 1. Option 1 is to institute a playoff system with either four or eight teams that would be selected at the close of the regular season. It is important that the selection of which teams to participate must be unbiased, thus the need for the development of an accepted standard methodology to produce the rankings, not just conference winners. To reinforce this point, consider the 2008 season summary ranking data presented in Table 10.2, for which the biased method of selecting BCS bowl teams is apparent. If the top 10 teams were to go to big-payday BCS bowls even with the BCS system, two schools were overlooked (Texas Tech and Boise State), resulting in a significant financial loss, especially for Boise State ($1.5 vs. more than $17 million) because it is not a member of a first-tier (one of the original six) BCS conference. The R

TABLE 10.2   2008 Final Regular Season Rankings (BCS and R Methodology) With BCS Bowl Matchups

Rank	BCS	BCS Bowl[a]	R Method
1	Oklahoma	**CHAMPIONSHIP**	Oklahoma
2	Florida	**CHAMPIONSHIP**	Florida
3	Texas[b]	**FIESTA**	Texas
4	Alabama	**SUGAR**	**Boise State**
5	USC	**ROSE**	USC
6	**Utah**	**SUGAR**	Penn State
7	Texas Tech	**Cotton (6)**	Texas Tech
8	Penn State	**ROSE**	**Utah**
9	**Boise State**	**Poinsettia (1.5)**	Alabama
10	Ohio State[b]	**FIESTA**	Ohio State
11	TCU	**Poinsettia (1.5)**	Ball State
12	**Cincinnati**	**ORANGE**	TCU
13	Oklahoma State	**Holiday (4.26)**	Pittsburgh
14	Georgia Tech	**Chick-fil-A (5.65)**	Oklahoma State
15	Georgia	**Capital One**	Missouri
16	BYU	**Las Vegas (2)**	North Carolina
17	Oregon	**Holiday (4.26)**	Georgia Tech
18	Michigan State	**Capital One (8.5)**	**Cincinnati**
19	Virginia Tech	**ORANGE**	Georgia
20	Pittsburgh	**Sun (3.8)**	Michigan State
21	Missouri	**Alamo (4.5)**	Virginia Tech
22	Ball State	**GMAC (1.5)**	Florida State
23	Northwestern	**Alamo (4.5)**	BYU
24	Boston College	**Music City (3.2)**	Mississippi
25	Mississippi	**Cotton (6)**	Nebraska

Note: Bolded teams are not from one of the original six BCS conferences.

[a]BCS bowls are in all caps (more than $17 million payout).

[b]$4.5 million payout for second team included from a BSC conference.

methodology, which is not subject to bias, in fact, has two non-BCS teams in the top 8 that should participate in a playoff system.

Of course, the primary hurdle facing this option is to accommodate the scheduling issues with respect to the existing bowl games. However, given the relatively modest prediction level for major bowl games of approximately 60%, a playoff system appears as a desirable and logical alternative.

Option 2 is potentially more interesting and may have more long-term economic potential as well as the advantage of not being as constrained by the scheduling issues required to implement a playoff system. Given the acceptance of a standard statistical framework, this methodology can be used to determine the final rankings after all the bowl games are completed. The fact is that the better teams play each other in bowl games, and the outcomes of these games are not currently factored in the national championship evaluation, which of course makes no sense. Clearly, this greatly minimizes their importance with respect to the media and fans, which serves to limit their overall financial performance. And, given that there were 34 bowl games in the 2009–2010 season, this economic reality is a major issue. The simple fact is that the amount of information provided by these games could have a significant effect on the overall evaluation of a team's record, especially if one considers how the quality of the opponents is factored at a high level (50%) into the R methodology formulation. For example, consider when all the opponents that Team A beat won their bowl games and the reverse for Team B. The quality of the indices of the opponents of Team A under the R methodology would increase greatly, thereby significantly increasing the overall rating of Team A in comparison to Team B.

It would appear that the outcomes of bowl games would and should add substantially to the determination of the "true order" of team performance. And if these bowl games become an integral part of the selection of a national champion, would not they become better attended and viewed by a much wider audience, especially for those fans for whom the outcome has an effect on the ultimate success of their team?

Herein lies a critical marketing-related insight resulting from this option. By increasing the interest in all bowl games because they directly factor in the final determination of which team is crowned the national champion, the entire bowl system would benefit economically. In fact, using the R methodology as a basis, after the regular season is completed as many as six teams in a recent season have had a statistical chance to win the national championship depending on the combination of bowl outcomes. (Note: With the six possible outcomes of the R methodology for a given game, 34 bowl games have 6^{34} combinations, which is 2.865117999807 $\times$ 10^{26}.) With the bowl games scheduled for the 2008 season, for example, the University of Texas team (ranked third), for example, could in fact conceivably be number 1 using the R methodology based on the several scenarios of possible bowl outcomes. Thus, using this information to determine the remaining scenarios in which one's favorite team could conceivably become the national champion would draw increased attention and involvement to the entire series of postseason bowls. To further this objective, the Internet could be used to provide the computational mechanism for determining the scenarios to accomplish the highest possible ranking for a given team at any given point in the bowl process. This presents the possibility of creating marketing programs to develop "what-if scenarios" that could literally be updated after each bowl game.

Accepting the idea that the bowl games should be included in the crowning of a national champion because of the increased importance of the minor bowls leads to Option 3, which is a hybrid of the first two options. This option involves first using the bowls as a statistical playoff system, then matching the top two teams as determined statistically at the completion of the traditional bowl system. Option 3, then, permits multiple teams at the end of the regular season to have a chance to become number 1 depending on the bowl outcomes, essentially giving a majority of bowl games a much higher level of interest due to their effect on determining the rating of a given team; it has the additional advantage of a head-to-head matchup with the top two to determine the national champion.

Whichever of the three options is implemented, it is clear that the revenue obtained from the chosen method should not be allocated in the biased manner it has been in the past and currently continues to be.[2]

Synopsis

The existential validity of the BCS method of determining team rankings was assessed using as a benchmark a transparent statistical ranking

---

[2] For example, the guaranteed payouts for the 2008–2009 season allocated to a conference if it was one the original six (one share each, $17+ million) and to the five second-tier conferences (one share in total), and to Notre Dame ($1.3 million), even if it does not play in a BCS bowl, and to two other independents, Navy and Army ($100,000 each), if they are simply available to play, leave only one school of the 120 in Division I-A, independent Western Kentucky, not part of the BCS payroll. The differential rates of these guaranteed payouts suggest an unfair competitive environment, which can be remedied by a simple performance-only-based system reflected by all of the three unbiased options presented.

methodology using only measures of the quality of wins with regard to the quality of opponents beaten. The BCS ranking methodology was determined over the 12-year term of its existence to provide no increase in terms of predictive validity over the conceptually simple benchmark R methodology and thus has no reason for existence. Thus, the assumption that the procompetitive benefit of the ranking system the BCS provides has merit, which has been noted as the reason the BCS should be exempted from the Sherman Act (Carroll, 2004), is false.

Potential future nonbiased options for determining how a national champion could be determined were presented. These were as follows: a playoff plan using an unbiased statistical model for team selection, a statistically derived ordering of teams producing a national champion after *all* the bowl games are played, and a hybrid approach that combines the two by computing the top two teams to play in a championship game after all the bowl game results are considered using an unbiased statistical analysis format like the R methodology.

Marketing Implications of Using the Transparent R Methodology

There are several outcomes and opportunities in using the R formula to compute team rankings. First, and perhaps most important, the R methodology can be easily updated after each bowl game in the public domain to provide the new rankings. Consequently, the importance of the non-BCS bowl games and perhaps some of the BCS games also will increase with the fans and viewers, translating into increased media attention (read this as revenue).

Second, the possibility of playing what-if games, by using this information to determine the remaining scenarios in which one's favorite team could conceivably become the national champion, will draw increased attention and involvement to the entire series of postseason bowls. To further this interest, the Internet could be used to provide the mechanism for determining the scenarios to accomplish the highest possible ranking for a given team at any given point in the bowl process. This presents the possibility of creating marketing programs and contests using this framework.

Third, recall that in utilizing the R formulation the championship title is determined by the results of all bowl games. Therefore, the possibility exists for multiple teams to be named national champion, and there is now the option to select BCS matchups that will maximize the number of potential champions, thereby further increasing fan interest in all bowl games.

Fourth, from a public policy perspective, the monopolistic nature of the team selection for the most lucrative bowls can be eradicated by using such a transparent, nonproprietary methodology. Of course, due to the increased involvement with the non-BCS bowls, increases in media revenue should result in the financial viability of many of these other bowls, including corresponding increases of the size of the financial rewards for other smaller conferences.

Acknowledgment

I would like to thank Rick McMullen for his many analytical contributions.

References

Carroll, M. T. (2004, Summer). No penalty on the play: Why the Bowl Championship Series stays in-bounds of the Sherman Act. *Washington and Lee Law Review.*

Cronbach, L. J. (1970). *Essentials of psychological testing.* New York: Harper & Row.

Pardee, M. (1999). *An artificial neural network approach to college football prediction and ranking.* Technical paper. Madison, WI: University of Wisconsin, Electrical and Computer Engineering Department.

Stern, H. S. (2006). In favor of a quantitative boycott of the Bowl Championship Series. *Journal of Quantitative Analysis in Sports, 2*(1), Article 4.

Trono, J. A. (1988). A deterministic prediction model for the American game of football. *ACM SIGSIM Simulation Digest, 19,* 26–53.

West, B. T., & Lamsal, M. L. (2008). A new application of linear modeling in the prediction of college football outcomes and the development of team ratings. *Journal of Quantitative Analysis in Sports, 4*(3), Article 3.

Appendix: R Methodology Computation

The first computational step to develop a measure of team performance is to construct a square matrix W that contains the outcomes for all of the Division I-A teams at a given point in time. The row designations of $W(i)$ define the winning team, and the column j indicates the loser. The row (win)/column (loss) entries in W reflect both the quantity and quality of wins against Division I-A opponents. In this framework, quality, or magnitude of a win, simply refers to three possible margins of victory that are meaningful: 1–8 points = $\sqrt{1}$, 9–16 points = $\sqrt{2}$, and 17 or more points = $\sqrt{3}$. Interestingly, the inclusion of a margin-of-victory statistic is not permitted in the BCS computer algorithms and has led to statisticians calling for a "quantitative boycott of the BCS" (Stern, 2006). However, the reason for the square root adjustment is simply to recognize that a win by more than 8 or 16 points is marginally better than the importance of gaining the win, resulting in possible scores of 1.000, 1.414, and 1.732, respectively. There is no predictive estimate of point spreads with the R methodology, which appears as the primary concern motivating the decision of the BCS to forbid such a commonsense statistic. Thus, a team's first-order performance score is the sum of the square roots of the number of points gained from Division I-A opponents divided by the total number of Division I-A games played—the total number of nonzero entries is the row and column for that team. (Note that non-Division I-A games have no impact on the overall quantity score.)

By using the total number of I-A games as the denominator, a loss, or a failure to gain points, is factored in to the calculation. Thus, the direct measure for the performance $W_{(1)}$ of a given team i can be considered the square root of the average number of "quality" points gained per opportunity. The direct win component may be summarized as

$$W_{i(1)} = \frac{\sum\left(\sqrt{W_{ij}}\right)}{n(W_i)}$$
(10.A1)

where W_{ij} corresponds to the margin of victory (1, 2, or 3) for team i over team j, and $n(W_i)$ equals the number of Division I-A games team i played.

The second step in the computation involves developing a summary measure that reflects the "quality of opponents," which refers to the strength of the competition that the team has beaten. This can be computed by determining the respective margin of victory for each W_{ij} (reflecting each opponent j beaten by i) and then multiplying it by the respective margin of victory rescaled (square root) for the first-order wins. This win component $W_{(2)}$, which denotes the quality of the wins, may be summarized as

$$W_{i(2)} = \frac{\left(\sum\left(\sum \sqrt{W_{ij}} \sqrt{W_j}\right)\right)}{n(W_i)} \qquad (10.\text{A}2)$$

where W_j reflects all the first-order teams that W_i beat, and $n(W_i)$ is the total number of Division I-A games that team i played, then yields an average of competition quality.

This logic can be extended to the second order of implied wins, again taking into account the respective margin of victory from each implied win, as

$$W_{i(3)} = \frac{\left(\sum\left(\sum \sqrt{W_{jk}} \sqrt{W_k}\right)\right)}{n(W_j)} \qquad (10.\text{A}3)$$

where W_{jk} is the (adjusted) margin of victory of team j over team k, which is multiplied by each (adjusted) margin of victory for W_k wins, and $n(W_j)$ is the total number of Division I-A games team j played.

11

Service Quality Perceived by Fans at Professional Sporting Events

Florian Riedmueller

Success Indicators at Professional Sporting Events

In today's society, sport has become an omnipresent mass phenomenon: More than 27 million people are members of the approximately 87,000 sports clubs in Germany, and more than 5 million Germans work out in approximately 6,000 fitness centers. The most spectacular segment within the sports market, which at the same time has the most public attention, is certainly top sporting events. Thousands of fans undertake extensive trips to see and support their favorite athletes during competitions. Televised sports reporting reaches blockbuster levels, earning the broadcasting stations record advertising profits. The Olympic flame is followed not only by current top athletes but also by the media and business enterprises from all over the world (Hermanns & Riedmueller, 2008). The high popularity that sporting events enjoy with the spectators, the media, and the advertising industry is quite impressively shown by the following statistical data:

- Of Germany's overall population, 45% over 14 at least occasionally visit sporting events (TDWI, 2008).[1]
- TV broadcasts of sporting events are watched at least occasionally by 76% of Germans (TDWI, 2008).
- International sporting events, such as the Olympic Games or world championships, earn record profits from the advertising industry despite the current economic crisis.

---

[1] TDWI is an online database, which enables users to analyze sociodemographic data for Germany with representative values (12,000 cases).

In the competition between the various different promoters of professional sporting events, a banal distinction is made between successful and less-successful events. To be able to determine whether an event has been successful, it is essential to determine criteria that can be used to measure the success of the event. These criteria to quantify success are referred to in this chapter as *success indicators.*

In business management terms, success normally refers to the business result that is measured by or reflected in monetary units. Besides such economic success indicators, an important role is also assumed by noneconomic success indicators. These are measuring units on which the economic indicators are based but that cannot be so easily quantified. Krueger (1998) illustrated this by comparing the profit of a company with the "tip of the iceberg," while the ensuing profits would be the "underwater part" of the profits. At professional sporting events, the performance of the athletes constitutes an exceptional case of noneconomic success indicators. While classic noneconomic success indicators, such as customer commitment or turnout, are a reaction of the audience to the offered event, the performance of the athletes is the central part of the event.

Economic success indicators (financial indicators), spectator-oriented success indicators (customer commitment, turnout, etc.), and performance of the athletes (speed, number of goals) are closely related in professional sporting events. The higher the performance of the athletes of the event is, the higher in general the turnout and the number of regular visitors will be. High utilization of the capacities of the event in conjunction with the positive side effects of customer commitment result in a positive financial result for the event. A high profit in turn enables promoters to contract highly competitive athletes, thus increasing the level of athletic performance (Brandmaier & Schimany, 1998). This correlation can also be called the *helix of success* (Figure 11.1).

The complementary relation of the various success indicators at sporting events helps to explain why athletic and economic success of such an event do not stand in contradiction with each other. Normally, significant athletic competitions in attractive sports are tantamount with high prizes, extensive media coverage, and high public attention, so that the athletic achievements pay off financially as well.

Success Factors at Professional Sporting Events

The influences on athletic performance, number of spectators, and economic success at professional sporting events are diverse and cannot be

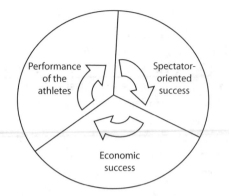

Figure 11.1   The helix of success at professional sporting events.

easily generalized. General market environment factors, such as the economic development, the status of sports in society, and the weather on the day of the event can have an influence on the performance of the athletes and on public demand. Specific features of the trade (e.g., the popularity of the type of sport with active athletes and spectators) may also be of high importance. A couple of years ago, for instance, the German Tennis Association had to realize that their sport, just like all other products and services, is subject to a classic life cycle: The impressive boom of the 1980s, revolving around tennis idols of the likes of Boris Becker and Steffi Graf, has been contrasted in recent years by a continuous drop in active tennis players, spectators, and sponsors (Riedmueller, 2003). Also, event-specific variables might have a great influence on the success of professional sporting events. "Some ... organizations sell out stadia every week and have long waiting lists of loyal fans who want to purchase season tickets, whereas others have difficulty selling out one game" (Gray, 2001, p. 310). In the German National Soccer League season 2008–2009, for instance, Borussia Dortmund could welcome an average 72,900 spectators to their 17 home matches, while Arminia Bielefeld only reached an average of 22,400 spectators. The great difference in numbers of spectators between the individual clubs of the German Football League shows that the formally identical service "organizing home matches in the German Football League" is offered by the organizing German clubs with varying success. In this case, the athletic competitiveness of the home team, the equipment of the stadium, and the supporting program of the football match are potential influences on individual success.

Despite the variety of influences on professional sporting events, there are some central variables to which success or failure can be traced. It is the aim of the research into the success factors to derive such key factors (success factors) that have a substantial impact on the success or failure of the business activities. A number of qualitative and quantitative studies have looked into the dimensioning of factors influencing the number of spectators of professional sporting events. The success indicators most generally applied are the customer-oriented indicators of the absolute number of spectators and their relation to the capacity of the venue. The authors of meta-analyses covering all types of sports have classified the factors leading to the success of such an event into the following categories:

- Economic factors (e.g., income, ticket price, etc.)
- Sociodemographic factors (e.g., number and composition of spectators at the venue, etc.)
- Quality-related factors (e.g., performance of players or teams, comfort of the seats)
- Residual factors (e.g., weather, time of match, etc.)

(see, e.g., Heinemann, 1999, or Lucerna, 1997). In the center of this heterogeneous variety of influencing factors, one factor has to be emphasized that in many studies has been explicitly or implicitly mentioned: the quality, or rather service quality, of a professional sporting event (Table 11.1).

TABLE 11.1 Studies of Factors of Success With an Explicit or Implicit Reference to Service Quality

Authors	Studied Subject	Reference to Connection Service Quality Success
Hansen and Gauthier, 1989	Home matches in U.S. leagues	Explicit: Quality of home team as dominating factor for success
Robertson and Pope, 1999	Home matches in football and rugby	Explicit: Atmosphere in the stadium, cleanliness, and suspense as most important factors for success
Voeth, Klein, and Lier, 2001	Football matches	Implicit: Safety in the stadium and participation of popular teams as factors for success numbers 1 and 3
Siegfried and Eisenberg, 1989	Home matches in baseball	Explicit: Quality of the home team as one of the most important factors for success
Cismar, 2001	Home matches of FC Bayern München	Explicit: Quality of the guest team as one of three important factors for success

Service Quality as Dominating Success Factor at Professional Sporting Events

The success-enhancing character of high service quality at professional sporting events first shows its positive effects on spectator-oriented key data, especially in the repeatedly mentioned number of spectators. If the quality of the event is rated positively, the spectators will visit the event more frequently, which is why the promoter can also profit from the positive effects of customer commitment. Furthermore, top-quality sporting events, such as the Olympic Games or world championships, are outstandingly prestigious and can attract spectators to visit the event who live outside the regional catchment area. A high service quality can also help to mobilize cross-selling potentials, which in themselves are an important indicator for customer penetration: Not only do satisfied customers buy again, but they also expand their purchases to other offers of the supplier. In a study covering several clubs of professional German sports leagues, it was found, for instance, that on a repeat visit spectators made more use of catering or other entertainment services than on their first visit (Hermanns & Riedmueller, 2008).

The connection between service quality and economic key data must be viewed in a differentiated manner. On the one hand, the positive effects on the spectator-oriented key data as a result of the helix of success at professional sporting events lead to a quantitative rise in income and thus turnover. With reference to the financial profitability of an event, high quality leads to lower costs for communication. Professional sporting events featuring an attractive field of athletes are broadcast extensively in the sports media, thus reaching a wide range almost free of charge. At the same time, higher prices can be charged for top-ranking professional sporting events. The uniqueness of such an event protects it from competition, and the price sensitivity of the demander is correspondingly lower. On the black market, tickets for the finals of the Soccer World Championship 2006 in Germany generally cost five times the official ticket prices of between EUR 120 and 600, thus showing how insensitive spectators can be to prices when extraordinary sporting events are involved.

Despite the positive effect of low communication costs and higher attainable prices, we should not overlook the fact that quality is primarily the result of high-cost input factors. In an empirical study on the cost distribution in the National German Soccer League, it was found, for instance, that 60% of the total salaries are paid to 20% of the assumed best players (Lehmann & Weigand, 1999). This distribution has also been

confirmed by empirical studies among the best tennis or basketball players, thereby deviating from salary structures typical for most other industries. In the sports universe, also, top quality costs top prices, which again
has a negative cost effect for the promoters.

The influence of high service quality on athletic success can be mainly
attributed to the indirect effect of the helix of success as described. In
addition, a high service quality can also influence the performance of the
athletes via the atmosphere at the venue. Many successful athletes have
pointed out in interviews that the spectators contributed largely to their
success by cheering for them.

Service Quality at Professional Sporting Events

After outlining the important role of quality for the success of a professional sporting event, it is now to be clarified what lies beneath this theoretical construct. Even though some of the quality parameters have been
mentioned (e.g., athletes, environment of the venue, etc.), a detailed reflection on and structuring of this multidimensional phenomenon is still
to be rendered. The etymological roots of the word are the Latin *qualis*,
which can be translated as "as it is." In everyday linguistic use, quality is
tantamount with good quality or high value of a product or service.

Definition of Service Quality

The standardization organizations ISO (International Organization for
Standardization) and DIN (Deutsches Institut für Normung e.V.) view
quality with their definitions from a service- and customer-related perspective. According to the performance-based quality term, quality is
the sum or level of present characteristics. This theory puts its emphasis
on objective performance parameters that can hardly be observed in the
case of services, to which type professional sporting events doubtlessly
belong from a goods-typological point of view. The quality term from the
customer's point of view, however, is centered on how quality characteristics are perceived by the demander: Those services that best satisfy the
individual requirements of the customers have the highest quality (Bruhn,
2008). The customer-focused quality term typical for marketing has thus
become the only permissible perspective as regards professional sporting events. Neither promoters or coordinators of an event nor neutral

test organizations can act as referee for the actual quality level. Quality is determined by the individual classifications of the spectators alone.

The more complex the offered range of services, and the higher the number of quality characteristics with which the customer is confronted in its wake, the more unlikely it will be that all features are perceived and evaluated by the customer individually. Based on the wide differentiation of quality perception, for instance, a spectator buying a sandwich at a professional sporting event would perceive the quality characteristics "sausage," "bread roll," "mustard," "salesperson," and so on independently from each other. The customer would then compile these characteristics and the quality characteristics of all other individual services to form an overall picture of the event. It is obvious that such a differentiated perception only takes place when relatively simple purchasing decisions are involved and does not apply to services, especially complex services (Benkenstein, 1993).

When quality is perceived at professional sporting events or other complex services, the customer's quality perception is more likely to be based on a narrow differentiation: When several quality characteristics are perceived at the same time and the perceptions made are associated with each other, it can be assumed that the perception of a number of quality characteristics by the customer will be bundled to form so-called quality dimensions on a higher aggregation level. A *quality dimension* is defined as the simultaneous perception of various different quality characteristics by target groups within and outside the company (Bruhn, 2008).

Basic Models to Illustrate Service Quality

Many of the first models to illustrate service quality were based on approaches that had been developed for the product industry (Gummesson, 1991). These models mainly focus on the technical output of the production process. Based on such a product-oriented approach, the quality dimensions of the U.S. telecommunication company Ameritech Corporation, for example, were divided into wire condition, speech reproduction quality, and invoicing system accuracy (Johnson, Tsiros, & Lancioni, 1995). Such a division into technically measurable dimensions that the customer, however, can hardly evaluate contradicts the customer-oriented quality approach. The following therefore concentrates on quality models that reflect the multidimensional character of service quality from a customer perspective.

Donabedian's (1980) model to illustrate different service quality dimensions was based on the approach developed by the author as early as 1966 to describe the quality of medical services. In *The Definition of Quality and Approaches to Its Assessments*, Donabedian introduced a differentiation of service quality into the structural and process- and result-oriented quality dimensions, which seems also to be applicable to other sectors. The dimensions are arranged according to the different levels of customer integration into the service creation process. This quality model shows that service quality is influenced not only by the result of the service rendered but also by the service creation process itself and the underlying structural potentials. Each of the three quality dimensions is perceived by the customer and evaluated with reference to the expected performance level. In a tennis tournament, for instance, the spectator forms an opinion on the quality of the players (structural quality), the quality of the match (process-oriented quality), and on the—in his or her opinion—"fair" result of the tournament (result-oriented quality). The judgments of these three quality dimensions form an impression of the overall quality. Since it can be assumed that there is a general linear connection between the individual dimensions, the separate analysis of the different dimensions has only limited meaningfulness (Woodruff, 1997).

Grönroos's (1984) quality model centers on the idea that the evaluation of quality by the service customer is based on a comparison of the customer's preservice expectations with the service quality perceived during rendering of the service. According to Grönroos, the basis for consolidation between expectations and perceptions are three dimensions: the technical quality of a service, the functional quality of a service, and the image of the individual supplier of the service. The dimension of the technical quality answers the question regarding "what" the consumer receives as part of the service creation process. This technical quality can be measured fairly objectively, such as by the number of stars of a hotel or restaurant or the classification of sports leagues (first, second, and third league). The manner in which the service is rendered is also important for the customer: "A bank may manage the affairs of a customer perfectly in a technical sense ... but if the customer is dissatisfied with the performance of the manager ... , he will probably feel unhappy with the service he gets from the bank" (Grönroos, p. 38). The question regarding "how" the service is rendered within the integration process is called *functional quality*. In addition to the technical and functional qualities, Grönroos's approach identifies the image of the company as a further quality dimension. The customer has expectations not only toward the quality of the service but also toward the image of the supplier of the service. For many spectators of the Grand Slam Tennis Tournament in

Wimbledon, for instance, it is not only the participating players and the supporting program that are important. It is rather important for them to attend the most well-known tennis tournament with the longest tradition. Unlike other tournaments, Wimbledon may also be able to afford to do without injured players since their missing "technical quality" can be compensated by the image of the tournament.

Other important quality models are the approaches of Berry (1986) and Brandt (1987), which are not identical but feature the same division into quality dimensions as the central idea. Berry divided service quality into "routine" and "nonroutine," whereas Brandt distinguished between "minimum requirements" and "value-enhancing" elements. According to Berry, routine quality covers all aspects of a service, which according to the demander are part and parcel of the normal scope of services, the "quality level at which the regular service is delivered" (Berry, 1986, p. 7). As far as professional sporting events are concerned, this would include elements that, according to the spectators, are more or less the same at all events, such as signposts to the venue, number of seats or standing tickets, and catering (drinks, food). The importance of this "standard" quality dimension was looked at in detail by Brandt. If the perceived quality of the various features of the routine dimension fails to meet the expected quality, this negative deviation is evaluated with penalty points ("demerits") in the quality judgment. Unlike the routine dimension, the nonroutine dimension refers to all additions above and beyond the standard scope of services. Here, Berry mainly specified services delivered by the supplier based on individual and extraordinary requests of the demander. If the supplier of the service manages to add exceptional components to the scope of services exceeding the ordinary standard of the trade, the supplier can thereby earn bonus points.

Much attention has also been paid to the quality model jointly developed by Parasuraman, Zeithaml, and Berry (1988), called SERVQUAL. The term *SERVQUAL* is an abbreviation for service quality. In a study, various influencing factors were reduced by a multistage alignment process of correction and ensuing factor analysis to five basic quality dimensions with 22 according items, which are applicable to all sectors of service.

- The quality of the *tangibles* is to be seen as the complete physical environment of a service covering, for instance, the physical appearance of the venue and the personnel.
- *Reliability* is the ability of the service provider to render the promised service reliably and accurately.

- *Responsiveness* answers the question about whether specific customer requests can be fulfilled. This includes the willingness to quickly assist the customer and the promptness of the actual reaction.
- *Assurance* is the ability of the service provider to render the service by means of the knowledge, courtesy, and trustworthiness of the provider's employees.
- *Empathy* is the willingness and ability of the service provider to respond to individual customer requests or specific situations (Parasuraman et al., 1988).

The more the anticipated quality and the perceived quality of these dimensions match from the customer's point of view, the higher the overall quality of the service is evaluated.

Critical Analysis of the Models Regarding the Measurement of Quality at Professional Sporting Events

A comparison of the quality models has shown that some models have a similar approach but vary from each other in the concrete dimensioning. The model of Donabedian (1980), for instance, is based on the course of events of rendering a service. The models of Grönroos (1984), Berry (1986), Brandt (1987), and Parasuraman et al. (1988) disregard the aspect of time when evaluating service quality. In the dimensions of these models, several performance characteristics reflecting the overall perception of the consumer are bundled, which is why they can also be called character-oriented quality models. The dimensions of character-oriented models are valid regardless of the creation process of the service and explicitly do not refer to a certain process phase.

Even if the quality of each service can theoretically be illustrated with any of the described models, they are not equally appropriate for the reflection of quality of a specific service. Resulting from the heterogeneous character of the service sector, there are a number of trade- and type-related performance specifics, so that depending on the type of service, a certain model can best illustrate the dimensions of perception and evaluation of quality from the customer's point of view.

Within the heterogeneous scope of services, professional sporting events can be allocated to the service type of adapted individual services with complete customer integration and high result insecurity. This allocation is the basis for deriving special marketing aspects for sporting events, as are the event-specific characteristics and the athletic content. From a marketing

TABLE 11.2   Evaluation of Approaches of Different Quality Models With a View to Incorporation of Special Features of Professional Sporting Events

	Donabedian, 1980	Grönroos, 1984	Berry, 1986, and Brandt, 1987	Parasuraman, Zeithaml, and Berry, 1988
Complexity	+	+	O	O
Course of phases	O	–	–	–
Individual entertainment value	–	–	O	+

Note: +, request fulfilled; O, request partially fulfilled; –, request not fulfilled.

point of view, the most important characteristics of a professional sporting event are its complexity, the phases of the event, and the individual entertainment value (Riedmueller, 2003). All three characteristics have a substantial influence on the perception and demand of sporting events by the spectators and the resulting paradigms of action for the suppliers.

The three characteristic-oriented quality models described have far more problems illustrating the quality of a professional sporting event from the spectators' point of view than a process-oriented model (Table 11.2). Because of their static nature, these quality models are not capable of recording the course of the sporting events in several phases and to illustrate the complex quality components within the dynamic subprocesses. The process-oriented quality model of Donabedian (1980) with its relatively simple structure is also incapable of illustrating the quality of a professional sporting event sufficiently. It only offers a very rough recording frame, which only insufficiently reflects the variety of the simultaneous processes of such an event and the corresponding quality perception by the spectators.

It is therefore logical to develop a performance-specific quality model that also incorporates the special requirements of the complexity, the course of events, and the individual entertainment values at professional sporting events. The quality models described are not disregarded in this process but are used as a theoretical framework to structure the quality dimensions and characteristics of a sporting event from the spectators' point of view.

The PROSPORT Model as an Approach to Illustrate Service Quality

PROSPORT is short for professional sporting event and symbolizes the level of knowledge that is to be specified by this term. The PROSPORT quality model tries to illustrate quality at a professional sporting event. According to the tradition of marketing and therefore customer-oriented quality models, the PROSPORT model focuses on quality as perceived by the spectators in the stadium. It is not unintentional that the chosen short-form PROSPORT also gives rise to associations with "professionally organized sports" as contrasted to the widespread ad hoc approach of many promoters on the sports market. By understanding the perception and evaluation of a sporting event from the spectators' point of view, the promoters of professional sporting events can better focus their concept of the event to customers' requirements, which should always be in the center of all planning from the marketing point of view.

Based on the model of Donabedian (1980), the first idea would be to differentiate quality into potential, process, and result quality to reflect the spectators' point of view. The spectators would, according to this differentiation, evaluate the quality of a professional sporting event prior to, during, and after their integration in the course of the events. This distinction, however, misleads us to believe that spectators evaluate potential quality only prior to their visit, process quality only during their visit, and result quality only after their visit to a professional sporting event. Since professional sporting events usually are a service with a fixed venue, the spectators have to integrate into the service process prior to the start of the real event to obtain their tickets and get to the venue. During the sporting event, the spectators are not integrated in a single service creation process but perceive several aspects of the service as a result of bundled individual services at the event, for which they might sometimes decide at the event itself based on the potential factors perceivable there. After the event, the way home has to be organized, so process quality influences the service evaluation even here (Stauss & Seidel, 1997). Based on the overlap described, it is clear that at the first level the quality dimensions of a professional sporting event should not be differentiated according to process phases of integration but according to the phases of the event from the spectators' point of view. For long-term services, it can be assumed that the quality dimensions orient themselves by the sequences of interaction as perceived by the spectator.

By means of a blueprint that is well known from general event marketing, the main phases of such an event are the preevent phase (the time prior to the event), the force event phase (the period during the event), and the postevent phase (the period following the event) (Wochnowski, 1996). In a phase-oriented approach, a professional sporting event can thus be distinguished into four quality dimensions, within which the spectators compare the anticipated with the perceived quality characteristics. In the preevent phase, the quality evaluation sets in with the spectator's decision to want to visit a certain sporting event and ends with the spectator entering the venue. It can be assumed that the spectator, who travels to the venue with high expectations, already takes in the impressions of this phase with high intensity. The quality evaluation of the force event phase by the customer starts with the customer entering the venue and lasts until the spectator leaves the site. The nonaction subphase covers all impressions of the spectators when they are not directly busy watching the athletic events. During these times, the spectators mainly perceive the entertainment program and supporting acts of the sporting event. In the action subphase, however, they concentrate on the athletic events of the competition. Depending on the rules of the sports in question and the program schedule of the promoters, the impressions of the spectators from the action and nonaction subphases alternate more or less frequently and extensively.

Even after leaving the venue, which marks the start of the postevent phase, the spectators still gather impressions on the quality of the event. Directly after the event, the spectators first evaluate the return trip home from the venue. Also, many professional sporting events are edited after the "final whistle" by a variety of media, thus offering the spectators of a sporting event the possibility to pass the events in review by consuming newspaper, news magazine, or TV reports. The overall quality from the spectator's point of view is composed of an evaluation of quality impressions from all four phases described for a professional sporting event.

The phase-oriented subdivision of the quality dimensions of the PROSPORT model (Figure 11.2) into preevent, force event action, force event nonaction, and postevent phase is empirically supported by the

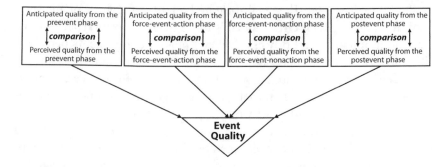

Figure 11.2   Dimensions of event quality in the PROSPORT model.

result of a study on a cultural event: During the 2½-day Main Street Festival in Fort Worth, Texas, Childress and Crompton (1997) conducted an exploratory quality measuring survey in which they questioned 822 of the approximately 50,000 visitors to the festival on their expectations and perceptions of various different aspects of the festival. Based on the 20 inquired quality characteristics, they conducted a factor analysis to clarify the joint evaluation of individual variables. The ideal solution was four quality dimensions summarizing 18 of 20 quality characteristics: information on the event schedule, quality of the event environment, quality of the supporting acts, and quality of the individual festival attractions.

To illustrate the evaluation process of the services from the spectators' point of view within each subphase, the PROSPORT model then differentiates the services classically into potential, process-oriented, and result-oriented quality (Figure 11.3). The potential quality within the phase of an event is determined by all persons and objects with whom and which the spectators are in contact during the service creation process. During the force-event-action phase of a professional sporting event, potential quality-determining factors are, for instance, the type of seats in the stadium or the participating athletes. The evaluation of all processes, however, is allocated to the process quality of the individual phase. The spectators evaluate different service processes according to their individual comparison of expected and perceived quality. Examples for quality-relevant service processes for the force-event-action phase would be the suspense of a competition or the atmosphere in the stadium: "Yet the games and sport itself have become inseparable from their atmosphere" (Rinehart, 1998, p. 7). Since visiting a professional sporting event is a linear experience for the spectators, with no immediate changes of the recipient of the service observed after termination of the event, the result-oriented quality can be neglected as an individual quality component in the various phases of the PROSPORT model. The result-oriented quality of a phase of an event, according to the PROSPORT model, is more likely a summarizing evaluation of all potential and process-oriented quality components perceived within this phase by the spectator. The more positive the judgment on correspondence between the anticipated and the perceived service potentials and processes of a phase of an event, the more positive will be the evaluation of the result-oriented quality of this phase of the event.

However, professional sporting events are not visited by "standard spectators" with identical expectations but by extremely different groups of spectators, each focusing their expectations on different aspects of the event. Supporters of a certain football team, for instance, will put more

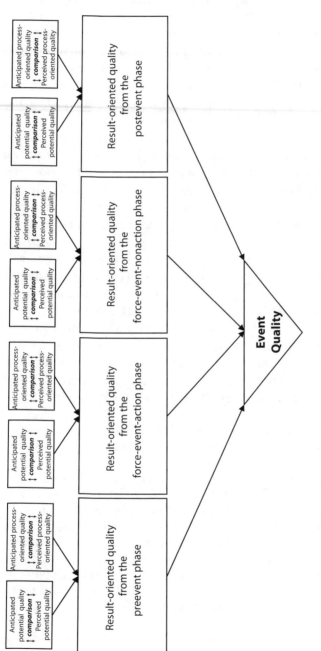

Figure 11.3 Integration of the differentiated view on potential, process-oriented, and result-oriented quality within the event phases into the PROSPORT model.

emphasis on the proximity to their team and the atmosphere in the supporter's block, whereas the neutral visiting family will mainly expect a balanced entertainment program and safety in the stadium. A quality model failing to incorporate these different expectations of the various groups of spectators into its structure will at best be a compromise: Although it can show the quality evaluations of all spectators of a professional sporting event as an average value, it cannot provide a detailed explanation on how this quality judgment has been determined.

The motivation to visit a professional sporting event comes from subjectively evaluated target means relations. The visit to an event is seen by the spectators as an appropriate means of realizing the motivation target "pleasant feelings" or "having fun" (Kroeber-Riel & Weinberg, 1999). Based on this at first sight relatively unspecific but easily understandable motivation target, many studies of the entertainment industry fail to look closely into the spectators' motivations. However, if we compare the different composition of spectators at different sporting events with each other (e.g., the spectators of an ice skating event and of a boxing event), it becomes clear that the motivation of having fun as a one-dimensional explanation for the visit to professional sporting events cannot be maintained, and that a more differentiated approach is needed. To summarize and structure the various different motivations for visiting a professional sporting event, it is helpful to revert to a categorization of motivations known from communication science into cognitive, affective, integrative, and interactive driving forces (Drabczynski, 1982):

- Pieces of information, new impressions, and uncertainty regarding the result refer to the knowledge of the processes and the result of an entertainment offer and can be summarized as cognitive motivations.
- Aesthetic experience, relaxation, distraction, thrill, suspense, stress relief, and entertainment stand in close connection to emotional and aesthetic experiences and can be called affective motivations.
- Prestige, appreciation, identification with, and experiencing of success refer to the consumers' faith in the stability of their environment and can be summarized as integrative motivations.
- Social or interhuman relations, sociability, interaction, enthusiasm, and common experience refer to contacts with the environment, which is why they can be assigned to interactive motivations.

The motives of each individual spectator to visit a professional sporting event are therefore a mix of motivations from cognitive, affective, integrative, and interactive driving forces (Figure 11.4). The different categories

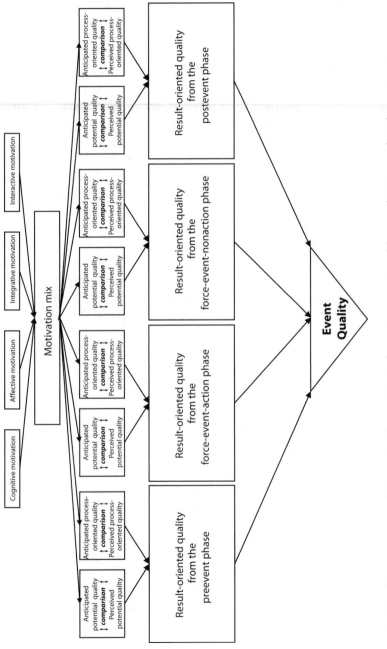

Figure 11.4   Incorporation of the motivation mix into the PROSPORT model as mediating quality determinant.

of motivations are not competing with each other but complementing one another. Altogether, they cover all possible driving forces for spectators to visit a professional sporting event.

Since the importance of the service quality from the spectators' point of view for the success of professional sporting events has been detailed, the PROSPORT quality model is now expanded to include the anticipated success potential of service quality. Although the expansion stands in no direct connection with the central target of a quality model, it forms a helpful supplement by providing the proof requested by quality management of the relevance of service quality to success. According to the PROSPORT model, the service quality of a professional sporting event is comprised of the evaluations of the four event phases by the spectators. Based on this evaluation process by the spectators, the success of an event will primarily be caused by changed consumer behavior. It can be assumed that spectators who give an especially positive evaluation of a professional sporting event stay longer on the premises of the event than others, recommend the visit to the event more frequently than others, and tend to visit follow-up events repeatedly. Such a change in behavior of the spectators is a positive result for the promoter of a professional sporting event and can be called, from the promoter's point of view, a success with the visitors.

Empirical Validation of the Postulated Connections

To be able to assess the validity of a theoretically derived model, the underlying research hypotheses have to be reviewed empirically. For this purpose, three surveys with more than 200 spectator interviews each were conducted at an international athletics meeting, an international judo invitation tournament, and a bicycle race. From the range of different survey methods, similar studies had envisaged written and oral interviews to survey quality judgments. Since spectators who are interviewed in writing usually have great difficulty with differentiating between the anticipated and perceived quality, personal in situ interviews were conducted with the spectators to validate the PROSPORT model.

The predicted composition of motivation factors of spectators to visit a professional sporting event could be confirmed at all three surveyed events. The questionnaire statements on the four dimensions received singular agreement values of more than 50%. The statements of the surveyed spectators on supplementary motivation factors were questioned openly;

no grounds could be found for possible additional motivations. The statements made rather corresponded with the agreement values for the type of motivation of an explicit statement. Depending on the composition of information, entertainment, integration, and interaction requirements, consumers decide to visit a certain sporting event that seemed to be the appropriate means, owing to the type of sports involved and the supporting acts offered, to realize the individual motivation aim. The study of the three events also showed that spectators with an above-average cognitive, affective, and integrative motivation had higher expectations regarding the suspense of the competition and the victory of preferred athletes.

On the basis of the results of the survey, the method of factor analysis used to validate the phase structure revealed a uniform structure of factors for the three events. When the contents of the allocated quality characteristics were analyzed, there was a considerable overlap with the theoretically predicted quality dimensions. Despite minor deviations that had to be accepted because of the chosen survey approach focusing on consistency and efficiency, the phase-oriented differentiation approach of quality dimensions in the PROSPORT model can be empirically validated. The central quality characteristics of the preevent, force-event-action, force-event-nonaction, and postevent phases were summarized by the spectators of all three events into one or two corresponding phase-specific subevaluations.

To be able to validate the structure of the spectators' judgment on the overall quality of the events from the evaluations of individual service potentials and processes within the preevent, force-event-action, force-event-nonaction, and postevent phases, ensuing regression analyses were conducted. The coefficient of determination r^2, on the basis of which the influence of the quality dimensions found on the overall quality can be judged, was at the significant level for all three events, between .63 and .69. The resulting explanation ratio of between 63% and 69% showed a "clear connection" between the evaluations of the phases of the event and the overall judgment of the corresponding event.

The surveys also showed that a positive quality judgment of the event did have a significant influence on the duration of the stay and the intention to visit follow-up events. Spectators who gave an above-average positive judgment of the sporting event tended to stay there longer. At the same time, spectators with an above-average positive judgment of the quality more frequently intended to visit follow-up events. The general effect of positive service quality judgment on the intention to visit events of other sports was studied at the judo tournament but could not be confirmed.

Theoretical and Practical Outlook

Besides explaining the process of quality judgments of the spectators, the PROSPORT model also furnishes proof of the relevance of service quality for the success of professional sporting events: High service quality leads to an increase in customer-oriented success indicators. The theoretical development and empirical validation of the PROSPORT model showed that the quality of professional sporting events can be explained on the basis of approaches and models known from general service marketing to illustrate quality. This proved that marketing theories can be applied to sports in general and especially to the illustration of quality at professional sporting events. The interaction between suppliers and demanders on the sports market is therefore not to be seen as an economic exception closed to economic theories and implications. It is, however, not possible to congruently apply quality models known from service marketing to the application spectrum of professional sporting events. It is rather necessary to differentiate specific market conditions and service characteristics for sports to adequately translate the theoretical foundation to practice.

Even if the PROSPORT model has primarily been developed to explain the process and effects of quality judgments of spectators, and even though the model itself cannot supply optimum solutions regarding possible decision scenarios within quality management, it supports decisions owing to its illustrating character. The understanding of the perception and evaluation of professional sporting events by the spectators helps promoters in this market to focus their event concept more directly on the requirements of this central clientele.

References

Benkenstein, M. (1993). Dienstleistungsqualität. Ansätze zur Messung und Implikationen für die Steuerung. *Zeitschrift für Betriebswirtschaftslehre, 11,* 1095–1116.

Berry, L. (1986). Big ideas in service marketing. In M. Venkatesan, D. M. Schmalensee, & C. Marshall. (Eds.), *Creativity in service marketing: What´s new, what works, what's developing* (pp. 6–8). Chicago: American Marketing Association.

Brandmaier, S., & Schimany, P. (1998). *Die Kommerzialisierung des Sports: Vermarktungsprozesse im Fußball-Profisport.* Hamburg: Lit Verlag.

Brandt, D. (1987). A procedure for identifying value-enhancing service components using customer satisfaction survey data. In C. F. Suprenant (Ed.), *Add value to your service* (pp. 61–65). Chicago: American Marketing Association.

Bruhn, M. (2008). *Qualitätsmanagement für Dienstleistungen, Grundlagen, Konzepte, Methoden.* Berlin: Springer.

Childress, R., & Crompton, J. (1997). A comparison of alternative direct and indirect discrepancy approaches to measuring quality of performance at a festival. *Journal of Travel Research, 3,* 43–57.

Cismar, T. (2001). *Erfolgfaktoren bei der Ausrichtung von Heimspielen in professionellen Sportliga-Wettbewerben—Eine empirische Analyse am Beispiel der Fußball-Bundesliga.* Master's thesis, University of German Federal Armed Forces, Munich.

Donabedian, A. (1980). *The definition of quality and approaches to its assessment.* Ann Arbor, MI: Health Administration Press.

Drabczynski, M. (1982). *Motivationale Ansätze in der Kommunikationswissenschaft.* Berlin: Spiess Volker.

Gray, D. (2001). Sport marketing: Strategies and tactics. In B. L. Parkhouse (Ed.), *The management of sports: Its foundations and applications* (pp. 300–336). Boston: McGraw Hill.

Grönroos, C. (1984). A service quality model and its marketing implications. *European Journal of Marketing, 4,* 36–44.

Gummesson, E. (1991). Service quality—a holistic view. In W. Stephen & E. Gummesson (Eds.), *Service quality. Multidisciplinary and multinational perspectives* (pp. 3–22). Lanham, MD: Lexington.

Hansen, H., & Gauthier, R. (1989). Factors affecting attendance at professional sport events. *Journal of Sport Management, 3,* 15–32.

Heinemann, K. (1999). Oekonomie des Sports—Eine Standortbestimmung. In H. Horch, J. Heydel, & A. Sierau (Eds.), *Professionalisierung im Sportmanagement* (pp. 13–47). Cologne, Germany: DSHS.

Hermanns, A., & Riedmueller, F. (2008). *Management-Handbuch Sport-Marketing.* Munich: Vahlen.

Johnson, R., Tsiros, M., & Lancioni, R. (1995). Measuring service quality: A systems approach. *Journal of Services Marketing, 5,* 6–19.

Kroeber-Riel, W., & Weinberg, P. (1999). *Konsumentenverhalten.* Munich: Vahlen.

Krueger, W. (1998). Die Erklärung von Unternehmenserfolg: Theoretischer Ansatz und empirische Ergebnisse. *Die Betriebswirtschaft, 1,* 27–43.

Lehmann, E., & Weigand, J. (1999). Determinanten der Entlohnung von Profifußballspielern—Eine empirische Analyse für die deutsche Bundesliga. *Betriebswirtschaftliche Forschung und Praxis, 2,* 124–135.

Lucerna, C. (1997). *Vermarktung von Sportereignissen.* Wiesbaden, Germany: Gabler.

Parasuraman, A., Zeithaml, V., & Berry, L. (1988). SERVQUAL: A multiple-item scale for measuring consumer perceptions of service quality. *Journal of Retailing, 1,* 12–40.

Riedmueller, F. (2003). *Dienstleistungsqualitaet bei professionellen Sportveranstaltungen*. Frankfurt, Germany: Lang.

Rinehart, R. E. (1998). *Players all—Performances in contemporary sport*. Bloomington: Indiana University Press.

Robertson, D., & Pope, N. (1999). Product bundling and causes of attendance and non-attendance in live professional sport: A case study of the Brisbane Broncos and the Brisbane Lions. *The Cyber-Journal of Sport Marketing*, 1. Retrieved January 10, 2006, from http//www.cjsm.com/vol3/robertson&pope31.htm

Siegfried, J., & Eisenberg, J. (1989). The demand for minor league baseball. *Atlantic Economic Journal, 3*, 59–69.

Stauss, B., & Seidel, W. (1997). Prozessuale Zufriedenheitsermittlung und Zufriedenheitsdynamik bei Dienstleistungen. In H. Simon and C. Homburg (Eds.), *Kundenzufriedenheit: Konzepte–Methoden–Erfahrungen* (pp. 185–208). Wiesbaden, Germany: Gabler.

TDWI. (2008). *Typologie der Wünsche Intermedia*. Retrieved October 26, 2008, from http://www.tdwi.com

Voeth, M., Klein, A., & Lier, M. (2001). *Akzeptanz und Einstellungen gegenüber dem Sportgroßereignis WM 2006*. Duisburg, Germany: University of Duisburg.

Wochnowski, H. (1996). *Veranstaltungsmarketing*. Frankfurt, Germany: Lang.

Woodruff, R. (1997). Customer value: The next source for competitive advantage. *Journal of the Academy of Marketing Science, 2*, 139–153.

12

Event Marketing and Sponsorship
Lessons Learned From the Tour
de Georgia Cycling Races

R. Zachary Finney, Russell Lacey, and Angeline G. Close

Introduction

In this chapter, we introduce an overview of event marketing and sports sponsorships with a focus on a compilation of their consumer research in the context of a professional cycling event.

Even in difficult economic times, sponsorships continue to grow at a remarkable pace that far exceeds the growth of other integrated marketing communications (IMC) methods (International Events Group [IEG], 2009). In fact, each year there are approximately 40,000 sponsored events in the United States alone. Of those sponsored events, approximately two thirds are sporting events ("Marketing Fact Book," 2008).

Understanding this growing phenomenon requires an appreciation of two related but distinct terms: event marketing and sponsorship. Both event marketing and sponsorship can be used to link the brand of a company or product to an event, but not all sponsorships involve an event. Event marketing offers consumers the opportunity to interact personally with, and thus experience, branded products and services. Sponsorship entails the support of individuals or groups participating in an activity or support of the activity itself. While they are independent activities, the synergistic characteristics of event marketing and sponsorship support their joint application (Lacey, Sneath, Finney, & Close, 2007; Walliser, 2003). When combined, sponsorship of sporting events and ancillary event marketing activities offer marketers the opportunity to engage consumers in an inherently personal way.

Both sponsorship and event marketing have emerged as central players in IMC strategies of various firms (Close, Finney, Lacey, & Sneath, 2006).

Marketers state that there are many reasons to like sponsorships and event marketing. Most marketing professionals concede that the majority of people are not particularly interested in products and brands; sponsorships, on the other hand, provide firms with an ability to engage consumers in the context of emotionally charged sporting events that are interesting to consumers (IEG Sponsorship Report, 2006). Sponsors and event marketers also benefit from the fact that event attendees voluntarily choose to interact with their businesses; moreover, the interactions are often personalized, two-way individualized exchanges of information, as opposed to standardized, one-way mass marketing messages (Whelan & Wohlfeil, 2006).

Sponsors and event marketers can choose to participate in a wide array of nonproprietary events (staged by an outside organization) and proprietary events (staged by the event sponsor) (Sneath, Finney, & Close, 2005). Managers indicate that nonproprietary events offer contacts with larger numbers of attendees and with attendees from more diverse backgrounds than the same marketer would likely interact with at a proprietary event. Also, because outside sponsors are less-strongly associated with nonproprietary events than with proprietary events, nonproprietary events offer sponsors more ways to transfer the image of the fun event activities to the sponsor's offerings. Finally, the cost of sponsorship rights for a nonproprietary event generally is lower than the cost of staging a proprietary event (Sneath, Lacey, Finney, & Close, 2006).

In spite of the rosy picture, practitioners have begun to raise questions about the effectiveness of sponsorships and event marketing amid associated rising cost and sponsorship clutter concerns. The measurement of financial returns vis-à-vis the expenditures required to support an event has been an acute concern (Sneath et al., 2006). The scholarly community, moreover, has been slow to focus its research on sponsorships and event marketing. A particularly glaring omission has been the lack of empirical research on sponsorships in field settings. (Notable exceptions include the work of Barros, de Barros, Santos, & Chadwick, 2007; Grohs, Wagner, & Vsetecka, 2004; Sirgy, Lee, Johar, & Tidwell, 2008.)

So, at present, spending on sport and event marketing continues to increase without sufficient empirical evidence to support such an occurrence. Given the increasing demands of industry that marketers link their spending to quantifiable results, this state of affairs is untenable (Stotlar, 2004). If sport and event marketing practices are to have any sort of empirical underpinning, scholars must carry out more research in this area.

In 2004, we began to gather data during the second year of a professional cycling event in an effort to conduct a set of empirical studies on effective methods of sports sponsorship and event marketing. Specifically, from 2004 to 2008, we conducted survey research at the five Tour de Georgia cycling races. Our research, therefore, begins to move sports sponsorships from unsubstantiated "common wisdom" to empirically supported best practices. Thus far, the five surveys have yielded seven research studies.

In this chapter, we review our findings from the Tour de Georgia data. First, we provide background on the Tour de Georgia and our efforts to gather data at the races. Second, we include an overview of our results to date. Finally, we conclude with suggestions for future research directions.

The Tour de Georgia: 2003–2008

History of the Event

The Tour de Georgia was an annual professional cycling race held from 2003 to 2008 ("Bring Back the Tour de Georgia!" 2009). The Tour de Georgia was a multistage, multicity event; cyclists competed each day over approximately 1 week on courses throughout Georgia and Tennessee. During its 6-year run, the Tour de Georgia multistage event was regarded as the premier professional cycling event in North America (Tour de Georgia, 2007). As a result, it attracted a renowned group of international cyclists, including Lance Armstrong, who won the race in 2004.

The event also drew attendees from across the world. There was no assigned seating at the venues or general ticketing. Attendees therefore had the opportunity and were encouraged to roam through sponsors' exhibits (Sneath et al., 2005). Other cycling enthusiasts followed the race on television, radio, the official Web site, cycling Web sites, and various blogs.

The event took considerable effort and money to stage and to promote. For example, in the tour's second year, Tour de Georgia sponsorship fees ranged from $10,000 for Friends of the Tour sponsorship (a cash and in-kind combination) up to $1 million (cash) for the title sponsorship. More than 4,000 volunteers and 550 staff members supported the 2004 event, which drew an estimated 750,000 spectators across the host cities (Sneath et al., 2006). Furthermore, thousands of media exposures were generated as a way to integrate the sponsorship with sponsors' marketing efforts and to promote the event.

Spectators attended the Tour de Georgia for free. As a result, the Tour de Georgia was heavily reliant on its sponsors: "Ninety-nine percent of its revenues ... [were] derived from sponsorship fees" (Sneath et al., 2006, p. 29). Three major sponsors supported the Tour de Georgia: Dodge (2003–2005), Ford (2006), and AT&T (2007–2008). There were also many smaller sponsors each year. The organizers of the Tour de Georgia recruited sponsors primarily from the consumer goods, health care, and transportation industries (Sneath et al., 2006).

The major sponsors received substantial publicity in exchange for their financial support. For instance, in the early years of the event, Ford went to considerable lengths to leverage its title sponsorship of the 2006 Tour de Georgia. Ford's marketing program began with a preevent publicity tour. During the Tour de Georgia, Ford's brand name and logo were visibly displayed on signage, banners, volunteer apparel, and large video screens that televised the race to the spectators. Event marketing activities showcased new Ford models (Fusion, Escape, and F150). New Ford vehicles served as pace cars and shuttles for cyclists, volunteers, and invited guests (USA Cycling, 2006). Many of the major sponsors also used their exhibits at the Tour de Georgia to interact with potential customers and to gather contact information from those who had an interest in their offerings (Sneath et al., 2005). For a tangible promotion, Ford gave attendees VIP-style ticket badges complete with an online link to access their photograph with the new Ford vehicles. This is a way Ford was able to engage consumers both at the event and subsequently offline on their Web site.

In 2009, the race organizers were unable to convince a major sponsor to finance the Tour de Georgia; as a result, there was no Tour de Georgia in 2009 (Williams, 2008). At this writing, the Tour de Georgia's organizers are hopeful that they can stage the Tour de Georgia again ("Bring Back the Tour de Georgia!" 2009). Collectively, the marketing research shows that the event benefits the state economically, and on a consumer and community level, consumers appreciate the event and the sponsor's financial contributions that keep the event alive in spirit until the next race.

Data Collection

The state of Georgia conducted surveys to measure the economic impact of the Tour de Georgia; we helped conduct these studies at the Tour de Georgia during the 2004–2008 races. The state's researchers asked us to provide student volunteers to collect surveys in the host cities. In exchange, the representatives allowed us to insert marketing scales into their surveys so that we could measure marketing-related variables. There were slight changes in the data collection process from year to year; the following paragraphs, therefore, constitute a general overview of the methods that we used from 2004 to 2008.

We recruited junior- and senior-level undergraduate business majors to collect data at the various Tour de Georgia venues; the students chose to participate to receive extra credit for the courses in which they were enrolled. The representatives of the Tour de Georgia also recruited volunteers through local contacts at the venues. Prior to each Tour de Georgia race, we worked with an event-marketing professional to train the students in data collection procedures.

The researchers primarily conducted survey research with attendees, but we also conducted a limited number of indepth interviews. We collected data at almost all of the host cities and towns of the Tour de Georgia races. Researchers wore shirts and hats to signify researcher status to attendees. In return for completing the survey, participants were offered official Tour de Georgia shirts, pens, meal vouchers, and other assorted items (Lacey, Close, & Finney, 2009b).

Depending on the year, nonresponse rates varied from approximately 5% to 10%. The most common reasons given for attendees' refusal to participate in the survey were that they had already participated in the survey, they were en route to an exhibit, and they wanted to witness cyclists start or finish the race (Close, Lacey, & Finney, 2009).

The survey results revealed that Tour de Georgia attendees were a diverse group. Attendees were of many different ages and from many different economic backgrounds. The samples tended to have more men than women and drew highest participation among people ranging between the ages of 20 and 39 years old (Lacey et al., 2009b). Tour de Georgia attendees were loyal and were willing to make an effort to attend. For example, over 55% of attendees surveyed in 2007 indicated that they had attended the Tour de Georgia before, and 40% indicated that they had traveled from out of state or from another country to attend (Close et al., 2009).

Framework of Tour de Georgia Research

In this section, we present a framework that summarizes our Tour de Georgia research to date and expound on this framework. As illustrated in Figure 12.1, event sponsorship is impacted by an array of event attendee- and event sponsor-related variables. Depending on alternative models of this framework, these variables have been shown to have a direct impact

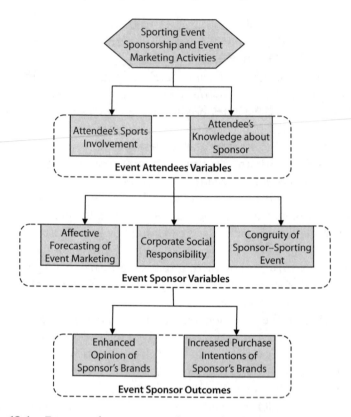

Figure 12.1 Framework summary of Tour de Georgia event sponsorship research.

or influence on event sponsor outcomes. Our research explores how attendees' knowledge about the sponsor and their level of sports involvement affect attendees' attitudes toward the event sponsor. Moreover, the research examines the respective impact of affective forecasting, corporate social responsibility (CSR), and sponsor-event congruity on event outcomes. As shown, event sponsorship effectiveness is gauged by two key outcomes: enhanced opinions of the brands or products and increased purchase intentions of the brands of the sponsor.

Event Attendees' Variables

Sports Involvement
Part of the lure of sporting events to sponsors is the strong emotional ties among its most highly involved fans. The attendance of highly involved

fans obviously makes a substantial impact on the ultimate success or fail-ure of any sporting event sponsorship. Managers believe that sporting event attendees who are (a) sports fans and who (b) participate in sports are better target markets for such events than are attendees who neither like nor participate in sports (Close et al., 2006). However, the evidence to support such beliefs is largely anecdotal.

Previously, focus group research showed a linkage between active par-ticipation in a social event and favorable attitudes toward sponsored activ-ities (Meenaghan, 2001). Limited empirical research on this topic does suggest that a consumer's attitude regarding sports plays an important role in determining his or her attitude regarding sports sponsorships. As long as a sporting event attendee is engaged in sports, he or she is likely to be more receptive to the messages at sporting events than would be an attendee who is not engaged in sports. Interestingly, the results do not show that it matters if the sporting event involves a sport in which the "sports-engaged" attendee participates (McDaniel, 1999). The study also finds no evidence that it matters whether sponsors are involved with nega-tively perceived or positively perceived sports (McDaniel, 1999).

On the strength of a large sample of Tour de Georgia attendees, our field study research confirmed the finding that event attendees who are more active in sports have more favorable attitudes regarding sporting events (Close et al., 2006). In assessing our study, moreover, we found it striking that attendees who were involved in sports and who were knowledgeable about the sponsor and its products were more likely to want the sponsor to be involved in their local communities. Managers should regard this result with care; it suggests that involved event attendees expect more out of event sponsors beyond financial donations.

Perhaps knowledge is power for the attendees. When firms spon-sor events, the firms cease to be faceless, multinational businesses. Knowledgeable attendees are likely to be better customers for the spon-sors, but such attendees also demand more of the sponsors.

One of the most advantageous aspects of our 5-year involvement with the Tour de Georgia is the ability to build longitudinal data sets from the large collected samples. We are able to include a number of variables in multiple versions of the Tour de Georgia survey. One thing that inter-ested us was whether we could find differences in the responses of Tour de Georgia attendees based on the number of years that they had attended the race. To that end, we used data collected during the Tour de Georgia's third year (2005) to examine whether first-, second-, and third-time attendees had different perceptions of Dodge, the title sponsor of the Tour de Georgia. (Dodge was the sponsor for all three Tour de Georgia races that had been held at the time of the survey.)

Intuitively, we expected that multiyear attendees would more likely be "hard-core" cycling fans who were very involved with the event at hand; attendees who had been to the races less frequently should have been, on the whole, less involved with the event and its sponsors. Our two specific research questions were "First, does repeat attendance enhance an event sponsor's brand image? Second, do repeat attendees indicate that they are more likely to purchase the sponsor's brand?" (Lacey et al., 2007, p. 244).

The results revealed that repeat Tour de Georgia attendees reported that they had (a) more favorable opinions of Dodge and (b) a greater likelihood of purchasing a Dodge in the future than did first-time race attendees. Perhaps commitment to the sponsor takes time to build. If so, the study helped support the idea that firms must commit to building their promotional programs for the long run; the impact of an individual sponsorship might be modest, but the impact improves when event attendees repeatedly encounter the sponsor's promotional messages. Another interpretation might be that the third-year attendees were simply more willing to support the sponsors due to their involvement with cycling. If this is the case, sponsors might want to focus on methods to identify and interact with the most involved event attendees rather than spending time with less-involved attendees. A final possibility could be that both interpretations have some degree of merit.

Knowledge About Sponsor

The marketing literature provides ample reason to suspect that knowledge of the event sponsor plays a role in attendees' assessments of the sponsor (e.g., Roy & Cornwell, 2004). Scholars have established that exposure to product knowledge alters consumers' perceptions; scholars hold that, as a consumer becomes more aware of a product, his or her opinion of that product becomes more positive. Researchers referred to this as the "mere exposure effect" (Zajonc & Markus, 1982). So, an informed consumer is more likely to come to an event with a favorable attitude toward the sponsor. Study of the literature also revealed that product knowledge is the basis of consumer commitment to a brand (e.g., Leung, Lai, Chan, & Wong, 2005).

Events are expensive for their sponsors. Beyond the costs for obtaining sponsorship rights, sponsors routinely incur higher expenditures in sponsorship activation to communicate the sponsorship and provide ancillary event marketing activities. In return, however, event marketing offers high potential payoffs to sponsors. A firm that pays to affiliate with an event and does nothing else will have less opportunity to impart product knowledge than will a firm that uses both sponsorship and event marketing (Wakefield, Becker-Olsen, & Cornwell, 2007). Indeed, scholars hold that event marketing can enhance the image of brands and improve event attendees' awareness of brands of these sponsors (Javalgi, Traylor, Gross, & Lampman, 1994). A key for event sponsors, then, is that their exhibits need serve not only to entertain event attendees but also to inform event attendees about the sponsor (Lacey, Close, & Finney, 2009a).

Event attendees differ in their knowledge of the offerings of event sponsors. Therefore, we decided to examine the degree to which attendees' knowledge about the offerings of an event sponsor influenced their feelings about the sponsor during their attendance at the Tour de Georgia. Our results established that attendees who have knowledge of the brands of an event sponsor (a) are more committed to the sponsoring organization, (b) are more committed to the brands of the sponsor, and (c) have greater intention to purchase the products of the sponsor (Lacey et al., 2009b). These results tell marketers that they should attempt to attract informed attendees to their events; perhaps event marketers can attempt to contact potential attendees before events and provide the attendees with knowledge about the offerings of the firm. An event marketer could also use the event itself to impart product knowledge to attendees, thereby creating the mere exposure effect.

Further research should separate knowledge that attendees have prior to attending an event from knowledge that they gain at the event. This research would help explain (a) the efficacy of the different methods of promotion and (b) whether the sponsored event or the differences among event attendees are responsible for the findings. Given the value that firms can derive from drawing potential customers who are positive about their offerings and who may become committed to their firms, researchers interested in event marketing should also examine which particular types of information have the biggest impact on attendees' perceptions, intentions, and behaviors.

Event Sponsor Variables

Affective Forecasting

An event attendee who plans to experience the event marketing activity of a sponsor in the near future may engage in affective forecasting. Affective forecasting occurs when people anticipate certain emotions before those feelings actually occur (Wilson & Gilbert, 2003). People may derive pleasure from those feelings, even if their later, actual feelings do not match the feelings that they anticipated experiencing. In fact, event attendees who just anticipate feeling a particular way about an exhibit of the sponsor may not even visit it but may still take home positive feelings about the sponsor after the event.

We have examined attendees' actual visits to these exhibits and their anticipated visits to them (Lacey et al., 2009a). Actual visits do enhance attendees' feelings about the sponsor, but anticipated visits have a strong impact on attendees' intent to purchase the products of an exhibitor and on attendees' perceptions of the brand of that exhibitor. The results suggest that attendees tend to overestimate the importance of current events when they look back on those events in the future.

More specifically, our results suggest that plans to experience the exhibits of a sponsor are more important than the actual experience at those exhibits. Attendees tend to overestimate the value of attending the exhibits. They are more apt to focus on the positive aspects of the exhibits while ignoring the negatives. Attendees seem to be skilled at predicting whether they will have negative or positive feelings about some aspect of an event. They are less skilled, however, at forecasting the "intensity and duration of the emotions" (Lacey et al., 2009a).

The research revealed the key role that consumer behavior outside the event plays in creating a satisfying event experience. To improve the attendees' experiences at sponsored events, sponsorship should be activated prior to the event and supplemented by marketing communication tools to enhance affect before, during, and after the sponsored event. Thus, hosting exhibits at an event is not enough alone to fully activate event sponsorship (Lacey et al., 2009a).

Corporate Social Responsibility

To maximize the effectiveness of an event sponsorship, ironically, the profit motives of an event sponsor cannot be overly obvious (Becker-Olsen & Hill, 2006). Event attendees expect event sponsors to make sincere efforts at CSR through community involvement. CSR is "the continuing commitment by business to behave ethically and contribute to economic development while improving the quality of life of the workforce and their families as well as of the local community and society at large" (The World Business Council for Sustainable Development, 2009). As a form of CSR, community involvement is "the amount of noncommercial interaction an organization has with individuals and organizations in the markets in which it operates" (Close et al., 2006, p. 423).

Sponsorships offer firms opportunities to show consumers that they are involved in the local community and that they practice CSR (Simmons & Becker-Olsen, 2006). Indeed, scholars have begun to write about "social sponsorships": "Social sponsorships are instances in which companies invest sponsorship money to promote social causes in order to 'play the good citizen' and 'give something back to society'" (Bovaird, Löffler, & Parrado-Díez, 2002, p. 422).

For the firm, then, a social sponsorship provides value in two ways: first it helps the firm promote its products and second it helps promote the firm as a good corporate citizen (Simmons & Becker-Olsen, 2006). Research confirmed that when customers believe that a firm takes actions that help society, the firm benefits (Maignan & Ferrell, 2001, 2004). More specifically, scholars found that when people either (a) begin to support the CSR activities of a firm or (b) already support a good cause adopted by a firm, those people are more likely to want to do business with the firm (Broderick, Jogi, & Garry, 2003; Du, Bhattacharya, & Sen, 2007; Sen & Bhattacharya, 2001).

Indeed, our research showed that consumers like that event sponsors do more than just sell products; moreover, respondents indicate that they "act on that appreciation" by supporting community-minded event sponsors (Lacey et al., 2007, p. 243). Results from another Tour de Georgia study (Close et al., 2006) indicated that when attendees viewed a sponsor as involved in the community, they were more likely to indicate that the event had changed their opinion of the sponsor for the better. Consumers whose opinions of the sponsors have improved are more likely to indicate that they will act on that appreciation and buy the products of the sponsor.

The results supported the position taken by those scholars who have asserted that firms should not view promotion and CSR as disparate activities (Docherty & Hibbert, 2003; Zablah, Bellenger, & Johnston, 2004). When event attendees assess the promotions of a firm, the attendees are more receptive to those promotions if they believe that the firm practices CSR and is involved in the community. Firms, therefore, must integrate the messages they send about CSR or community involvement with their other promotional messages. Firms, unfortunately, have been slow to adopt such a practice (Du et al., 2007).

Our studies also examined the role of product knowledge in influencing event attendees' perceptions of a sponsor as socially responsible and involved in the community (Lacey et al., 2009b). Research revealed that when consumers have knowledge of the sponsor of an event it has an impact on how they connect the sponsor to the sponsored event (Meenaghan, 1991). More specifically, informed consumers can better link a sponsoring brand to its CSR and community activities (Algesheimer, Dholakia, & Herrmann, 2005).

We extended the previous research by examining two specific issues. First, we studied how existing knowledge of the products of an event sponsor influenced attendees' assessments of the sponsor as socially responsible (Lacey et al., 2009b). We also asked how attendees' product knowledge and perceptions of social responsibility had an impact on their level of commitment and intentions to purchase the products of the sponsor (Lacey et al., 2009b). Event attendees with more product knowledge did have more favorable views of the event sponsor; consumers' perceptions of the degree to which the sponsor engaged in CSR activities mediated this relationship. In turn, perceptions of a sponsoring firm as socially responsible also drove commitment to the firm and its brands.

Congruity

To enhance an organization's image, event sponsorship helps to create or reinforce brand associations of the events themselves (Cornwell, Humphreys, Maguire, Weeks, & Tellegen, 2006). Scholars hold that some firms are better candidates for a given sponsorship than are other firms. Researchers posited that a congruent sponsorship will be more effective than an incongruent sponsorship. Congruity represents the degree to which an attendee perceives that a sponsoring brand and a sponsored event have comparable images, values, and a rational connection (Simmons & Becker-Olsen, 2006).

Scholars typically found that congruity has desirable effects (Shaver, Schwartz, Kirson, & O'Connor, 1987). Congruity theory deems that the value of a less-positive facet (e.g., a large corporation) will be strengthened when linked to a more positive facet (e.g., community-oriented sporting event). However, this result holds only when the facets are similarly viewed on a highly salient dimension or as long as consumers are not cued to focus on a specific dimension (Close et al., 2009).

Congruity can also be natural or contrived. Natural congruity is "the extent to which the sponsored (event) is perceived as being congruent with the sponsor's image, independent of marketers' efforts to create a perceived congruity between the organizations" (Simmons & Becker-Olsen, 2006, p. 156). Scholars hold that natural congruity is better than contrived congruity because sponsors do not have to spend time and money trying to create natural congruity.

As a rule, consumers expect that sponsors and events will be congruent. Low congruity forces consumers to make more mental effort assessing the sponsorship and generally leads to a lower opinion of the sponsorship (Simmons & Becker-Olsen, 2006). (In some instances, increased elaboration can be positive; please see Mandler, 1982).

In one study (Close et al., 2009), we predicted that a high-congruity sponsorship would positively benefit both the event and the sponsors of the event. Our results were surprising. We found that when attendees perceived fit between the event and the sponsor, there were better perceptions of the sponsor. However, there were no indications that event-sponsor congruity had an impact on attendees' opinions of the event. (Specifically, attendees indicated that fit influenced their opinion of the brands of the sponsor and their plans to use these brands.) So, our results revealed some occasions when fit mattered in consumers' perceptions. In conclusion, we posited that perhaps attendees used different criteria for assessing the event than for assessing the event sponsor (Close et al., 2009).

Event Sponsor Outcomes

Measuring the impact of event sponsorship on awareness levels is a relatively straightforward task. However, organizations want to be able to assess the impact of these marketing activities on the bottom line. Marketing personnel increasingly struggle to quantify the gains (or return on investment, ROI) that their organizations reap from specific marketing activities (cf. Cook & Talluri, 2004; Court, 2005; Stewart, 2008). And yet, it is often difficult to connect marketing activities to measurable outcomes. Our results suggest, moreover, that sponsored event marketing activities often produce desirable outcomes only after considerable periods of time (Lacey et al., 2007).

Professional organization studies conducted thus far have indicated that event marketing offers businesses an attractive return for their investment. For example, a 2004 study found that U.S. executives believed that event marketing offers better returns than more conventional forms of promotion (MPI Foundation, 2004). One of the main difficulties in assessing the outcomes associated with event marketing is that too many firms choose to focus on outcomes related to consumer purchases or market share of their products (Sneath et al., 2005). In many instances, communication goals, such as "recall, awareness, and attitudes," may be more appropriate measures (Sneath et al., 2005, p. 375; see also Hulks, 1980, and McDonald, 1991).

The primary focus of our studies to date has been on the variables related to the event itself and the event attendees that we have discussed. As noted, however, marketers must increasingly connect marketing expenditures to some "bottom-line" outcomes. We offer here, therefore, some insight into key outcomes that managers may expect to derive from their event sponsorship and event marketing expenditures.

Enhanced Opinions of Sponsor

The discussion of affective forecasting noted that, for attendees, anticipation of the exhibits of an event sponsor is often more important than are their actual experiences with those exhibits. We can also ask what impact actual experience with the exhibits produced among attendees.

Measures pertaining to the exhibits of a sponsor did predict attitude changes among Tour de Georgia attendees (Sneath et al., 2005). Specifically, those who had experienced these exhibits were more likely to indicate that their attitudes toward the sponsor had changed for the better as a result of their attendance at the Tour de Georgia. Experience with the exhibit was only a marginally significant predictor of whether attendees liked the fact that the company had served as the sponsor of the Tour de Georgia. One could interpret the results to mean that fewer attendees felt the need to experience the exhibits to assess the *act* of sponsorship, but that more attendees felt the need to interact with the exhibits of the sponsor (and to gain information) to assess the sponsor.

The sponsor could take away positive feelings about the bottom-line impact of its sponsorships. Those who had experienced the exhibits indicated that chances were that they would buy one of the vehicles of the sponsor the next time they shopped for a car. Remarkably, just one fourth of attendees who had not experienced the exhibits of the sponsor would consider buying one of its cars for the next purchase; among those who had experienced the exhibits, over 55% would consider the sponsor when buying their next vehicle.

As noted, connecting the promotions of a firm to the bottom line is a difficult task. One could interpret the results to mean that the exhibits of the sponsor made a significant difference in attendees' attitudes toward the sponsor. Just as plausibly, however, one could argue that those who sought out the exhibits of the sponsor were more interested in its vehicles prior to their attendance at the Tour de Georgia. The 2005 study could not identify the specific factors that drove the differences between those who had experienced the exhibits and those who had not. Also, one might note that the 2005 study concerned only one sponsor; therefore, the results might generalize only to certain sponsors.

Increased Purchase Intentions
We have discussed purchase intentions as an outcome variable in several of the previous sections. In fact, purchase intentions served as an outcome variable in several of our research studies. Here, we provide a short overview of what our studies have taught us about the connections between event marketing and purchase intentions.

In spite of the managerial interest in the impact of event sponsorships on purchase intentions, relatively few scholars have accepted the challenge of connecting the two (Close et al., 2006). Unfortunately, those studies that do exist offer only inconclusive results on the link between sponsorship activities and buyers' purchase intentions. Some studies, including ours, purported to find links between the two variables (e.g., Close et al., 2006; Cornwell & Coote, 2005; Sneath et al., 2005). Other studies, meanwhile, found no evidence of a connection between the two variables (Hoek, Gendall, Jeffcoat, & Orsman, 1997; Javalgi et al., 1994; Pitts & Slattery, 2004).

Our results did establish the intuitive hypothesis that a better opinion of an event sponsor was connected to higher purchase intentions regarding the offerings of the sponsor. As with any study of purchase intentions, one must bear in mind that a survey respondent who indicated an intention may not actually follow through on that intention. It is also intuitive that the attitudes that attendees held regarding an event sponsor were important in regard to purchase intentions. Not surprisingly, attendees who felt committed to the sponsor had higher purchase intentions regarding the products of the sponsor than did those who were less committed (Lacey et al., 2009b). Results suggested that commitment tended to be built over the long run and not as a result of a one-time experience (Lacey et al., 2007). Event sponsors, therefore, should integrate the event marketing experience with the other promotional campaigns of the event sponsor; attendees who come to events with positive feelings about (or even commitments to) the sponsor are more likely to form purchase intentions for the products of the sponsor.

Scholars hold that people can experience three different types of utility at an event: predicted utility, experienced utility, and remembered utility (Kahneman & Snell, 1992). Predicted utility measures personal beliefs regarding how much one will enjoy a future event, whereas experienced utility measures satisfaction during or immediately following an event. In contrast, remembered utility is how an experience will be retrospectively recalled with the passage of time (Kahneman & Snell, 1992).

The discussion of affective forecasting dealt with predicted utility. In this discussion, we want to focus on the role of experienced utility. Our analyses established that attendees' opinions of the brand of the sponsor were linked to their purchase intentions for the products of the sponsor. Moreover, the analyses showed that consumers' actual experiences with the exhibits of the sponsor positively moderated this relationship (Lacey et al., 2009a). The results, then, support the idea that firms should combine event marketing with their sponsorships to enhance attendees' purchase intentions.

Future Directions

It has become an axiom that any time a researcher answers a question, an exponential number of additional questions arise. It comes as no surprise, then, that such is the case with our investigations into sports sponsorships and event marketing. As noted, the literature on event marketing is particularly "thin" and leaves much room for future work. With this line of research still in its infancy, opportunities to add to our knowledge base are almost limitless. Clearly, many factors may influence the success of a promotional program of a firm. Scholars conducting future studies should look at the impact of multiple factors on the success of sponsorships and event marketing. The following discussion, therefore, in no way constitutes a complete list of future research topics on these issues.

We divide our suggestions for research into three sections:

1. "The Sponsor-Event Interface," with discussions of (a) transfer and (b) fit
2. "Human Side of Event Marketing," with discussions of (a) involvement with sports, (b) human resources and relationship marketing, and (c) attendee behaviors
3. "Methods and Measures," with discussions of (a) longitudinal measures and (b) experimental designs

The Sponsor-Event Interface

We open with two of the basic issues—transfer and fit—that challenge all event marketing practitioners and scholars.

Transfer

"Sports sponsors often hope that the 'cool,' 'active' image of sporting events will transfer from the event to the sponsor's brand" (Close et al., 2006, p. 423; see also Bennett & Lachowetz, 2004). A close look at the literature regarding transfer reveals that we lack key knowledge about some basic issues. We still do not know how the image of the event transfers to the sponsors of the event or how the image of the event transfers to the offerings of the sponsors (Close et al., 2006). A related question concerns how potential event sponsors should quantify the value of the link between the event and the sponsors (or the brands of the sponsors) (Close et al., 2009).

Clearly, these issues concern some of the most basic (and, therefore, pressing) issues pertaining to marketing effectiveness for an event. We expound on some of the other measurement challenges facing researchers in a subsequent section.

Fit

Our results illustrate that *fit* (the degree to which event attendees believe that there is a natural connection between an event and a sponsoring firm) mattered when attendees assessed the sponsor of an event. We could not show, however, that fit made any difference when attendees assessed the event itself (Close et al., 2009). Our studies involved well-known sponsors (Dodge, Ford, and AT&T); it would be interesting for scholars to examine how the value of fit changes for a lesser-known sponsor.

Suppose there is a fit between a sponsor and an event, but the fit would ordinarily go unnoticed by attendees. In this case, the sponsor may inform (or "cue") the attendees to the connection between the sponsor and the event (Cornwell et al., 2006). This raises a whole host of potential research questions about the tradeoffs between the cost of informing consumers versus the benefits gained. It would also be interesting to examine the payoffs from cued low-fit sponsorships versus "uncued" higher-fit sponsorships.

Researchers might also wish to examine whether the impact of perceived fit changes depending on whether the researcher measures fit before, during, or after the event (Close et al., 2009). One might argue that as long as an attendee *remembers* that there was a logical connection between the event and the sponsor, the fit would be sufficient for the sponsor. However, if consumers perceive a high degree of sponsorship *prior* to the event, it would seem logical to argue that the sponsor would not have to work as hard during the event at convincing the attendees that the sponsorship makes sense.

A final suggestion would be to examine whether a low-fit sponsorship might make sense. Research confirmed that consumers spend more time trying to figure out low-fit sponsorships. Scholars posited that the extra work needed to figure out a low-fit sponsorship generally results in negative feelings among consumers (Mandler, 1982). And yet, promotion professionals complain about the prevalence of clutter that keeps consumers from paying attention to their messages. Is it possible that a low-fit sponsorship could, under the right circumstances, cause consumers to become more engaged with the sponsor (Close et al., 2009)?

Human Side of Event Marketing

Our studies at the Tour de Georgia convinced us that the characteristics of event attendees influenced the success of event marketing (Sneath et al., 2005). We continue with a discussion of the "human inputs" (variables pertaining to event attendees and sponsor personnel) that determine the success of sponsored events.

Involvement With Sports

Sports sponsorships continue to evolve, and the number of sports sponsorships continues to increase (Lacey et al., 2007). The rationale for all of these sponsorships is that the passion of the world for sports puts sporting event attendees into more receptive moods for exhibits of the sponsors (Close et al., 2006). Given the spread of sports sponsorships into lesser-known niche sports and the high sponsorship fees for the most visible sports, it would be interesting for scholars to focus on whether (or how) ROI changes as firms move from sponsoring expensive, top-tier sporting events to sponsoring cheaper, less-popular sporting events.

McDaniel's (1999) findings were certainly surprising in this regard. He could not find any evidence that the popularity of a particular sport or an event attendee's participation in a *particular* sport made a difference in the attendee's perceptions of a sponsored sporting event. Attendees' perceptions differed based on whether they were engaged in *any* sport, not just the type of sport at the sponsored event. It would be intriguing to see if attendees' involvement with a particular sport mattered if researchers also measured attendees' degree of involvement with the products of the sponsor; to date, our studies have focused on relatively high-involvement products. It would be interesting to see if our results changed if sponsors were promoting medium- or low-involvement products (Lacey et al., 2007).

Human Resources and Relationship Marketing
Through sporting events and experiences, marketers have the opportunity to link their brands to personally relevant moments in consumers' lives and to broaden and deepen relationships with consumers (Pine & Gilmore, 1999). Yet, contrary to our expectations, our results did *not* show that attendees' experiences with the exhibits of Ford at the 2007 Tour de Georgia strengthened the link between attendees' knowledge of products made by Ford and their opinions of the brand of the company (Lacey et al., 2009a). We speculated that the relatively small number of Ford personnel at the event may be responsible for this result. Our results to date suggest that perhaps attendees have one set of criteria for assessing the sponsor of the event and another set of criteria for assessing the event itself (Close et al., 2009). Sponsors that do not provide personnel at the event site, therefore, may make little impression on attendees. Firms often fail to devote sufficient human resources to sponsored events (Sneath et al., 2006).

Firms need to make better use of their opportunities to interact with event attendees; after all, these opportunities are the reasons that the firms pay to become sponsors. A more fundamental issue is that researchers still do not know which event activities matter to event attendees (Lacey et al., 2009a). We advocate that researchers interested in these issues adopt a relationship marketing perspective (Lacey et al., 2007); relationship marketing, with its emphasis on the bonds between firms and their customers, is ideally suited to study links between event attendees and event sponsors.

Attendee Behaviors
We know that event attendees indicate that they like the contributions of sponsors to events. Attendees frequently report that they intend to purchase the products of event sponsors. What we do not know is how (or whether) purchase intentions and good feelings translate into actual attendee behaviors (Sneath et al., 2005). The literature indicates that people often overstate their intention to buy products (Jones & Sasser, 1995). In the future, therefore, researchers need to focus on event attendees' actual behaviors and purchases of the products of the sponsors instead of relying on self-reported purchase intentions.

Scholarly studies to date reported conflicting results on whether we can link event attendance to purchases of the offerings of event sponsors (Lacey et al., 2007). Reports from the field indicated that results from sponsorships are often dismal; for instance, roughly two thirds of the sponsors of the 1996 Olympic Games indicated that they failed to reach the sales goals that they had set for their sponsorships (Helyar, 1997). The fact that multiple factors that occur at different points in time may influence attendees' future purchase decisions makes it difficult to isolate the impact of a particular sponsored event. Nonetheless, firms increasingly demand that marketing personnel compute ROI from sponsored events. We still have much to learn about the long-term impact of sponsorships (Close et al., 2006); a focus on attendee behaviors can help answer these questions.

Methods and Measures

We conclude with a discussion of some measures and methods that can provide new insight into the issues raised in this chapter.

Longitudinal Measures

As the previous discussion concerning behaviors indicated, scholars have much to gain by examining relevant event marketing variables at different points in time. Given that the literature contains so many (largely unanswered) calls for longitudinal research, we hesitate to make this suggestion. All of the usual practical difficulties that researchers encounter in conducting longitudinal studies (time, effort, measurement, etc.) also apply to longitudinal research on sponsorships and event marketing. Nevertheless, without a longitudinal approach we may have reached the limits of how much we can say about some questions.

Scholars have established that there are short-term gains from event marketing sponsorships. Many scholars, however, believe that the primary benefits that firms derive from event marketing are long term (Sneath et al., 2005). Longitudinal studies can help explain the long-term impact of event marketing. We encourage scholars interested in event marketing to examine Kahneman and Snell's (1992) work indicating that consumers may derive benefits before (predicted utility), during (experienced utility), and after (remembered utility) an event. Studies that measure all three types of utility can explain the actual contributions that attendance at a sponsored event contributes to attendees' perceptions of the event sponsor.

Researchers interested in conducting longitudinal studies should focus on how attendees' product knowledge changes as a result of their attendance at sponsored events. Our studies helped reveal that knowledge of the products of an event sponsor is a key to attendees' perceptions of the sponsor and of the commitment of the sponsor to CSR (Lacey et al., 2009b). It would be particularly interesting to compare the product knowledge that attendees have before and after an event to assess the effects of such knowledge on sponsorship outcomes.

A final suggestion is for researchers to consider examining the impact of affective forecasting from a longitudinal perspective. Our results revealed that event attendees' plans to visit the exhibits of a sponsor are often more important than are their actual visits to such exhibits (Lacey et al., 2009a). Given that this is the case, it would be fascinating to study how the accuracy of affective forecasting influences event attendees' perceptions. If the anticipation of visits is more important than are actual visits, it might suggest that event marketers should "build up" their exhibits as much as possible in promotions prior to the event regardless of whether the actual exhibits can deliver on the promises the sponsor makes. (Such an approach, if implemented, would involve an ethical dilemma in that it might be inappropriate for an event sponsor to make promises about its exhibits that it knows it cannot keep.)

Experimental Designs

The fact that we conducted our research in field settings has helped us gain insight into event marketing. As noted, such studies are surprisingly rare. We are convinced that field study offers unique opportunities for researchers. Pham (1991), on the other hand, called for researchers to examine the sponsorships through experimental designs. We echo his call. Experimental designs offer researchers opportunities to clarify many of the issues raised by field studies.

Over the course of our examinations of event sponsorship, we have been struck by how often the questions raised by our studies reminded us of the old saw: "Which came first, the chicken or the egg?" That is, our data collection at the Tour de Georgia allowed us to establish relationships between variables. We were often left, however, with competing (and equally plausible) explanations for why such relationships existed.

For instance, research helps establish that attendees' contact with the exhibits of a sponsor is linked to their perceptions of the sponsor (Sneath et al., 2005). But, attendees may (a) become interested in the sponsor after they experience the exhibits or (b) experience the exhibits because they were interested in the sponsor prior to their attendance. It is logical to expect that some attendees followed path a to the exhibits, while others followed path b. We have not, however, distinguished between these different attendees. More important, we have not controlled for any extraneous variables that may influence attendees' interest in the exhibits. Experimental designs can establish causality by overcoming concerns about extraneous variables.

One particular issue, among many, that scholars should study through experimental design is the effectiveness of different forms of IMC at sponsored events. Firms often do not even attempt to assess the impact of the various IMC methods that they use at sponsored events. Sales and market share, while important in many contexts, are not the most appropriate measures of the impact of IMC (Sneath et al., 2005); yet, managers often assess the effectiveness of IMC only through sales and market share. This is due, in part, to the difficulties managers have in discerning the individual impact of each form of IMC. Experimental designs would help identify the impact of each IMC method. Experiments would also help answer the call that we made for scholars to assess which event activities matter to event attendees.

References

Algesheimer, R., Dholakia, U. M., & Herrmann, A. (2005). The social influence of brand community: Evidence from European car clubs. *Journal of Marketing, 69*(3), 19–34.

Barros, C. P., de Barros, C., Santos, A., & Chadwick, S. (2007). Sponsorship brand recall at the Euro 2004 soccer tournament. *Sport Marketing Quarterly, 16*(1), 161–170.

Becker-Olsen, K. L., & Hill, R. P. (2006). The impact of sponsor fit on brand equity: The case of nonprofit service providers. *Journal of Service Research, 9*(1), 73–83.

Bennett, G., & Lachowetz, T. (2004). Marketing to lifestyles: Action sports and generation Y. *Sport Marketing Quarterly, 13*, 239–243.

Bovaird, T., Löffler, E., & Parrado-Díez, S. (2002). Finding a bowling partner: The role of stakeholders in activating civil society in Germany, Spain and the United Kingdom. *Public Management Review, 4*, 411–431.

Bring Back the Tour de Georgia! (2009). Retrieved August 25, 2009, from http://www.tourdegeorgia.com

Broderick, A., Jogi, A., & Garry, T. (2003).Tickled pink: The personal meaning of cause-related marketing for customers. *Journal of Marketing Management, 19*, 583–610.

Close, A. G., Finney, R. Z., Lacey, R., & Sneath, J. Z. (2006). Engaging the consumer through event marketing: Linking attendees with the sponsor, community, and brand. *Journal of Advertising Research, 46*, 420–433.

Close, A. G., Lacey, R., & Finney, R. Z. (2009). *Fit matters? Why fit impacts sponsorship and not events.* Unpublished working paper.

Cook, W. A., & Talluri, V. S. (2004). How the pursuit of ROMI is changing marketing management. *Journal of Advertising Research, 44*, 244–254.

Cornwell, T. B., & Coote, L. V. (2005). Corporate sponsorship of a cause: The role of identification in purchase intent. *Journal of Business Research, 58,* 268–276.

Cornwell, T. B., Humphreys, M. S., Maguire, A. M., Weeks, C. S., & Tellegen, C. L. (2006). Sponsorship-linked marketing: The role of articulation in memory. *Journal of Consumer Research, 33,* 312–321.

Court, D. C. (2005). Boosting returns on marketing investment. *McKinsey Quarterly, 2*(May), 36–47.

Docherty, S., & Hibbert, S. (2003). Examining company experiences of a UK cause-related marketing campaign. *International Journal of Nonprofit and Voluntary Sector Marketing, 8,* 378–389.

Du, S., Bhattacharya, C. B., & Sen, S. (2007). Reaping relational rewards from corporate social responsibility: The role of competitive positioning. *International Journal of Research in Marketing, 24,* 224–241.

Grohs, R., Wagner, U., & Vsetecka, S. (2004). Assessing the effectiveness of sports sponsorships—An empirical examination. *Schmalenbach Business Review, 56*(April), 119–138.

Helyar, J. (1997, February). No gold for Summer Olympic sponsors. *The Wall Street Journal,* 14, p. B11.

Hoek, J., Gendall, P., Jeffcoat, M., & Orsman, D. (1997). Sponsorship and advertising: A comparison of their effects. *Journal of Marketing Communications, 3*(1), 21–32.

Hulks, B. (1980, December). Should the effectiveness of sponsorship be assessed, and how? *Admap,* pp. 623–627.

International Events Group (IEG) Sponsorship Report. (2006). 06 activation spending to match all-time high. *25,* 1, 4.

International Events Group (IEG). (2009). Retrieved June 2009 from http://www.sponsorship.com

Javalgi, R. G., Traylor, M. B., Gross, A. C., & Lampman, E. (1994). Awareness of sponsorship and corporate image: An empirical investigation. *Journal of Advertising, 23*(4), 47–58.

Jones, T. O., & Sasser, W. E. (1995). Why satisfied customers defect. *Harvard Business Review, 73*(6), 88–99.

Kahneman, D., & Snell, J. (1992). Predicting a changing taste: Do people know what they will like? *Journal of Behavioral Decision Making, 5*(3), 187–200.

Lacey, R., Close, A. G., & Finney, R. Z. (2009a). *How affect and event experiences impact linkages among product knowledge, brand opinion, and purchase intent for the sponsor.* Unpublished working paper.

Lacey, R., Close, A. G., & Finney, R. Z. (2009b). The pivotal roles of product knowledge and CSR on event sponsorship effectiveness. *Journal of Business Research.*

Lacey, R., Sneath, J. Z., Finney, R. Z., & Close, A. G. (2007). The impact of repeat attendance on event sponsorship attendance. *Journal of Marketing Communications, 13*(4), 243–255.

Leung, T. K. P., Lai, K. H., Chan, R. Y. K., & Wong, Y. H. (2005). The roles of xinyong and guanxi in Chinese relationship marketing. *European Journal of Marketing, 39,* 528–559.

Maignan, I., & Ferrell, O. C. (2001). Corporate citizenship as a marketing instrument. *European Journal of Marketing, 35,* 457–484.

Maignan, I., & Ferrell, O. C. (2004). Corporate social responsibility and marketing: An integrative framework. *Journal of the Academy of Marketing Science, 32*(1), 3–19.

Mandler, G. (1982). The structure of value: Accounting for taste. In M. S. Clark and S. T. Fiske (Eds.), *17th Annual Carnegie Symposium on Cognition* (pp. 17–26). Hillsdale, NJ: Erlbaum.

Marketing fact book. (2008, July 15). *Marketing News,* p. 26.

McDaniel, S. R. (1999). An investigation of match-up effects in sport sponsorship advertising: The implications of consumer advertising schemas. *Psychology and Marketing, 16*(2), 163–184.

McDonald, C. (1991). Sponsorship and the image of the sponsor. *European Journal of Marketing, 25*(11), 31–38.

Meenaghan, T. (1991). The role of sponsorship in the marketing communications mix. *International Journal of Advertising, 10*(1), 35–47.

Meenaghan, T. (2001). Understanding sponsorship effects. *Psychology and Marketing, 18*(2), 95–122.

MPI Foundation. (2004). As events unfold: Event trends 2004. In *MPI Foundation/The George P Johnson Company report on the changing role of events in corporate America's marketing mix.* Retrieved September 2006 from http://www.mpiweb.org

Pham, M. T. (1991). The evaluation of sponsorship effectiveness: A model and some methodological considerations. *Gestion 2000, 7*(4), 47–65.

Pine, B. J., & Gilmore, J. H. (1999). *The experience economy: Work is theatre and every business a stage.* Boston: Harvard Business School Press.

Pitts, B., & Slattery, J. (2004). An examination of the effects on time on sponsorship awareness levels. *Sport Marketing Quarterly, 13*(1), 43–54.

Roy, D. R., & Cornwell, B. T. (2004). The effects of consumer knowledge on responses to event sponsorships. *Psychology and Marketing, 21*(3), 185–207.

Sen, S., & Bhattacharya, C. B. (2001). Does doing good always lead to doing better? Consumer reactions to corporate social responsibility. *Journal of Marketing Research, 38*(May), 225–243.

Shaver, P., Schwartz, J., Kirson, D., & O'Connor, C. (1987). Emotion knowledge: Further exploration of a prototype approach. *Journal of Personality and Social Psychology, 52,* 1061–1086.

Simmons, C. J., & Becker-Olsen, K. L. (2006). Achieving marketing objectives through social sponsorships. *Journal of Marketing, 70*(4), 154–169.

Sirgy, M. J., Lee, D. J., Johar, J. S., & Tidwell, J. (2008). Effect of self-congruity with sponsorship on brand loyalty. *Journal of Business Research, 61,* 1091–1097.

Sneath, J. Z., Finney, R. Z., & Close, A. G. (2005). An IMC approach to event marketing: The effects of sponsorship and experience on consumer attitudes. *Journal of Advertising Research, 45*, 373–381.

Sneath, J. Z., Lacey, R., Finney, R. Z., & Close, A. G. (2006). Balancing act: Choosing between event and sponsorship marketing requires careful consideration. *Marketing Health Services, 26*(1), 26–32.

Stewart, D. W. (2008). How marketing contributes to the bottom line. *Journal of Advertising Research, 48*, 94–105.

Stotlar, D. K. (2004). Sponsorship evaluation: Moving from theory to practice. *Sport Marketing Quarterly, 13*(1), 61–64.

Tour de Georgia. (2007). Tour de Georgia partners with Ford. Retrieved September 2009 from http://tourdegeorgia.s3.amazonaws.com/public/pressreleases/release2008hostvenueannounce12-5-07f.pdf

USA Cycling. (2006). Retrieved September 2009 from https://www.usacycling.org/news/user/story.php?id=2072

Wakefield, K. L., Becker-Olsen, K., & Cornwell, T. B. (2007). I spy a sponsor. *Journal of Advertising, 36*(4), 61–74.

Walliser, B. (2003). An international review of sponsorship research: Extension and update. *International Journal of Advertising, 22*(1), 5–40.

Whelan, S., & Wohlfeil, M. (2006). Communicating brands through engagement with "lived" experiences. *Brand Management, 13*, 313–329.

Williams, D. (2008, November 14). Tour de Georgia cancels for 2009. *Atlanta Business Chronicle.* Retrieved August 2009 from http://www.bizjournals.com/atlanta/stories/2008/11/10/daily115.html

Wilson, T. D., & Gilbert, D. (2003). Active forecasting. In M. Zanna (Ed.), *Advances in experimental social psychology* (Vol. 35, pp. 345–411). New York: Elsevier.

The World Business Council for Sustainable Development. (2009). *Business role: Corporate social responsibility (CSR).* Retrieved September 2009 from http://www.wbcsd.org/templates/TemplateWBCSD5/layout.asp?type=p&MenuId=MTE0OQ

Zablah, A. R., Bellenger, D. N., & Johnston, W. J. (2004). Customer relationship management implementation gaps. *Journal of Personal Selling and Sales Management, 24*, 279–295.

Zajonc, R. B., & Markus, H. (1982). Affective and cognitive factors in preferences. *Journal of Consumer Research, 9*, 122–131.

Author Index

Subject Index

A

Academic development, sport contributions to society, 44
Acceptable social behavior, 91
Accomplishment, 192, 194
   as Hoopfest participant value, 191
   sense of, 193
Achievement, as motive for amateur sport participants, 186, 193–194
Activation theories, 170, 171
Add-on activities, at amateur sporting events, 196, 198
Adrenaline rush, 129
   impedance from slope congestion, 130
   as primary motivation of winter sports participants, 115, 116
   in snowboarders, 111
Adults, reduced team sport engagement among, 184
Aesthetics
   as motivation in nonaggressive and individual sports, 185
   and pleasure needs, 74
   as spectator motivation, 185
   as sports fanship motive, 68–69
Affective consequences, inability to forecast, 66
Affective forecasting, 269–270
Affective motivations, to attend sporting events, 254–255
Affiliation
   and BIRGing/CORFing behaviors, 6, 8
   depth of, 2
   intensity of consumer, 3
   level of, 5
Age
   and risk-taking propensity, 113, 123
   skiers vs. snowboarders, 108, 125
   and slope behavior, 113
Aggressive behavior, 88
   as defense strategy to restore self-esteem, 90
   in park and pipe users, 125
   physiological conditions disposing to, 89
   priming through sports spectatorship, 68
   in skiers vs. snowboarders, 123
Alabama Crimson Tide, 90
Alcohol consumption
   importance as revenue source, 93

sales curbing initiatives, 94–95
   and spectator rage, 93, 94
Allegiances
   heightening through fan enjoyment, 77
   permanence and stability, 61
Alma mater
   belongingness and common bonds to, 73
   support for, 62
Altruism, by NPOs, 40
Amateur Athletic Union (AAU), 200
Amateur sporting events
   augmenting with add-on activities, 198
   community support reasons, 195
   economic development motives, 195
   ensuring sport long-term viability through, 199
   future research, 199–202
   Hoopfest strategic redesign, 195–197
   leveraging social values in, 197–199
   long-term sustainability, 194
   marketing differences from professional sports, 187
   motivational influence on youth, 184
   motivational properties of social values, 188–191
   motivations of attendance and participation, 183–184
   participant and spectator social values, 191–194
   role in promoting healthy lifestyles and fitness, 184
   role of social values in, 190–191
   social vs. skill components, 187
   success dependence on community support, 195
Ambush marketing, 218, 219
Ameritech Corporations, quality dimensions, 245
Antisocial behaviors, of fans, 67–68
Antitrust litigation, 226, 230, 234
Appraisals, role in elicitation of emotions, 7
Arousal
   fanship facilitation through, 66
   as fanship need, 74, 75
   physiological effects, 66
   skiers vs. snowboarders, 108–109
   sports appealing to need for, 79
   strategies informed by, 77–78

297